From Panthers to Promise Keepers

New Social Formations

Series Editor:
Charles Lemert, Wesleyan University

Forthcoming

From Panthers to Promise Keepers

Rethinking the Men's Movement

Judith Newton

ROWMAN & LITTLEFIELD PUBLISHERS, INC.
Lanham • Boulder • New York • Toronto • Oxford

ROWMAN & LITTLEFIELD PUBLISHERS, INC.

Published in the United States of America
by Rowman & Littlefield Publishers, Inc.
A wholly owned subsidiary of The Rowman & Littlefield Publishing Group, Inc.
4501 Forbes Boulevard, Suite 200, Lanham, MD 20706
www.rowmanlittlefield.com

P.O. Box 317, Oxford OX2 9RU, UK

British Library Cataloguing in Publication Information Available

Library of Congress Cataloging-in-Publication Data

Newton, Judith Lowder.
   From Panthers to Promise Keepers : rethinking the men's movement / Judith
Newton.
      p.   cm.—(New social formations)
Includes bibliographical references and index.
   ISBN 0-8476-9129-2 (cloth : alk. paper)—ISBN 0-8476-9130-6 (pbk. : alk.
paper)
   1. Men's movement—United States. 2. Masculinity—United States. 3. Sex
role—Political aspects—United States. 4. Gay liberation movement—United States.
5. Million Man March (1995 : Washington, D.C.). 6. Promise Keepers (Organization).
I. Title. II. Series.
   HQ1090.3.N493 2005
   305.32'0973—dc22

                                                                    2004013004

Printed in the United States of America

∞™ The paper used in this publication meets the minimum requirements of American
National Standard for Information Sciences—Permanence of Paper for Printed Library
Materials, ANSI/NISO Z39.48-1992.

Contents

Introduction

Close Encounters

On a warm Friday afternoon in September 1995, I found myself driving on a Northern California freeway in a sea of vans and sports utility vehicles, their interiors packed with clean-cut, seemingly middle-class white men, some wearing baseball caps and not a few sporting matching t-shirts as well. These men were headed, it was readily apparent, to the Oakland Coliseum for the twelfth of thirteen Promise Keepers Conferences for Men that year, and I was going with them or, at least, in their midst. As a professor of Women and Gender Studies at a local university, specializing in the study of masculinities and men, I had been intrigued by what already promised to be the largest "men's movement" in history. Seven hundred thousand men were expected at Promise Keepers "stadium events" that year, and by 1999 over three million men would have attended.

Further intrigued that this phenomenon was visiting the Oakland Coliseum, only an hour or so from my home, I had racked my brains for a way to see, for myself, what "they" were up to. Like some other feminists, I was to discover, I briefly considered the possibility of disguising myself as a man—another woman was to prove quite successful at this male masquerade—but I reluctantly dismissed the idea on the grounds (1) that I would look ridiculous and (2) that I would never pull it off.[1] Instead, I persuaded my obliging hometown newspaper to send me as "press." In return I had offered to write an op-ed on the movement.

The Coliseum parking lot was a maze of vans and men, and it took me a while to find a spot to park, find the press gate, secure my pass, and join the lines of men filing into the stadium. I was uncomfortably aware at this point not just that I was the only woman in a crowd of men—now wearing sunglasses and carrying Bibles—but that these men, by all official accounts at least, held political views directly opposite to those of feminists like myself. By September of 1995, indeed, several accounts of the Promise Keepers, written by men regularly engaged in "watching" the Right, had decisively pegged the organization as a quasi-militaristic movement, a "third wave of the religious right," that was secretly or not so secretly engaged in various forms of "spiritual warfare."[2]

Various accounts had argued that Promise Keepers' leaders, by means of a stealth operation concealed by the organization's "beatific" public image, aimed to fuse church and state, take over local school boards, and restore male domination—"women are to submit absolutely to their husbands or fathers"—while also organizing men into larger networks against abortion and gay civil rights.[3] Rife with citations from men who had spoken at various Promise Keepers events, the essays had documented remarks on the topic of abortion (an "epidemic"), on homosexuality (an "abomination"), and on national politics ("We are going to war as of tonight").[4] They had also presented evidence of disturbing links between Promise Keepers leaders and such right-wing spokesmen as Jerry Falwell and Pat Robertson and political organizations such as the Christian Coalition and the Coalition on Revival.[5] Reading these wake-up calls had already given me more than one clammy wave of anxiety about the organization I was about to encounter.

Still, I was not entirely ready to write Promise Keepers off. As an erstwhile born-again Christian, between the ages of twelve and eighteen, I had sung "Onward Christian Soldiers" enough times and had heard enough sermons about our "warfare" on sin not to be unduly alarmed by religious military metaphors, although, in the context of a politically organized religious right, "taking the nation for Jesus" now had a more ominous ring.[6] The fact that Jerry Falwell and Pat Robertson expressed support for Promise Keepers was unnerving, but I also felt they could be counted on to tout anything that might be given an antifeminist twist. "Real men are back," Robertson's monthly newsletter was to crow, while Falwell thanked God that "America's anti-Biblical feminist movement is at last dying" and being replaced possibly by "a Christ-centered men's movement which may become the foundation for a desperately needed national and spiritual awakening."[7]

Although it had given me a turn to read about the links between Promise Keepers speakers and various right-wing organizations, I also knew from experiences in the 1960s how easy it is to build assumption upon assumption on the basis of sometimes slender association. I was to learn, moreover, from another scholar of the Right, that one of the organizations, regularly portrayed as the headquarters for a conspiracy to take over America, the Coalition on Revival, had mainly functioned in the last few years as a clearing house for its founder's position papers and as a network of pastors each busy with his own projects. As a political organization, according to sociologist Sara Diamond, it was largely inactive.[8]

Still, if the fact that Promise Keepers opposed abortion and saw homosexuality as a sin did not come as a surprise, given the conservative evangelical tradition out of which it stemmed, it had been profoundly disturbing to read that the founder of Promise Keepers, Coach Bill McCartney, had once called gay people "stark raving mad," had served on the board of Colorado for Family Values, and had actively campaigned to pass Colorado's Amendment II, which denied various forms of civil rights to gays.[9] Virtually all the essays I read, finally, had quoted the African-American minister Tony Evans, whose 1994 essay on "Spiritual Purity" in the official Promise Keepers publication *Seven Promises of a Promise Keeper* contained what have to be the most frequently cited lines ever penned by anyone involved in the organization—the lines urging men not to ask for their leadership role at home but to "*take it back*."[10] Needless to say, I was planning to take careful notes on the session billed as "Raising the Standard in Our Marriages."

I was not to be the only feminist or progressive to spend my first weekend at a Promise Keepers conference trying to reconcile what I saw with what I had read.[11] It was not an easy process. For one thing, there were several moments during the fifteen hours of conference activities when I seemed to be having feminist hallucinations—fifty thousand men in a sports arena wearing jeans, shorts, and baseball caps, hugging, holding hands, talking intimately in small consciousness-raising-like groups, men audibly urging each other to "serve" their wives, men ritually repeating the words "I was wrong," "I am sorry," "Can you forgive me?" Sights and sounds like these evoked memories of the personal transformations that feminists had once dared to hope for from men.

At this conference, moreover, Promise Keepers rhetoric did not justify its reputation for overt political position taking. Abortion and homosexuality, for example, were never mentioned—although the latter was alluded to in the exhortation that participants "come out" as Christians. By 1995, it would appear, conference rhetoric upon these issues was being more tightly controlled. (Some four years and eight conferences later, indeed, I still found direct references to both topics to be rare.) Somewhat uneasily, I began to be aware that, although Promise Keepers unquestionably did support men in maintaining conservative positions on these issues, its energies were not organized around them at this conference.

I was also also provoked by the tendency of Promise Keepers' man-as-citizen rhetoric to erase gender inequality and, indeed, women themselves, from the public sphere—a tendency that it unfortunately shared with many male-led movements past and present, not excluding those on the Left. Nonetheless, what I heard that day on marriage relations did not alarm me. (I compared notes with a feminist reporter at the end of the second day—Did *you* hear anything? Did *you*? We agreed, somewhat hesitantly, that we had not.) What I did hear that particular day was men being urged to stop "acting like children" and to stop having "temper tantrums." Only children are "insensitive" and "can't be reasoned with." Maturity was "accepting responsibility," participants were told. "Act like men!" Now, there was a version of that injunction I thought I could get behind. Nothing I read, moreover, had prepared me to hear a stadium full of largely conservative, white, Evangelical males being told that antiracism was a foundation for being godly men. If this was the "beatific" public image of Promise Keepers, its "subtle presentation," someone had forgotten to mention that this was the image of Promise Keepers for most of its participants that day as well.[12]

My interior conflicts that September weekend were not allayed by conversations and interviews with the men whose vans and SUVs I had noted en route. I had concluded, after sorting through various approaches to my interviews, that it was best just to be up front about being a professor gathering materials for a book on men's efforts to invent or revise masculine ideals. (I had no intention at the time of giving Promise Keepers more than a passing reference.) Although this revelation, it seemed to me, was often met with a subtle pause—the pause would get longer after NOW became more active in its criticism of the organization—the men proved friendly and willing, even eager at times, to talk. Unbiblical feminists, I was relieved to find, were not automatically to be shunned. Far from seeming dupes of some sinister organization, the men I talked with often struck me as reflective and sometimes critically acute. A number of them, for example, expressed resentment of media efforts to lump Promise Keepers with "the religious right," whose "hate rhetoric" and political self-seeking they intensely disliked. "I don't keep up with the Christian Coalition," said one. "Are you familiar with the term *pharisee*?" asked another.

The men also seemed a lot more open about themselves than I had been prepared for or was, myself, prepared to be. On the first evening, for example, between dutifully scribbling notes on the speakers, I fell into a long, sporadically interrupted conversation with one of the Promise Keepers volunteers. White, in his thirties, married, born-again, and middle-class, Mark, who lived in southern California, fit the Promise Keepers profile to a T. Mark told me early on in our conversation that he had been a faithful listener to the right-wing psychologist James Dobson since 1984 and that he felt he had learned some concrete strategies for being a better husband and father. Religion teaches men how to live, he explained to me, adding, "Lots of men are jerks!" I asked Mark about his marriage, which, in the ideals he entertained for it, at least, turned out to be quite different from what I would have expected from a Dobson fan. Mark and his wife were professionals who worked full-time, with Susan earning the greater salary. As Mark put it, "There's no way I'm going to tell her what's what."

Still later in the evening, Mark observed that Dobson had become "more political" of late and that Dobson had been severe about some talk at the Women's International Conference in Beijing about there being "five genders." We talked a bit about gender systems, I noting that many academics, including myself, thought of gender as socially constructed and explaining that some cultures did indeed recognize more than two. Mark, to my surprise, conceded that there might be something to this point of view. Still later, turning the tables on our interview, he inquired about my own religious background. I told him about losing my faith, after reading about pre-Christian religions during the first quarter of my Western Civilization class at Stanford in my freshman year. Mark looked at me for a moment and then confessed: "Sometimes I've wondered about that, too." This was the enemy? I was beginning to wonder what kind of ally this open and reflective man would make.

Although, overwhelmingly, the fifty-five Promise Keepers men I interviewed over the next five years would command considerable liking and respect, not all my interviews left me fantasizing about crossing borders. A month later, for example, at the Dallas conference—I had decided after all that Promise Keepers would require an entire chapter—I was to learn much more about the role that local cultures played. If, in Northern California for example, some Promise Keepers had told me about gay neighbors whom they professed to love, men from the Bible Belt had far greater difficulty with Promise Keepers' love-the-sinner rhetoric. One man completely lost his composure when I broached the subject of Promise Keepers' stance on gay men, and our long, steady interview careened to an abrupt end as he burst into an angry rail against the unnaturalness of homosexuals and their "disrespect for life."

In 1996, finally, the year that I began to think that I would focus on Promise Keepers in my book, several articles on the organization by progressive men either dismissed or glossed over Promise Keepers' racial reconciliation efforts.[13] Although no white-dominated organization escapes racist tendencies for very long, the rhetoric and practices of the Promise Keepers conferences I had attended were also suggesting a strong effort on the part of the organization to be patently antiracist instead.

I would learn at the Los Angeles conference that spring that men of color, like white men, said they attended Promise Keepers events to strengthen their faith, to become better husbands and fathers, and to have Christian fellowship with other men. What *was* different, however, was that men of color universally mentioned antiracism and race reconciliation as the reasons they had affiliated themselves with the Promise Keepers organization. A man I shall call

Chris, for example, a black man who had been to several Promise Keepers conferences and belonged to a Promise Keepers men's group, felt he had never heard "anything so aggressive" on racial reconciliation as what Promise Keepers had developed. "Dwight," also black, had only attended conferences, but he felt that "Promise Keepers walked the walk" and gave him "strength" to continue his work with inner city youth: "It's lonely on the frontier."

Promise Keepers of color, however, representing 6 to 14 percent of the participants at the conferences I attended, were not the only ones to see potential in Promise Keepers' racial reconciliation work. My last conversation of the day in Los Angeles was with a journalist, not a Promise Keeper, named Eduardo, a young Latino who belonged to a small inner-city church and to a band of young people who have devoted themselves to working with the marginalized and the poor. Eduardo and his group had taken care of children while their crack-addicted mother went through rehabilitation; they counseled and mentored young people and helped to keep them out of jail; they pooled their salaries, gave to the poor, and talked a lot about issues of race, gender, and class.

Eduardo's take on gender, race, and class, indeed, impressed me so much that for a moment I thought he sounded like a student in one of my Women and Gender Studies classes. He was not, of course. He was an evangelical whose belief provided the energy and inspiration for his politics, although he did not call it that, since "politics" and the government in his opinion had failed. I asked Eduardo what he thought of Promise Keepers, and he said, "You must have introductory courses at the university on gender, like Gender 101." I said, "We do," and he told me that Promise Keepers is an introductory course to his group's work: "They are getting baby steps out of right-wing Christian men. Last year the course was 101. This year it's 102."

LEARNING TO LISTEN

I begin with this story of a close encounter, this fable of seeing "others" differently from the way I had expected that I would, because in many ways it characterizes the disconcerting nature of my research for this book. My reading, interviews, and participant observation, that is, continually required me to readjust my expectations and my focus. Sometime in the summer of 1996, for example, I momentarily decided to limit my study of men's organized efforts to revise masculine ideals to a short book on the Promise Keepers organization. My continuing ambivalence about the movement, however—it had links to the religious right but, as I was soon to discover, it had unexpected ties to progressive Christian networks as well—my distrust of several progressive and feminist takes on what it was about, and Promise Keepers' unsettling resemblance to some of the secular men's networks with which I was acquainted, eventually propelled me to reconsider the focus of my inquiry. To make any sense of Promise Keepers, I began to understand, I would need to have a handle on many of the other organized efforts to invent or revise masculine ideals that had come before and after.

A short book about Promise Keepers, therefore, became a long book on a series of organized efforts to refashion masculine ideals in the last forty years of the twentieth century. In the end, the groups and networks that I came to study included black men and women associated with Black Power, with later forms of black cultural nationalism, with black fathering organizations, and with the black academic Left. My study also came to include black and other men of color associated with Promise Keepers, as well as the largely white gay networks and/or authors associated with the Radical Faeries, Manifest Love, and gay liberation theology. Finally, I also reflected upon the largely white, middle-class networks involved in "men's liberation," the National Organization of Men Against Sexism (NOMAS), men's rights, the mythopoetics, and Promise Keepers.

The political affiliations of participants in the groups I studied varied wildly. A longtime member of the Radical Faeries described the "conservative" wing of that network as "being a Democrat." The profeminist NOMAS was Left to liberal, and the mythopoetics were largely liberal. Participants in Black Power and black cultural nationalisms were often radical or liberal on race and conservative on gender and homosexuality, and 61 percent of the Promise Keepers at the Washington, D.C., Stand in the Gap Assembly identified themselves as "conservative" to "very conservative."[14]

I had expected at the beginning of my work that these politically disparate groups would produce insights, values, and behaviors that a feminist like myself would find to be aligned somehow with their political differences—and to some degree they did. The dominant political affiliations of participants in the groups did not, however, necessarily line up with the group's effectiveness in getting large numbers of men to change—and to change in what I found to be personally progressive directions, such as defining antiracism as fundamental to a masculine ideal or getting men to alter their day-to-day practices with respect to sharing housework, childcare, and the emotional labor of working on intimate relationships with women. My study of these groups, indeed, produced several disconcerting, paradigm-shifting revisions of my expectations—revisions that were, by turns, painful, frustrating, encouraging, and a continuing challenge to my organizational skills. My reading, my interviews, and my participant observations, for example, not only compelled me to give value to the achievements of seeming Others, even when they had been "deeply wrong" on many things; they also forced me to confront the limitations of groups with which I identified and which I deeply wanted to support.[15] My research, in short, became an unsettling journey into the perception that "close encounters" can reveal a complexity, and a downright messiness, in life for which one's political assumptions and desires may not have prepared one. I shall return to these themes in the chapters to come.

FEARS OF FALLING: THE SHIFTING GROUNDS OF MASCULINE IDEALS

National dialogue over masculine ideals has been common to U.S. history— so common, indeed that a recent anthology suggests that models of manhood in the United States have been "in crisis in the sense of being constantly engaged in [their] own redefinition" since the founding of the nation.[16] Certainly, the latter half of the twentieth century, like the latter half of the century before, was characterized not only by conversations about masculinity but by a series of organized efforts to revise, reinvent, and/or revive masculine ideals. Several of these efforts were launched in the late 1960s and 1970s and had their origins in the struggles for social justice that were so prominent at the time. Later efforts, those that emerged in the 1980s, 1990s, and beyond, had ties to the social movements of the past as well, but they also constituted a response to post-sixties economic, social, and cultural developments. These developments had gradually eroded many of the grounds on which dominant masculine ideals had once been based.

From the early 1970s on, for example, deindustrialization and a profit-driven restructuring of global and local economies led to a decrease in men's real wages and initiated a decline in secure, well-paying jobs for U.S. men and women both. These developments, in turn, promoted an increase in the number of married women and mothers entering the labor force, especially as low-paid workers. Inflation, escalating consumption standards, the expansion of coeducation on the college level, and the persistence of high divorce rates also fueled the continued entry of women and mothers with small children into labor outside the home. Feminism, according to the sociologist Judith Stacey, by encouraging female economic and personal autonomy, acted as unwitting "midwife" to these changes.[17] Each of these developments had tended to reduce the cultural resonance of, and the feasibility of performing, what had been dominant markers of manhood for U.S. men—primary breadwinning and being head of house.

A dominant ideal of masculinity had also implicitly assumed men's right to greater power and privilege than women. Feminisms' hard-won gains for women, however—the growth of gender consciousness, an increase in the percentage of women in higher education, greater access for some women to traditional male-dominated forms of employment, laws against gender discrimination, and many other social and political inroads into traditional gender arrangements—further challenged the unquestioned acceptance of such inequality. The gay liberation movement, the proliferation of gay masculine ideals, and the influence of gay culture on male bodies and fashions also complicated the automatic equation of heterosexuality with being a "masculine" man. Changing racial demographics, meanwhile, and continuing struggles for racial equality shed greater light upon the race privilege that had often functioned as another foundation of a dominant masculine ideal. By the late 1980s, when the media-hyped figure of the angry white male began most fully to appear, the category "white, middle-class, heterosexual, and male" was still a privileged category but a much less secure or celebrated one than before.

The more precipitous drop in wages and employment for black men of the middle and lower classes, along with the dismantling of affirmative action and worker safety nets, contributed to an even greater loss of material security for black and many other men of color. These developments strengthened the already existing barriers to their attaining the economic well-being, not to mention the primary-breadwinner/head-of-household status that had been identified historically with dominant models of being a man.[18] Feminists of color had also criticized race liberation leaders for sexist attitudes and behaviors, focusing national attention on men of color as persons more complex than simple victims of racial and economic discrimination—but as far more worthy of respect than the absent husbands, failed fathers, and criminals that political discourse often made them out to be.[19] Gay men of color, finally, had challenged the identification of heterosexuality not just with manhood itself but with racial authenticity as well.

MALE REVOLT, OR A FAILURE TO EMBRACE THE CAUSE OF MEN?

Scholarly accounts of men's responses to the political, economic, social, and cultural developments of the past forty years have been ambivalent about what men have been able to accomplish with respect to reinventing or restoring masculine ideals. Barbara Ehrenreich's 1983 *The Hearts of Men* wittily uncovered what she described as a "male revolt"—albeit one "hardly organized and seldom conscious of its goals"—against the marriage-and-breadwinner ethic on the part of white "professional-managerial class" men.[20] Ehrenreich found traces of this revolt as early as the 1950s in accounts of the organization man, in medical writing on the type A personality, in the construction of the *Playboy* man, in the Beat rebellion and then later in the human potential movement, in the counterculture, and in literature by spokesmen for "men's liberation," most particularly those later identified with men's rights.

The outcome of this revolt, however, was, to say the least, mixed. On the one hand, it participated in humanist liberation struggles by striking some blows against "a system of social control that operates to make men unquestioning and obedient employees." Through its production of a more androgynous masculine ideal, moreover, it increased somewhat the possibility of "honest communication between the sexes" and the possibility that men might take on "more of what have been women's traditional tasks . . . or so we may hope." On the other hand, the revolt was marked both by childish flights from responsibility and by accommodation to consumer society. In the end it offered "no more uplifting a vision than a little more leisure and good times for men." From this perspective, men "won their freedom first."[21] Susan Faludi's 1999 *Stiffed,* while echoing some of the themes in *Hearts of Men*, distinctly did not endorse the concept of a male revolt but focused instead on men's sense of betrayal and loss. In being deprived of "economic authority" and in witnessing the breakdown of "loyalty in the public domain"—the loyalty of corporations, for example, to their male employees—men in the post–World War II period felt abandoned by public and personal fathers both. Since men's personal worth was no longer judged much on the basis of "inner qualities" but was being measured in "ornamental terms"—such as being sexy, being known, and having won—men had lost a sense of public usefulness as well.[22] Worst of all, perhaps, men lacked a well-defined enemy and a clear frontier and had, therefore, not risen up "in protest against their betrayal." Promise Keepers and the Million Man March, however, offered hope that men were "seeking a place where they could start to think about their situation afresh."[23]

Sally Robinson's 2002 *Marked Men,* in some tension with Faludi's *Stiffed,* turned a critical eye upon "a dominant or master narrative of white male decline in post-sixties America."[24] This master narrative, the book argued, grew out of 1960s liberation politics and did involve men in shared processes of transforming gender and race ideals. Still, narratives of white male wounding and victimization, while they could not be dismissed as simple backlash or elevated to a male revolt, primarily called attention (sometimes masochistically) to white men's loss of social status and centrality. In so doing, these narratives had repositioned white, middle-class men as primary objects of the nation's fond attention.

The sociologists Lynne Segal and Michael Messner followed Ehrenreich to some extent in that they, too, documented what men had done in taking up the cause of gender change. Segal's 1990 *Slow Motion*, citing many British sources, focused on the complexities and contradictions of the way masculinities were being constructed in research on sex differences, in psychoanalytic theory, popular culture, the new fatherhood, and gay and black communities, and in the organized efforts of some progressive men to change. As the title might suggest, the book documented the leisurely pace at which men's attitudes and practices, not to mention social structures, had changed. It also emphasized the need for alterations in public policy—such as the institution of family leave—that might support men in moving forward on what the sociologist R. W. Connell has called a "long and winding road."[25]

Messner's 1997 *Politics of Masculinity* examined several men's networks "mostly in terms of their actual or potential political impact." The networks he examined included the mythopoetics, Promise Keepers, men's liberation, men's rights, radical and socialist-feminist men, racialized masculinity politics, and gay male liberation. Messner lucidly mapped these groups with respect to their stand on men's institutionalized privilege, on the costs attached to sticking with "narrow conceptions of masculinity," and on "differences and inequalities among men." Messner's fundamental question—to what extent the actual or potential political impact of such networks will "impede or advance movements for social justice"—is the question that ultimately shapes *From Panthers to Promise Keepers* as well.[26]

RETHINKING THE "MEN'S MOVEMENT"

From Panthers to Promise Keepers also focuses upon men's efforts to organize around their own transformation, but, in contrast to many popular accounts of these efforts, it largely avoids a "men's movement" framework. This framework, I found, made it difficult to identify, and to justify the inclusion of, gender work by marginalized or subordinated men.[27] The efforts of black men to reinvent ideals of black masculinity, for example, largely took place within movements or networks that men and women shared. Efforts to theorize and practice a radical ideal of male homosexual personhood in the 1950s and 1960s, moreover, could not sensibly be referred to as constituting, or even as participating in, something as well defined as a "men's movement." In *From Panthers to Promise Keepers,* therefore, I use the term "men's movement" only in quotation marks, relying instead on versions of "men's organized efforts to transform masculine ideals." This homely but useful phrase allowed me to widen my lens and, in so doing, permitted me more easily to see how networks of men of color or of white gay men had promoted more fully human and, in different ways, more egalitarian ideals of masculinity for men.

In *From Panthers to Promise Keepers,* moreover, I attempt to see white men and men of color in more dialogue with each other than has been common in the past. Indeed, my initial desire to make sense of Promise Keepers' mixed-race leadership, which in the mid-1990s included several high-placed black men, compelled me, in particular, to explore the mutual histories of white and black efforts to refashion masculine ideals. Once I set upon this road, I saw more meeting points than I had anticipated. Early on, for example, in tracing black men's organized attempts, in the late 1960s and beyond, to transform models of black manhood, I began to see that black men and women had significantly contributed, through the Civil Rights Movement and especially the Student Nonviolent Coordinating Committee (SNCC), to later projects that would consciously focus on masculine ideals. Not unexpectedly, the men and women of SNCC helped lay the groundwork for revised ideals of black masculinity in the late 1960s and beyond, but they gave renewed political resonance to preoccupations that would predominate in largely white networks as well. (I turn to the subjects of SNNC, Black Power, and black masculine ideals in chapter 2.)

The first of these preoccupations—a variously articulated criticism of individualist, economically focused, competitive, self-making values—had many precedents in U.S. history, among them being the old Left and some articulations of Ehrenreich's male revolt. The second preoccupation—giving value to, and attempting to define, ideals of personhood that were characterized by collectivity, compassion, and care, and by the more open expression of tender emotion—had historical precedents for men as well as for women, for example, in the abolition and temperance movements.[28] The civil rights movement, however, and especially SNCC, gave those preoccupations renewed political resonance in re-identifying them with passionate, self-sacrificing activism and transcendent social ideals.

These dual concerns, for example, characterized the work of activist Harry Hay in his attempts to theorize a loving and self-sacrificing ideal of male homosexual personhood in the 1960s and 1970s in particular. (I turn to Hay and to the Radical Faerie network that he helped to construct in chapter 3.) To some extent, moreover, since many of those who participated in "men's liberation" in the early 1970s had also participated in, or been touched by, civil rights, the dual preoccupations to which SNCC gave resonance entered directly into the development of "men's liberation" and into NOMAS, its profeminist offshoot, as well. For the younger men who became involved in "men's liberation" and profeminist male networks, the women's movement and gay liberation were more direct influences. Both of these movements, however, had themselves been inspired by values derived from the civil rights struggle. (I turn to these topics in chapter 4.)

Later networks, as I was to discover, also shared these dual concerns—a critique of self-making values and an effort to construct ideals of personhood that were more nurturing and more open to expressions of tender emotion. Because there were so many of these networks and because the preoccupations they had in common seemed *potentially* conducive to social justice, I chose to focus mainly on these groups and not on others. *From Panthers to Promise Keepers*, therefore, has relatively little to say about groups organized around creating more competitive, career-oriented, aggressive, or racist masculine ideals.

The overlap in concerns among the groups I studied seemed surprising to me at first, given the marked differences in the political affiliations of their members (from Far Left to "very conservative"). Indeed, a far more common approach to the study of groups bent on transforming ideals of masculinity has been to emphasize the differences among them and to yoke those differences to the political affiliations of the groups' participants. This approach has been immensely helpful in mapping the terrain, and I have employed it myself from time to time. In my research for this book, however, what struck me more were the commonalities across political divisions, and in the end, despite some initial hesitations on my part, I came to feel that it was precisely in exploring the commonalities across groups that I could contribute most to ongoing conversations about men's organized efforts to transform masculine ideals.

Once I ventured down this path, I found many explanations for the fact that politically disparate groups shared similar concerns. To some extent, for example, the shared criticism of self-making values and the shared project of inventing more tender, more openly expressive ideals of masculinity had been passed from one group to another. They were "in the air" and in the media as issues for men. Bill McCartney, the founder of Promise Keepers, began to ponder the idea of a specifically Christian congregation of men in March 1990, a mere two months after Bill Moyer's television documentary brought fame to Robert Bly's mythopoetic gatherings. Three years later a much smaller experiment with a Christian-based revision of masculine ideals directly borrowed Bly's mythical "Iron John" to create an "Iron Jesus," who would model, among other things, a radical devotion to the poor. Bly himself, moreover, had held his first conference for men at the Lama Commune in New Mexico in 1981, two years after the First Spiritual Conference for Radical Faeries in nearby Arizona.

That groups shared issues and that they at times employed similar concepts and language may also be explained by the fact that some members of these networks had participated in the same 1960s political movements. Some of the men who had been active in civil rights, for example, went on to participate in "men's liberation" and in NOMAS in the 1970s and 1980s. Others became active in black cultural nationalist groups and black fathering projects in the 1980s and 1990s. Some black and white evangelicals who had been civil rights activists as well became involved in Promise Keepers in the 1990s. (I turn to Promise Keepers' work on race in chapter 9.)

Men in one network also read literature produced by men who belonged to other groups. Both black cultural nationalists and Promise Keepers, for example, read and cited white "men's liberation" texts, and black speakers at Promise Keepers conferences sometimes employed concepts that were intensely familiar to me from black cultural nationalist literature—such as the nesting relation of family, community, and nation. Men might also have ties to several networks or organizations. Some participants in men's rights, for example, began their activism in NOMAS. Radical Faeries also showed up at NOMAS, for a time, and there were NOMAS members who were also active in the mythopoetics.

To some extent, finally, the overlap of issues across politically disparate groups was a function of the fact that, as many men have testified, dominant ideals of masculinity exert a dehumanizing pressure on many men. Indeed, since the values that perpetuate the inequalities of our economic system are values that have been identified with dominant ideals of manhood in the United States, both system and ideals call upon men to be self-interested, competitive, materialistic, and emotionally tough, thereby pressuring men to give up aspects of their humanity in ways that are limiting, uncomfortable, and often painful as well. As the British philosopher Victor Seidler puts it,

> salvation as something external is replaced within a secular capitalist culture by individual achievement and success. Life becomes an endless struggle and we are denied any sense of intrinsic fulfillment and satisfaction. We are locked into competitive relationships with others and plagued by feelings that whatever we do is not good enough.[29]

As for feelings, Seidler continues, "we have learnt to be suspicious of them. We often fear they will make us less effective in the world where we have to struggle to prove ourselves. This is part of an estrangement from self that has become part of our masculine inheritance, and that is so taken for granted that its injuries are rendered invisible."[30] Many men in the groups I studied focused on a critique of self-making values and embraced the production of more openly vulnerable and caring modes of being men because they were responding to the ways in which they had been limited or damaged as human beings.

Not surprisingly, many men involved in organized efforts to reinvent masculine ideals were men who had been particularly vulnerable to the impact of dehumanizing norms. Their race, class or economic fortune, sexual identification, and /or personal histories, for example, had often deprived them of some, or even many, of the material or social privileges that relinquishing parts of one's humanity as a man can also bring. Black and gay men are two obvious examples of men in these categories, but white, heterosexual men who had participated in mythopoetic groups spoke of experiencing forms of economic, social, and personal damage as well.

Other men I studied were already critical of dominant ideals of masculinity before they joined, not just because they had suffered from the limitations of attempting to live out those ideals, but also because they were immersed in belief systems, such as black cultural nationalisms, leftist ideologies, pro-feminisms, countercultural politics, and/or some forms of Evangelical Christianity that had sharpened their assessment of the personal and social costs of dominant norms. Promise Keepers, for example, frequently expressed the view that being "born again" set them apart from many of the values of dominant masculine ideals.

The political affiliations of participants, of course, did matter, as *From Panthers to Promise Keepers* will relate. The groups might interpret and weight their common concerns differently. Most groups had concerns that other groups did not share, and some groups took opposing positions with respect to the same issue. Support for homosexuality, for example, was an emphatic dividing line. Some groups were more concerned with race than with gender or sexual justice, and other groups did little on race despite official concerns about it. The groups also differed in the degree to which they theoretically embraced and actively worked toward public or private structural social change. In the end, however, differences among the groups seemed to have had less influence on mainstream culture and on political imaginations than did the repetition of their shared concerns. That a critique of self-making values and an investment in producing more caring and more emotionally expressive masculine ideals appeared and reappeared in politically disparate networks over a period of some forty years had cultural resonance. That resonance, I will argue, had, and still has, political potential. I shall return to this theme shortly.

MALE ROMANCE

Most of the networks on which I did research shared common processes or practices as well. Over and over, for example, I discovered that the groups of men I studied, although very different when it came to the political affiliations of their members, had been involved in separating from women, creating ritual space, risking intimacy and disclosure with each other, and undergoing a species of rebirth, most often through the agency of male figures or other men. I encountered versions of this phenomenon so often, indeed, that

I found it necessary to find a term to refer to it. The term I choose is "male romance."

"Romance," defined as a story of (typically male) heroic deeds, adventure, and love and sometimes incorporating supernatural events, evoked many of the qualities that characterized these latter-day phenomena.[31] There *was,* for example, an air of adventure for men in going off with other men for the purposes of redefining masculine ideals, an air captured in Spike Lee's film about the Million Man March, *Getting on the Bus.* For many men, moreover, the very attempt to redefine ideals was cast as a heroic effort or journey. There were also pronounced elements of love in the male bonding that was a primary goal and outcome of many ritual activities. The potential or actual homoeroticism of such gatherings also contributed to their romantic nature, although this potential was handled in very different ways. In many cases, finally, the evocation of a higher cause or higher power (sometimes conceived of as supernatural and other times as not) played a central role in facilitating men's efforts to change their attitudes and behaviors.[32] I look more closely at some of the meanings and histories of male romance—those most pertinent to my study—in chapter 1 and in several chapters devoted to individual networks or organizations.

THE PERSONAL AS THE POLITICAL

After the decline of Black Power in the mid-seventies, and after what many have called the mid-seventies "end of politics" for white progressive men, the sense of political possibility that had been originally linked to revising ideals of masculinity began to fade. Although this was less true in black circles than in white, the relation between the revision of masculine ideals and the active pursuit of structural change became more tenuous in networks attempting, in some organized way, to transform masculine ideals.

A good many of men's organized energies with respect to masculine ideals were devoted, from the mid-seventies on, to more personal kinds of alteration—identifying and mourning the costs of dominant masculine codes, articulating new ideals of being a proper man, giving and receiving support in making individual change, developing closer relations with other men, and/or practicing more caring attitudes and behaviors in the fathering, or mentoring, of children. Although many of these networks theoretically, and unevenly, supported gender, race, sexual, and/or economic justice, activism—and public activism on behalf of women's equality, in particular—would characterize only a minority of organized efforts to refashion masculine ideals. (NOMAS would be the only organization I studied to organize around activism on women's behalf.) As the sociologist Linzi Murrie observed in his study of a group of profeminist Australian men, men "had their own agenda" with respect to "patriarchal culture."[33]

As others have pointed out in previous reflections upon men's organized efforts to transform masculine ideals, changes in the ideals one lives by and even in one's day-to-day behaviors are not sufficient in themselves to effect public, structural social change. As Lynne Segal rightly cautioned, "the difficulty of changing men is, in part, the difficulty of changing political and economic structures." Without such change and indeed even with it, new, more caring men might still "retain, if less infallibly than ever before [their] hegemony over women and over other subordinated groups of men."[34] Men's organized efforts to transform masculine ideals, moreover, did sometimes serve to reaffirm the privilege of heterosexual men over women or gays, to make class division and extreme economic inequality invisible, or to recenter white men and men of color both as representatives and as the true citizens of a "nation."

Still, changes in ideals and in day-to-day behaviors do matter. Dominant ideals of U.S. masculinity, for example, have been deeply identified with being aggressive and competitive, with making it and being on top, and with suppressing empathy for others. These are the values that shore up the economic and other structures that sustain the economic, racial, gender, and sexual inequalities from which our culture suffers. As Seidler put it, "people often fail to appreciate how deeply forms of masculinity are tied into the very organization of production. . . ." "A men's politics," he continues, "that challenges these aspects of male socialization cannot avoid challenging the larger structures of power in society."[35]

Changed ideals, if they give rise to alterations in day-to-day behaviors, can also help to create conditions that make structural change possible. In this, as in most things, we are without guarantees, but as the British social critic Anthony Giddens put it, "a world in which men no longer value economic success in the way they once did and where they live more for love and emotional communication—the least one can say is that this would look very different from the present one."[36] If radically changing men's ideals and behaviors depends on changing structures, changing structures is dependent upon significantly altering dominant masculine ideals and men's day-to-day practices.

It is crucial to remember, moreover, that families are structures, too, and that they are the site of a good deal of inequality for women. Networks that promoted ideals of masculinity requiring men to share more of the housework and childcare, as well as the emotional labor of sustaining intimate relationships, cannot be dismissed as having had no interest in structural change—not, that is, if one is to take families and social justice for women and children, along with their happiness and well-being, into serious account. The personal realm of love and emotion is also a realm of power. As Seidler puts it, "justice does not only have to do with the distribution of resources within the public realm, but also with the just treatment of people in our personal relations with them."[37] This is a connection that is still too often forgotten or dismissed.

Performing emotional labor and doing "housework," or mundane day-to-day tasks, moreover, are key to political alliances. Women's vigorous complaints about men in the social movements of the 1960s and 1970s often focused on men's refusal to do mundane labor or on their unwillingness to attend to the personal as the political. These resistances on the part of men helped consolidate their role as movement leaders or "heavies." Despite the lessons of those times, moreover, the realm of "serious" politics is still too often conceived of as separate from feeling and from the day-to-day. Thus some male allies, who may in fact share housework and emotional labor in the home, still burden women in political alliances with the task of doing behind-the-scenes work and of building the relationships that hold such alliances together. Even younger feminists, in my travels, have repeatedly complained that in their own alliance politics much of this work, if it is done at all, is left to them.

Increasingly, moreover, political alliances with weight require emotional labor—working with others across racial, gender, and sexual lines—and this at a time when members of subordinated groups have raised their expectations with respect to the treatment they are to receive in political, and all other, venues. My own ten-year experience in a cross-racial, cross-gender political community has convinced me that "working on the relationships" was the single most important element in our getting together in the first place, in our staying together, and in our getting anything done at all. The experience has also convinced me that, as the literary critic Wendy Ho puts it, the labor of "earning one's relationship to others who are different from oneself" can no longer be left to women alone. In their fondness for grand gestures, for large-scale protest, and for focusing on structures in the public sphere, male allies sometimes devalue, and/or studiously avoid, the relationship work that makes alliances, and therefore structural social change, possible.

"EMOTION WORK"

Male self-transformation of the kind studied here does not operate on the level of willful political choice alone. Many of the men I studied seemed to require therapy, or "emotion work" of some other kind, to manage egalitarian and nurturing relationships—because of the power of dominant ideals, because of conscious and unconscious investments in those ideals, and because men feared losing not just their privilege but their identity altogether if they deviated from what they were accustomed to as the norm. Seidler, writing in 1991 about men's "precarious relationships" with women who changed through the women's movement, suggested that "in some strange way, men can cease to exist at all, as their sense of self has been so undermined they cannot be the way they used to be, nor do they know *how* they want to be."[38] Radical therapy, a form of emotion work, was central to Seidler's own process of self-transformation.

"Emotion work" in general, however, has often been characterized by men and women both as apolitical. It has been interpreted as implying that the release of feeling is being defined, in and of itself, as evidence of structural social transformation. Engaging in emotion work has been seen as a means of disguising the absence of efforts on the part of men to promote structural, social change. More negatively, emotion work has been interpreted as a means of establishing white, middle-class, heterosexually identified men as victims, thereby excusing them from political responsibility altogether, and it has been constructed as a means of recapturing some of white men's lost social status and centrality. All of these elements, to be sure, did surface to different degrees and at different times in some of the groups on which I did research. Still, these readings of emotion work do not capture its complexity or political potential.

What I refer to as "emotion work," of course, is not a simple release of feeling. "Emotion work" refers here, rather, to the practices in which the men I studied primarily engaged—the deliberate adoption of less competitive, less materialistic, and more compassionate and caring ideals, the behavior-modifying practices that were often ritually performed, the repeated attendance at events in which both processes were repeated, and participation in small groups that reaffirmed the changes that were being aimed at. Sociologist Arlie Hochschild has written of the way in which dominant ideals of masculine identity in the United States have involved perpetual and compulsive performance, or "deep acting" in which certain feeling rules such as "don't feel fear, don't feel grief, don't feel sad, remain cool under stress" are repeatedly practiced.[39] It may well require behavior-modifying practices and emotional investigation of the kind that takes place in group emotion work or in private therapy for older men, in particular, to reverse even some of the effects of a "deep acting" that took center stage in distant childhoods.

A POLITICS OF FEELING

Although men in the groups I studied did not comprise a "men's movement," the forty-year repetition of shared concerns in groups that, politically speaking, were widely diverse did seem to have had cultural effect. Indeed, the groups I worked on seemed to have contributed to a shift in consciousness with regard to masculine ideals. By the late 1990s and beyond, a less competitive, less individualistic, more vulnerable and compassionate ideal of masculinity had indeed become more common and acceptable in mainstream culture, as was evidenced in the discourse around masculinity just after 9/11. While gender liberals celebrated the fact that firemen weeping at Ground Zero displayed an "an element of self-sacrifice and tenderness," gender traditionalists tried to cast these 9/11 heroes as representing a return to a tougher, more rugged masculine ideal and as a decided break with the legacy of men's organized efforts to reinvent masculine ideals. The latter efforts were dismissed as "touchy-feeliness" and "the last decade's gender-neutral sex roles."[40]

The production of more compassionate and less selfish masculine ideals also appears to have touched progressive imaginations, creating the conditions of possibility for visions of progressive politics that would boldly insist upon compassion, love, and personal relationships as central to political alliances and to structural social change. The most progressive of these calls, those of the black literary critics bell hooks and Cornell West, of the gay liberation theologian J. Michael Clarke, of the British social critic Anthony Giddens, of the Jewish activist Michael Lerner, and of the Evangelical activist Jim Wallis, would pronounce male self-transformation a necessary, and unavoidable, part of bringing that politics into being. I turn to this politics in chapter 10.

It was also in the context of men's organized efforts to construct more fully human masculine ideals that the United Nations began its ten-year effort to eradicate violence in every form, a project that it launched in the explosive year 2001. It was in this context, some three years earlier, that UNESCO sponsored a conference devoted to masculine ideals and men's practices as seen from the perspective of constructing "a culture of peace." A central question of the conference was how to engage masses of ordinary men in the work of constructing peace-making practices and gender ideals.

It is another, perhaps modest, argument of this book that the subjects of my study, in their organized efforts to refashion masculine ideals, helped bring into being hundreds and thousands of "good hearted," or more caring, men who might potentially be drawn upon for such labors. How men such as these might be tapped for the work of nonviolence, antiracism, antisexism, economic justice, and other forms of progressive social change remains a question, although the Million Man March, cultural nationalisms, the Christian Left, progressive grassroots movements, and NOMAS have all made gestures in just those directions. These efforts seem ever more vital in the context of current efforts to forge a more aggressive, less compassionate, more force-dependent masculine ideal—an ideal unsuited to the production of either peace or justice. I shall return to these themes in chapter 10.

CAUTIONARY NOTES

My focus in this book is on the masculine ideals and performances of male-bodied persons who identified as lifelong men because these groups were bound, to some degree, by similar psychic, social, and cultural constraints. I do not take up the important subjects of female masculinities or of transgendered persons that have been explored elsewhere.[41] Nor do I focus evenly on men in every racial category. When I began this book in the mid 1990s, black men were the most prominent men of color in the Promise Keepers organization, which was the original focus of my research. The literature on the masculinities of black or African-American men was overwhelming, while the now burgeoning literature on Latino and Asian-American masculinities was only beginning to develop.

Studies of the participation of the latter groups in men's organized efforts to invent or transform masculine ideals are crucial to the fullest understanding of this phenomenon. Accounts of Native American masculine ideals from Native points of view are particularly pertinent as well, both in their own right, and as a comment upon the repeated ways in which various groups of largely white men have referenced them as models. Like many worthy subjects of research, however, these histories are beyond the scope of the present book.

Although I make use of psychoanalytic concepts and theories, I do *not* assume that unconscious psychic phenomena are universal and/or determining of one's identity. They are but *one* influence among many—most especially the economic and social circumstances under which we live—on our performance of our own identities. Gender identities are not universal, either, but are constructed differently by different people—and by the same people—in different times. Thus I try consciously to use the plural term "masculine ideals" to signal that there is not one masculine ideal but many. I see attempts to live out all gender ideals, moreover, as continuing projects that we pursue day by day and, in the process, often change.

Having lived with men who were ostensibly supportive of feminism but who did not necessarily behave in feminist ways, I am familiar with the distance between ideal and behavior. I am familiar, indeed, with that distance in myself. Ideals of masculinity are ideals like those of femininity and are "never quite inhabited by any one."[42] I do not assume, therefore, that men's ideals are always lived out or that men's accounts of their actual behaviors are objectively "true." Although I have documented some practices through interviews with wives and through my own participant observation, I am mainly focused here on the relationships among the ideals that men have constructed for themselves and among the behaviors they claim to practice.

Ideals, nonetheless, do matter. As the writer Tim Beneke has also argued, it is in repeatedly attempting to live out an ideal, by, for example, repressing one's desire to cry or to show other soft emotions, swearing, rehearsing toughness, and otherwise "taking it" like a man that ideals of masculinity become male "character," are internalized "in one's body, brain, and nervous system."[43] Because attempting to act out ideals of masculinity is an ongoing project, however, the ideals and practices may be changed or be intervened in at any moment, as men involved in efforts to transform models of manhood would certainly attest. Indeed, the behavior-modifying rituals frequently employed by these networks were designed to intervene on this level of practice in particular.

Because I wanted to produce a book that some of the nonacademic men I studied might also read, I wrote this book with a general audience in mind, at the cost of a good deal of anxiety and revision. ("Face it," one agent told me upon reading an early draft, "this is an academic book.") I have tried since then to put more distance between myself and some of my more mystifying academic habits. This book, moreover, as the reader has discovered, was written from a point of view. Although I have tried to interpret my reading, my interviews, and my participant observation as fairly as I can, the "truth" that I have produced is always situated. My gender, my whiteness, my age, my politics, and my sexual identification, my living in California, and other facets of my personal history constrained what I could and chose to discover, what I gave value to, and what I hoped for in the future. ("Face it," a friend of mine observed, "you're writing about the kinds of [masculine ideals] we long to see.")

My research, which was based on diligent reading, on participant observation, and on interviews when possible, reflects the varied nature of my access to the subjects of my study. As a straight-identified, lower-middle-class girl growing up in Compton, California, I had no known encounters with gay radical networks in the 1950s, and although I supported the Black Panthers and certainly encountered them on an almost daily basis for about two years, during which time I was an English graduate student at UC Berkeley, my relations with them were shyly indirect. I have relied most in these and other chapters about the past on reading texts. My whiteness, my politics, and my profession, however, gave me easy access in the 1990s to participant observation in NOMAS, to interviews with a cluster of fifty-to-sixty-year-old progressive, white academic men, and to acting as "press" and conducting interviews at Promise Keepers events. In these chapters I rely more on participant observation and on interviews. My research, then, is a quilting of different forms of knowledge and includes some appreciative readings of what some might view as unexpected, and, indeed, suspect, texts.

In interviewing men I had originally conceived of myself as "studying up," that is, as studying those with greater social power than I. As with so many facets of my research, however, this did not prove to be the case in quite the way I had imagined. First, as interviewer I had power as She Who Asks the Questions, and with nonacademic men I often had authority for being a professor and a writer—and with men of color of being white, to boot. Even with highly successful white academic men, however, I experienced an unexpected edge as a feminist who intended to use their interviews in my published work. I attempted to offset the distance this produced by engaging in friendly and nonjudgmental exchange, but this set of power dynamics operated to some degree even with academic men who were my friends. As one friend put it, "Even now with you I worry. I worry about what you think."

I began to take for granted that the men I studied would attempt to present themselves in their best light. Given the profeminist, academic, and, with Promise Keepers, the religious nature of many of my subjects, however, being at their best seemed to include a heightened respect for, and willingness to struggle toward, some kind of situated accuracy, or with Promise Keepers, "truth." As I shall suggest throughout this study, my ethnographic experience brought home to me the realization that many feminists, myself included, have not owned up to their influence and authority with respect to feminist-sympathizing men and to the ways in which feminist women have shaped men's response to gender politics. This is not a perspective with which all feminists, by any means, will agree, but I could not speak for all feminists even if I tried.

I am particularly conscious that I write as a woman mature enough to have participated in 1960s politics, and that, to a great degree, this study is shaped by my having belonged to this particular generation. I have lived long enough by now to have moved through a sustained state of anger in the 1960s and early 1970s (not entirely absent in the present day), through witnessing dramatic changes of the kind I never could have dreamed, through seeing movements backwards that have made me weep. I have lived to see white feminist work, first taken as gospel, then rigorously, and rightly, challenged for its rigidities and failures, most particularly with respect to racial privilege and bias. The experience has been humbling and has contributed to what I think of here as taking a long view. This is, then, a partial history, and it takes its place in other histories, also partial. I have struggled to see beyond my limitations—the book is about the unexpected—but inevitably, this is the book of a white, female feminist whose coming of age politically—my second go at being "born again"—was initiated when I was supposed to be studying Renaissance poetry in the graduate reading room at UC Berkeley in 1963. Instead, I was pouring over James Baldwin's "Letter from a Region in My Mind."[44]

NOTES

1. See, for example, Donna Minkowitz, who disguised herself as a sixteen-year-old boy, "In the Name of the Father," *Ms.* (November/December, 1995), 64.

2. Joe Conason, Alfred Ross, and Lee Cokorinos, "The Promise Keepers Are Coming: The Third Wave of the Religious Right," *The Nation*, 7 October 1996, 11; "'Promise Keepers' Declare Spiritual Warfare in Colorado," *Church & State* 46, no. 9 (October 1993): 20.

3. Hans Johnson, "Broken Promise?" *Church & State* (May 1995), 9; Russ Bellant, "Promise Keepers: Christian Soldiers for Theocracy," in *Eyes Right! Challenging the Right Wing Backlash,* ed. Chip Berlet (Boston: South End Press, 1995), 81.

4. Johnson, "Broken Promise?" 10, 11.

5. The conservative ties are certainly there, but, as I suggest in chapter 8, what gets presented in official Promise Keepers settings runs the gamut from conservative to liberal. As I note in chapter 9, Promise Keepers also has ties to liberal and progressive Christian networks.

6. Johnson, "Broken Promise?" 10.

7. Johnson, "Broken Promise?" 12, 11.

8. Sara Diamond, *Facing the Wrath: Confronting the Right in Dangerous Times* (Monroe, Me.: Common Courage Press, 1996), 50.

9. Johnson, "Broken Promise?" 10.

10. Tony Evans, "Spiritual Purity," in *Seven Promises of a Promise Keeper* (Colorado Springs, Colo.: Focus on the Family Publishing, 1994), 79.

11. For work that focuses on the complexity of Promise Keepers, see Minkowitz, "In the Name of the Father," 71; Suzanne Pharr, "A Match Made in Heaven: Lesbian Leftie Chats with a Promise Keeper," *The Progressive* (August 1996): 28–29; Sara Diamond, "The New Man: The Promise Keepers Are on the Road to Stardom," *Z Magazine* (December 1995): 16–18; Michael S. Kimmel, "Promise Keepers: Patriarchy's Second Coming as Masculine Renewal," *tikkun* 12, no. 2 (March/April 1997): 49; Dane S. Claussen, ed. *Standing on the Promises: Promise Keepers and the Revival of Manhood* (Cleveland, Ohio: Pilgrim Press, 1999); Rhys H. Williams, *Promise Keepers and the New Masculinity: Private Lives and Public Morality* (Lanham, Md.: Lexington Books, 2001).

12. Johnson, "Broken Promise?" 9; Conason et al., "The Promise Keepers," 19.

13. See Sara Diamond, "The New Man," 17 (noting that many progressives were loath to recognize Promise Keepers' racial reconciliation theme, preferring "to cast evangelicals as uniformly racist.)

14. "Promise Keepers Poll Results," *Washington Post*, 5 October 1997, A19.

15. See Michael Lerner's *The Politics of Meaning: Restoring Hope and Possibility in an Age of Cynicism* (Reading, Mass.: Addison-Wesley, 1996), 130.

16. Mary Chapman and Glenn Hendler, eds., *Sentimental Men: Masculinity and the Politics of Affect in American Culture* (Berkeley: University of California Press, 1999), 9.

17. Judith Stacey, *Brave New Families: Stories of Domestic Upheaval in Late Twentieth Century America* (New York: Basic Books, 1990), 11, 18, 12.

18. See Clarence Lusane, "To Fight for the People: The Black Panther Party and Black Politics in the 1990s, in *The Black Panther Party (Reconsidered),* ed. Charles E. Jones (Baltimore: Black Classic Press,1998), 443, 446–51; Donna L. Franklin, *Ensuring Inequality: The Structural Transformation of the African-American Family* (New York: Oxford University Press, 1997), 182, 188, 192–207.

19. See Toni Cade [Bambara], *The Black Woman: An Anthology* (New York: Signet, 1970); Beverly Guy-Sheftal, ed., *Words of Fire: An Anthology of African-American Feminist Thought* (New York: The New Press), 1995; Johnnetta Betsch Cole and Beverly Guy-Sheftall, *Gender Talk: The Struggle for Equality in African American Communities* (New York: Ballantine Books, 2003).

20. Barbara Ehrenreich, *The Hearts of Men: American Dreams and the Flight from Commitment* (Garden City, N.Y.: Anchor Books, 1983), 13.

21. Ehrenreich, *The Hearts of Men*, 170, 171, 172. Ehrenreich quotes Deirdre English, "The War against Choices," *Mother Jones* (Feb/March 1981): 6, on men winning their freedom first.

22. Susan Faludi, *Stiffed: The Betrayal of the American Man* (New York: Morrow, 1999), 595, 596, 598.

23. Faludi, *Stiffed*, 604, 605, 603, 606.

24. Sally Robinson, *Marked Men: White Masculinity in Crisis* (New York: Columbia University Press, 2000), 2–4.

25. Lynne Segal, *Slow Motion: Changing Masculinities, Changing Men* (London: Virago, 1990); R. W. Connell, "Long and Winding Road; An Outsider's View of U.S. Masculinity and Feminism," in *Masculinity Studies & Feminist Theory: New Directions*, ed. Judith Kegan Gardiner (New York: Columbia University Press, 2002).

26. Michael A. Messner, *Politics of Masculinities: Men in Movements* (Thousand Oaks, Calif.: Sage Publications, 1997), 12, 13. See also Kenneth Clatterbaugh, *Contemporary Perspectives on Masculinity: Men, Women, and Politics in Modern Society,* 2nd. ed. (Boulder, Colo.: Westview Press, 1997). For work on black men, see Joseph L. White and James H. Cones III, *Black Man Emerging: Facing the Past and Seizing a Future in America* (New York: Routledge, 1999), and anthologies: Devon Carbado, *Black Men on Race, Gender, and Sexuality: A Critical Reader* (New York: New York University Press, 1999); Darlene Clark Hinc and Earnestine Jenkins, eds., *A Question of Manhood: A Reader in U.S. Black Men's History and Masculinity*, vol. 1 (Bloomington: Indiana University Press, 1999); Rudolph P. Byrd and Beverly Guy-Sheftall, eds., *Traps: African American Men on Gender and Sexuality* (Bloomington: Indiana University Press, 2001); and Maurice O. Wallace, *Constructing the Black Masculine: Identity and Ideality in African American' Men's Literature and Culture, 1775–1995* (Durham, N.C.: Duke University Press, 2002).

27. The terms are R. W. Connell's in *The Men and the Boys* (Berkeley: University of California Press, 2000), 30–31.

28. See, for example, Chapman and Hendler, eds., *Sentimental Men,* 12, 9, 11.

29. Victor J. Seidler, *Recreating Sexual Politics: Men, Feminism and Politics* (New York: Routledge, 1991), xv.

30. Seidler, *Recreating Sexual Politics*, 172.

31. *The Random House Dictionary* (New York: Random House, 1978), 779.

32. See Michael Schwalbe on the use of similar rituals in mythopoetic men's groups, *Unlocking the Iron Cage: The Men's Movement, Gender, Politics, and American Culture* (New York: Oxford, 1996), 82–96.

33. Linzi Murrie, *Feminism as 'Men's Business': The Possibilities and Limitations of Profeminist Politics in Men against Sexual Assault."* diss., University of Queensland, August 2002, 33.

34. Lynne Segal, *Slow Motion*, 309.

35. Seidler, *Recreating Sexual Politics*, 21.

36. Anthony Giddens, *Beyond Left and Right: The Future of Radical Politics* (Cambridge, England: Polity Press, 1994), 195.

37. Seidler, *Recreating Sexual Politics*, 235.

38. Seidler, *Recreating Sexual Politics*, 20.

39. Arlie Hochschild, *The Managed Heart: Commercialization of Human Feeling* (Berkeley: University of California Press, 1983), 24.

40. Patricia Leigh Brown, "Heavy Lifting Required: The Return of Manly Men," *New York Times,* 26 October 2001: 5.

41. See, for example, Judith Halberstam, *Female Masculinity* (Durham, N.C.: Duke University Press, 1998); Dawn Atkins, ed., *Looking Queer: Body Image and Identity in Lesbian, Bisexual, Gay, and Transgender Communities* (New York: Haworth Press, 1998).

42. Judith Butler, "Melancholy Gender/Refused Identification," in *Constructing Masculinity*, ed. Maurice Berger, Brian Wallis, and Simon Watson (New York: Routledge, 1995), 32.

43. Timothy Beneke, *Proving Manhood: Reflections on Men and Sexism* (Berkeley: University of California Press, 1997), 41–43, 66.

44. James Baldwin, "Letter from a Region in My Mind," *New Yorker*, 17 November 1962.

1

Men, Masculinity, and Mourning on the Mall

National Manhood and Male Romance

> What matters now is what ordinary men do with their feelings of grief, of outrage, of affection for each other, and of longing for lives richer in meaning. My hope is that men will channel these feelings toward riskier social action and farther-reaching change.
>
> —Michael Schwalbe, *Unlocking the Iron Cage*[1]

The latter days of the twentieth century witnessed two remarkable mass meetings of men on the National Mall in Washington, D.C., each involving an estimated seven hundred thousand to one and a half million participants and each, despite pointed differences in constituencies and agendas, enacting rituals of tears and atonement with regard to men's neglect, abandonment, and abuse of women and children. The October 16, 1995, Million Man March, defined as a "day of atonement, reconciliation, and responsibility," featured a long line of speakers, from very different political perspectives, urging black men throughout the day to stop making excuses, to "straighten their backs," to be responsible husbands and fathers, to atone for misusing women, children, and each other, and, in the words of the poet Maya Angelou, to engage in the "love" work of practicing "courtesy in the bedroom, gentleness in the kitchen, and care in the nursery."

Two years later, at the Promise Keepers Stand in the Gap Assembly, also in Washington, Bruce Fong and Isaac Canales, an Asian-American and a Latino seminarian professor, respectively, called upon participants to take out pictures of family members whom they had wronged and to "admit mistakes"— to confess, atone, and ask forgiveness for abuse, selfishness, spiritual and psychological absence, pushing children away, letting wives take responsibility for children, and for sacrificing family on the "altar of machismo," greed,

27

and pleasure. A final speaker, the African-American minister Tony Evans, urged participants to assume "a second job" of doing dishes, caring for children, and working on the (marriage) relationship: "You come home to dry the dishes as she wants you to. You come home to get the kids ready for bed." The "language of marriage," he cautioned, may take a lifetime to learn.

As I watched the Million Man March, with its close-ups of serious-looking men, their eyes turned upward to children who took the podium one by one and two by two, to call for their "protection," "clean devotion," and "unconditional love, and as I attended the Stand in the Gap Assembly, where a sea of men knelt or lay prostrate in the pleasant October sun, family pictures before them, crying with remorse, I could not help thinking both of the changes that feminists had once hoped for from men and of the fact that no feminist I know of had ever imagined gatherings such as these! Over a million and a half men admitting to faults at the nation's capital? Truly contrite men asking women's forgiveness, a short walk from the White House? Men, in the shadow of the Houses of Congress, dedicating themselves to a "second job" of child care, dishes, and working on relationships? It seemed an almost hallucinatory end to a decade marked by an historical outpouring of dialogue on "new" masculinities, manhood, and men.

These epic assemblies, of course, gathering hundreds of thousands of men to the nation's seat, could not help evoking traditional associations between citizen, nation, and manhood, with all the gender inequality that these associations have historically implied. Because both gatherings were staged on men's behalf, because they took place at the nation's capital, and because media coverage featured multiple long shots of the overwhelmingly male crowds that filled the National Mall, both events did tend at times to render women invisible as citizens. This was particularly true of the Promise Keepers Stand in the Gap Assembly, at which references to "church," "community," "nation," and "leaders" often focused, unreflectingly, on males, and at which Bill McCartney, then president of the organization, spoke only of "men" advancing the "kingdom of God," sharing the burdens of "community," and "sweeping the nations."

At the Million Man March, in contrast, many speakers addressed the gathering as "brothers *and* sisters," invited women and daughters to participate in political struggle, and made reference to the sacrifices of men and women both on behalf of their communities. Most of the eight women who spoke in the "Affirmation of Our Brothers" segment of the proceedings were emphatic about women's contributions to public and private life. Dr. Betty Shabazz, widow of the Muslim leader Malcolm X, maintained that "women do most of the world's work." Dorothy Height, leader of the National Council of Negro women, observed that "African-American women seldom do what they want but always what they have to do" and called for "strong partnership" between women and men. Attorney Faye Williams, one of the Washington, D.C., co-ordinators of the march, remarked that women "hold up the sky" but that the task would be easier with black men and women working "side by side in harmony."

While black men were exhorted by cultural nationalist professor Maulana Karenga to practice "more egalitarian" familial relations and to "atone" for sexism as well, Jesse Jackson referred to a rising tide of "race justice, gender equality, and feminist ability" and called for a movement of men and women to battle the "sin" of racism and of sexism both. But the massive numbers of men and stray allusions, largely by Nation of Islam spokesmen, to men as "heads of house" and "God's representatives on earth," as well as the unquestioned equation of citizenship with the maintenance of traditional heterosexual relations, diluted the more utopian elements of the day with bracing reminders of how often progressive gestures made by men, and movements led by them, have held on to gender and sexual inequalities.

Both events, nonetheless, despite their man-as-citizen rhetoric and effects and despite their exclusion of gay men as subjects of address, gave male citizenry a partially forward-looking cast. Both assemblies presented male citizens not just as sensitive new men, as men who feel, but, more importantly, as men who feel regret about their mistreatment of women, children, and each other and who pledge themselves to act more compassionately, more responsibly, and, at times, more justly in the future. At the Stand in the Gap Assembly, for example, men were urged to extend their capacity for "admitting mistakes," apologizing, and asking forgiveness, so dramatically displayed with respect to family members earlier in the day, to their racism and racial bitterness toward each other. Thus, the African-American pastor, A. R. Bernard, urged the massive gathering of men to drop to their knees once more and to ask God for help in ridding themselves of the "disease" of racism and racial bitterness, while Raleigh Washington, Promise Keepers' African-American Vice President of Reconciliation, challenged each individual to engage in the "love work" of building at least one "committed relation" to a man of another race as part of a larger strategy for "changing the face of the Church overnight."

At the Million Man March exhortations to action were more overtly political, as speakers like Ron Sailor of the NAACP youth organization and Representative Donald Payne called on black "prodigal sons" to "go home" not only to individual and familial relations but also to the homeless and the poor, to local school boards, to voting booths, and to antiracist and antisexist political organizations. Both events, moreover, in linking an improvement in men's personal behavior toward women, children, and each other with their public identity as citizens, attempted to regenerate the personal as a basis for a more public social and political, thereby promoting something more than a sentimental politics of getting men to cry in public.

For the same two days, male citizens were also imagined as something more than white and middle class. The Million Man March, as might be expected, affirmed the identification of its participants with a black "nation" while also laying claim to first-class citizenship for black men, including poor black men, within the U.S. nation as a whole. "This capital belongs to each of you," Congressman Charles Rangel assured the crowd. The overwhelmingly white Promise Keepers gathering, moreover, with its mixed-race speakers, its 14 percent African-American attendance, its lengthy session on antiracism, and its exhortations to enter into committed cross-race relationships, challenged the historical association of *citizen* with the white and the middle class as well.

These mass gatherings at the nation's capital, indeed, with their mixture of prayer, politics, and love, brought to mind an earlier assembly that I had listened to but not attended— the 1963 March on Washington during which Martin Luther's King Jr.'s "I have a dream" speech prompted men and women both to tears and to a deepening involvement in issues of racial and economic equality. Several speakers at the Million Man March, moreover, and at the Stand in the Gap Assembly—as well as media coverage of both events—directly invoked King's memory, the memory of the civil rights movement, and the memory of the 1960s as a whole. ("This is how the sixties should have been!" one Promise Keeper exclaimed to me.) At the Million Man March, for example, the year 1963 was frequently recalled both for purposes of inspiration and as a challenging reminder that King's dreams had never been fulfilled. Thus, Pastor Henry Hardy, drawing upon the memory of Dr. King, enjoined black men to "rise up, rise up, rise up and soar, and soar, and soar," while Congressman Kweisi Mfume reminded the crowd that two hundred years after the nation's founding and thirty-two years since the March on Washington, "racial justice is receding" and "economic justice is denied."

At the Stand in the Gap Assembly, by the same token, Raleigh Washington echoed Martin Luther King by proclaiming "I have a *new* dream," a dream of "oneness," while A. R. Bernard recalled King's bitter disappointment at the many white Christian ministers who maintained a studied silence about racial justice "behind stained glass": "those that he thought would be his strongest allies, the Christian church, they became his greatest opponents." King brought the nation under "the conviction of racism," Bernard continued, but a generation later Christians must still repent, not just the sins of "omission" but those of "commission" as well. That the March on Washington of 1963, staged in the name of far-reaching social change, appeared to haunt these latter day gatherings on masculinity and men only contributed to the giddy experience of feeling, however momentarily, and with whatever contradictions, that masculine reform, in relation to the mistreatment of women, children, and other men, had, for once, been raised to the level of a national moral and political priority.[2]

FEMINIST ENCOUNTERS WITH MALE ROMANCE

Although the Million Man March and the Stand in the Gap Assembly challenged their participants to become less selfish, more nurturing, and more socially responsible to women, children, and each other, and though the Million Man March did call for structural social change with respect to race and, at times, gender as well, both events were met with feminist suspicion, and at times, with feminist alarm. Some black women, for example, supported the Million Man March, but many also worried that "the role African American women are given in this march is to tend the bake sale, raise the money or stay at home and take care of the children." Others feared that the bravado of an all-male march might drown out meaningful dialogue between women and men.[3] Two years later the National Organization for Women (NOW) vigorously protested Promise Keepers' Stand in the Gap Assembly by carrying "Patriarch Keeper" signs, shouting "Ominous!" Dangerous!" and "Patriarchal!" a few blocks away, and denouncing the Promise Keepers organization as a dangerous "stealth male supremacist group" quietly building a mass movement in the United States.

It was, in part, the leadership of these events that prompted understandable feminist concern. Louis Farrakhan, convener of the Million Man March, and Bill McCartney, founder and president of Promise Keepers, were both firmly associated with antigay positions and activities and with gender conservatism. In part, however, it was also the very form of the gatherings that provoked unease, for both assemblies of men embodied elements of what I have called "male romance," a sometimes actual, and often fictionalized, phenomenon that involves men going off with other men, ritually bonding with each other, and being "reborn" within a community of males.[4]

Both gatherings on the mall, for example, involved men going off with other men and leaving women, for the most part, behind. This was an element of male romance that Spike Lee took some trouble to foreground and defend in *Get on the Bus*, his 1996 road film about black men journeying to the Million Man March. As Lee registered in this film, men "getting on the bus" with other men is in itself enough to make many women pause. When getting on the bus, moreover, leads to male-only rituals of bonding and of being born again in each other's presence, it can lead to the troubling impression not only that men are consolidating gender privilege but that women are being decentered, emotionally and politically, from men's lives. Masses of men at both assemblies on the mall, for example, held hands, embraced, prayed together, shared feelings with each other, and, at the end of the Million Man March, repeated the words, "I love you. I'm sorry," to the men nearby. Speakers at both gatherings exhorted participants to be reborn symbolically within a community of men: "You can rise up. You can walk in the newness of life," Pastor Hardy assured the Million Man March while Bill McCartney called on Promise Keepers participants to be "a brotherhood of believers" who were "born again."[5]

The language of these particular exhortations, moreover, may have seemed benign, but male romance, whether purely imaginary or concretely enacted, had so often functioned to affirm men's privilege with respect to women and had so often served to justify women's exclusion from social, political, and economic power—as in some nineteenth-century fraternal organizations, for example—that even the preponderance of tears and repentance during these two days on the mall failed to allay many forms of feminist mistrust. The latter included the perception that masses of men on the National Mall constituted a symbolic claim on the capital itself, the fear that men's mourning signaled little more than a softer expression of male domination, and the half-joking suspicion, in the words of the cartoon character Cathy, that "when men change it's into something worse." Thus, the *New York Times* columnist Maureen Dowd assured her readers: "Don't get me wrong. I'm not at all alarmed, as Patricia Ireland of NOW is, that the Promise Keepers will force women into submission. It's way too late for that. I'm just tired of men exploring their fragilities. It usually leads to trouble."[6]

"NATIONAL MANHOOD" AND WHITE MALE ROMANCE

Actual and purely fantasized versions of male romance—involving separation from women, ritual bonding with other men, and the promise of being transformed or renewed in each other's presence—are easy to come by in U.S. history. Elements of male romance have shaped the formation of the state, fraternal brotherhoods, street gangs, boys' clubs, gay circuit parties, and heterosexual weekends or evenings with the guys. Elements of male romance, moreover, have appeared in dozens of American novels and Hollywood films. One has only to think here of Huck Finn and the escaped slave Jim running away together to drift "down the big, still [Mississippi] river, laying on our backs looking up at the stars," or of Burt Reynolds, Jon Voigt, Ned Beatty, and Ronny Cox as four Atlanta businessmen momentarily buoyant and bonded after navigating the first set of rapids on the Cahulawasse River in the 1972 film *Deliverance* (just before this particular male romance goes bad). According to some scholars of masculinity, indeed, various forms of purely fictive and concretely realized male romance have played a central role in U.S. history, where they have functioned to help produce and sustain dominant ideals of masculinity that were based on the implicit belief that economic, gender, sex, and race privilege constituted true manhood for white, property-owning men and that the latter represented the U.S. nation as a whole.

The cultural critic Dana Nelson, for example, argued in *National Manhood: Capitalist Citizenship and the Imagined Fraternity of White Men* that the proponents of the as yet unratified U.S. Constitution, which called for a strong central government rather than direct, face-to-face democracy, implicitly offered white, property-owning, heterosexual men a form of "bribe." Nelson traced the outlines of this "bribe" in the arguments of the Federalist Papers, the collective title for the eighty-five essays, mainly written by Alexander Hamilton, James Madison, and John Jay, that were published in New York newspapers between 1797 and 1788 as a strategy for persuading New Yorkers to support ratification of the Constitution.[7] This bribe involved a fantasy form of what I call male romance.

The Federalist Papers, according to Nelson, invited white, propertied men who were willing to be ruled by a strong central government to imagine themselves as members of a fictional brotherhood that would represent the nation as a whole. Those entering into this brotherhood would be free to devote themselves to economic self-advance, just as the nation devoted itself to gaining territory. At the same time members of this brotherhood would enjoy an imagined unity with other men that promised to offset the competitive relations of the market. Participation in this fictive brotherhood would also bestow upon its members a newly "vigorous, strong, undivided manhood."[8]

Each man would enact this manhood ideal by managing or exercising control over his own passions, his household, and disorderly "others" such as white women, men and women of color, and national "foreigners." This individual practice of management, in turn, would prepare men for further civic duties such as managing the terms on which the rest of the world would relate to the nation itself.[9] Unequal powers and privileges, therefore, were written into an ideal of (white, property-owning) masculine "character" that was often assumed to be bestowed by nature or assigned by God.

This privileged model of masculinity, however, which Nelson refers to as "national manhood," was impossible to perform. White, propertied men were unable to stand for the "Good of the Whole," and in accepting the bribe of imaginatively locating themselves within this "privileged spot" they foreclosed a whole range of human connections—with women, blacks, Native Americans and foreign "others"—that would come back to haunt them.[10] The fantasied unity of brotherhood, moreover, could not really protect men from the competitive rigors of the real world market. Thus, the imaginary possession of national manhood required continual forms of reaffirmation or proof.

In the nineteenth century, in particular, according to Nelson, white men's social space began to rely on "rituals" that would perform this reaffirming function. These rituals might be informal—jokes and complaints about women being "key" activities at men's dinners and clubs—or they might take a more formal shape in the "extraordinarily elaborate and explosively popular secret ceremonies and rites" of fraternal orders.[11] These orders, though replete with fantasy, constituted concretely realized forms of male romance that functioned, by and large, to provide a form of escape from, and preparation for, attempts to live out this self-achieving, nation-representing, unequally privileged ideal.

MALE ROMANCE AND "THE SELF-MADE MAN"

Michael Kimmel traced a related set of masculine ideals that he referred to as those of "the Self-Made Man." The values of the self-making masculine ideal, according to Kimmel in *Manhood in America*, came into real prominence with further shifts from an agrarian to an industrial economy in the early to mid nineteenth century. Manhood was "no longer fixed in land or small-scale property ownership or dutiful service" but was increasingly located instead in individual achievement, success in the market, mobility, and wealth. If the nation represented "political autonomy," the ideal of self-making masculinity embodied "economic autonomy," an autonomy that must be continually earned and re-earned in the uncertain and competitive arena of the market.[12] Values on which a competitive, capitalist economy depended, therefore, became identified with ideals of manhood that were then seen as natural. Men's deep-seated desire to be identified as men, a privileged category with respect to women, and their need to survive in a competitive economic system fueled their identification with the ideals and behaviors that sustained the system itself.

According to Kimmel, however, most men's attempts to perform a self-making masculine ideal were "less about the drive for domination" and more about the fear of being dominated or controlled by others. Anxiety, restlessness, and loneliness were implicit in attempts to live out this ideal.[13] White, middle-class men, moreover, who aspired to live out this ideal had two basic choices: they might stay put and compete or they might try to escape the rigors of the marketplace and begin over again in the company of other men. If they stayed, they usually tried to "stack the decks in their favor" by defining themselves as superior to women and to other men— men of color and working class or immigrant males—and by struggling to exclude these "others" from economic and social power. The second strategy—escape—often meant leaving for some uncharted territory, in the mid-nineteenth century, perhaps, the actual frontier. There, in concretely enacted versions of male romance, men might try to "make themselves all over again" and to prove themselves anew with other men.[14]

When white, middle-class men took off for uncharted territory, however, they did not seek to escape the pressures of the marketplace alone; they also ran way from women. A major factor in what Kimmel saw as white men's repeated efforts to go off with other men and to leave domesticated women, like wives and aunts, behind, were the increasing divisions between white, middle-class, heterosexual men and women's lives. Industrialization, in having separated much of men's work from the home, had ushered in the ideal and reality of "separate spheres," and as men's work was disassociated from the home and from the rhythms of family life, white, middle-class husbands ceded to their women increasing domestic authority and responsibility. The white, middle-class home became the domain of wives. Mothers edged out fathers as primary parents, becoming specialists in love, and home itself became an emblem of what were now seen as specifically feminine habits of the heart—love and sacrifice rather than aggression and self-interest. Emotional expressivity and noneconomic relations of love and nurturing were often squeezed to the margins of men's social lives.[15] Some men, finding the home place dominated by values and emotional registers now linked with women, took off for less female-identified spaces.

This emphasis on the suppression of feeling in dominant masculine ideals, although it certainly captures familiar elements of masculine performance, past and present, can also mask the history of male emotionalism in the United States. *Manhood in America* itself, for example, acknowledged that the newly feminized white, middle-class home also served men as a "balm to soothe men from the roughness of the workday" and that social movements such as abolition involved men in alternative visions of American manhood that emphasized "inclusion and self-expression." *Manhood in America* also recognized that some literature about male bonding and homosocial intimacies did not involve fantasies of escape from women.[16] More recent work on the emotional history of U.S. men, moreover, identifies a virtual "cult of sentiment" among men that was expressed in abolitionist rhetoric, appeals for philanthropy, temperance testimonies, literature and advice manuals, and even in the world of commerce.[17] Although this male emotionalism could be evoked both to challenge and reaffirm men's power over subordinated others, it also constituted an alternative set of ideals for masculinity on which later efforts to humanize masculine ideals might draw.

THE GOLDEN AGE OF MALE ROMANCE

Nelson and Kimmel both suggest that unsettling social transformations might provoke widespread "crises" over attempts to live out the ideals of self-making masculinity and the struggle to live up to the larger ideal of national manhood, with its identification of white man with the nation itself. These crises then produced fresh waves of longing to begin again. At the end of the nineteenth century, for example, increasing industrialization, the women's movement, the entrance of white, middle-class women into the public sphere along with newly freed black men and women, an influx of immigrants, and the closing of the frontier all led many white men to feel that the traditional foundations of their manhood were uncertain: "Such a large-scale loss of control as a civil war, the new political and social claims of women and freed blacks, and failed attempts at escape all signaled the inadequacy of the various strategies [white] American men had developed upon which to ground a secure sense of themselves as men."[18] This sense of uneasiness with respect to white manhood prompted a swell of membership in fraternal organizations where largely white, middle-class men sought to make themselves anew.

At the turn of the century an estimated five and a half million men out of a total adult male population of about nineteen million belonged to largely white, fraternal orders such as the Odd Fellows, the Freemasons, the Knights of Pythias, and the Red Men. More than one scholar has deemed the late nineteenth century "'The Golden Age of Fraternity'" or one might say the Golden Age of Male Romance.[19] What characterized many white, middle-class fraternities, according to the historian Mark Carnes, was the gathering of men away from women and the performance of an "emotionally charged psychodrama" in which the initiate was brought through the "stages of childhood" and encountered ritual threats from lodge members playing the role of elderly patriarchs. The initiate might also endure a symbolic near-death experience, complete a successful quest for approval by surrogate father figures, and be ultimately surrounded by "brothers" who would lavish the "utmost affection and kindness" upon him and welcome him into a new family consisting of men.[20]

The intent of these rituals, according to Carnes, was not "to reform the initiate but to remake him entirely" and to offer him a "secondary male identity" that would enable him to approach the enactment of manhood ideals with "greater self-assurance."[21] In the 1860s, for example, the order of Red Men featured an initiation ritual in which the prospective member was momentarily reduced to the status of a mere "pale face" or "squaw" and required to pad around the lodge in moccasins, following the guidance of a lodge member acting the part of "scout." In the meantime other lodge members, playing "Red Men of the forest," threatened to torture and burn him and ultimately tied him to a stake. A "prophet" then saved the initiate from the threat of death and the latter was lectured to, given an eagle feather as proof of his courage, and finally adopted into the "bosom" of the fold.[22]

Another function of these rituals, according to Carnes, was that they offered white, middle-class men "solace" from the rigors of the market. Fraternal organizations, that is, allowed men to enter an alternative or "liminal" world of ritual and secret symbols that expressed partial opposition to existing social rules for men by, for example, espousing the value of noncompetitive and collective community.[23] Some fraternal organizations, according to Kimmel, even prompted participants to express "feminine emotions like compassion, nurturance, and charity," forms of expression that might also be ascribed to an earlier and purer tribe.[24] Nelson suggests that such rituals allowed white, middle-class men momentarily to connect with idealized images of the feminine and of Native American men and thereby with those "others" whom national manhood excluded.[25]

Ultimately, however, any "solace" that fraternal organizations might have offered, according to Carnes and Nelson both, functioned in the main to ensure the survival of the status quo. White, middle-class fraternal organizations did not officially promote structural social transformation, but, rather, offered men a sense of heightened power and confidence about living out self-making ideals. According to Nelson, the rituals of such organizations also incorporated and affirmed the naturalness of hierarchy by enacting hierarchical relations between the initiated and the uninitiated and between imaginary "fathers" and their "sons." This, in turn, helped to naturalize hierarchies of race, class, and gender in the world outside.[26]

Nelson also argues that the affirmation of hierarchy within fraternal brotherhoods functioned to identify the love between men, which such fraternal organizations encouraged, as something different from what was increasingly perceived to be the social disorder represented by homosexuality. According to the historian George Chauncey, a gay male subculture had become visible in working-class neighborhoods of New York by the 1890s. The association of homosexuality with working-class districts, Nelson maintained, contributed to its being linked with middle-class fears of the "depravity" of the working class itself.[27]

At the same time that fraternal organizations allowed white, middle-class men to enact "feminine" emotions, however, they also provided "elaborate sequences of initiation rituals" in which boys raised in father-absent Victorian homes "effaced the religious values and emotional ties associated with women" while undergoing a species of rebirth at the hands of men. Such rituals, according to Carnes, affirmed "that while woman gave birth to man's body," male-controlled initiation "gave birth to his soul."[28] All in all, Nelson concluded, if fraternal rituals allowed white, middle-class, ostensibly heterosexual men to experience symbolic connection to the feminine and to nonwhite men and emotional closeness to each other, connections which the ideal of national manhood called upon them to suppress, the ritual activity itself allowed members to experience a sense of acting in unity as white, relatively privileged men. To Nelson, indeed, the experience of fraternal rituals provided a kind of "narcotic" for the conflict men faced outside the lodges.[29]

BLACK MEN, NATIONAL MANHOOD, AND MALE ROMANCE

The identification of men with nation, however, and with self-making values, along with participation in male romance, was not the province of white, middle-class, heterosexual men alone. From the late nineteenth century forward, representing the nation, controlling women and various unruly others, pursuing self-interest and economic self-advance not only constituted the most dominant ideals of what it meant to be a "man" in U.S. terms, but also defined dominant notions of "the citizen" and of the "American" as well. Marginalized men, therefore, such as male members of the white working class, enfranchised black men, and immigrant men sought full status as citizens and as Americans by aspiring to self-making masculine ideals, despite the tremendous barriers that racism, xenophobia, and poverty presented. According to the sociologist Mary Ann Clawson, for example, white working-class men participated in fraternal orders that "exerted a special appeal to any one seeking to establish or reaffirm a symbolic relationship to the figure of the producer and proprietor."[30] I will focus here on some of the ways in which black men have related to these ideals and practices.

After Emancipation, according to the sociologist Donna Franklin, freed black men were also anxious to take on dominant understandings of what it meant to be a citizen and a "man," and by 1867 some black men were able to enact the role of citizen. Black men, but not black women, for example, could hold office, serve on juries, vote, and take leadership positions in the Republican party. This division promoted the identification of black men as representatives of the black community, though hardly of the nation as a whole.

Black male citizens were also encouraged to assert their position as heads of families. Thus the National Negro Convention of 1855 declared, in significantly gendered terms, that "as a people, we have been denied the ownership of our bodies, our wives, home, children, and the products of our own labor."[31] The Freedman's Bureau, moreover, which was created in 1866 to help freemen make the shift from slavery to freedom, officially designated black men as head of households, granted them the right to sign contracts for their family's labor, and set women's wages lower than those for men. Although many black women were eager to stay home and tend to their children, some also protested the new forms of control that black men were awarded over the labor of their female relatives.[32]

Racism and white agricultural interests, nonetheless, did much to counter the attempts of black men to live out the ideals of self-making masculinity, let alone the ideal of representing the nation as a whole. Since the white-dominated agricultural economy, benefited from a large pool of laborers, the Freedman's Bureau actively encouraged men to persuade their wives to work. The sharecropping/tenant farmer system kept black families in constant debt, often making the labor of women and children crucial to the family's survival. By the end of the nineteenth century, moreover, 80 percent of all black families were living in the south in rural areas and nine-tenths of those were tenants, sharecroppers, or contract laborers. For many black men, therefore, nation-representing, self-making status was beyond reach.[33]

For a small number of black men, however, fraternal organizations, much like those which white men sought, offered opportunities to consolidate a more self-confident masculine identity in the face of stressful self-making efforts and in the face of black men's exclusion from representing the nation at all. In 1775 some fourteen free men, led by the War of Independence veteran, Prince Hall, founded their own blacks-only Masonic lodge (ultimately chartered in 1784 by British but not by white American Freemasons).[34] By 1865 fourteen states had Prince Hall Lodges, and by the 1890s W. E. B. Dubois reported that there were nineteen such lodges in Philadelphia alone. Both Booker T. Washington and Marcus Garvey had Masonic ties.[35]

According to the literary critic Maurice O. Wallace, white American Freemasonry celebrated the figure of the artisan, who personified the values of "muscular labor, capitalist productivity, economic independence, and masculine self-sufficiency." In Prince Hall Freemasonry, black men — who shared a long history of labor — were ritualistically transformed into "symbolic artisans, and thus members of the masculine body politic." Prince Hall Freemasonry, indeed, reflected the "extraordinary aptitude of African-American craftsmen, slave and free," to turn labor on behalf of their employers into training and profit for themselves, thereby transforming "the perfunctory, labor-intensive practices of everyday black life into self-affirming, self-expressive exercises of freedom and identity."[36]

Prince Hall Freemasonry achieved these goals in part by symbolically applying architectural principles to "the construction of male subjects." The ideal lodge, for example, was built at some distance from other buildings, had "lofty" walls to isolate it, was characterized by both a public (outer) and private (inner) door, and was linked symbolically to both male and female principles (sun and universe). Described as "one enduring and connected mass," the lodge represented a secret, cohesive masculine black self. Within its walls, moreover, black initiates were said to be "'born again' into the light of Masonic truth."[37] Barring women, Prince Hall Freemasonry also "'enacted 'a compensatory male response to [an ostensibly] threatening female productivity'" by making "real" men out of those whom slavery had made "in a manner of speaking, mama's boys."[38]

A CONTEMPORARY FORM OF BLACK MALE ROMANCE

Like white male romance, black male romance was not a product of the nineteenth century alone nor was it the exclusive province of middle-class men. Contemporary working and lower-class men have also created forms of male romance that imitated and posed alternatives to the ideal of the nation-representing, self-making man, while also expressing rebellion against the ways in which white, elite and middle-class men had stacked the deck against them. As in nineteenth-century, middle-class, fraternal organizations, the content of these ideals was largely determined by male peers: "A man must be considered a man among his peers, and therefore he must achieve this status through the rules established in the environment around him."[39]

To give an example that will be especially pertinent to the groups I studied, I will turn for a moment to the 1994 autobiography *Makes Me Wanna Holler.* In this work the *Washington Post* journalist Nathan McCall described the role of a version of male romance—involving separation from women, male bonding, and ritualized identification with a "secondary" masculine ideal—in his own life as an adolescent in a black working-class neighborhood in Portsmouth, Virginia, in the 1960s. (A version of this masculine ideal was to be recast by the Black Panther Party in the late 1960s, as I suggest in chapter 2.) The standards for this masculine ideal, according to McCall, were set by older boys, the "slick" dudes who "ran the school and hung in the streets," the most powerful of whom was Scobie-D: "Scobie-D stood out from the other hoods because he was super-baad, meaning he took flak from no man, white or black." McCall frequently describes his own and Scobie-D's "baad," street masculinity as a response to the racism that made black men's efforts to support their families and/or themselves exercises in humiliation and despair.[40]

McCall consolidated this masculine ideal through being part of an all-male group or brotherhood—"everywhere we went we traveled in packs of seven to fifteen boys"—and through obtaining the approbation of his own group and that of others. This masculine ideal was partially enacted through mastering elements of style, such as "jonin" the stylized and creative "putting down of others"; the "pimp," "a proud, defiant bouncy stride"; and "gettin' clean" or dressing hip. As in nineteenth-century fraternal organizations, trying to achieve this ideal involved risk and threat, but this time it was real risk and real threat rather than a fantasy enactment of them. Stealing, for example, became a "hanging rite, a challenge to take something from somebody else and get away clean."[41]

Fighting, to emphasize self respect and power, was also key, its importance being particularly enhanced by the blatant racism of the 1960s, and near-death experiences were common. Taking these risks was one sign of having performed a "higher," or in this case tougher, masculine ideal. Unfortunately, however, the imaginative possession of the qualities identified with this ideal of manhood required continual reaffirmation or "proof." After a serious fight at the bus stop, for example, Nate considered asking his mother to drive him to school "but I couldn't bring myself to do it. How could I turn punk after having been so baad before? How could I face all the people I'd tried to impress at the bus stop the previous week? I *had* to go."[42]

Although the all-male group did encourage boys to bond emotionally with each other, it also required suppression of anything identified as "feminine," such as emotions like love and grief. Separation from and devaluation of women also played a central role. Getting sex from women "without giving love" and participating in gang rapes or "trains" left McCall feeling "sick and unclean" at first but both ultimately consolidated a sense of having acted according to a tougher and more powerful masculine ideal: "It was a macho thing. Using a member of one of the most vulnerable groups of human beings on the face of the earth—black females—it was another way for a guy to show the other fellas how cold and hard he was."[43]

Although McCall's cool, street masculinity implied a rejection of traditional self-making masculine ideals, it also incorporated elements of the tough, individualistic, and economically oriented values associated with them. On the one hand, McCall's attempts to enact a baad masculine ideal offset his humiliating efforts to work his way up in a racist culture. On the other hand, McCall's experiments with the underground economy of "hustling"— in this case alternately stealing and selling drugs—functioned as the "black urban answer to capitalism."[44] This model of black, working-class, street masculinity may have expressed rebellion against racism and the barriers it posed, but structural, social transformation was not its central project. I will return to this ideal in chapter 2.

MULTIPLICITIES: THE MANY FORMS OF MALE ROMANCE

Although feminists have been known, half-jokingly, to pronounce that "men in men's groups are men in bad company," what I am calling male romance cannot be written off historically as a mere vehicle for reproducing male dominance, promoting separation from and/or mistreatment of women, or prompting foolish behavior on the part of men. The cultural meanings of male romance seem to have been far more complex than that. The anthropologist David Gilmore, for example, found phenomena that resembled what I have referred to as male romance in many Western and non-Western cultures, past and present, and argued convincingly in 1990 that their social and psychic functions have varied. Ritualized activities involving separation from women, entry into a brotherhood of men, and rebirth through male agency, he suggested, may have served as "modes of integrating men into their society" or may have supplied "codes of belonging, in a hard, often threatening world." Most especially, when times were difficult, these ritualized activities may have induced men to take on high performance, not just for personal aggrandizement but for the collective good as well: "the harsher the environment and the scarcer the resources the more manhood is stressed as inspiration and goal."[45]

A second, related purpose of these ritualized behaviors, according to Gilmore, was to enforce a separation from "boyishness" and most particularly from an "ambivalent fantasy/fear" of re-merging with the mother or mother figure. These male-only initiation rituals might function as a defense against "the eternal child within."[46] Although rituals involving separation from women and bonding with other males had certainly involved the production of violent masculinities, male domination, the devaluation of females, and enforced heterosexuality, they did not *necessarily* involve any of the above.

Phenomena resembling what I have called male romance were found in cultures that espoused violent and aggressive masculinities and in those that espoused gentle and nonviolent gender ideals for men. The Tewa people of New Mexico, for example, known as the Pueblo Indians, gave up warfare in the last century, according to Gilmore, and were known for their serene culture, yet Tewa boys as part of their initiation into manhood were lashed with a yucca whip which drew blood and left permanent scars. Tewa girls had their own nonviolent initiation but "there is no parallel belief that girls have to be *made* into women."[47]

Forms of this phenomenon, moreover, were found in those cultures that emphasized male dominance and in those that made room for something approaching gender equality. Among the !Kung Bushmen of southwest Africa, men and women were said to be "equal in most things," but boys among the Bushmen were also subject to a ritual form of testing and rebirth. They were separated from women for about six weeks, were forced to fend for themselves in the bush, and then were required to kill an antelope before being accepted into the world of men.[48] Phenomena resembling what I have called male romance, finally, have not been restricted to the production of purely heterosexual masculinities. The Sambia of New Guinea incorporated ritual homosexuality as part of a boy's passage to manhood, and, as I shall suggest in chapter 3, contemporary U.S. gay men have also drawn upon elements of what I call male romance as a means of taking on secondary ideals of gay masculinity or personhood.[49] Although most forms of the phenomena resembling what I have called male romance seemed to have reaffirmed men's participation in the category "man," a privileged category with respect to "woman" in most cultures, these same phenomena supported a multiplicity of masculine ideals and different kinds of social relations.

PROVING MANHOOD AND MALE ROMANCE

There are strong indications that, in some cultures, fantasy and concretely achieved forms of what I have called male romance have also played a role in addressing psychic conflicts over the construction of gender identities by men. Gilmore, for example, while he carefully avoided claiming any universal model for manhood, did note that masculinity was widely regarded as something to be proved among the cultures that he studied. There was a strong suggestion, he argued, that in many Western and non-Western cultures attempts to live out ideals of masculinity, however those ideals might be defined, were "precarious." Masculinity was a "Holy Grail to be seized by long and arduous testing."[50]

Many scholars in the humanities and social sciences, of course, now think of all gender identities as unfixed, as continually evolving, and as acted or performed. According to the literary critic Michael Uebel, "you are constituted by what you do (and have done) and how you are interpreted doing what you do (and have done)."[51] In the words of the philosopher Judith Butler, masculinity and femininity both are accomplishments and are acquired "in relation to ideals that are never quite inhabited by any one."[52] Many scholars of U.S. masculinities, however, have identified (gay and straight) men's attempts to live out gender ideals as more insecure, more driven, and

more arduous than those of women.[53] The explanations offered for these differences have varied.

Nelson and Kimmel, for example, both explained the anxious, compulsive,
and labor-intensive nature of efforts by largely white, middle-class men to
live out dominant masculine ideals as a function of the fact that ostensibly
representing the nation as a whole was an impossible task, making it difficult
"for any human to fit into a full sense of compatibility" with the ideal.[54] Enjoying uncommon power and privilege, excluding others, and engaging in
competitive economic advance also produced the fears of those below that
contributed to a defensive need for continual reaffirmation.[55]

Scholars of U.S. black masculinity, such as Carl F. Nightingale, have argued that the compulsive efforts of many lower-class black men to live out
dominant masculine ideals might be centrally explained by racism and by the
effects of global restructuring. According to Nightingale, the collapse of the
urban industrial economy, which attended the growth of global restructuring
beginning in the 1970s, "left young, unskilled black men without the opportunities to create identities as family breadwinners" and thereby saddled them
with "lifelong memories of frustration and humiliation." Young, poor black
men, in consequence "have created a gendered class and racial identity"
largely derived from selected values and images of mainstream American culture. This masculine ideal involved "particularly enthusiastic and often desperately driven forms of mainstream conspicuous consumption."[56]

Still other scholars of masculinity have emphasized the role of unconscious
psychic processes in making insecurity, compulsion, and struggle central to
the performance of a whole range of U.S. masculine ideals. Believing, as the
philosopher Martha Nussbaum puts it, that "adult human emotions cannot be
understood without understanding their history in infancy and childhood,"
these scholars have turned to psychoanalytical accounts of gender to explain,
in the words of the philosopher Iris Young, "why gender meanings are so
deep seated in the individual identity and cultural categorization."[57] In his
1997 book *Proving Manhood*, for example, the writer and activist Tim
Beneke focused on the largely unconscious psychic processes that he believed informed efforts to live out dominant, and marginal, masculine ideals
in the United States.

Drawing on the 1970s work of the late psychologist Dorothy Dinnerstein
and the 1970s and 1980s work of the psychoanalyst Nancy Chodorow, in particular, Beneke argued that a certain compulsiveness, insecurity, and struggle
did indeed characterize a wide range of attempts to live out dominant masculine ideals, as *Manhood in America* had claimed.[58] These qualities were partially linked, Beneke argued, to men's unconscious fears of the all-powerful
and controlling primary parent of their infancy, a role that women predomi-

nantly played and which women in domestic relationships with men frequently came to represent. What also informed these qualities, however, was men's unconscious longing to remerge with that mother, a longing that had its roots in infancy and in the male infant's primary identification with his caretaker.[59]

The feminist object relations work on which Beneke drew maintained that identity formation took place in relation to the early "objects" with whom infants interacted, such as their primary caretakers, who in U.S. culture have been primarily mothers or female figures. At first, infants made no differentiation between themselves and mother, who was perceived only as an object rather than as a self, but an early task in the infant's development of an ego was to experience the mother or primary caretaker as a person who was connected but also separate from the infant's needs and wants.[60] Despite this ego development, however, according to Dinnerstein, most men and women retained a naive, egoistic attitude toward the early mother throughout their lives, and both harbored largely unconscious desires to re-create those early merged experiences.

These psychic processes, however, were constructed by and interacted with specific social formations. Dominant forms of male and female socialization in the 1970s, for example, heavily subscribed to the idea that women should be primary parents of the young. Dominant gender norms also affirmed women's nurturing role and men's right to be at the emotional center of women's lives. All of this provided what Nussbaum called a "facilitating environment" for men's ongoing sense of entitlement with respect to women. Psychologist Ronald F. Levant has also suggested that men, especially, developed what he calls a sense of "destructive entitlement" in relation to women. Unable to acknowledge or mourn the loss of the "holding environment" that good-enough mothers provided to their infants, men often felt that others, especially women in domestic situations, should make up for the original loss.[61]

According to feminist object relations theory, these largely unconscious desires for the mother's continued care produced anxiety in men and women both, because they threatened the separate, though connected, sense of self that they had achieved. The anxiety, however, was more intense for men than for women.[62] Male gender identity, it was theorized, was more conflictual for men than for women because "underlying, or built into, core male gender identity [was] an early, nonverbal, unconscious, almost somatic sense of primary oneness with the mother, an underlying sense of femaleness" that, in a culture that posited masculinity as opposite to femininity, "continually, usually unnoticeably, but sometimes insistently challenge[d] and undermine[d] the sense of maleness."[63]

Thus in theory the boy's and man's core gender identity, therefore, was insecure, and this insecurity often prompted boys and men to emphasize their separation from others and to define themselves as not female. A girl's gender identity, in contrast, was usually modeled on her mother's and thus built upon her primary sense of oneness and identification with her primary parent. Girls were primed to grow up with a sense of continuity and similarity to their mother and a relational connection to the world. They were primed to identify as "I who am female" rather than as "not men," and they were primed to hear multiple cultural messages to the effect that connection and nurturing were "natural" attributes of women.[64] These psychic promptings, of course, were not determinant of men's or women's gender performances. Many other factors could shape how such promptings were experienced and what an individual might do with them.

Building on this general understanding of U.S. men's gender formation, Beneke theorized that many boys and men formed a defense against the ego-threatening elements of a recurring desire to return to primary identification with the early mother or mother figure by "institutionalizing a compulsion to prove their manhood, through creating and conquering stress and distress." The process of creating and conquering stress, for example, might include taking risks, competing with other men, acting tough, disparaging the feminine in various ways, and many other kinds of activities, not excluding the risk-taking, near-death, and born-again experiences that have characterized many forms of U.S. male romance. Since this longing for the mother continually recurred, however, many men experienced the imagined possession of manhood as something that must be compulsively performed and re-performed: "One is momentarily a man and then the doubts reassert themselves—you're only as masculine as your last demonstration of masculinity."[65]

Although feminist object relations theorists originally based their conclusions on case studies of white, heterosexual, middle-class families—a fact that laid them open to a good deal of criticism—scholars of color have since applied similar assumptions to Latino and African-American families and gender relations as well.[66] Black therapists such as Audrey B. Chapman, Derek S. Hopson, and Darlene Powell Hopson, as I suggest more fully in chapter 7, used many of these assumptions in their work with black, middle-class clients.

Assumptions about early merging with the primary parent, the infant's need to become a separate, although relational, being, and the effects of a gender system that defined masculinity as opposite to femininity were seen as having a bearing on the gender identity formation of gay men as well. Gay boys and men also undergo merger with, and partial separation from, the mother, and they have historically been subjected to the same socializing forces as heterosexual boys and men. Although some studies have suggested that the ability and/or desire of gay boys to live out the "proving manhood" practices of dominant boy culture in the United States are less pronounced than those of heterosexual boys, others have argued that some gay boys are also conditioned to engage in constant self "proving," to experience "performance anxiety," and to depend on "constant, external approbation or support for [their] sense of self worth or self-esteem," and to engage in competition.[67] Gay boys and men, like heterosexuals, moreover, have had good psychic and social reasons for struggling over their relation to the feminine. As the gay activist Allen Young once put it, in an exploration of gay men's complex relationships with women: "One thing is certain: male homosexuals are preoccupied with the fact that on some level we are womanly, or we are considered womanly by this society."[68]

Another objection to feminist object relations theory was that it could be, and has been, used to suggest that a boy's "need" to separate from women and the feminine is a natural and irreversible phenomenon—a use of the argument that neglects to take the social and cultural into much account. A more cogent argument, from my perspective, is that it is in cultures that polarize male and female, as U.S. culture does (though less so than in the past), that men's identification with what is regarded as "feminine" becomes most problematic and most productive of insecurity and of a compulsive need to prove the opposite. According to Chapman, "for a boy to develop as masculine in our culture, he must abandon the feminine style of the mother in favor of the more action-oriented individualistic style of what this society defines as masculine. Unfortunately, in this process of individuation 'fighting the feminine' becomes a way of life for too many black men."[69]

What Chapman suggested, without completely articulating it, was that if the boundaries between ideals of masculine and feminine were more fluid in U.S. culture, if the categories more resembled each other, a whole range of behaviors requiring separation from the feminine might no longer be necessary.[70] Were the gender system to be changed or even eroded, through active effort, were traditionally "feminine" qualities seen as part of a proper gender ideal for men, much of the compulsive quality of masculinity in men might be diminished. As I shall suggest in the chapters to follow, men's organized efforts to transform masculine ideals have often worked, however unevenly, toward this very goal.

While the behavior and testimonies of the men I studied seemed to require some way of talking about the operation of unconscious or barely conscious anxieties and desires, it is important to emphasize that these psychic processes were but one thread in the formation of their gender ideals. What men *did* with these desires and with the anxieties they provoked had much to do with their personal histories, with the historical moment, and with their relation to such phenomena as the structures that perpetuate competitive economic relations, the dominance of nation-representing, self-making masculine ideals, and the multiple forms of male socialization that call on men to prove their masculinity from boyhood on. Multiple economic, social, and cultural phenomena have contributed to the fact that being a "real man" in U.S. culture has often involved insecurity, compulsion, and arduous performance.

SOME UNLOOKED-FOR LEGACIES OF MALE ROMANCE

Although most forms of U.S. male romance lend themselves to being read as exercises in consolidating an identification with the privileged category "man," insofar as a masculine rather than a human ideal is being affirmed, the social and political effects of male romance, along with the ideals of masculinity that they have helped produce and sustain, would seem to have been contradictory and historically variable. Indeed, elements of male romance have been used not only to sustain but also to resist the values of national manhood and the self-made man. They have been used not only to reinforce racism and homophobia but to protest them. They have been employed not just to escape women and the family but to rearticulate a relationship to both. Men have engaged in male romance not only to consolidate male dominance but to promote more egalitarian and respectful relations with women, children, and other men. Less frequently, men have taken up elements of male romance to work toward greater gender justice as well.

Many of these elements, for example, unevenly characterized two of the earliest organized efforts to transform masculine ideals that had their origins in the social activism of the 1950s and 1960s. One of the first was that of Black Power, which drew upon the values of the Civil Rights Movement and especially SNCC to construct a revised set of ideals for black masculinity. Both the Million Man March and Promise Keepers Stand in the Gap Assembly, with their evocations of the March on Washington in 1963, were heirs of this legacy. The white-led "Men's Liberation Movement" of the 1970s was also preceded by the radically gay theorizing of Harry Hay, who helped produce the gay Radical Faerie and related networks of the mid 1970s.[71] The Million Man March and the Stand in the Gap Assembly, for all their neglect, or rejection, of homosexual men, were unwitting heirs of this legacy as well.

NOTES

1. Michael Schwalbe, *Unlocking the Iron Cage: The Men's Movement, Gender, Politics, and American Culture* (New York: Oxford, 1996), 245.

2. Other critics have had similar experiences. The Promise Keepers conference Donna Minkowitz attended reminded her of "a gay pride rally—or the Michigan

Womyn's Music Festival," she notes in "In the Name of the Father," *Ms.* (November/December, 1995).

3. Michel Marriott, "Black Women Are Split Over All-Male March on Washington," *New York Times*, 14 October 1995, 1, 8.

4. See Introduction, 15–16.

5. Schwalbe documents similar ritual activity among the mythopoetics, *Iron Cage*, 60.

6. Maureen Dowd, "Promises, Promises, Promises," *New York Times*, 4 October 1997, A 21.

7. Dana D. Nelson, *National Manhood: Capitalist Citizenship and the Imagined Fraternity of White Men* (Durham, N.C., and London: Duke University Press, 1998), 34.

8. Nelson, *National Manhood,* 38, 46, 39, 34.

9. Nelson, *National Manhood,* 14, 37, 46.

10. Nelson, *National Manhood*, 28, 203.

11. Nelson, *National Manhood*, 178.

12. Michael Kimmel, *Manhood in America: A Cultural History* (New York: Free Press, 1996), 23.

13. Kimmel, *Manhood,* 6, 23.

14. Kimmel, *Manhood*, 44, 59.

15. Kimmel, *Manhood*, 52–53.

16. Kimmel, *Manhood,* 53, 70–71.

17. Mary Chapman and Glenn Hendler, introduction to *Sentimental Men: Masculinity and the Politics of Affect in American Culture,* ed. Mary Chapman and Glenn Hendler (Berkeley: University of California Press, 1999), 9, 10, 11, 12.

18. Kimmel, *Manhood*, 78.

19. W. S. Harwood, "Secret Societies in America," *North American Review* 164 (May 1897), cited in Mark C. Carnes, "Middle-Class Men and the Solace of Fraternal Ritual," in *Meanings for Manhood: Constructions of Masculinity in Victorian America*, ed. Mark C. Carnes and Clyde Griffen (Chicago: University of Chicago Press, 1990), 38. It is not clear from the source if the figure represents all men or white men alone.

20. Carnes, "Middle-Class Men," 45, 48, 49.

21. Carnes, "Middle-Class Men," 44, 47, 50.

22. Carnes, "Middle-Class Men," 41–42.

23. Carnes, "Middle-Class Men," 51.

24. Kimmel, *Manhood*, 173.

25. Nelson, *National Manhood*, 187.

26. Carnes, "Middle-Class Men," 51; Nelson, *National Manhood,"* 186–87.

27. George Chauncey, *Gay New York: Gender, Urban Culture, and the Making of the Gay Male World, 1890–1940* (New York: Basic Books, 1994), 36; Nelson, *National Manhood*, 187.

28. Carnes, "Middle-Class Men," 38, 48.

29. Nelson, *National Manhood*, 187, 186.

30. Mary Ann Clawson, *Constructing Brotherhood: Class, Gender and Fraternalism* (Princeton, N.J.: Princeton University Press, 1989), 14.

31. Howard Bell, ed., *Proceedings of the National Negro Convention, 1830–1864* (New York: Arno Press, 1969), 33, cited in Donna L. Franklin, *Ensuring Inequality: The Structural Transformation of the African-American Family* (New York: Oxford University Press, 1997), 31.

32. Franklin, *Ensuring Inequality,* 29–33.

33. Franklin, *Ensuring Inequality,* 29–30.

34. Maurice O. Wallace, *Constructing the Black Masculine: Identity and Idealist in African-American Men's Literature and Culture, 1775–1995* (Durham, N.C.: Duke University Press, 2002), 55.

35. Wallace, *Constructing,* 78; Stephen Howe, *Afrocentrism: Mythical Pasts and Imagined Homes* (New York: Verso, 1998), 69, 70.

36. Wallace, *Constructing,* 64, 65, 66.

37. Wallace, *Constructing,* 67, 77–78.

38. Wallace cites Mark Seltzer, *Bodies and Machines* (New York: Routledge, 1992), 28, *Constructing,* 80.

39. Marlene Kim Connor, *What Is Cool? Understanding Black Manhood in America* (New York: Crown, 1995), 11.

40. Nathan McCall, *Makes Me Wanna Holler: A Young Black Man in America* (New York: Vintage, 1994), 28.

41. McCall, *Makes Me*, 35, 23, 24, 26, 38.

42. McCall, *Makes Me, 70, 69.*

43. McCall, *Makes Me*, 79, 42, 49, 50.

44. McCall, *Makes Me*, 90,102.

45. David D. Gilmore, *Manhood in the Making: Cultural Concepts of Masculinity* (New Haven, Conn.: Yale University Press, 1990), 224.

46. Gilmore, *Manhood,* 28–29.

47. Gilmore, *Manhood*, 15.

48. Gilmore, *Manhood*, 115, 168.

49. Gilmore, *Manhood*, 154–56.

50. Gilmore, *Manhood*, 11, 19.

51. Michael Uebel "Men in Color: Introducing Race and the Subject of Masculinities," in *Race and the Subject of Masculinities,* ed. Harry Stecopoulos and Michael Uebel (Durham, N.C.: Duke University Press, 1997), 9.

52. Judith Butler, "Melancholy Gender/Refused Identification," in *Constructing Masculinity*, ed. Maurice Berger, Brian Wallis, and Simon Watson (New York: Routledge, 1995), 32.

53. Jay Mechling notes that "boys constantly have to prove their masculinity; it is always a process, never an achieved goal. What others see as arrogance in boys covers the fragility of the masculinity they are attempting to construct and repair daily." *On My Honor: Boy Scouts and the Making of American Youth* (Chicago: University of Chicago Press, 2001), 279.

54. Nelson, *National Manhood*, 28.

55. Kimmel, *Manhood*, 6.

56. Carl F. Nightingale, "The Axes of Oppression," in "The Crisis of African American Gender Relations: A Symposium on the Crisis of Gender Relations among African Americans," *Transition* 66 (1995): 146.

57. Martha C. Nussbaum, *Upheavals of Thought: The Intelligence of Emotions* (Cambridge, U.K.: Cambridge University Press, 2001), 178; Iris Marion Young, "Is Male Gender Identity the Cause of Male Domination?" in *Mothering: Essays in Feminist Theory*, ed. Joyce Treblicot (Savage, Md.: Rowman & Littlefield, 1983), 135.

58. Dorothy Dinnerstein, *The Mermaid and the Minotaur: Sexual Arrangements and Human Malaise* (New York: Harper & Row, 1976).

59. Timothy Beneke, *Proving Manhood: Reflections on Men and Sexism* (Berkeley: University of California Press, 1997), 34–35.

60. Nancy Julia Chodorow, "Gender, Relation, and Difference in Psychoanalytic Perspective," in *The Future of Difference*, ed. Hester Eisenstein and Alice Jardine. (New Brunswick, N.J.: Rutgers University Press, 1980), 5–6.

61. Martha C. Nussbaum, *Upheavals,* 186; Ronald F. Levant and Gary R. Brooks, "Nonrelational Sexuality in Men," in *Men and Sex: New Psychological Perspectives*, ed. Ronald F. Levant and Gary R. Brooks (New York: John Wiley & Sons, 1997), 21.

62. Nancy Chodorow, *The Reproduction of Mothering: Psychoanalysis and the Sociology of Gender* (Berkeley: University of California Press, 1978), 81, 79.

63. Chodorow, "Gender, Relation, and Difference," 15. Cited in Beneke, *Proving Manhood*, 34.

64. Chodorow, *Reproduction of Mothering,* 14.

65. Beneke, *Proving Manhood*, 35, 43.

66. Denise A. Segura and Jennifer L. Pierce, "Chicana/o Family Structure and Gender Personality: Chodorow, Familism, and Psychoanalytic Sociology Revisited," *Signs* 19, no. 1 (Autumn, 1993):62–92. Audrey Chapman's work on black middle-class men and women employs many of the same concepts. See Chapman, *Entitled.*

67. J. Michael Clark, "Men's Studies at the Margins: Doing the Work of Love, Part 1," *Journal of Men' Studies* 5, no. 4 (May 1997): 315. Available online at melvyl@popserv.ucop.edu.

68. Allen Young, "Some Thoughts on How Gay Men Relate to Women," in *After You're Out: Personal Experiences of Gay Men and Lesbian Women*, ed. Karla Jay and Allen Young (New York: Gage Publishing Limited, 1975), 197.

69. Chapman, *Entitled*, 30.

70. Chodorow, *Reproduction*, 13.

71. See Harry Hay, *Radically Gay: Gay Liberation in the Words of Its Founder,* ed. Will Roscoe (Boston: Beacon Press, 1996).

Revolutionary Men

*Civil Rights, Black Power, and the
Reconfiguration of Black Masculine Ideals*

Let us go on outdoing ourselves; a revolutionary man always transcends
himself or otherwise he is not a revolutionary man, so we always do what
we ask of ourselves or more than what we know we can do.

—Huey P. Newton, *Revolutionary Suicide*[1]

DREAMING MANHOOD

David Hilliard, the twelfth child of Lee and Lela Hilliard, was born in
Rockville, Alabama, sometime in the early 1940s. Although the family was
poor, and often hungry, and although they, like other Southern blacks, lived
in fear of violence under the racist regime of Jim Crow segregation, David
remembers his life in the black South as "the place where life is lived as it
should be." The pride and dignity of his hard-working father, the "unconditional love" of his mother, the security of knowing that in his family and community people were accepted with all their foibles, stayed with Hilliard as a
touchstone of how life should be carried on long after he left Alabama. In
1955 the Hilliard family relocated to California, a "golden" land, in David's
imagination, that promised escape from the "obstacles, hatred, and vicious-
ness that limit my life" in the South.[2] This golden place, however, turned out
to be a working-class neighborhood in the Oakland "flatlands," a crowded
and rundown section of the city that David's friend Huey Newton was to call
"a ghost town with inhabitants." Home to some two hundred thousand blacks,
nearly half the city's population, the flatlands everywhere bore evidence to
the "indifference" with which middle-class whites regarded "the plight of the
city's poor."[3]

Despite poverty, however, despite his struggles in the Oakland school system—which, according to Newton, taught young black children to be ashamed of being black—and despite his experiments in heavy drinking with his teenaged "hanging partners" from junior high on, David clung to the strong sense of family and community that he associated with his Southern, rural past. Thus, when he married Patricia Parks, who was pregnant with his child, the young David felt a new content: "A kind of sweetness mellows me as I lie in bed in my new house. I feel I'm a man. My other partners are still on the corner. But I've got a house and a wife. My whole life is getting meaning. My dream is coming true."[4]

Hilliard's dream of feeling like a "man," however, by providing for his wife and child, would prove as difficult for a working-class black to achieve in Oakland as in the South. Lacking skills and living in a city with one of the highest unemployment and welfare rates in the country, as well as a history of police corruption and brutality toward blacks, David experienced the futility that so many blacks encountered in their attempt to escape the racism and economic inequities of the South.[5] Influenced by the heightened consciousness of racial inequity that the movement for black civil rights had produced and finding only "the plainest, meanest tasks" to perform, David felt no pride in "earning money for Pat and myself; I resent the fact that this tiring, spiritless slaving is the only way I can make an income." As he drifted from one low-paid, unskilled job to another, his frustration and "bitter, blind anger" would lead him to "give up on jobs altogether. I no longer need real reasons to quit."[6]

In 1965 the Watts riot initially gave Hilliard a feeling of release—"we should never accept our situation! . . . my rage and contempt pour out, as though they're a song or a kind of exuberant, defiant love." In the end, however, he felt that life hadn't really changed and that "that's what I want, a different existence, a calling, something that removes me from my aimlessness, gives my days and weeks purpose."[7] The Black Power movement, which emerged in 1966, as an alternative to the nonviolent strategies of the early movement for civil rights, would supply the calling or higher cause that Hilliard was looking for. By extending provision for family into service of the black community as a whole and by enlarging personal rebellion into a militant, collective struggle for structural social change, Black Power would supply new strategies for feeling "I'm a man."

A related ideal of manhood, moreover, embodying these very values was already presenting itself in the figure of Malcolm X, the charismatic Nation of Islam spokesman who had riveted the nation with his angry denunciation of U.S. racism, his call to black empowerment, and his advocacy of armed self-defense. Hilliard had first heard Malcolm X speak in a 1963 television interview with Mike Wallace, during which Malcolm had declared that "in this society the victim is called the criminal and the criminal is turned into the victim." "You're making sense out of my years of frustration," had been Hilliard's immediate response: "Now I know where I'm going."[8] Then, during the summer of 1966, Hilliard read Malcolm's *Autobiography,* which had been published in 1964, "feeling I am not reading Malcolm's life but my own.[9] As in many narratives by young, black men, such as that of Nathan McCall, reading the *Autobiography of Malcolm X* would prove a life-changing experience.

It was during this same period that Huey Newton, Hilliard's hanging partner and boyhood friend, who had begun to take an interest in Black Power politics, proposed a new organization based on Malcolm's call for militant antiracism and community self-defense. By patrolling the streets and observing police interactions with ordinary citizens, by openly, and then legally, carrying a shotgun or rifle, and by arming himself with law books, from which he cited pertinent sections of the penal code, Newton hoped to protect members of the community from the police harassment and brutality that were so infamously common in the flats. In October of that year Huey Newton and Bobby Seale would draw up their Ten Point Program for the new organization, and in January of 1967 they would hold the first meeting of the Black Panther Party for Self Defense (BPP). The BPP would become the leading Black Power organization and the first nationally prominent movement of the 1960s to make the transformation of masculine ideals a conscious and explicit political goal.

Hilliard's engagement with the Black Panther Party would eventually lead him to embrace an ideal of masculinity that combined the militancy of the Northern and urban figure of Malcolm X with values represented by Hilliard as belonging to his rural, Southern origins.[10] (Malcolm, too, had in fact been born in the South.) Despite the Black Panther's emphasis upon an urban, warrior-like masculine ideal involving black leather jackets and guns, the Black Panther identification with community, as expressed in their breakfast, health, and education programs as well as in their armed protection of black citizens from the police, also represented to Hilliard a continuation of a Southern, rural past and of its traditions of communal care:

> The work that went into the Party, our dignity as an independent people, the communal ideal and practice that informed our programs, all stem in part from the civilization of which my mother and father were so representative.[11]

In crafting what they saw as a higher masculine ideal, the Black Panthers would attempt to translate elements of the individualistic, "baad," and often criminal, masculinity of the city streets into self-sacrificing militancy on behalf of the black community as a whole. At the same time they would hold on to the more nurturing forms of personhood that informed black, rural, Southern culture and the movement for civil rights.

THE CIVIL RIGHTS MOVEMENT: SNCC AND A CIRCLE OF TRUST

The emphasis on community and care that Hilliard identified with black, Southern rural life was similar to the values that informed the early civil rights movement and the Student Nonviolent Coordinating Committee (SNCC), in particular. According to African-American studies professor Michael Thelwell, who served as field secretary of SNCC between 1963 and 1964, SNCC "was fundamentally an expression of Afro-American culture, Afro-American Southern culture, in its principles and its values and its character."[12] Emerging from the lunch-counter sit-ins staged by college students in Greensboro, North Carolina, in 1960, inspired by longtime civil rights activist Miss Ella Baker, this group of largely black, working-class, college-educated activists organized the black voter registration drive in the South while also participating in direct action demonstrations that drew national attention to the civil rights effort. Combining these two highly publicized activities with food distribution and historical, political, and cultural education programs (in "Freedom Schools"), labor organizing, and demands for economic justice, SNCC was central in inspiring "a populist rebellion by lower-class Negroes."[13]

Although neither SNCC nor the civil rights movement as a whole explicitly focused on male gender transformation, both struggled to extend the rights of citizenship to black men and women, thereby breaking with the ideal of "national manhood" that identified citizens with white, property-owning males. In revealing how deeply implicated the ideals of national manhood and of self-making masculinity had been in racial and economic injustice at home and imperialism abroad, the civil rights movement also helped produce disillusion with, and rebellion against, "the system" and the implicitly masculine ideals that it represented. The alliance between SNCC and the largely white New Left Students for a Democratic Society (SDS), according to the sociologist and activist Todd Gitlin, represented "an alliance with brothers and sisters against the old white men who deadlocked the Democratic Party and fueled future wars."[14] As Eldridge Cleaver was to observe in his 1968 bestseller, *Soul on Ice*, "the white race had lost its heroes. . . . A new generation of whites was rejecting the panoply of white heroes, whose heroism consisted in erecting the inglorious edifice of colonialism and imperialism."[15]

The civil rights movement, however, and SNCC, in particular, did not merely promote critical insights about the bad fathers of the past but, like many organizations for social change, offered an alternative model of male and female personhood both, based on the idea that self-realization was to come through sacrifice, through "action in common," and through putting one's "body on the line" for social justice. SNNC also tied the personal to the political by defining love and personal bonds as the bases for a political movement devoted to structural social change. According to Diane Nash, director of SNCC's direct action wing in 1961, SNCC was a "beloved community," "a band of brothers and sisters, a circle of trust."[16] SNCC also expressed the belief that "private feeling" was public in its origins and "should therefore be expressed where it belongs, in public."[17] Many elements of this personhood ideal were to be taken up in the New Left, in the antiwar and student movements, and in the women's, gay, and men's liberation movements as well. (I shall return to these links in chapter 4.) It was these same elements, moreover, that laid the groundwork for a differently organized ideal of black masculinity that was consciously and deliberately articulated, albeit with multiple contradictions, in Black Power.

BLACK POWER

Black Power emerged in 1966 as a response to a growing sense that something more than the strategies employed by the nonviolent civil rights movement were required in the fight for social justice. "Black Power" was in the first instance a "new consciousness" or vision that called on black people "to unite, to recognize their heritage, to build a sense of community," to form an imagined nation set apart from the U.S. nation as a whole. As such it was linked to the earlier forms of black nationalism. The closed ranks of Black Power constituted a mental enclave in which racist hierarchies, institutions, values, and rules were to be systematically rejected and in which the traditional values of individualism and economic self-making were to be replaced by an alternative set of values identified as black and, in some instances, as African in origin: "reorientation means an emphasis on the dignity of man, not the sanctity of property. . . . 'free people, not 'free enterprise.'"[18] The latter, of course, were values that already informed SNCC and the civil rights movement as a whole.

Black Power called on blacks to search for "new and black controlled forms of political structure to solve political and economic problems," to embrace armed "self-defense," and to reject nonviolence as "an approach black people cannot afford and a luxury white people do not deserve."[19] Entering into this new consciousness, which was seen as drawing strength from "a history which predates [blacks'] forced introduction into this country . . . a long history beginning on the continent of Africa" and entering into the imagined community that this consciousness formed constituted a mode of rebirth and re-identification for men and women both: "many blacks are now calling themselves African-Americans, Afro-Americans or black people because that was *our* image of ourselves."[20] Black Power, therefore, was to replace racist constructions of blackness and of black and African culture with an emphasis on black pride and self-respect. Revised ideals of black masculinity, however, were to receive particular emphasis in Black Power organizations.

BLACK NATIONAL MANHOOD

Despite the fact that the Black Power movement was organized on behalf of the black community as a whole, the rhetorical shift from concepts of a "beloved community" or of a group of brothers and sisters standing in a "circle of trust," to celebrations of a black "nation" evoked long-standing narratives that identified nation and citizenship with men. The 1965 Moynihan report on "The Negro Family: The Case for National Action," moreover, would reemphasize the traditional association between male citizen and head of house. Taking as its theme the fact that one-quarter of black households were headed by women, the report argued that this "matriarchal" black family was a "tangle of pathology" threatening to strike even black middle-class families.[21]

The solution was both to get poor black men jobs and to "restore" the black man to his rightful place as family head. Only then, by implication, would black men and women both rise above the status of second-class citizen and would black, heterosexual men, in particular, be included in the concept of national manhood—an ideal that had historically required men to exercise control over the little "commonwealth" of the family. The national attention that the report directed to black men's ostensible failures as husbands and fathers (and therefore as citizens) contributed to the tendency of Black Power to focus on ideals of masculinity, to call for limits on black women's agency, and to identify the leadership of the movement with heterosexual males.

Black Power's rejection of nonviolence, its embrace of armed self-defense, and its identification with global, anticolonialist struggles for political liberation also prompted a new reliance on metaphors of colonialism and armed revolt. Black women certainly participated in this rhetoric—Diane Nash felt for many years that "violence was the way to go"—but the rhetoric of armed struggle was also traditionally associated with men, and Black Power, like the New Left, often postulated its warrior figures as male.[22]

Huey Newton would also conceive of the Black Panther Party as the "vanguard" of a "revolution" that he did not expect to survive. The titles of his 1972 and 1973 books, *To Die for the People* and *Revolutionary Suicide*, were not mere romanticization.[23] The violence of white racism and of the FBI counterintelligence effort (Cointelpro) to put an end to organizations like 'anther's Central Committee, the Panthers represented "a new black men, divorced completely . . . from the old, the civil ent of the NAACP and the Urban League and Martin Luther rn Christian Leadership Conference." This new leadership ing the question but making a demand, a demand it declared king up with armed force, as symbolized in the hero of that t: Huey P. Newton."[30]

lcolm X as a model for a manhood ideal, the BPP deliberately urage the spontaneous and disorganized outbreaks and riots l in 1964 and to transform the tough, angry, often aimless mas- the lower-class streets. "Brothers on the block," like Newton ad been robbing banks, pimping, and peddling dope as alter- self-advance, were to be initiated into a revolutionary mascu- med not just by individual defiance but by disciplined self- alf of the oppressed.[31] Like members of SNCC who thought with reason, as living sacrifices to the cause of justice, New- e concept of dying "for the people." This constituted a break ominant norms of self-making masculinity but with the indi- f much street masculinity as well.

McCall's black street version of male romance, which I dis- l, the Black Panther Party originally targeted only men and ed its own ritual ways of initiating its "brothers" into a sec- e ideal. (Brothers were soon joined by sisters.) One ritual, for at of political education, of schooling Black Panther initiates of racism, economic inequality, revolutionary political strug- ve social ideals.[32] Just as older brothers on the block taught s how to fight (and just as SNCC activists were trained in the nviolence), initiates into the BPP were trained in the virtues d organized armed self-defense. Hilliard recalls a tense con- he police when "the party rules help me keep my composure. and practice endow me with discipline and purpose; without on like this, I'd probably cuss furiously and get myself into

s all-male groups, risk-taking behaviors were central to be- h within the BPP these behaviors were officially to be un- llective and political common good. In October of 1967, af- th the police during which Newton had been wounded and a n Frey, killed, Eldridge Cleaver proposed that Hilliard reen- rieve bloody clothing from Newton's house. Hilliard was re- aring that he, too, would be taken or shot, but ultimately he because "in Eldridge's mind I hang out with the Party. But

SNCC and to destroy the Black Power
gers that were quite real. Black Pov
might also be seen as a strategy for in
formance not just for personal aggrai
nificant component of that—"but foi
Power organizations were sites for p
ways do what we ask of ourselves or

"BROTHERS ON THE BLOCK"

Two of the most central organizatic
were the socialist-identified Black P
ganized by Huey Newton and Bobb
and the cultural nationalist organiz
which was founded by Ron Maulana
Angeles. Both groups were organi
Black Power with the masculine ide
Black Panther Party's minister of de
the spirit of Malcolm." For Ron K
"the highest form of Black manhoc

Malcolm X had been, in his own
over racism and poverty and havin;
raphy put it, "from hoodlum, thie
most dynamic leader of the Black
Malcolm X represented, however,
ualist ethos of economic autonom;
dividualist "baad" brother on the b
with a self-sacrificing but also de
behalf of the oppressed. For writer
ing in 1970, it was Malcolm X wh
pimp, the hustler, the entertainer,
but "along came Malcolm and Mu
we tend to think of a Man in term

Martin Luther King Jr., of co
liberation leaders, such as Fred
also exemplified a masculinity b
colm X represented a more def
civil rights fathers like King. H
which to black liberation was
"armed self-defense."[29] To Elai

on the Black
generation of
rights movem
King's South
"was not beg;
that it was ba
new moveme

In taking M
aimed to disc
that had erupte
culine ideals o
himself, who
native forms o
line ideal info
sacrifice on be
of themselves,
ton embraced t
not just with d
vidualist ethic

As in Nathar
cuss in chapter
quickly develo;
ondary masculi
example, was t
about the nature
gle, and alterna
younger brothe
principles of no
of disciplined ar
frontation with t
The philosophy
them, in a situat
more trouble."[33]

As in McCall
longing, althoug
dertaken for a co
ter a shootout wr
police officer, Jo
ter Oakland to re
luctant at first, f
could not refuse

I'm still not a member. I haven't passed my initiation, my test of courage. . . . I'm still Huey's man, his running buddy, undeserving to be included on my own merits into the Party leadership. If I reject this invitation, I'll be shunned forever. I tell him I'll go."[34]

As in McCall's experience, mastering elements of style was another sign of belonging to the group. The standard Panther dress of black leather jacket, black pants, sunglasses, berets, and guns was the intended outward sign of a disciplined, defiant—and consciously white-intimidating—revolutionary masculine ideal, with the characteristic powder-blue shirts perhaps hinting at the Panthers' softer sides, and there *were* softer sides. To Hilliard, for example, his BPP comrades became "closer to me because of our shared ideas than my biological relatives." They were "Revolutionaries. In deed as well as speech. My family. My home."[35] Like Hilliard, Newton also referred to the BPP as supplying "the closeness and love of family life, the will to live in spite of cruel conditions. . . . I have found that to be an outsider is to be alienated and unhappy."[36]

Community and nurturing, I shall argue, were integral to the ideal of Panther masculinity as Newton and Hilliard conceived it and to some of the Panther's political priorities as well.

REVOLUTIONARY MANHOODS

The ideals of Black Panther masculinity, however, along with Panther political priorities, were conceived of differently by different men. Newton and Cleaver, for example, although they embraced elements of a warrior-like masculine ideal that took community defense and world-wide revolution as its stated goals, split over whether the revolution was to be waged by focusing on armed conflict in the near future or by focusing on service to the people over a longer haul. In the end, it was service to the people rather than organized revolutionary battle that took concrete form. Thus, in 1970 the California Panthers, as with SNCC before them, began a series of community projects that emphasized nurturing and care. These included a free breakfast program for children, food and clothing giveaways, an elementary school, a free community health clinic, free ambulance service, and free shoe manufacturing. Huey Newton would characterize all of these as "*a survival program*" necessary to sustain "the people" in a longer process of revolution.[37] To the political scientist Errol A. Henderson "the survival programs taught through practice the ethics of love, caring, diligence, reciprocity, community, creativity, responsibility, and struggle—all of these representative of the best aspects of a truly African American culture."[38]

From Hilliard's perspective these two emphases were differently represented in Eldridge Cleaver and Huey Newton. For Cleaver, armed conflict
was the pressing business of revolution. To Huey Newton, by 1971, Cleaver's
focus was not properly revolutionary at all because it undermined community
support: "under the influence of Eldridge Cleaver the Party gave the community no alternative for dealing with us except by picking up the gun."[39] The
split over defining revolution as armed conflict or as primarily day-to-day
service to the people in the interest of a larger cause involved different ideals
of masculinity as well, or, if not different ideals, a different weighting of the
elements of which they were composed.

Cleaver, for example, "fell in love with the Black Panther Party immediately upon [his] first encounter with it" in February of 1967, when four Panthers showed up for a meeting to organize a memorial for Malcolm X, at
which his widow, Betty Shabazz, was to appear. The Panthers were wearing
"black berets, powder blue shirts, black leather jackets, black trousers, shiny
black shoes—and each with a gun!" To Cleaver, who also noticed that the
four men produced a gleam "of total admiration" in the eyes of one of the
women present, the Panthers in their warrior gear were "the most beautiful
sight I had ever seen."[40] What most attracted Cleaver to the Black Panthers
was their "courage to kill," their willingness to stand up to white authorities
such as the police and to back up their stance with force.

To Cleaver the courage, power, and implied virility of Black Panther masculine performance primarily represented a recovery from black men's prior
"impotence" and "conquered manhood," a recovery all the more to be prized
because it prompted women's sexual appreciation and respect.[41] Cleaver's
celebration of this masculine ideal, moreover, was initially bound to conservative gender politics and to an unabashed homophobia as well. Thus, having
shed his rapist past, Cleaver praised black women in his early writing as
queens, mothers, and daughters of Africa but emphasized their need for male
protection. To Cleaver, moreover, homosexual black men were not properly
men at all—or even black. The black homosexual, according to Cleaver's essay on James Baldwin, was not only "castrated," but was also "an extreme
embodiment" of a "racial death wish."[42] Cleaver's own physical appreciation
of the Panthers and of other men may have contributed to the defensive, un-
compromising nature of his stance.

Huey Newton, while certainly aspiring to revolutionary courage and power, as
well as to women's sexual appreciation, found elements of this warrior masculinity harder to embrace. Made fun of in his youth for his baby face, his pale
or "yellow" skin, and his high-pitched voice, Newton had compensated by becoming tough and prone to fight.[43] However, while Cleaver loved the famous
poster of Newton sitting like an African king in a rattan chair, armed with rifle

and spear, Newton ostensibly hated it and was terrified of having to live up to the ideal that the famous poster projected. For Newton, who confessed to Hilliard that he was "'a scared little fucker, and that's why I fight,'" guns were a "badge of his defiance, proof he's not fronting," but his preferred strategy for revolution—that of gaining "the support of the people through serving their needs"—was accompanied by an emphasis upon more nurturing values and behaviors.[44]

To Die for the People, for example, a collection of Newton's writing between 1967 and 1971, visually promoted these elements of Newton's masculine ideal, and not, I think, just as an effort to hoodwink the public, as some critics of Newton suggest. Published in 1972, the book included the famous poster of Newton, but with a bullet hole through the middle of it, and prominently featured some ten pages of photographs illustrating the free food, shoe, and clothing programs and showing images of Newton alternately meeting world leaders and interacting with Chinese children. *To Die for the People* also contained Newton's 1970 essay, "The Women's Liberation and Gay Liberation Movements," in which he suggested that the women's and gay movements should be considered potential allies, that homosexuals might be "the most oppressed people in the society" and that "maybe I'm now injecting some of my prejudice by saying that 'even a homosexual can be a revolutionary.' Quite the contrary, maybe a homosexual could be the most revolutionary."[45]

Newton's autobiography, *Revolutionary Suicide*, published in 1973, continued these themes. Dedicated to Newton's mother and father, the book also emphasized a masculine ideal that was deeply invested in familial, brotherly, and communal ties. Out of thirty-seven photographs, there were at least ten pictures of Newton as a youth and of his family and there were seven pictures of Black Panther community programs. The pictures of Newton's Black Panther colleagues were head shots featuring reflective-looking men or photos of men embracing each other. There was also a group shot of Black Panther brothers attending a barbeque. Newton himself was pictured as speaking, observing, greeting, or embracing others. There were only four pictures alluding to violent encounters. Two were of George Jackson's funeral, and one was a picture of Newton lying wounded and handcuffed to a gurney in the emergency room of Oakland's Kaiser Hospital while a white police officer stood guard. The fourth was the famous poster of Newton, but it was the copy with the large bullet hole through the middle of it. As such, it suggested Newton's vulnerability and the magnitude of the forces arrayed against him. The photographs in both of Newton's books, therefore, emphasized responsible and dignified social activism and loving ties to family, friends, and community, along with vulnerability, sensitivity, and thoughtfulness as part of a masculine ideal. Several of these values would be central to Harry Hay's gay revolutionary hero and to "men's liberation" as well.

GENDER CONFLICT IN THE BPP

The complex and sometimes conflicting elements of the Black Power masculine ideal, and of attempts by different men to perform it, were echoed in the
complex and contradictory nature of the attitudes toward women that it espoused. Initially, for example, both Huey Newton and Bobby Seale had imagined the Black Panther Party and Black Liberation in terms of "the black
man's search for unity of his body with his mind, in order 'to gain respect
from his woman because women want one who can control.'"[46] The early focus of Panther recruitment efforts in 1966–1967, therefore, was "brothers on
the block." When women asked to join, however, they were allowed to do so,
and they began to swell the movement in large numbers. By 1968, according
to Bobby Seale's estimate, women represented approximately 60 percent of
the BPP membership.[47]

African-American women were no strangers to political activism and leadership. In the civil rights movement, for example, according to the sociologist
Belinda Robnett, it was Miss Ella Baker who was principally responsible for
founding SNCC and for its having adopted principles of collective, nonhier-
archical leadership. It was women like Baker and Septima Clark who developed programs for building a mass base in rural communities, employing
door-to-door contact and emotional ties as mobilizing tools. Such activism,
Robnett convincingly demonstrated, constituted a crucial form of leadership
in the civil rights movement. This leadership, moreover, was mainly responsible for the emotionally expressive and self-sacrificing personhood that
SNCC in particular offered to men and women both.[48]

Women continued their activism within the Black Panther party by often taking major responsibility for community service programs—free breakfasts for
children, free health clinic projects, "liberation schools," and community political education, although men also participated in these programs.[49] These programs, moreover, were the lifeblood of the organization. According to historian
Tracye Matthews, an FBI memo from Director J. Edgar Hoover in 1969 described the free breakfast program as the "best and most influential activity going for the BPP and as such, . . . potentially the greatest threat to efforts by authorities . . . to neutralize the BPP and destroy what it stands for." According to
a former Panther, Malika Adams, "women ran the BPP pretty much."[50]

Some women took on more prominent leadership roles as well. Kathleen
Cleaver, for example, was assistant editor of the Black Panther newspaper,
the first woman to serve on the Panthers' Central Committee, and its national
communications secretary. Pat Hilliard, David Hilliard's wife, was the national finance secretary, and Elaine Brown served as editor of the newspaper,
sat on the Central Committee, and ultimately became chairperson of the BPP

in 1974 when Newton left for exile in Cuba. During Brown's tenure, moreover, women increased their participation in party affairs and the BPP expanded its role in local Oakland politics.

Like white men on the New Left, however, black brothers brought sexist baggage to a movement that otherwise called for revolutionary social transformation.[51] More than one black feminist saw a disturbing form of male romance in a movement that was prone to reduce "discussions of 'black community' or 'black people' to references to black males, the struggle against racism to essentially a struggle against black male subordination."[52] According to activist Frances Beale in 1970, Black Power organizations were also given at times to asking black women to "step back into a domestic submissive role" so that black men could move forward."[53]

Women's participation in formal leadership roles, moreover, did not come automatically and was often accompanied by accusations that women were taking over or by pressure on women to play out traditional gender roles by, for example, serving food to, and providing sex for, male revolutionaries. During his 1968 presidential campaign, indeed, Eldridge Cleaver had promoted the idea of "pussy power," "women's ability to withhold sex in order to compel men to political activism."[54] Hilliard, however, insisted that the BPP made real efforts to keep male Panthers from demanding sex in return for their role in the revolution and testified that he personally had struggled to resolve conflicts with his wife "in a more humane, rational way than the brutal, desperate ones we've been given and taught."[55] Despite efforts like these, nonetheless, many men felt free to harass women for sex and some to physically abuse their girlfriends and wives.

The subject of women in the movement had become a topic for discussion in the Black Panther newsletter by 1969. In that year, for example, Cleaver himself, writing from exile, introduced gender equality as an important part of BPP goals: "If we want to go around and call ourselves a vanguard organization, then we've got to be . . . the vanguard also in the area of women's liberation."[56] In 1969 Panther women also began to make more public pronouncements on gender relations. Although some women emphasized the importance of living for "your man," of helping black men realize their ambitions, and of avoiding "the White ways of trying to be equal to the Black man," Roberta Alexander, speaking on "women in the struggle" at a BPP sponsored forum, observed that black women were oppressed as a class.[57]

In an anonymous interview, six Panther women called on black men to rethink their definitions of manhood so as to make it independent of keeping black women subordinate.[58] Women like Brown also made their resentment of male sexism known: "We had no intention . . . of allowing Panther men to assign us an inferior role in our revolution." Some brothers continued,

nonetheless, to complain of women's bad attitudes and to regard female leaders as "eroding black manhood" and as "hindering the progress of the black
race." Ultimately, during Newton's mid-seventies decline, Brown began to
fear that her leadership role was endangering her physical safety. For Brown,
Black Power had come to symbolize "the denial of black women in favor of
the freedom of 'the black man.'"[59]

REVOLUTIONARY SUICIDE: HUEY NEWTON'S DECLINE

The Black Panther's ideal of masculinity as well as attempts to perform that
ideal were nothing if not contradictory. Huey Newton, in particular, had, or
developed, a severe internal split in which his investment in familial, brotherly, and communal ties and his serve-the-people ideals began to clash with
the individualistic, violence-prone street masculinity that he had attempted to
harness to those ideals and thereby transform. Newton became increasing violent and self-serving after he was released from prison in 1970 and plunged
into alcohol and cocaine addiction.

According to black journalist Hugh Pearson, in a book highly critical of the
Oakland leadership of the BPP, Newton, Seale, and Hilliard maintained a distance from the community projects that rank-and-file members, often women,
actually ran. The Oakland leadership generally was responsible for the fact
that reluctant merchants were sometimes "boycotted, firebombed or beaten"
into making donations of food to the breakfast program, and Newton himself,
according to Pearson, eventually sanctioned a Panther-run underground economy involving drugs and prostitution. Pearson also claimed that Newton beat
or sanctioned the beating and even murder of disgruntled members.[60] At the
same time, Pearson notes, Newton began an even more communal phase in
the Panther party agenda by declaring that the Panthers had been wrong to attack the police as they had, by trying to reconcile with black churches, and by
initiating a new wave of survival programs for the community.[61]

Newton's decline into addiction and violence has been linked by several
commentators to his long stretches in solitary confinement, which, they argue, contributed to a mounting paranoia. Newton's paranoia, however, has
also been explained by the fact that he had much to fear. Struggles over
racism and the Vietnam War were often violent in the 1970s on all sides. This
was an age in which police officers viciously beat and shot peaceful demonstrators as well as black citizens going about their business (a practice that has
not disappeared) and in which the FBI facilitated assassination attempts
against Black Panthers sleeping in their beds (Chicago Panthers Fred Hamp-
ton and Mary Clark). Elements of the white Left, such as the Weathermen,

were also robbing banks and firebombing buildings. Almost from its inception, moreover, the BPP was the target, along with other Black Power organizations, of FBI infiltration and violent Cointelpro tactics.[62] Cointelpro tactics included infiltration of Black Power organizations by undercover agents, the promotion by these agents of violent and abusive behaviors, the provocation of conflicts between Black Power groups, and the facilitation of murders.

Pearson acknowledges these realities and notes that Panther leaders in other cities did not exhibit Newton's failures of self-transformation, but he chiefly blames the "gang" or street mentality of Newton and of many members of the Oakland leadership for acts of violence and corruption. "Gang mentality" of a kind was certainly at work in Newton's violence and underground activities, but the term does not quite get at the psychic stakes that must have been involved. What Pearson calls "gang mentality" was also a familiar form of masculine self-proving, one that Newton had performed as a younger man and one that he fell back on as other forms of demonstrating manhood become increasingly difficult to sustain.

The pressure on Newton to live up to a heroic, warrior-like masculine ideal, for example, became more and more intense and therefore increasingly productive of anxiety during his prison years. While imprisoned, Newton became identified with the warrior hero of the famous poster, and many Panther supporters came to believe that Newton's release from prison would mark the real beginning of "the revolution." Newton, however, felt conscious of the fact that he was not the heroic warrior figure, or even the dynamic public performer, that the role required. According to Alex Hoffman, "Huey was scared of getting out. . . . 'I'm not that poster,' he said. 'That's Eldridge's poster of who I am. That's not me. They're gonna expect me to come out of here as that poster. I can't even speak in public.'"[63]

Newton also expressed anxiety about what he perceived to be his greater distance from the community:

> There was now an element of hero worship that had not existed before I got busted. But I wanted our rapport to get back to where it was before I went to jail, that is, a relationship based on face-to face communication between people working together for survival. . . . The earlier family tie has been enlarged by an image of me created through publicity and the media.[64]

Thus, Newton's partial reversion to the performance of an individualistic and violence-prone masculine ideal may have been driven in part by his fear of not living out the heroic masculine ideal with which he had been saddled and that he had also taken on.

Newton's anxiety may have had some roots in his ambivalence over his Southern heritage as well. Like Hilliard, Newton had been born in the South, in

Monroe, Louisiana, in the early 1940s and, like Hilliard, Newton admired his father for his constant work, for the fact that he commanded "dignity and respect," for his "strong belief" in family, and for being a strong protector. At the same time, however, Newton insisted that his father was "not typical of southern Black men in the thirties and forties" because of the dignity and pride he represented and because "he never let a white man humiliate him or any member of his family"—because, in effect, he showed qualities that Newton felt were seldom seen in black men from the South: "Although many other Black men in the South had a similar strength, they never let it show around whites."[65]

As the inheritor of the ideals of Malcolm X, and as a leader of the Black Power movement, Newton divorced himself from the nonviolent strategies of the Southern-focused civil rights movement and from the man who, despite the disdain that Black Power leaders often directed at him, could not help being experienced as an ideological and political father figure, Martin Luther King Jr. Malcolm X, as the literary critic Riché Richardson points out, had explicitly placed black Southern masculinities at the bottom of a hierarchy of black masculinity by identifying Southern men as house Negroes and Uncle Toms.[66] The suppression by Newton of this Southern heritage, like the suppression of fear itself, may also have taken a psychic toll.

As unusual a figure as Newton was, however, he was not unlike more ordinary men. He too was subject to that fear of failure, to that anxiety over not living up to one's potential, to those "memories of shame about blackness," and to the need for a "'front' of bluster, masculine boasting and aggression" that have characterized the lives of so many black men—men who were cruelly caught between dominant masculine ideals requiring self-promotion and success, the structural impossibility of their living out even a modest version of those ideals, and a gender system that required men to prove manhood no matter what.[67] Such considerations, although they certainly do not excuse Newton's acts of violence and corruption, do help us to understand Newton's unintended form of "revolutionary suicide." Newton was not the first black man to embrace self-destructive behaviors in an effort to ask "of ourselves . . . more than what we know we can do."[68]

BLACK NATIONAL MANHOOD, CULTURAL NATIONALIST STYLE

Related tensions in masculinities informed US cultural nationalism, which officially emphasized the importance of black separateness rather than socialist coalition and the creation of specifically black values, institutions, and cultural productions over economic revolution. Nonetheless, the cultural nationalist masculine ideal, as represented by US, shared many features with that of the

Panthers. The cultural nationalist masculine ideal was also a warrior masculinity in that "cultural" was to be followed by "political" revolution." US security personnel were visibly armed, engaged in shootouts with Panthers, and were accused of assassinating Black Power rivals. The preferred dress of US security men—shaved heads, olive drab uniforms, and African talismans—according to Baraka, gave them a neo-African military quality.[69] Discipline was also a key feature of the masculine ideal. According to Baraka, the worst thing a person could be for Maulana Karenga was "Ovyo, a Swahili word meaning 'random,' a person acting random, disorganized, and unpredictable."[70]

Although US was often identified as a more middle-class organization than the BPP, even middle-class blacks like Baraka, who was allied with Karenga early on and who was central to the cultural nationalist Black Arts movement, identified with ideals of tough, lower-class street masculinities. Like Cleaver, many also vilified homosexuals and defined white (and less radical black) masculinities as weak and/or gay. Much male-authored cultural nationalist and Black Arts writing, as literary critic Philip Brian Harper put it, positioned the cultural nationalist author as a "politically aware, racially conscious" and also a "phallic" or powerfully virile male subject, while it addressed noncultural nationalist, black, male readers with an implied taunt: "*I* am a man, but *you*?"[71]

Karenga's seven principles of Kawaida—one for each of the seven days of Kwanza, the African holiday that Karenga also created—called for an ethos of community devotion that was not dissimilar to the values of Newton's serve-the-people philosophy. The seven principles, for example, included *Ujmaa,* or cooperative economics; *Umoja,* or unity; *Kujichagulia,* or self-determination; *Ujima*, or collective responsibility; *Kuumba,* or creativity; *Nia,* or purpose, and *Imani,* or faith.[72] Like the Black Panther masculine ideal, the ideal of Karenga's cultural nationalist masculinity embraced both warrior-like and more nurturing elements.

Gender discourse, however, appeared to have been more traditional in US circles than in the BPP. In Baraka's early promotion of Karenga's Kawaida doctrine, women were "the divine complement" for their men. Men and women each had "natural" functions. Women were principally to inspire men, teach children, and create a beneficial "environment." Women were also to "submit" by crossing their arms on their breast and slightly bowing to Karenga when he passed.[73] Angela Davis, for example, while working with a series of black political groups in 1967, was "criticized very heavily, especially by male members of Karenga's organization, for doing 'a man's job.' Women should not play leadership roles they insisted. A woman was supposed to 'inspire' her man and educate his children."[74]

Elaine Brown also recalls a dinner she attended in Los Angeles at which women were required to eat after the men. When she and her female companion resisted giving up their place in line, a cultural nationalist brother "advised us that it was not only 'unsisterly' of us to want to eat with our Brothers, but it was a sacrilege for which blood could be shed."[75] As in the Panthers, there were instances of woman beating and accusations of torture as well. Although cultural nationalist leaders challenged many of the values of self-making masculinity—materialism, competitiveness, self-interest, suppression of feeling, lack of spirituality, and racism—when it came to women and their own gender relations, their revolutionary imaginations, like those of male Panthers, often sputtered or failed to start.

Although black women were initially reluctant to challenge the unity of the movement by going public with their critiques, there is testimony about black women's resistance to and struggle over male chauvinism in cultural nationalist circles. Belle, for example, a friend whom I interviewed in the early 1990s, had participated in both the student and the New York Black Arts movements. She recalled that men became upset at women taking on leadership roles in the Columbia student strike of 1968 and that she began thinking "wait a second cause we thought we were doing this for all of us and all of a sudden the men . . . were telling me how they'd been castrated and deserved all this attention." There was "a lot of resistance within and anger and rage" and "I was . . . troubled already about the amount of emphasis being put on manhood." Although Belle, like other Black Arts girlfriends and wives, willingly typed her male partner's manuscripts, when her partner brought home a list of "ten commandments," one of which required women to be silent in front of men, "of course I threw it on the floor and started jumping." For her, black feminist consciousness-raising groups proved to be crucial in those early years, while the publication in 1970 of Cade's *The Black Woman* had seemed a "turning point."

SONS OF BLACK POWER

Given the multifaceted ideals of Black Power masculinity, and given that Black Power leaders often fell short of the self-transformation that the highest ideals of their organizations espoused, it is hardly surprising that the legacy of Black Power masculine ideals has been complex. With the destruction of the Black Power movement, for example, generations of working-class and lower-class young men, beset by racism and economic injustice, as well as by their own choices, took on elements of Black Power warrior masculinity—guns, toughness, the courage to kill—without political direction or the goal of serving the people. Politically pointless violence and criminal behavior were sometimes cast as a form of struggle. Nathan McCall, for example, remembers randomly shooting through the window of a white home, feeling that "I had fought in the real war and contributed to the Cause."[76]

Popular media also celebrated and glamorized violence, drugs, and misogyny on the part of black men in 1970s black exploitation films. Black-directed but white-produced films such as *Sweet Sweetback's Bad Asssss Song*, *Shaft*, and *Superfly*, for example, emphasized various forms of the hero's identification with or connection to lower-class black communities, but downplayed the significance of organized political struggle and sometimes celebrated individualistic acts of violence or of marketing drugs. They also relentlessly portrayed black women as persons needing protection from the hero or as supporters, lovers, or objects of his sexual interest rather than as agents in their own right.

Elements of warrior masculinity, also entered into the phenomenon of "gangsta rap." According to Barbara Ransby and Tracye Matthews, the masculine posturing of the latter has often combined the political warrior with the pimp and antiracism with misogyny and has both celebrated and condemned "the kind of black woman who is presumably undeserving of either respect or protection, the bad girl, Jezebel, whore, bitch." At the same time, the warrior legacy of Black Power, along with the veneration and commodification of Malcolm X, has led to the continuing identification of politics with the "militant posturing" of black male heroes and to the erasure of grassroots politics as carried on by black women and men both during civil rights and Black Power eras.[77]

Another legacy of Black Power masculinity, however, has entered into the continuing construction of an ideal of black manhood based on a critique of individualist, self-advancing masculine ideals and on the embrace of political struggle involving service to the community, nurturing, and care. Performances of this ideal are still to be found in many grassroots movements organized around urban peace and justice, gang truces, and community development, many of which, according to Errol A. Henderson, have former members of the BPP at the core of their cadre of community organizers.[78]

FROM BROTHERS ON THE BLOCK TO FAMILY MEN

From the late 1970s onward, cultural nationalists seeking to reinvent a black political movement and a new model for the nationalist, black, male citizen have made Kawaida doctrine the basis for a differently constructed but related masculine ideal. This ideal, like that of Black Power, also drew on the example of Malcolm X, but it was focused more on his domestic role as a benevolent patriarch than on his warrior role as an advocate for armed self-defense. The ideal would be developed in the context of the FBI-facilitated destruction of the Black Power movement, which involved many acts of violence against Panther families. Mary Clark, for example, had been pregnant when she was shot in bed. The new familial ideal would also be developed in the aftermath of the Moynihan report, which targeted black women's supposedly unnatural power in the household as a major source of black suffering. It would be developed as well in the context of the active dismantling of affirmative action programs, the deleterious effects of economic restructuring, and the transformation of "cool" street masculinities into something colder, more self-destructive, and more misogynist. It would develop, finally, within the context of at least a decade of black feminist criticism of the more patriarchal and more violent elements of Black Power masculine ideals.[79]

This more gentle and more family-oriented masculine ideal emphasized respect for women along with protection and provision for families, but it did not initially endorse equality between men and women. By 1978, for example, writer Haki R. Madhubuti, who had been influenced by black cultural nationalism and most particularly by Karenga's *ngzo saba* or Kawaida doctrine, extolled the "family" as the foundation upon which "the new black consciousness and community can be built."[80] In contrast to earlier, more patriarchal models of cultural nationalist organizations, however, Madhubuti emphasized "the equal work and decision making responsibilities of both men and women at all levels of the institution" and while stopping short of endorsing full equality within the family, urged black men "to take care of their children."[81]

In 1982 Jawanza Kunjufu, an education consultant with African-American Images who had been mentored by Madhubuti and would be likewise influenced by Karenga, Baraka, and the Kawaida doctrine, published the first of three widely quoted short volumes on *Countering the Conspiracy to Destroy Black Boys.* Citing literature from the largely white "men's movement," most notably Herb Goldberg's *The Hazards of Being Male,* Kunjufu criticized familiar elements of a specifically Euro-American self-made masculine ideal to which African-American men were often brought up to aspire: "African-American men, like European men, are taught to be aggressive, to not cry, show little emotion and affection toward male children, ignore health symptoms and continue to bring home the bacon."[82]

Kunjufu proposed an alternative set of masculine ideals that he associated with Africa and specifically with male African leaders: "I strongly advocate that we redefine manhood." In place of "'bringing home the bacon' and letting mama bring home the emotion," Kunjufu wrote, "I believe being a man may be best expressed by telling your wife 'I appreciate you,' by bringing your son to your chest, and by telling your fellow brothers when you are hurting and need their help."[83] In his 1988 edition of *Afrocentricity,* Molefi Asante, professor of African American studies at Temple University and a well-known advocate of Afrocentric nationalism today, also urges black men to adopt the Kawaida values of *nija,* which include "feeling before belief," cooperation, gentleness, and equal respect for men and women. Haki Madhubuti—in his 1990 *Black Men: Obsolete, Single, Dangerous?*—once again made close family ties and the display of love and caring the foundation of a black nationalist politics.[84]

This shift from "brother on the block" to family man is reflected in the narrative structure of McCall's autobiographical *Makes Me Wanna Holler* as well. In 1975, according to McCall, he had been sentenced to twelve years in prison for armed robbery when he began to renounce the misogynistic, physically dominant masculine ideal of his youth. Eleven years after David Hilliard, McCall would also read *The Autobiography of Malcolm X*, preceded by Richard Wright's *Native Son,* and would undergo a life-changing experience, concluding that if Malcolm X "could pull his life out of the toilet, then maybe I could too."[85]

Like Malcolm before him, McCall joined the Nation of Islam, which he felt helped him to see women with respect, and he read the psychologist Na'im Akbar, who rejected a manhood based on self-absorption, greed, and material possessions and advocated a male identity that would extend "concern beyond self to other beings." McCall would leave the Nation of Islam because it discouraged questioning and because it enforced traditional gender roles, but he would devote himself to raising a son who would treat women with respect and reject "pseudo-macho hip-hop fads."[86] This masculine ideal, as I detail in chapter 6, would become the basis of a new black fatherhood as well.

Nevertheless, many versions of this more nurturing, but still political, masculine ideal continued to enact the conservative gender roles of the 1960s, by, for example, continuing to emphasize a notion of men and women's (unequal) complementarity and by remaining staunchly antigay.[87] It has been these unevenly conservative positions on gender and homosexuality, I would suggest, that have tended to obscure the fact, in many histories of men's efforts to transform masculine ideals, that Black Power and later black cultural nationalisms articulated ideals of masculinity that were less materialistic, more communal, more nurturing, and more emotionally expressive than the ideals of white national manhood and the self-made man. Although gender politics among black men and women would be an ongoing and vigorous concern, with some cultural nationalist men embracing antisexism in the 1990s, black men did not simply trail behind white men in the effort to construct less materialistic, more communal, and more emotionally expressive models for being a man. Indeed, in the very act of naming the transformation of masculine ideals as one of its overt goals, Black Power lent authority to idea that the reform of masculine ideals might become a legitimate political project for other men—this despite the fact that these later projects might reject some, or even several, elements of Black Power masculine performance.

NOTES

1. Huey P. Newton, *Revolutionary Suicide* (1973; reprint, New York: Harcourt Brace, 1995), 200.
2. David Hilliard and Lewis Cole, *The Autobiography of David Hilliard and the Story of the Black Panther Party* (Boston: Little, Brown, 1993), 53.
3. Newton, *Revolutionary*, 15.
4. Hilliard, *Autobiography*, 99.
5. Newton, *Revolutionary*, 14.
6. Hilliard, *Autobiography*, 101, 109.
7. Hilliard, *Autobiography*, 114, 115.
8. Hilliard, *Autobiography*, 112.
9. Hilliard, *Autobiography*, 115.
10. I wish to thank the literary critic Riché Richardson for first alerting me to the importance of region in thinking about black masculinities and for insights about the role of Southern black masculinity in the Black Panther Party.
11. Hilliard, *Autobiography*, 27.
12. Cited in Cheryl Lynn Greenberg, ed., *A Circle of Trust: Remembering SNCC* (New Brunswick, N.J.: Rutgers University Press, 1998), 205.
13. Greenberg, introduction to *Circle*, 7.
14. Todd Gitlin, *The Sixties: Years of Hope, Days of Rage* (New York: Bantam Books, 1987), 128.
15. Eldridge Cleaver, *Soul on Ice* (1968; reprint, New York: Random House, 1991), 90.
16. Gitlin, *Sixties*, 85; Greenberg, introduction to *Circle*, 4, 21, 4.
17. Gitlin, *Sixties*, 135.
18. Stokely Carmichael and Charles V. Hamilton, *Black Power: The Politics of Liberation in America* (New York: Vintage Books, 1967), 39, 44, 42, 41.
19. Carmichael and Hamilton, *Black Power*, 39, 53.
20. Carmichael and Hamilton, *Black Power*, 38, 37.
21. Cited in Robert L. Griswold, *Fatherhood in America: A History* (New York: Basic Books, 1993), 214.
22. Cited in Greenberg, *Circle*, 19. For the language of anticolonialist struggle, see Carmichael and Hamilton, *Black Power*, 3, 5, 13, 34, 35, 53.
23. Huey P. Newton, *To Die for the People: The Writings of Huey P. Newton* (1972; reprint, New York: Writers and Readers Publishing, 1999).
24. David D. Gilmore, *Manhood in the Making: Cultural Concepts of Masculinity* (New Haven, Conn.: Yale University Press, 1990), 223, 224, 223.
25. Newton, *Revolutionary*, 200.

26. Newton, *Revolutionary*, 113.

27. Malcolm X, *The Autobiography of Malcolm X* (New York: Grove Press, 1964).

28. Toni Cade [Bambara], ed., *The Black Woman: An Anthology* (New York: Signet, 1970), 106.

29. Bobby Seale, *Seize the Time: The Story of the Black Panther Party and Huey P. Newton* (New York: Random House, 1970; Baltimore: Black Classic Press, 1991), 31.

30. Elaine Brown, *A Taste of Power: A Black Woman's Story* (New York: Anchor Books, 1992), 126, 127.

31. Newton, "Brothers on the Block," in *Revolutionary*, 73.

32. Hilliard, *Autobiography*, 118–20.

33. Hilliard, *Autobiography*, 155.

34. Hilliard, *Autobiography*, 132.

35. Hilliard, *Autobiography*, 209.

36. Newton, *Revolutionary*, 96.

37. Newton, "Speech Delivered at Boston College: November 18, 1970," in Newton, *To Die*, 20, 21.

38. Errol A. Henderson, "The Lumpenproletariat as Vanguard? The Black Panther Party, Social Transformation, and Pearson's Analysis of Huey Newton," *Journal of Black Studies* 28, no. 2 (November 1997): 186.

39. Newton, "On the Defection of Eldridge Cleaver from the Black Panther Party and the Defection of the Black Panther Party from the Black Community: April 17, 1971," in *To Die*, 51.

40. Eldridge Cleaver, "The Courage to Kill: Meeting the Panthers," in *Post-Prison Writings and Speeches* (New York: Vintage Books, 1969), 23, 29.

41. Cleaver, "To All Black Women from All Black Men," in *Soul*, 237.

42. Cleaver, "To All Black Women," 236, 239; Cleaver, "Notes on a Native Son," in *Soul*, 128–29.

43. Newton, *Revolutionary*, 13.

44. Hilliard, *Autobiography*, 140, 180. Newton, *To Die*, 52.

45. Newton, "The Women's Liberation and Gay Liberation Movements: August 15, 1970," in *To Die*, 153.

46. Tracye Matthews, "'No One Ever Asks, What a Man's Role in the Revolution Is': Gender and the Politics of The Black Panther Party: 1966–1971," in *The Black Panther Party (Reconsidered)*, ed. Charles E. Jones (Baltimore: Black Classic Press. 1998), 280.

47. Angela D. LeBlanc-Ernest, "'The Most Qualified Person to Handle the Job': Black Panther Party Women 1966–1982," in *The Black Panther Party*, 309.

48. Belinda Robnett, *How Long? How Long? African-American Women in the Struggle for Civil Rights* (New York: Oxford University Press, 1997), 86–114.

49. See Matthews, "'No One,'" and LeBlanc, "'The Most Qualified Person'" in *The Black Panther Party*, 267–304, 305–34.

50. Cited in Matthews, "'No One,'" 291, 292.

51. Hilliard, *Autobiography*, 222.

52. Joy James, "Antiracist (Pro)Feminisms and Coalition Politics: 'No Justice, No Peace,'" in *Men Doing Feminism*, ed. Tom Digby (New York: Routledge, 1998), 249.

53. Frances Beale, "Double Jeopardy: To Be Black and Female," *The Black Woman*, 93.

54. Matthews, "'No One,'" 281.

55. Hilliard, *Autobiography*, 221, 235, 251.

56. Eldridge Cleaver, "Message to Sister Erica Huggins of the Black Panther Party, Excerpt from Tape of Eldridge Breaking His Silence from Somewhere in the Third World," *The Black Panther,* 5 July 1969, cited in Matthews, "'No One,'" 283.

57. Cited in Matthews, "'No One,'" 283.

58. Matthews, "'No One,'" 284.

59. Brown, *Taste*, 192, 357, 368.

60. Hugh Pearson, *The Shadow of the Panther: Huey Newton and the Price of Black Power in America* (Reading, Mass.: Addison-Wesley, 1994), 259–68; 271–73.

61. Pearson's book has been sharply criticized on the grounds that it relies on the testimony of former FBI informants, but the information about sanctioning beatings and some Panthers' growing interest in Mafia-like underground activities are corroborated by Elaine Brown's *A Taste of Power*.

62. Mattias Gardell, *In the Name of Elijah Muhammad: Louis Farrakhan and the Nation of Islam* (Durham, N. C.: Duke University Press, 1996), 86.

63. Cited in Hilliard, *Autobiography*, 179.

64. Newton, *Revolutionary*, 291–92.

65. Newton, *Revolutionary*, 11, 30. I am indebted for these insights to conversations with Riché Richardson.

66. Riché Richardson, "Black Southern Masculinities on the Margins," unpublished research proposal, 2001.

67. Carl H. Nightingale, "The Axes of Oppression," in "The Crisis of African American Gender Relations: A Symposium on the Crisis of Gender Relations among African Americans," *Transition* 62, 1993: 142, 143, 146.

68. Newton, *Revolutionary*, 200.

69. Amiri Baraka, *The Autobiography of Leroi Jones* (Chicago: Lawrence Hill Books, 1997), 355–58.

70. Baraka, *Autobiography*, 358, 357.

71. Phillip Brian Harper, *Are We Not Men? Masculine Anxiety and the Problem of African-American Identity* (New York: Oxford University Press, 1966), 48, 52, 53.

72. Baraka, *Autobiography*, 356.

73. Imamu Amiri Baraka, *The New Nationalism: Studies by Imamu Amiri Baraka* (Chicago: Third World Press, 1972), 24, 25; Baraka, *Autobiography*, 359.

74. Angela Davis, *Angela Davis: An Autobiography* (New York: Random House, 1974), 161.

75. Brown, *Taste*, 109.

76. Nathan McCall, *Makes Me Wanna Holler: A Young Black Man in America* (New York: Vintage, 1994), 83.

77. Barbara Ransby and Tracye Matthews, "Black Popular Culture and the Transcendence of Patriarchal Illusions," in *Words of Fire: An Anthology of African-American Feminist Thought*, ed. Beverly Guy-Sheftall (New York: New Press, 1995), 531, 528, 529.

78. Henderson, "Lumpenproletariat," 193.

79. On "cool" turning "cold," see Marlene Kim Connor, *What Is Cool? Understanding Black Manhood in America* (New York: Crown Publishers, 1994).

80. Haki Madhubuti,"The Redevelopment of the Dead Black Mind: The Building of Black Extended Family Institutions," in *Enemies: The Clash of Races* (Chicago: Third World Press, 1978), 119.

81. Haki Madhubuti, "The Quality of Sharing," *Enemies*, 157.

82. Herb Goldberg, *The Hazards of Being Male* (New York: Signet, 1976); Jawanza Kunjufu, *Countering the Conspiracy to Destroy Black Boys*, vol. 1, rev. ed. (Chicago: African American Images 1985), 23.

83. Kunjufu, *Countering*, vol. 1, 24.

84. Molefi Kete Asante, *Afrocentricity* (Trenton, N.J.: Africa World Press, 1988), 109, 111, 116, 114; Haki R. Madhubuti, *Black Men: Obsolete, Single and Dangerous? Afrikan American Families in Transition: Essays in Discovery, Solution, and Hope* (Chicago: Third World Press, 1990).

85. McCall, *Makes Me*, 165.

86. McCall, *Makes Me*, 217–19, 410.

87. See Clarence E. Walker, We *Can't Go Home Again: An Argument about Afrocentrism* (Oxford: Oxford University Press, 2001), 121–27, on homophobia in Afrocentric thinking.

3

A Circle of Loving Companions

Radically Gay

> This shared commonality of outlook is a world view totally unfamiliar to the accrued experience of our Parent Society. It is a view of the life experience *through a different window*.
>
> —Harry Hay, *Radically Gay*[1]

BACHELORS ANONYMOUS

In August 1948, in the Silverlake District of Los Angeles, the germ of a new fraternal order came into being. Alternatively referred to as "Bachelors Anonymous" (an allusion to its grassroots, self-help origins) and "Bachelors for Wallace" (announcing its support of the Progressive Party presidential candidate Henry Wallace), the organization was eventually entitled the "International Bachelors Fraternal Order for Peace and Social Dignity," or IBFO. By June 1950, according to its founding document, this new brotherly order was to be structured on the venerable traditions of the Masons. Like its model, the IBFO planned to shroud its membership in secrecy, maintain a hierarchy of orders—into which members, after a period of initiation, might gradually advance—and create an "insignia" that could be worn at "an unconventional angle" as a symbol of distress.[2]

Like its older sibling, the IBFO was to stress fraternity among its members, universal brotherhood abroad, and a sense of spiritual mission in life. Finally, like the Masonic order, which had worked toward consolidating the identity of its members as upstanding citizens and as representatives of the nation, the IBFO aimed to improve the civic standing of its own white, middle-class, male participants. Through uniting, educating, and leading them and through developing what would later be called "a highly ethical" group culture among them, the IBFO would work to secure their "basic and protected right to enter the front ranks of self-respecting citizenship." The front-ranking citizens of the IBFO, however, in contrast to their Masonic elders, were to be forged from what the IBFO founder, Harry Hay, had called "an oppressed minority culture"—that of male, and sometimes female, homosexuals.[3] The IBFO, indeed—which was renamed the Mattachine Society in November of 1950— has often been called the beginning of the gay liberation movement.

The birth of the Mattachine Society in the 1950s had much to do with the revived visibility of homosexual subcultures in the post–World War II era and with subsequent efforts to contain them by undermining the citizenship rights of their members. As the historian George Chauncey illustrates in *Gay New York*, homosexual male subcultures had emerged in urban areas like New York by the 1890s, had risen to particular prominence during Prohibition, and had suffered increasing harassment and regulation in the 1930s. The military mobilization of World War II, however, had brought homosexual men and women into single-sex environments, had increased their opportunities for exploring same-sex relations, and had prompted many to stay in cities when the war ended. The war, therefore, had contributed to the renewed expansion of homosexual subcultural worlds.[4]

Predictably, perhaps, the noticeable growth of homosexual subcultures in the 1940s provoked further efforts at regulation and containment, as did increasing national awareness of the number and variety of persons engaged in same-sex activities.[5] The Kinsey Report, published in 1948, for example, significantly contributed to national consciousness of homosexuality by revealing, among other things, that 37 percent of the adult men it surveyed had experienced at least one post-adolescent homosexual experience. The Cold War and the domestic anticommunism of the late forties and early fifties provided other contexts in which homosexual men and women could be controlled and their rights as citizens further curtailed. "As the anticommunist wave in American politics rose," according to the historian John D'Emilio, "it carried homosexuals with it."[6]

By 1947, for example, President Truman had established a loyalty program for federal employees; the Justice Department had compiled a list of allegedly subversive organizations, and the House Un-American Activities Committee had conducted hearings in search of traitors. By December of 1950 the Committee on Expenditures in Executive Departments had claimed, in its report on the "Employment of Homosexuals and Other Sex Perverts in Government," that homosexual men and women were "'outcasts' thoroughly unsuitable for government service even as its civil servants."[7] Then, in 1953,

President Eisenhower issued Executive Order 10450, making "'sexual perversion'" sufficient and necessary grounds for disbarment from federal employment. Within these three years, thousands of job seekers were denied employment because of suspected homosexuality and thousands more lost their jobs in the federal government and in the military.[8]

By the early 1950s, when the Mattachine Society began operations, many white, middle-class homosexual men had achieved wealth and status in Los Angeles. Newly enforced and newly created regulations, however, curtailed their rights as citizens while dominant forms of the national imagination barred them from participation in the fantasy brotherhood that represented "the nation"—and denouncing them, along with their lesbian sisters, as potential enemies of the state. To Harry Hay, indeed, it seemed that homosexuals might well become the new national scapegoat and that organizing on behalf of citizen rights was now necessary for survival.

RADICAL AND GAY

As a gay man and a Communist to boot, Harry Hay was doubly targeted by the rising tide of anticommunist and antigay hysteria, although in many ways his early life had been that of a conventional, though homosexually identified, upper-middle-class boy. (Hay had been deeply influenced at the age of eleven by the work of Edward Carpenter, a nineteenth-century British writer who combined socialism, profeminism, and spirituality with a sense of the positive social role to be played by homosexuals or "the intermediate sex."[9]) Born in 1912 in Worthing, England, to American parents, Hay had spent most of his boyhood and adolescence with his wealthy family in Southern California and had been duly sent to Stanford University in 1930. While at college Hay developed an interest in drama and became acquainted with homosexual male friendship circles among actors, musicians, artists, and writers in nearby San Francisco. When a severe sinus infection forced him to withdraw from Stanford in 1932, he returned to Southern California, finding work as an actor and singer.[10]

In 1934, however, an affair with the actor Will Geer led Hay to become involved in agitprop theater during the general strike in San Francisco, and this contact with the economic battles of "hungry people" against "greedy businessmen" awakened Hay's political conscience. Upon discovering that many of his political associates were members of the Communist Party, Hay was drawn to the party too. The party, according to Hay's biographer, Stuart Timmons, appealed to Hay's idealism as "a community that went beyond national boundaries and differences of race and creed; it was driven by certainty that man's sojourn on earth could be happier if only his social relations were transformed from competition to cooperation."[11]

Initially, however, Hay's sexuality put him at odds with the party that he wished to join, for the latter, having abandoned its earlier sexual tolerance, was not only denouncing homosexuals as degenerate but, like the U.S. government, forbidding them to join. Troubled by this conflict between his personal and political lives, Hay revealed his homosexuality to party leaders, who promptly counseled him to suppress it, and, on the further advice of a therapist, Hay attempted to do just that. He married a fellow party member, Anita Platky, in September 1938, adopted two daughters with her, and for the next twelve years devoted himself to family life and to the party. In 1951, however, after meeting Rudi Gernreich, with whom he began a serious affair, and after seeing the Mattachine Society beginning to take shape, Hay realized that his life "as a heterosexual, a pseudo-heterosexual, was coming to an end." He and Anita were subsequently divorced, and Hay asked the party for an official release from membership.[12]

Hay's Old Left experience, nonetheless deeply influenced the initial organization and goals of the Mattachine Society and Hay's later work on gay politics and identity as well. (Ironically, Hay was forced to resign from the society he founded in 1953 because of anticommunist sentiments among the members.) A busy activist and avid intellectual eclectic, Hay borrowed ideas and concepts from a wide range of movements and organizations—the Masons, the Communist Party, black cultural nationalism, the women's movement, "men's liberation," and gay liberation as well. Characteristically, however, Hay "radically queered" the ideas and concepts he borrowed, not just by applying them to homosexual men, and often women, but by imagining them in relation to a set of values and beliefs that Hay conceived of as "radically gay." Among these values and beliefs was a commitment to the possibility and necessity of replacing an economic system and society based on "competition" with alternatives based on "cooperation." For Hay, being homosexual meant having a different vision of social relationships and politics than that of the mainstream. It meant challenging the values of the self-made man. It meant looking at the world "through a different window."[13]

A GAY NATION

Hay's early theorizing about a homosexual male ideal emerged during the first stirrings of the civil rights movement and was deeply informed by the early history of black nationalisms and by the Communist Party's reflections upon that history. In 1928, for example, the Sixth World Congress of the

Communist Internationale had defined African-Americans as a "national minority," a group with its own language, a shared territory (the U.S. South), a similar psychological makeup, and a common culture.[14] Hay was to extend this model to homosexual Americans, arguing that they, too, shared a common language and psychological profile. As in black cultural nationalisms, Hay also uncovered a submerged history for his cultural group or nation. If the lost history of black men and women lay in Africa, however, the lost history of gay men and women lay in Native American cultures, such as those of the Iroquois, the Plains Indians, and the Pueblo Indians of the Southwest, as well as in subcultures of Europe, Asia, Africa, and South America.[15]

Like black cultural nationalists, Hay sometimes imagined the homosexual nation as male. Although the Mattachine Society was open to women, and although Bay Area chapters involved a number of lesbians, Southern California chapters of the society largely consisted of men, almost universally white men, and of the middle to upper-middle class.[16] Hay certainly acknowledged lesbians as part of a homosexual nation or community, but he took care at times to stipulate that he was qualified to speak only from a *male* perspective and that it would be presumptuous of him to speak *for* women. His writing, therefore, although it often referred to men and women both, was uneven in this regard. In its focus on homosexual male experience and identity, indeed, it sometimes postulated a community or nation in which citizenship was unthinkingly attributed to men.

Hay's national "man," however, inhabited that category far more tenuously than the men implied by the Black Power masculine ideal. Indeed, Hay's national citizen was represented by figures who deeply challenged the concept of a gender system based on two categories. Hay, for example, often cited the berdache as an early model of the modern homosexual. *Berdache* was a term applied by European explorers to men living and working as women, or to women living and working as men, among North American Indian Tribes. Native people sometimes used the term "Two Spirit" to refer to these individuals.[17] Hay limited but also extended the reference of this term by applying it to gay men around the world.

Another version of the berdache, according to Hay, was the European Fools, who were unmarried men belonging to societies or guilds known, in Renaissance France at least, as *sociétés joyeuses*. One articulation of the Fool tradition in the thirteenth and fifteenth centuries was the all-male, French folk-dance societies known as Les Bouffons or Les Mattachines—hence the name of the Mattachine Society. These folk-dance societies, Hay argued, continued the traditions of the Medieval Feast of Fools by performing dances that involved parodies of "warlike posturing" and that sometimes featured a figure who was cross-dressed or dressed in both male and female clothes. This figure, Hay argued, like the Native American Two Spirit figure, was a symbol of the power to bridge opposites.[18]

Like the African (or black Southern) culture that would be honored by Black Power groups in the 1970s, these lost homosexual subcultures constituted a source of values that ran counter to those of the self-making masculine ideal. According to Hay, "the Berdache . . . never produced for himself but primarily for others." The Fool, moreover, was centrally involved in resistance to the Church and to the oppression of laboring people by the upper orders.

The continuation or revival of these traditions within a gay cultural minority, Hay argued in the 1950s, might have revolutionary potential with regard to contemporary social change. Just as Communist Party members had suggested, in the 1940s, that blacks might be replacing the working class as the true revolutionary force in U.S. culture, so, as early as 1953, Hay was proposing that a gay cultural minority might comprise a vanguard, too.[19]

REVOLUTIONARY HEROES

By 1970, for example, four years after the advent of Black Power, Hay was increasingly distressed by the talk of violence as a means to social change. It was at this time that he described his own version of a revolutionary man, a concept that he partially borrowed from black cultural nationalism but that he deliberately conceived of as an antithesis to the warrior elements of the Black Power masculine ideal. Hay's revolutionary man was a lover but *not* a fighter, too. Gay heroes, Hay theorized, would seek to undermine the aggressive, competitive, and imperialist values of capitalist society through tenderness rather than through combat, through "the grace and tenderness *behind* that competitive strength, the humility and compassion *behind* that territorial ruthlessness."[20]

In conceiving of a revolutionary gay hero, Hay emphasized the link between the personal and the political that SNCC and Black Power had embraced and that the women's movement was also taking as a central feature of its vision. One, among many, expressions of this concept was the idea that one's experience as a subordinated person often produced insights about dominant culture that people in the mainstream rarely, if ever, entertained. Thus blacks were able to see white privilege and racism as most whites could not, and women could see the sexism that men were blind to. A related argument was that subordinated people might also develop special capacities because of their struggles to get on in life or even to survive.

Although Hay never ceased to assert the citizenship rights of gay men and women, he did, nonetheless, believe that their outcast status, and the suffering that their being scapegoats entailed, endowed them with the potential for unusual insight, compassion, and love. Hay explained the marginalized status of gay men and women as a function of the gender systems of early patriarchal cultures that maintained strict divisions between the masculine and feminine. This strict gender division, Hay argued in 1967, was unsuited to a tiny percentage of persons—male and female homosexuals—who were stigmatized but permitted to subsist "on the fringes of the horde or just 'outside' the village camp." Living between the horde or village and the great unknown, such "deviant outcasts" were eventually institutionalized by the village or horde itself, as intermediators between the unknown and the known.[21]

The homosexual's place of exile, therefore, became consecrated ground, and homosexuals themselves, who were begrudged subsistence on the one hand, selflessly served the community on the other by seeming to ease the relations "between Gods and men" through special rituals. These "institutionalized outsiders," according to Hay, were "exempted from the social bonding of marital and reproductive institutions with all their joys as well as their exactions." As a consequence they turned in "upon themselves to discover higher reaches of personal and intimate inter-relationships . . . those of sexual and psychic love *between equals* on a subject-to-subject basis."[22] This special capacity for imagining intimate, egalitarian relation, which Hay would call "analog vision," "gay consciousness," and "the gay window" in the early 1970s, was, in his eyes, the gay community's gift to human civilization.[23]

SNCC had also embraced an ethic of egalitarian and redeeming love, so familiar from Christian traditions. Hay, however, "radically queered" this concept by locating the capacity for egalitarian love in the very structure of same-sex desire: "He who answers, she who answers, our call into being is our *like*, *our similar—the one who finds in our aspect the ideal we find in his.*"[24] The potential for healing mainstream culture, then, lay precisely in the same-sex nature of gay men and women's (widely vilified) love and desire. This formulation, of course, directly rejected the contradiction between homosexuality and radical politics that the Communist Party had imposed on Hay himself.

As in SNCC, moreover, loving, intimate relationship became a necessary foundation for political alliance and for successful efforts at social change. Hay's inspiration for this point of view, however, was not just the discourse of 1960s political movements, or the writings of Edward Carpenter or Walt Whitman, but also the fact that in 1963, the year of the March on Washington, he also discovered the love of his life—John Burnside, a science major turned inventor and a manufacturer of a mandala-producing kaleidoscope. During the 1960s Harry and John quickly became a model of the gay committed couple, often wearing flamboyant matching outfits, engaging in political activism, and writing pamphlets together. When in 1965 Hay founded "the Circle of Loving Companions," a gay political and social collective that sometimes included friends and that sometimes consisted of only John and Harry, it was meant as a living embodiment of the principle that political alliance was necessarily grounded in loving relation.[25]

The capacity for subject/SUBJECT relationship, however, as a foundation for radical political change, was not an automatic consequence of oppression and suffering or of same-gender desire. Indeed, what Hay generalized as "gay experience" was nothing if not ambiguous as a resource for personal life and politics. On the one hand, the fact that gay adolescents were forced to learn heterosexual relationship rules and then had to invent new rules for gay relations —what Hay would call the "twice patterning" of gay experience in 1991— meant that gay men and women had a mutational potential that might be developed in the service of themselves and others.[26]

On the other hand, that heterosexual socialization was imposed upon gays also meant that gays had to work hard to be different. The gay window, therefore, with its connotations of looking in from without, might have some origins in the history and individual experiences of gays, according to Hay, but it was also something to be sought after and developed through long practice. (Hay's own cantankerousness at times may have given him special insight with regard to the necessity of working on the relationship.)

Hay borrowed insights from the women's movement as well, "radically queering" them, too, by imagining a vanguard position for enlightened gay men in combating sexism and in making harmonious heterosexual relations possible. Male chauvinism, Hay wrote in 1970, during the early days of the women's movement, was a perversion of the social order that gay men had experienced alongside women.[27] So long and so continuous had this history of chauvinism continued that ordinary, heterosexual men wanting to relate to women on an equal basis had to unlearn 2,500 years of dominating practice in order to begin.[28] Fortunately, Hay concluded, the ordinary heterosexual man, and the feminist woman too, might look toward the model of the enlightened gay men for alternatives, for as Hay would (rightly) observe in a 1980 essay, "the Women of Women's Liberation would give their eye-teeth to know how to develop some measure of subject/SUBJECT relations with their men."[29]

Gay men (and women, although Hay focused once again on men) differed from heterosexual men (and women) in being capable of egalitarian relationships with their lovers. Enlightened gay men, Hay proposed in 1967, might model another way of relating for their heterosexual brothers and sisters. Indeed, as the gay liberation movement would soon testify, enlightened gay men might also be required to model less sexist ways of relating for some of their gay brothers, since gender tensions and inequalities, it would become clear, were not confined to heterosexual communities.

A THIRD GENDER

In rejecting many elements of a dominant masculine ideal—individualism, competition, making it, toughness, aggression, the suppressing of tender feeling, and a pronounced tendency to avoid the work of sustaining intimate, personal relations—Hay anticipated and shared many of the concerns of "men's liberation" networks in the 1970s. Hay's politics, moreover—antiracism, antisexism, and a belief in replacing a competitive and unequal system with a system based on cooperation—also linked him to the politics of many men who participated in the development of profeminist networks of men. Hay's own efforts to imagine a gay male ideal, however, differed from these efforts to revise masculine ideals, and from most efforts at such revision, in that Hay increasingly rejected, rather than embraced, the category "man."

This response obviously capitalized on the fact that gay men at the time had already been barred from the "man club," but Hay turned that barrier into an opportunity for partially disowning the unequal privileges that attend to the category of man in U.S. culture and for radically challenging the dualistic gender system that made *man* into the opposite of *woman*. This dualistic system, of course, contributes in a significant way to the anxiety most men feel about proving their masculinity by, for example, suppressing the more compassionate and vulnerable aspects of their humanity.

In emphasizing the capacity for tenderness and love as central to a more fully human, gay male ideal, Hay embraced qualities that had often been identified with the feminine in mainstream culture or with being a "sissy" or effeminate if displayed by boys or men. In a 1980 essay, for example, Hay recalled that as a child he had felt a sense of "beauty, an excitement" that seemed "different" from what other boys had felt. His father, however, had not been pleased and had attempted to "*unmake* the Sissy in me by teaching me to use a pair of boxing gloves. . . ." "I simply *couldn't* understand," Hay wrote, "why he wanted me to hit somebody else . . . . I didn't want to hurt other boys, I wanted to be tender to them in the same way I wanted them to be tender to me . . . . " In celebrating the capacity for tenderness in gay men, Hay saw himself as embracing "that beloved little Sissy" as he was and telling "that *different* boy that he was remembered . . . loved . . . and deeply respected."[30] Hay's sissy remains a boy in this formulation, but Hay would go further in challenging received gender categories.

Another identity that Hay attempted to embrace and rework was that of "fairy," a category that had characterized some early twentieth-century homosexual subcultures. George Chauncey, for example, convincingly argues that our current division of homosexual and heterosexual into two separate categories is a fairly recent social construction that came into being between the

1930s and 1950s. From the late nineteenth century until the 1930s, Chauncey demonstrates, different kinds of divisions had been in play in homosexual working-class subcultures of New York. The more dominant divisions, for example, were between "fairies," "queers," and "trade" or "normal" men.

"Fairies" were men who performed elements of a feminine gender role, sometimes cross-dressing, sometimes using feminine language or body posture. These men preferred sex with men but often sought out men who were not regarded as homosexual. "Trade" was the name given to men who performed a recognizably masculine ideal, who occasionally had sex with "fairies," but who were nonetheless regarded as "normal." "Queers" referred to men who preferred sex with men but who did not see themselves as "normal." At the same time, they did not perform feminine gender behavior and were often careful to distinguish themselves from "fairies," who were denigrated by mainstream culture. By the 1940s, however, these differentiations were being lost, and the word *gay* had come to reflect a major reconceptualization of "homosexual." All men who had sex with men were now "homosexual" or "gay."[31]

Although Hay employed the terms "gay," "homosexual," and "queer," he would eventually choose "fairy," as in Radical Faerie, to characterize the gay male personhood that he continued to develop as an ideal. He also suggested that aspects of modern-day "fairy" culture, such as "camp," had had venerable antecedents in the traditions of the European Fool. Like earlier Fool traditions, for example, camp might also involve the wearing of female dress, the performance of feminine mannerisms and speech, implicit or explicit satire of mainstream gender norms, and barbed witticisms. For Hay, however, whose own mastery of camp had earned him the nickname "the Duchess," camp was not to be used meanly or irresponsibly. It was to be "gently mocking healing laughter-magicks," he wrote in 1976, a self-mocking but self-loving laughter.

Camp, moreover, was to be endowed with a conscious political purpose — helping to correct and heal the "mostly unconscious Hetero community gender-role interplays" and in the process helping "our Hetero brothers and sisters learn the art of penetrating criticism and self-criticism as a way to help the loving-sharing society function more truly." Hay's homosexual male ideal, then, imbued twentieth-century "fairy" culture with a kindly political significance.[32] (Although Hay would surely not have approved its consumerist values, the wildly popular television program *Queer Eye for the Straight Guy* employs aspects of this gently mocking but also friendly camp mode to, among other things, make heterosexual relationships smoother.)

Eventually, however, Hay would insist that his ideal of gay male personhood was neither masculine nor feminine but something "other." The real threat of homosexuality to mainstream culture, Hay argued, as early as 1952, was to the gender system, according to which men who love men must be feminine men, a frightening inversion of the gender order. This stereotype, Hay argued, prompted homosexual men either to "allow ourselves to be caricatured as feminine" or to "waste our days running around trying to persuade the world that we are 100% he-men studs with real balls."[33] It is in his break with a gender system that polarized masculine and feminine and that restricted gender identities to only two that Hay proved most radically gay of all.

Initially, Hay would use the word *androgyne* to describe homosexual male and female identity. Then in 1980 he would identify his gay gender ideal as that of "not MAN." In 1994, finally, he would embrace the concept of a "Third Gender" for gay men and lesbians both. Characteristically, this revision of gender identity took on a global, political significance:

> I am proposing that we take a hand-up example from our potential allies in the Third and Fourth Worlds, whose cultures may well be overtaking, and even outnumbering, our Hetero Western so-called Free World sensibilities in the not-too-far distant first decades of the twenty-first century. I propose that we Gay Men *of all colors* prepare to present ourselves as the gentle non-competitive Third Gender men *of the Western World* with whole wardrobes and garages crammed with cultural and spiritual contributions to share.[34]

Although "third gender" reverts here to meaning gay male, Hay did at least divorce "gay" from "white" and suggested that revising dominant ideals of masculinity should be not just a national but a global project. (UNESCO itself would embrace a global revision of this sort in 1999, although without the vanguard position of gay men with overflowing wardrobes.)

If Hay fused being gay with an embrace of his Old Left belief in the possibility and necessity of radical economic change, he also imagined a "radical queering" of leftist and indeed all activist and alliance politics. Radical Faeries, for example, were not just to be compassionate and caring models of intimate, egalitarian relationship in the private lives of individuals; they were to transform, through their own example, the nature of political activism itself. Hay and Burnside, indeed, were to suggest, in a coauthored pamphlet in 1976, that Gay Radicals might "find themselves called upon to constitute an *independent*, collectively, self-motivated, self-disciplined caucus in every radical organization or group" where they would challenge heterosexuals to make the leap to "ANALOG PERSPECTIVES." The compassion and care of subject/SUBJECT relations, Hay argued, had been implicit in Marxism all along in its conception of the ultimate communist relationship: "From each according to his abilities, to each according to his needs." In practice, however, this "political appreciation of compassion" had been "totally missed" by the hetero-male-dominated Second and Third Internationales "to their ultimate disaster and defeat." Radical Faeries were to restore this emphasis on compassion and personal relations to radical politics.[35]

RADICAL FAERIES, 1979

Radical Faeries were more than an idea in Harry Hay's head. They were a network of men who came together in the late 1970s and who, in various forms and with changing membership, have attempted ever since to put Hay's theorizing into practice. Although Hay appears to have coined the term Radical Faerie, other gay activists in the 1970s had been pursuing similar lines of thought. Arthur Evans, for example, an activist in the early gay liberation movement, began to publish a series of essays in 1973 and then a book in 1978, *Witchcraft and the Gay Counter Culture.* In this book Evans would assert that the fairies of European folklore had had an actual existence as nature-worshiping people who celebrated the Great Mother with sacred, sexual rites. Although ancient religions devoted to the Great Mother had been increasingly suppressed by the Christian church, their adherents had persisted underground, becoming known in folklore as fairies and later as heretics and witches. The latter, along with horned gods, fools, wildmen, shamans, and berdaches—had been identified with male homosexuality.[36] (Similar figures would reappear, heterosexualized, in mythopoetic evocations of "the wild man," a topic I turn to in chapter 5.)

The early 1970s had also seen groups of gay men and women, wishing to escape heterosexual culture and/or burned out by gay liberation politics or by gay urban life, establishing small rural communities as their homes, often influenced by countercultural spiritualism and the hippie back-to-nature movement.[37] Evans himself had attempted to form a homesteading collective called the Weird Sisters Partnership in Washington State, on a patch of forest land that he had fondly renamed the New Sodom.[38] In 1974 another community outside Grinnell, Iowa, established *RFD: A Country Journal for Gay Men Everywhere* that advocated gay country living, a separate gay culture, and radical politics. Its third issue arrived with packets of pansy seeds stapled to the back cover. (Hay would publish several essays in the pages of this journal.)

The Northwest, meanwhile, witnessed several rural gatherings of radical gay men, such as the "Faggots and Class Struggle" conference at Wolf Creek in September 1976. Still other groups of outrageously dressed gay men, who refused to be ghettoized in the cities, were trying "to keep some sort of gay spirit alive" by traveling across country in cars painted with slogans such as *Gay Power* or *Faggots against Fascism.* One man, according to the editor and writer Mark Thompson, went a year and a half, in the spirit of the times "without wearing men's clothing, including the time he worked for the federal government."[39] Each of these networks and phenomena would contribute to what became known as the Radical Faeries.

By 1970, finally, Hay and Burnside themselves had taken up life in a rural community of their own, in northern New Mexico near San Juan Pueblo. Here Hay continued to expand on his concept of faerie identity in talks and papers, and the couple was visited by gay activists, including Doug Kilhefner, one of the founders of the Los Angeles Gay and Lesbian Community Services Center, and Mitch Walker, a San Francisco writer and counselor who also emphasized the importance of finding a unique gay identity for gay men. When in 1979 Hay, Burnside, Kilhefner, and Walker announced "The First Spiritual Conference for Radical Fairies," there were several like-minded networks upon which to call.[40]

The first Radical Faerie conference was held at the Sri Ram Ashram in the Sonora desert near Tucson, Arizona, in 1979, predating the mythopoetic leader Robert Bly's first gathering for men in Lama, New Mexico, in 1981. (Previously Bly had been holding gatherings for women.) The conference was billed as a response to countercultural talk about "New Age Politics— beyond Left and Right—a synthesis of the political and spiritual movements of the past two decades" and the conference call looked toward a politics "in which we learn to assume personal and collective responsibility for the ways we treat one another, and nature, and ourselves."[41]

The purpose of the conference, as announced in the call, was to explore the merging of the political and spiritual as a "paradigm shift" for gay men, a shift that would be prepared for, perhaps, by such conference activities as renewing "our oaths against patriarchy/corporations/racism," talking about "the politics of gay enspiritment," and by rediscovering and reinventing "our myths." The loving, personal relations and personal healing that formed the basis of politics for Hay were suggested, as well, in the call "to hold, protect, nurture and caress one another" and "to find the healing place inside our hearts." Some two hundred and twenty men attended—many, according to Timmons, progressives, and most, feminists.[42]

Radical Faerie gatherings also featured familiar elements of male romance in order to create a liminal space in which men would feel free to express and/or develop aspects of themselves that were usually policed in mainstream culture. As in nineteenth-century fraternal organizations, these elements included separation from women and the creation of ritual space, as gay men were invited "to dance in the moonlight," and to "sing, sing, sing."[43] As in many versions of male romance, among the groups I studied, the structure of Radical Faerie conference activities plainly represented a suspension of ordinary rules and a contestation of the self-making, hierarchically oriented, mainstream masculine ideal.

In the spirit of rejecting corporate culture, for example, there were no "workshops" at this conference, which was quickly renamed "a gathering."

Rather, there were "Faerie Circles" loosely based upon different themes. A blackboard was used for proposing circle topics that carried through on the promised areas of interests and that included overtly political topics such as "rape and violence" as well as topics devoted to personal healing, "nutrition," "healing-energy," and "massage."[44] Small groups devoted to "male bonding" and "stories of growing up gay" suggested a familiar emphasis on building a sense of community among men, as did what came to be known as a "heart circle." In heart circles men sat in a circle while a talisman was passed. One after another the holders of the talisman would "speak [their] heart[s]" without interruption. No one was to answer but only to listen to and receive the speakers' words. Heart circles were to become a primary focus of Radical Faeries gatherings, often lasting half a day or even all day long. The heart circle at the 1979 gathering, for example, is reported to have lasted five hours.[45]

Conference activities also included rites of re-identification and affirmation that seemed designed to compensate for the favor and for the rites of initiation that fathers often withheld from gay sons. These Radical Faerie rites also focused upon rebirth into a "secondary" identity, but, rather than "proving manhood" by imaginatively endowing participants with tougher, more robust powers, the rites involved acceptance of the feminized sissy boy within.[46] Group activities such as "ritual makeup," "country dancing," and "silly sissies" reaffirmed this acceptance as did the way men dressed. As more men arrived, according to Timmons, a "Faerie aesthetic" developed, involving rainbows trailing from eyebrows and nipples, feathers, beads, bells, and less and less clothing, an evocation of the flamboyant and gender-bending dress that Hay and Evans both claimed as an ancient gay inheritance.[47]

The Radical Faerie conference featured loving brothers galore, but this loving brotherhood maximized the erotic potential that had been repressed in nineteenth-century organizations. As if capturing the spirit of pagan worship, which Evans claimed as an ancient gay male tradition, celebrations of sexuality, including a guided orgy and instruction in autofellation, were also featured. Dances broke out, as did drumming, howling, and a collective bath in the mud.[48] Thus, at least a decade before the media prominently discovered the mythopoetic movement, with its woodsy gatherings for largely heterosexual men, Radical Faeries went off together into the wilderness, where they drummed, danced, and sang to create ritual space, challenged each other to share feelings and intimate knowledge about their lives, and radically disrupted traditional gender divisions by embracing the sissy boy within.

The 1979 Spiritual Conference for Radical Faeries, according to Thompson, had a profound impact on many of those who came, and during the next six years over a hundred gatherings of Radical Faeries were held across the United States, with gatherings subsequently reported in Europe and Australia.[49] In the early 1980s, moreover, a caucus of Radical Faeries did indeed attend several Men & Masculinity conferences sponsored by the National Organization of Men Against Sexism. NOMAS members recall Radical Faeries as gentle, sweet, and antiviolent men, given to wearing outlandish costumes involving skirts, feathers, and jewelry. Radical Faeries, according to another NOMAS source, exuded love and fun, chanted chants, drummed drums, and created dramas and performances to create group interactions. One woman recalled that they had a "loving spirit"; "they just walked up to you and hugged and touched." They were also remembered for having well-formed political analyses that were antisexist and antiracist as well as antihomophobic.

Although Hay's penchant for rejecting the category "man" did not catch on, even in NOMAS, the loving spirit and gender play of Radical Faeries did seem to have had a liberating effect on more traditional men's willingness to experiment with gender norms. Next to them, one member of the leadership recalled, everyone else "seemed like middle America." As I observe in chapter 4, a NOMAS spokesman was to evoke the Radical Faeries in the year 2000 as inspiring models of men who had been both profeminist and positive about being who they were.

GAY LIBERATION

By 1979 Radical Faeries considered themselves to be alternative not just to the dominant ideals of heterosexual masculinities but to a differently constructed ideal of gay masculinity as well. This ideal emerged in the context of a national gay liberation movement and in the context of the political divisions between gay men and women that quickly developed. The beginning of a national, grassroots gay liberation movement is often dated from June 27, 1969, when the New York Police Department raided a gay bar, the Stonewall, on Christopher Street in Greenwich Village, and when patrons of the bar—many drag queens, transsexuals, and/or gay men of color—fought back. This resistance led to several days of rioting and struggle between mainly homosexual crowds and the police and to the formation of new gay liberation organizations and of a national movement.

As John D'Emilio and other gay historians have observed, the national movement that Stonewall sparked had many of its roots in the political organizing of the homophile movement that had gone before. The Mattachine Society and the lesbian Daughters of Bilitis, founded in 1955, had formed the center of this older movement. The Gay Liberation Movement also drew upon the political analysis, sympathies, and strategies that civil rights, Black Power, the New Left, the counterculture, and the emerging women's movement had called into being. Indeed, many of those who became gay activists in the early 1970s had already allied themselves with these causes.[50] As with several earlier movements, however, this commitment to umbrella politics alliance was to fade.

As in the homophile movement, the membership and leadership of gay liberation, although including strong, activist women, were predominantly male and, in this case again, white and middle-class as well. The movement emerged, moreover, just as black women were forming their own women's groups within and outside of Black Power organizations and as white feminists were leaving male-dominated New Left groups. It is not surprising, therefore, that from the beginning, the predominance of gay men and of gay, white, middle-class male leaders, along with the sexism of many of the above, were lively issues for lesbian activists in the Gay Liberation Front and in the more conservative homophile movement.

Feminist issues, indeed, had been raised in the latter as early as 1966 when Shirley Willer, of the Daughters of Bilitis, proclaimed, at a meeting of the North American Conference of Homophile Organizations (NACHO), that "lesbian interest is more closely linked with the women's civil rights movement than with the homosexual civil liberties movement." The next year Del Martin, cofounder of the DOB, was to write that the "'battle of the sexes' which predominates in American Society prevails in the homosexual community as well and the Lesbian finds herself relegated to an even more inferior status." Finally, in 1968 the new leader of the DOB, Rita LaPorte, warned against a "a sort of group 'marriage' . . . to the male homophile community" and pressed for a withdrawal of DOB from NACHO on the grounds that "the real gap within humanity is that between men and women, not that between homosexual" and heterosexual.[51]

Gender tensions, moreover, surfaced almost immediately within the new and largely white gay liberation organizations. Since men in the Gay Liberation Front far outnumbered women, for example, the political agendas of the new organization seemed dominated from the beginning by a focus on the special concerns of gay males—such as having sex free of shackles, overturning sodomy laws, and securing freedom from political harassment for public cruising. As Karla Jay put it, "the LA GLF hardly seemed to notice that lesbians had lifestyles and issues distinct from those of gay men."[52] Like women in the New Left, women in the gay liberation movement also seemed to be called upon to run the mimeograph machines and to get coffee. Jay, for example, recalls that at Columbia in 1968 women on the Left were relegated to "supporting roles—raising money for the cause, donating our own food for the 'true revolutionaries' (or preparing theirs), and cleaning up the mess they made of the building. Did I look like Dial-a-Maid?" The same sexism continued in the Gay Liberation Front: "If we were going to be there, . . . a few men thought we might as well make ourselves useful by baking some cookies and making coffee."[53]

Although some men in the GLF were sympathetic to feminisms and through some struggled with their own sexism, gay men and women both observed that many gay men felt threatened by women's liberation. Thus some gay men expressed distaste for lesbians because of their perceived "'butchness' or toughness," that is, their deviation from a traditionally feminine role. Other gay men, moreover, those who engaged in feminized behavior, sometimes pronounced that *they* were better women than lesbians.[54] Still others found feminism, rather than sexism, to be a polarizing force, and many saw lesbians as "anti male," "hostile," and guilty of "female chauvinism."[55]

In 1970, the same year in which *The Black Woman* and *Sisterhood Is Powerful* appeared with trenchant critiques of sexist leadership in the Black Power and New Left movements, the usually moderate Del Martin published a piece in the gay journal *The Advocate* that bade "goodbye to the male chauvinists of the homophile movement" and to the women who accepted "women's status" in these groups—"making and serving coffee, doing the secretarial work, soothing the brows of the policy-makers who tell them, 'We're doing it all for you, too.' Don't believe it, sisters, for you are only an afterthought that never took place."[56]

Many lesbians, finding antilesbian sentiments rampant in NOW and in other areas of the women's movement as well, separated from both the women's and gay liberation organizations to form a separate lesbian feminist movement that then asserted vanguard status with regard to feminism. By 1975 Karla Jay was observing that "the majority of lesbians" were choosing to work in separate groups and that many had "shut off the entire gay male race."[57] Reflecting on the year 1980, Torie Osborn also noted the continuing "deep divide between the gay men's community and the lesbian community."[58]

Dominant forms of gay community, moreover, while including men of color, were also predominantly white. Reginald Shepherd, writing about Boston in 1976, reports that "I finally *met* gay men in numbers greater than *two* or three. . . . Most of the gay men I met were white . . . and most of them were just not as welcoming of their oppressed darker brothers as I had been led to believe they would be by the gay liberation tracts that were already outdated by the time I got my hands on them in 1976 or so."[59] The gay black writer David Frechette also observed that "most white gays pretend that racism doesn't exist even as they practice it. . . ." "Mention gay racism to most white gays," Frechette writes, "and their eyes roll toward heaven as they attempt to stifle yawns. . . . The only thing more boring, however, than hearing about incidents of gay racism is being victimized by them."[60]

While the era of AIDS did bring gay men and lesbians together in a series of community-based projects, divisions among gays and lesbians and white gays and gays of color persisted. The lesbian activist Urvashi Vaid, writing in the nineties, felt that "the atmosphere of trust and respect that is requisite for work across racial lines is sorely lacking in the gay and lesbian community's struggles with its own diversity. Instead of dialogue, we engage in public attack."[61] Most gay and lesbian people, she felt, did not sufficiently value the importance of multiracial and multi-issue politics. Echoing the work of Harry Hay, Vaid also called on gays and lesbians to define "an ethical code of conduct toward each other as movement activists" that would include moral commitment "to the creation of community" and to broaden alliances or to find "the new path, creating what I call a 'common movement.'" Gay male writers in the 1990s and beyond would echo these sentiments and call for differently constructed ideals of gay masculinity as well.[62] I shall return to these writers in chapter 10.

GAY NATIONAL MANHOOD: THE GAY CLONE

Although some lesbians did continue to work with gay men in political organizations, the "deep divide" to which Osborn refers could not help having an impact on the shape of gay liberation politics, facilitating, for example, the identification of gay liberation at times with white, middle-class, gay, male concerns and with a differently constructed gay male ideal, the gay clone. According to the late sociologist Martin P. Levine, "by the end of the 1970s, the clone look was *the* look for the . . . urban denizen of the gay ghetto."[63]

The ideals of the gay clone, the related, but later, ideals of circuit masculinity, and the norms of the public gatherings in which these masculinities were most often performed have been the subject of heated debate. Criticisms of clone and circuit masculinities, for example, have rightly emphasized their resemblance to the competitive, emotionally repressed, and male-dominant ideals of self-making masculinity. Other gay writers, however, have celebrated the sexual practices of these masculinities as politically revolutionary and have angrily denounced criticism as antisex and antigay. Most recently, David Nimmons's *The Soul Beneath the Skin: The Unseen Hearts and Habits of Gay Men* (2002) attempts to take a middle road, by acknowledging some of the limitations of gay clone and circuit culture, while also making a case for its richly creative, robust, sexuality. I shall return to Nimmons's arguments in chapter 10.

In contrast to Hay's ideal of gay male personhood, which represented a political transformation of the "fairy," this new gay ideal represented a rejection of what "fairy" had stood for in mainstream culture—a demeaning stereotype and an emblem of the "failed man." The new ideal of the gay clone has also been read as a reinvention of a working-class "trade" masculine ideal in that it was based on a gym-defined body that emphasized physical strength and power and on clothing that was often borrowed from blue-collar wardrobes—whether it was Western gear, leather, or the clone uniform with which I was most familiar—501 Levi's, flannel shirts, short hair, a mustache or close beard, and a leather bomber jacket worn over a hooded sweatshirt. The clone also drew on traditions of dress and behavior adopted by men who had once defined themselves as "queer," the leather garb of 1950s queer biker clubs being one example.[64]

This masculine dress, of course, was worn with a difference that, it has been rightly argued, helped erode traditional masculine ideals by challenging the equation of manhood with heterosexuality. Thus if gay men wore clothes that straight men might also wear, they wore them tighter and often highlighted their genitals by going without underwear. Gay clones might also stylize their look until it verged on caricature or a form of drag. As Daniel Harris put it, "the feminine body of the dandy" collided head-on with "an implausibly studied machismo."[65] Certain traditionally masculine behaviors were also popular with the gay clone, especially in the context of gay bar life. According to Levine, these might include taking up space, talking loudly and coarsely, or conveying emotional distance through exhibiting a blank stare. Here again, however, the behaviors were sexualized for a male audience. At the same moment, therefore, that elements of traditional masculinity were affirmed, they were forcibly disassociated from heterosexuality, and therefore functioned, to some degree, as a mode of calling dominant understandings of masculinity into question.

The contradictions between heterosexual and homosexual codes, however, went deeper than that. Some men who had once performed more feminine gender styles and who had adjusted their appearance to fit the clone image of masculinity continued to acknowledge that underneath "we're still girls." Gay cool pose, moreover, might give way in private friendship circles to the kind of camp associated with men who once identified as fairies. The gay men I knew best in the 1970s did enact clone masculinity at gay bars and social events, but they performed a fairly straight, profeminist masculinity at work and in everyday conversations. No ideal, as philosopher Judith Butler puts it, is ever fully inhabited.[66]

Clone masculinity, as has been often pointed out, also took heterosexual male socialization with regard to sex to a new extreme. Many U.S. men in the 1960s were still being brought up to see genitally focused, frequent, emotionally distant sexual performance as a sign of manhood. Heterosexual men, however, had to negotiate with women over the way in which sexual relations were to be carried on. Homosexual men did not. As Levine put it, gay men did what men had traditionally been empowered to do—they were sexually adventurous and self-indulgent. The cultural experimentation of the 1960s and 1970s with respect to sexuality and drugs also contributed to the development of a gay party culture in which drugs and frequent, often anonymous, sex with multiple partners was the rule. Within the gay evening life of the "circuit"—a network of bars, baths, discos, and sex clubs where gay men gathered for sex but also for socializing—the one-upmanship and anxiety of mainstream, self-making masculinity were also translated into new forms of competition—over having the best body, the most and the hottest sex partners, and the most highly developed sexual skills.

Clone gatherings, however, despite the different masculine ideal that they celebrated, offered many of the same resources that heterosexual and Radical Faerie forms of male romance had done—going off with other men, the establishment of ritual space, a journey into childhood, a sense of rebirth and affirmation, entrance into a larger community, and participation in an energy or purpose that extended beyond the self. Signorile, for example, suggests that clone and later circuit culture offered a return to the merry-making of childhood or adolescence that gay men had often missed. Clone culture, however, rather than embracing the sissy boy within, let alone a third gender, as Harry Hay's ideals of gay male personhood had done, replaced the sissy with a figure whose pumped-up physique offered a sense of power and control that gay boys and men had often been deprived of in their youths.

The outbreak of AIDS in the early 1980s disrupted many elements of the public gatherings at which clone masculinity was performed, as bathhouses were shut down, safer sex was practiced, and attention and energy were shifted to tending the sick and dying. After 1996, however, when protease inhibitors made it possible to live with AIDS, the public gatherings that had grown up around clone masculinity and the ideals of clone masculinity themselves made a reappearance in exaggerated form. Indeed, the very steroids used to combat wasting in those who had AIDS became a means to building even more buff bodies than before, and standards of physical perfection grew more rigid and more difficult to attain. Circuit masculinity, named after the long weekend parties that drew national and international participants, now required a body that was perfectly chiseled, hairless, and tan and that was accompanied by a good deal of attitude.[67] (The buffed gay body, of course, would profoundly influence heterosexual body styles in the 1990s as well.) Circuit culture in the 1990s, from Signorile's perspective, was more even competitive and status-conscious than the clone culture of the 1970s and more hostile to those who, in age or physical appearance, did not measure up. These were values that Hay's Radical Faerie ideal would continue to call into question.

RADICAL FAERIES, 2001

There is a blue, cloudless sky over Davis, California, and from the window of my study I can see the last yellow leaves on a walnut tree outside. I am drinking green tea, or rather I am thinking I should be drinking it, for I am trying to connect with the spirit of modern-day Radical Faeries, who often begin their e-mail posts with a description of the weather, the view, and their beverage. Earlier this fall I interviewed Daniel, the friend of a friend who attended several Radical Faerie gatherings between 1993 and 1999, two in Clearlake, California, and three at Wolf Creek, Oregon. Later on I would also interview Ben, who had been active in the Radical Faeries since 1996, had attended faerie gatherings on a regular basis, and who was centrally located in Radical Faeries networks.

According to Daniel, modern-day faerie gatherings drew men from a wide range of ages, with the youngest appearing to be no more than eighteen to nineteen years old and the oldest appearing to be in their eighties. Ben felt that the average age of Radical Faeries was somewhere in the forties. Most of these men, Daniel felt, had been seemed urban-based and were often from San Francisco and the Bay area. Gatherings were "pretty white," with lots of "computer nerds" and men in mental health professions, but with many also in entertainment, music, poetry, and art. Ben also noted that of perhaps 170 men only ten to fifteen would be men of color. According to Daniel most Radical Faeries were "to the Left" although there were some who appeared "comfortable" with the status quo. Ben reported that the conservative end of the Radical Faerie spectrum was represented by being a Democrat.

Daniel, or to give him a Radical Faerie name, Spirit Quest, did not feel that politics played a major role in Radical Faerie gatherings—a change from the Radical Faeries of the late 1970s. The gatherings, he felt were, largely about "relationship." Still, Spirit Quest did acknowledge that the norms of Radical Faerie community life, with their emphasis upon building intimate relationship between men, were informed by political logic. Spirit Quest's own motivations for attending Radical Faerie gatherings, moreover, seemed to echo Harry Hay's overtly political criticism of materialism and competition: Spirit Quest, that is, had been "repulsed" by a gay male culture that emphasized "consumerism" and "looking pretty" and had been attracted to the Radical Faeries because they were about "getting back to basics," because they emphasized "spirituality," and because they valued "being yourself." Ben, or

"Sky," who had never been attracted to, and who had never attended, a circuit event, was drawn to the Radical Faeries for their community and spirituality as well. Sky felt that Radical Faerie gatherings were "transformative," but that one changed "from within." Hay's influence on the network, therefore, appeared to live on in the form of rejecting materialism as a central value but not in the form of emphasizing activism on behalf of structural social change. That might be said of many ex-activists, of course, at the beginning of the millennium.

Modern-day Radical Faerie gatherings, like the conference in 1979, still appeared to be organized so as to contest the ideal of self-making, hierarchical, and time-managed masculinity that undergirds corporate values. Although some groups do charge an attendance fee for gatherings, according to Sky, it is part of Radical Faerie culture that no one be turned away for lack of funds. No one was assigned work, either, according to Spirit Quest. Those who enjoyed kitchen work took charge, with self-designated "kitchen queens" often assigning "princesses" their tasks. There was no schedule of activities. People wrote down suggestions for faerie groups on big sheets of paper, with groups having as much or as little structure as the participants desired, the goal being to pursue "sharing and consensus." There were no watches—"after breakfast" being as close as Faeries came to designating the hour—and, not surprisingly, groups often overlapped and ran longer than at first intended. Radical Faerie gatherings ran on "faerie time."

As in the past, activities such as drumming, poetry reading, touring and blessing the grounds, decorating sacred areas, and staging AIDS memorials seemed to prepare a ritual space. The small groups that Spirit Quest most vividly remembered, moreover, were those that seemed to be devoted to community-building through having fun—tie-dying, hair coloring, and mud rituals. Traditions such as heart circles provided space in which men might take the "risk" of appearing vulnerable or of showing love, empathy, and compassion to those who were. According to Sky, heart circles were "the primary reason we gather." Men still discussed their difficulties with embracing the sissy boy within—how "it doesn't feel right at times" or how some felt they needed to strike a balance. Hay's focus on antisexism, however, did not seem evident. In keeping with Hay's emphasis upon the faerie tradition of flamboyance and cross-dressing, most men brought sparkles and bright clothing to gatherings, with nail polish, skirts, and fashion parades being well-established traditions.

Body acceptance was also a common theme, continuing earlier Radical Faerie criticism of clone masculinity. Bodies at Radical Faerie gatherings, according to Spirit Quest, ran the gamut from buff to flabby to overweight. Radical Faeries also adopted norms with respect to sex and drugs that were different from those prevalent in circuit culture. According to Spirit Quest, participants in Radical Faerie gatherings were free to express themselves sexually, but sexual contact, he felt, became an expression of crumbling boundaries, of experiencing someone on "a deeper level." Sex was not anonymous but more about "wanting to share." Although some men did drugs on the side, mainly marijuana, and although there were sometimes organized "trip outs" on mushroom tea, Spirit Quest felt that this was rare.

Spirit Quest himself felt that his experiences at Radical Faerie gatherings had made him more willing to be emotional, more sensitive, and more creative and that he had incorporated these qualities into his professional activities. He also felt that he had worked out his own relation to the feminine. By the time of our interview, however, Daniel/Spirit Quest was no longer attending Radical Faerie gatherings, having found another spiritual community—at a local church. This combination of faerie spirituality and major religious traditions would be replicated in other circles, such as those of gay liberation theologians that I turn to in chapter 10.

During the same fall in which I interviewed Daniel, I was given permission to read a Radical Faerie e-mail list, a kind of "heart circle" on line, where men identifying as Radical Faeries shared thoughts and feelings about a range of topics. I read this website every day between August 2001 and January 2002 and by September I was looking forward to it as a source of intellectual and political debate, of warmth, high spirits, and fun. Is Radical Faeriedom a religion? What is the nature of masculinity? How is intimacy formed? How do intentional communities work? What is the future of Social Security? These are among the topics that were addressed.

The list was also political, and although there was a range of political opinion, Radical Faeries clearly leaned to the Left. As with most of the lists to which I belong, there was a good deal of discussion of the terrorist bombings on September 11 and of the subsequent and alarming erosion of civil liberties and of a domestic agenda for the non-elite. While a few Faeries expressed dismay at what they felt was the intrusion of gloomy political discussion into the support network devoted to "our queer experience of culture, spirit, and sexuality," most others maintained that the very legacy of the Radical Faeries dictated a concern with national and international political affairs: "The Fae community is not a bubble to hide in," wrote "Ginger Tea." "My Faerie nature makes me a (r)evolutionary," wrote "Moon Spirit."

Discussions of personal intimacy, moreover, often merged into emphases upon the relation of personal compassion to social justice: "Intimacy is now about seeing into the starvation around the world, while Americans get fatter and richer." Political debate, by the same token, often affirmed the necessity for compassion, care, and attention to subject/SUBJECT behavior: "The needs of our more yin brothers and sisters should be heard and respected rather than subjected to sarcasm and ridicule as has happened here recently," wrote "Heart Circle." "I just don't have the heart or stamina to be around the few that continue to make statements about social justice or spirituality but haven't learned anything about compassion and honoring one another's paths," wrote "Wild Dancer."

Indeed, what was most different about this list, most particularly in contrast to one of the cultural leftist lists I also read, was the high level of concern for listening and for practicing sensitivity and compassion in political debate. Although individual Radical Faeries were not above sarcasm, personal attack, and threatening to leave in a huff, the group regularly practiced the emotional labor of trying to maintain what they still referred to as subject/SUBJECT relationship, treating the other as a respected and cared-for equal. The tensions that arose over the tone of some of the contributions to the 9/11 debate were eventually worked through with forthright talk, expressions of hurt, reminders of Radical Faerie ideals, humor, solicitation, apologies, and e-mailed hugs. These were men who, at the very least, did struggle to practice Gandhi's advice about the political day-to-day: "We must become the change we want to see in the world."[68]

The Radical Faerie list not only valued noncompetitive and supportive exchange and the expression of grief, vulnerability, compassion and care, but it was also a reliable source of high spirits and fun. This was another contrast to the fairly unrelenting sobriety of the cultural leftist lists and to the uneasiness often implied there, especially by men, about expressions of grief or vulnerability, and even at times about being light of heart. Aside from the Radical Faeries' humanizing attention to weather, place, and beverage and their penchant for sharing recipes—largely involving persimmons, lentils, and pears—I have enjoyed, in serious discussions of circuit masculinity and its obsessive body concerns, the occasional suggestion, that "yes, get plastic surgery! I just read this amazing article in *Harpers* where you can now have wings put on or an extra thumb, or turn yourself into a lizard or a cat."

That one member attended a gay event, dressed in an animal caftan, looking "fabulous" in a sea of more conservative and more traditionally masculine-looking gay men, struck a chord in someone so bored by the dressed-down norms of her college town that she has taken to carrying a red, orange, and aqua beaded purse to official college functions. The last Cultural Left event I attended, several years ago, could have used a liberal dose of subject/SUBJECT relationship, not to mention sparkling nail polish, animal caftans, and perhaps beaded purses as well. Where's a Radical Faerie caucus when you really need one?

Radical Faeries, nonetheless, scarcely command the attention of the gay or the heterosexual mainstream, not to mention the gay or straight Left. Although as individuals Faeries hold strong political opinions, political alliances do not seem of much interest to many of the participants on the e-mail list. As Sky put it, "You have to go find the Radical Faeries and they like it that way." There was "no big desire to be more public," and change was "individual." Radical Faeries, moreover, do not seem to interact much, as a group, with women. Although some gatherings admit female-bodied women, the gathering Sky favored was "male space," and to Sky the significance of gatherings lay in the different ways that men related to each other. Gatherings were "temporary autonomous zones" in which normal rules were suspended and men were free to touch, hug, and kiss. With men's defenses down, men's sensitivity and spirituality increased, and men talked about carrying these expanded capacities back home.

Although, as Sky reflected, some people think the Radical Faeries are dying off, I believe their values, in the radical forms that Hay first conceived of them, live on in unexpected quarters. Indeed, beginning in the late 1980s and continuing into the 1990s and beyond, at least a dozen books called for what I refer to as a politics of feeling, arguing that love, compassion, and working on relationships must now be fundamental to political alliance and political activism, much as Hay had believed and claimed. Although only gay authors of this literature appeared to have read Harry Hay and although only gay authors imagined gay men and women as leading the way, it was clear that many straight men and women, black and white, shared Hay's a vision of a radical politics that was deeply rooted in working on the relationship and in reinventing masculine ideals. I shall return to this political vision in chapter 10.

NOTES

1. Harry Hay, "Western Homophile Conference Keynote Address," 13–14 February 1970, in *Radically Gay: Gay Liberation in the Words of Its Founder,* ed. Will Roscoe (Boston: Beacon Press, 1996), 196.

2. Harry Hay, "Preliminary Concepts: International Bachelors' Fraternal Order for Peace & Social Dignity, Sometimes Referred to as Bachelors Anonymous, July 7, 1950," in *Radically Gay,* 70–72; Stuart Timmons, *The Trouble with Harry Hay: Founder of the Modern Gay Movement* (Boston: Alyson Publications, 1990), 135, 151, 152.

3. Timmons, *Trouble,* 154; Harry Hay, "Mattachine Society Missions and Purposes, April 1951," in *Radically Gay,* 131; Harry Hay, "Slogan: 'Children and Fools Speak the Truth': Les Mattachines (The Society of Fools)," 1950, in *Radically Gay,* 79; Timmons, *Trouble,* 151.

4. George Chauncey, *Gay New York: Gender, Urban Culture, and the Making of the Gay Male World, 1890–1940* (New York: Basic Books, 1994), 1, 8, 10, 11.

5. Timmons, *Trouble*, 146–47.

6. John D'Emilio, *Sexual Politics, Sexual Communities: The Making of a Homosexual Minority in the United States, 1940–1970* (1983; reprint, Chicago: University of Chicago, 1998), 35, 40, 41.

7. *New York Times*, 15 June 1950, 6, cited in D'Emilio, *Sexual Politics*, 41; United Senate, 81st Congress, 2nd session, Committee on Expenditures in Executive Department, "Employment of Homosexuals and Other Sex Perverts in Government" (Washington, D.C., 1950), 3–5, cited in D'Emilio, *Sexual Politics*, 42–43.

8. *Executive Order 10450*, reprinted in *The Bulletin of Academic Scientists*, April 1955, 156–58, cited in D'Emilio, *Sexual Politics*, 44. See also D'Emilio, *Sexual Politics*, 40, 42, 44.

9. Timmons, *Trouble*, 27–28.

10. See Roscoe, *Radically Gay*, 355–59, for a chronology of Hay's life.

11. Timmons, *Trouble,* 69.

12. Roscoe, *Radically Gay,* 357–59, cited in D'Emilio, *Sexual Politics*, 60.

13. Harry Hay, "Western Homophile," 196.

14. Roscoe, *Radically Gay*, 40–42.

15. Harry Hay, "The Homosexual and History . . . An Invitation to Further Study," 1953, in *Radically Gay*, 100–101.

16. D'Emilio, *Sexual Politics*, 72.

17. Roscoe, *Radically Gay,* 47.

18. Timmons, *Trouble*, 129–30.

19. Hay, "The Homosexual and History," in *Radically Gay*, 111, 114–15.

20. Harry Hay, "Western Homophile," in *Radically Gay*, 196.

21. Harry Hay, "The Homosexual's Responsibility to the Community," originally published in *Concern* 6, April 1967; in *Radically Gay,* 164.

22. Hay, "The Homosexual's Responsibility," in *Radically Gay*, 165.

23. Harry Hay and John Burnside, "Gay Liberation: Chapter Two, Serving Social/Political Change through Our Gay Window," 20 April 1976, in *Radically Gay,* 209.

24. Hay, "Western Homophile," in *Radically Gay*, 196.

25. Timmons, *Trouble*, 209, 213, 214.

26. Hay, "What Gay Consciousness Brings and Has Brought to the Hetero Left!" delivered at conference entitled "Queer Relations: the Lesbian/Gay Movement and the U.S. Left," 26 June 1991, in *Radically Gay*, 289.

27. Hay, "Western Homophile," in *Radically Gay,* 194.

28. Hay, "The Homosexual's Responsibility," in *Radically Gay,* 163.

29. Hay, "Toward the New Frontiers," in *Radically Gay,* 260.

30. Hay, "Toward the New Frontiers of Fairy Vision . . . subject/SUBJECT Consciousness," 5 July 1980, in *Radically Gay*, 256, 255.

31. Chauncy, *Gay New York*, 13, 16, 21–22.

32. Hay and Burnside, "Gay Liberation: Chapter Two—Serving Social/Political Change through Our Gay Window," signed Harry and John, 20 April 1976, in *Radically Gay*, 213.

33. Harry Hay, "Homosexual Values vs. Community Prejudices," delivered at Mattachine discussion group, August 1952, in *Radically Gay*, 85.

34. Hay, "Preliminary Concepts," 64; Hay, "Toward the New Frontiers," 263; Hay, "Remarks on Third Gender," 2 March 1994, in *Radically Gay*, 299.

35. Hay and Burnside, "Gay Liberation," in *Radically Gay,* 213, 208; Hay, "What Gay Consciousness Brings," in *Radically Gay,* 292.

36. Mark Thompson, "This Gay Tribe," in *Gay Spirit: Myth and Meaning* (St. Martin's Press, 1988), 262; Arthur Evans, *Witchcraft and the Gay Counter Culture* (Boston: Fag Rag Books, 1978), 69, 70, 92, 101, 103.

37. Thompson, "This Gay Tribe," in *Gay Spirit*, 262, 264.

38. "Arthur Evans: Biographical Sketch," 25 July 2001, http://www.webcastro.com/evans1.htm.

39. Thompson, "This Gay Tribe," in *Gay Spirit*, 263, 264, 266, 267.

40. Thompson, "This Gay Tribe," in *Gay Spirit,* 267.

41. Don Kilhefner, "Spiritual Conference for Radical Fairies: A Call to Gay Brothers," 1979, in *Radically Gay*, 239.

42. Kilhefner, "Spiritual Conference," in *Radically Gay*, 240; Timmons, *Trouble*, 265.

43. Kilhefner, "Spiritual Conference," in *Radically Gay*, 240.

44. Timmons, *Trouble*, 267.

45. Timmons, *Trouble*, 271.

46. Hay, "Towards the New Frontiers," in *Radically Gay*, 255.

47. Timmons, *Trouble*, 267, 266.

48. Timmons, *Trouble*, 267.

49. Thompson, "This Gay Tribe," in *Gay Spirit*, 268.

50. D'Emilio, *Sexual Politics*, 233, 234.

51. D'Emilio, *Sexual Politics*, 228, 229.

52. Karla Jay, *Tales of the Lavender Menace: A Memoir of Liberation* (New York: Basic Books, 1999), 179.

53. Jay, *Tales,* 14, 82.

54. Allen Young, "Some Thoughts on How Gay Men Relate to Women," in *After You're Out: Personal Experiences of Gay Men and Lesbian Women,* Karla Jay and Allen Young, eds. (New York: Gage Publishing Limited, 1975), 195, 198; "Can Men and Women Work Together: A Forum?" in *After You're Out*, 184, 186.

55. Alexandra Chasen, *Selling Out: The Gay and Lesbian Movement Goes to Market* (New York: Palgrave, 2000), 84; Jim Bradford, "Letter to the Editor," in *Long Road,* 58.

56. Del Martin, "Good-Bye, My Alienated Brothers," in *Long Road to Freedom: The Advocate History of the Gay and Lesbian Movement*, ed. Mark Thompson (New York: St Martin's Press, 1994), 42.

57. "Can Men and Women Work?" in *After You're Out,* 181–82.

58. Torie Osborn, "Calm before the Storm," in Thompson, *Long Road*, 195.

59. Reginald Shepherd, "Coloring outside the Lines," in *Fighting Words: Personal Essays by Black Gay Men*, ed. Charles Michael Smith (New York: Avon Books, 1999), 28.

60. David Frechette, "Why I'm Not Marching," in Smith, *Fighting Words,* 132, 131.

61. Urvahsi Vaid, *Virtual Equality: The Mainstreaming of Gay and Lesbian Liberation* (New York: Anchor Books, 1995), 278.

62. Vaid, *Virtual Equality*, 383, 381, 303.

63. Martin P. Levine, *Gay Macho: The Life and Death of the Homosexual Clone* (New York: New York University Press, 1998), 58.

64. Daniel Harris, *The Rise and Fall of Gay Culture* (New York: Hyperion, 1997), 94, 181.

65. Harris, *Rise and Fall*, 95.

66. Judith Butler, "Melancholy Gender/Refused Identification," in *Constructing Masculinity*, ed. Maurice Berger, Brian Wallis, and Simon Watson (New York: Routledge, 1995), 32.

67. Michelangelo Signorile, *Life Outside: The Signorile Report on Gay Men: Sex, Drugs, Muscles, and the Passages of Life* (New York: HarperCollins Publishers, 1997), 68.

68. Citation taken from www.gurteen.com/gurteen/gurteen.nsf/0/8EAD6302 FF4AA5AB80256848005AD6B0.

4

Reenchanting (White) Masculinity

The Profeminist Heritage of "Men's Liberation"

What strikes me now is how American masculinity has become a disenchanted symbol. . . . Any attempt to get American men to take responsibility for rape and violence against women must find a way to ennoble and enchant manhood while retaining a sense of equality with women. *This* will not be easy.

—Tim Beneke *Proving Manhood*[1]

"THE REVOLUTION"

The escalation of the Vietnam War in the mid-1960s and the emergence of Black Power—which called upon whites to organize in their own communities —marked both a transition and a continuation in the politics of many white, activist men. As participants in the civil rights movement, for example, white men had followed the lead of politicized black men and women, often embracing their self-sacrificing politics and adopting their implied critique of national manhood and of individualistic, self-making values. Tom Hayden, for example, a state senator in California for many years, was a cofounder of the leading New Left organization, Students for a Democratic Society (SDS), in Ann Arbor, Michigan, and in 1963 a staff member of the Student Nonviolent Coordinating Committee (SNCC). Hayden spent two years with the civil rights movement in the South and was later to recall that experience as a species of rebirth: "I started in the South, not in Ann Arbor. . . . My life was changed, I would say totally, by my experience in the South."[2] Although Hayden had initially aspired to a career as a newspaper editor or foreign correspondent, after his years below the Mason Dixon Line he "never went back to a conventional career, ever." As a consequence, he suffered a fifteen-year break with his father, who, in his more traditional aspirations for his male heir, "could not understand how he had created a person who went to college, got a degree, and went to Mississippi, Georgia, and Newark to work among blacks."[3]

Many white activist men also admired and took on some of the community-oriented, emotionally open, and caring attitudes and behaviors that SNCC, in particular, had celebrated. For the sociologist and sixties activist Todd Gitlin, "what existentialist radicals of the New Left cherished was variously what they saw as the stoicism, wholeness, community, and expressiveness of the poor [black] farmer which stood for alternatives to suburban blandness, middle-class impersonality, and folding-spindling-and-mutilating universities."[4] For Hayden SNCC's strength came from "the humanism of rural people who are immune to the ravages of competitive society." For the historian and activist Howard Zinn, SNCC had renounced "the fraud and glitter of a distorted prosperity" and had recaptured "an emotional approach to life, aiming, beyond politics and economics, simply to remove the barriers that prevent human beings from making contact with one another."[5]

Like SNCC, SDS also opposed egoistic individualism, marketplace masculinity, the organization man, and the career in "plastics" that would be offered to Benjamin Braddock in the 1967 film *The Graduate*. In their place, according to the founding document of SDS, the 1963 Port Huron Statement, participants in SDS expressed longing to explore "our unfulfilled capacities for Reason, Freedom, and Love." For Michael Kimmel, the Port Huron Statement was "an anxious plea for a new definition of manhood," a manhood based both on the struggle for social justice and on the capacity for love and care.[6]

As participants in the student and antiwar movements, of course, many white, activist men constructed a leadership of their own, but (despite the fact that, as one activist put it, "it was harder to feel intimate with Malcolm and the Panthers than with SNCC") some white male activists continued to model themselves upon politicized black men during the era of Black Power. If in civil rights struggles many white men had adjusted their performance of masculine identity to emphasize the values of love and self-sacrifice or "putting your body on the line" for the oppressed, so during the advent of Black Power many would follow black male leaders in adopting a more epic, although still self-sacrificing, masculine ideal. The white, male Left, according to sociologist Todd Gitlin, supported SNCC when it proclaimed Black Power in 1966 and by 1968:

> The main white movement "heavies" chose the Black Panther Party as their leading black heroes and allies. Alongside the posters of Che Guevara ("At the risk of seeming ridiculous, let me say that a true revolutionary is guided by feel-

ings of love") and Malcolm X . . . there appeared on movement walls the poster of Huey Newton in a black beret, seated in a fan-shaped wicker throne, spear upright in his left hand, rifle in his right.[7]

The identification of white antiwar movement leaders with revolutionary struggles throughout the globe imaginatively positioned them alongside their black counterparts as co-leaders of "the revolution," a movement that they hoped would sweep away unjust regimes and bring peace and justice not only to the United States but also to the world.

Modest traces of this heroic masculine ideal surfaced in a series of oral histories that I and sociologist Judith Stacey collected in the early 1990s from twenty-seven white, middle-class, heterosexually identified men who had been activists in the 1960s and who had become academics in the mid-1970s. One account of our research focused on the life stories of seventeen of these men, all of whom had been politicized by the civil rights movement and all of whom went on to participate in the student and antiwar movements as well.[8]

Fourteen of these men had been involved in Southern freedom rides, had gone south to register voters with SNCC during the Freedom Summer of 1964, had organized community protests, and/or had consistently engaged in other forms of civil rights activities. After 1966, when SNCC became an all-black organization, five of these men became Panther supporters and identified with Black Power (at least one of them sleeping under a poster of Malcolm X). Most of the fourteen, however, participated less directly or less often in antiracist struggles after the emergence of Black Power. It was the antiwar movement, which developed during the advent of Black Power, that was to prove, for most, the high point of their political experience.

The fall of 1964, for example, had marked the beginning of the free speech movement at the University of California–Berkeley, which was followed by student movements on other campuses. The years 1964 and 1965 also saw an escalation of the conflict in Vietnam and the growth of an antiwar movement. The latter would offer young white men a politics that involved their own self-interest as well as that of the oppressed. Young white men themselves, for example, were potential, or active, victims of the draft and, therefore, of the long-standing imperialist relations that Vietnam represented and of ruling-class men whom many regarded as "evil."[9]

Although not all the men we interviewed identified with Black Power, they did describe their political involvement in the antiwar movement in ways that evoked the genre of revolutionary autobiography—a form of writing in which Panthers like Huey Newton, Bobby Seale, and Eldridge Cleaver had all engaged. Thus, the antiwar movement was "thrilling and scary," a "high adventure," a "revolutionary moment" that justified "sacrifice," a time that exposed them to "danger," changed their lives and other people's, and involved them in struggle with the "evil" and "horror" of the war. A tie between ideals of masculinity and the war was also suggested in fond, if ironic, memories of revolutionary fervor. One man remembers taking PhD orals at an Ivy League university dressed in a work shirt and red arm band. For others, a sense of masculine failure attended this link. Simon felt his decision not to renounce citizenship was a "lost moment," and Ted, who had a medical deferment, linked this to his "vulnerability in terms of manhood." Like the civil rights movement, Black Power had a shaping influence upon the masculine ideals of white males in the New Left.

By 1968 and 1969, however, SDS, which had been central to sustaining an ideal of self-sacrificing, revolutionary (and implicitly masculine) political identity, was beginning to unravel. Between 1960 and 1967 it had grown from a small, controlled group to a sprawling network of thirty thousand and had begun to splinter into warring factions, each vying for theoretical control of "the revolution." By 1969 SDS had imploded from within.[10] Although the antiwar movement did continue for some years, after 1970–1971 the number of antiwar demonstrations declined. Nixon's "Vietnamization" policy reduced the number of U.S. combat troops in Indochina, a draft lottery replaced the draft, and the FBI stepped up its program of dirty tricks, disinformation, and harassment of antiwar contributors and celebrity allies. Violence toward demonstrators continued.[11] The subsequent decline both of the antiwar and New Left movements contributed to the loss of a political moment in which many white men had "proved" their manhood by playing what they and others saw as heroic roles.

It was the emergence of feminism, however, and the abandonment of the movement by many white women that would bring this heroic moment to a decided close, leaving many men who had lived their adult lives in the "movement" with "a powerful sense of loss and disorientation."[12] As early as 1964, for example, according to historian Ruth Rosen's account, Casey Hayden and Mary King, then members of SNCC, had circulated an anonymous position paper on informal male domination within that organization, complaining that women were assigned menial tasks and were undervalued.[13] Then, in December of 1965, Hayden and King, who had begun to organize white communities in Chicago with SDS, circulated another memo on sex and caste that argued that women, like blacks, were an oppressed caste in society and in the movement. According to Rosen, for example, Hayden had observed that the white SDS males attempting to organize men who had recently arrived in Chicago from Appalachia seemed taken by the latter's retrograde attitudes toward women: "the (SDS) men seemed fascinated by the violence; they even tried to imitate the men's swaggering and violent postures. Worst of all, some of the men tried to pressure SDS women into sleeping with community men."[14]

Drawing on what they had learned in SNCC about the oppressed defining their own freedom, the authors also raised pointed questions with regard to a range of movement assumptions about who "cleans the freedom house, . . . who accepts a leadership position, . . . who does secretarial work, and . . . who acts as spokesman for groups.'" A reading of the memo at an SDS conference that year was followed by discussion that lasted well into the early morning, some of it by women who formed their own group. One activist, Nanci Hollander, remembers thinking, "We've just started a women's movement."[15]

In 1967, once more, SDS women wrote a resolution for the liberation of women, describing themselves as having a colonial relation to men. Then in August of that year, at a conference meant to reunify the "movement," the National Conference for New Politics, Jo Freeman and Shulamith Firestone rewrote the document and asked to present it to the participants. The resolution, which was eventually read to the gathering, in a monotone, by a man, promptly met with derision and ridicule. Later that year in Chicago and New York small groups of women, sparked by SDS and SNCC veterans, began meeting in what became known as consciousness-raising groups, that took inspiration from the peasants' "speak bitterness" groups of the Chinese revolution.

Between the fall of 1967 and the end of 1968, movement women turned their organizing skills to creating women's liberation groups in nearly every city in America.[16] Black and white feminist organizing, moreover, overlapped. In 1968, for example, Frances Beal recommended the formation of a Black Women's Caucus within SNCC, which by 1969 had split from SNCC into the Black Women's Alliance, focusing on the needs of black women. The organization then established links to Asian, Chicana, Native American, and Puerto Rican women based on anti-imperialist ideology and became the Third World Women's Alliance (TWWA). The TWWA's position papers on women's liberation were also circulated in white feminist circles.[17]

The resistance of many New Left men to white feminist criticism, Rosen writes, was to become more hostile over the next two years as men on the Left spread word of the women's liberation movement through derision and ridicule. One year later, at a January rally against the Vietnam War, Marilyn Salzman Webb, who had remained on the New Left and who had been invited to speak to the gathering on the subject of the burgeoning women's movement, began her address only to see fistfights breaking out in the audience and to hear leftist male comrades yelling, "Fuck her! Take her off the stage! Rape her in a back alley." None of the male leaders tried to subdue the crowd, and many New Left women saw this as the last straw. Between 1969 and 1971, many white women, having decided that working for women's liberation in a movement with men was a waste of time, followed the example of Black Power by declaring their independence and separation from the white male left. According to Todd Gitlin, "the time was agonizing for movement men, exhilarating for tens of thousands of women." Women "had been the cement of the male-run movement; their 'desertion' into their own circles completed the dissolution of the old boys clan."[18]

THE END OF POLITICS

For many white feminists such as myself, the women's movement represented a logical, culminating, and thrilling next stage in the development of a struggle for social justice that had begun with civil rights. Sometime in 1963, for example, I first read James Baldwin's "Letter from a Region in My Mind," an experience that would lead to the born-again dedication of my own life to issues of social justice. Shortly after my encounter with Baldwin's text, I joined a chapter of The Friends of SNCC and began to register voters in Oakland's black neighborhoods. (Like Hayden's father, my parents were predictably aghast.)

As with many white men and women in the 1960s, my dedication to racial justice was deepened by hearing Malcolm X speak and then by reading and teaching his *Autobiography* and other Black Power texts. The political activities and glamour of the Black Panthers—whom I regularly encountered on the Berkeley campus—had similar effects. These engagements with civil rights and then Black Power also influenced my participation in the New Left, student, and antiwar movements. All of these engagements, moreover, would lead somewhat later to another born-again moment in 1971, when, during my first women's consciousness-raising session, I would feel once more that the "scales had fallen from my eyes."

For many white leftist men, however, the women's movement might have been a logical next stage, but it was scarcely thrilling in the way it was for me. Feminist politics, for one thing, extended the meaning of a personal politics involving egalitarianism, emotional openness, and self-sacrifice to men's relationships with women. This was something that the white, male-led left had never really contemplated in a systematic way and that many New Left men resisted when feminists began to articulate a criticism of the New Left from within. For many New Left men, indeed, feminism's personal politics was hard even to recognize as "politics."

Simon and Daniel, for example—their names, like those of others I interviewed for this study, are fictitious—recalled feeling support for women's equality in the early 1970s because it was consistent with the politics of equality that had initiated their participation in civil rights, but they confessed that they found feminist criticism of men's daily behaviors hard to take, and hard even to see as "politics." Simon claimed that, from his first encounter with feminism in the late 1960s, he agreed that women should have the same rights as men, that he defended the women's movement, gave support to women colleagues, and opposed stereotypes, but that he had had difficulty seeing himself as "an oppressive male." He found it particularly hard to adjust his speaking style or to self-consciously make room for women to talk in meetings.

Daniel reported that "the political stuff always, the things that were positions, things that could be remedied by public policy in some way, always made sense to me; they weren't a problem. The more difficult things were the politics of everyday life." Now, with belated appreciation, he defined this criticism as the difference between feminism and other politics. In the words of Isaac, "no other theory forces you to look at daily life." As Harry Hay had also argued, "Marxism could do this, but doesn't."

Feminism's version of personal politics, moreover, was too close to home. White men could deal with black hostility by evading direct engagement with it, by vicariously identifying with it from a distance, or by agreeing–from the same distance—that "they deserved it." In the words of Paul, "Although I was generally a Panther supporter, you know, there's a whole romance that's further away from home than the question of feminism for men." From Paul's perspective it had been easier for white men to be better on civil rights and the race question than on the woman question. It had cost them less. As Simon also put it, "Civil rights didn't challenge whites in the same ways; it wasn't in bed for the most part."

Early white feminisms, moreover, directed a good deal of (understandable) anger at white leftist men and insisted, in no uncertain terms, that white men should change, and in the ways that feminists prescribed. These developments, in many cases, gave concreteness and immediacy to whatever anxieties leftist men, like other men, might already entertain about women's (and their mothers') attention and control. Simon, for example, noted that feminism had decentered white men and observed that "the ego doesn't like this. The kid in us wants to be attended to. It's hard to become an adult." George, reflecting on his inability to remember his first encounters with feminism, speculated about the role that unconscious anxieties might have played: "But you know, you don't remember something, you figure there might be a reason for that, that there's a lot of anxiety there."

Feminist politics, moreover, did not offer white activist men the heroic, political roles to which many had become accustomed. The civil rights movement had been situated within the context of a long legacy of national shame

and organized protest, including that of civil war. It had also been characterized by dramatic encounters and mass demonstrations and, though led by
black men and women, had initially offered white men and women both historically familiar and sometimes dramatic roles to play. Early white feminisms, offered a far less familiar legacy to white men—that of being antisexist as well as antiracist and of following women's leadership alone. The
women's movement, moreover, although it involved some mass demonstrations, relied upon a mode of organizing—intimate, emotionally revealing,
consciousness-raising groups—that was not as easily compatible with earlier,
and especially antiwar, cultures of politically heroic manhood. As Isaac reported, the women's movement did not offer many opportunities "to put your
body on the line." Some white feminisms, of course, did not welcome men's
bodies in the women's movement on any level.

White feminisms also questioned the status of white men's heroism in the
past, insisting that radical men own up to the frequently sexist, egocentric,
and self-making terms of their political engagements with women. If by 1970
black feminists like Frances Beale and Toni Cade were criticizing black male
leaders for vehemently rejecting white, mainstream values on the one hand
and taking their ideas about gender relations from the *Ladies Home Journal,*
on the other, in the same year white feminists like Marge Piercy were accusing SDS chapters of acting like "fraternities" and of enacting with women the
egoistic individualism they otherwise purported to reject.[19]

White male leaders, or "machers," according to Piercy's "Grand Coolie
Damn," engaged in the egocentric careerism and sexism of self-making masculinity in refusing as "professional" revolutionaries to "haul garbage, boil
potatoes, change diapers and lick stamps" while conceiving of women in
terms of "bed, board, babies," as well as in terms of "typing and running
[their] office machines and doing [their] tedious research." Such machers
were also willing to use women "as props for a sagging ego," to create a
"harem atmosphere" in which they were the center of attention.[20] Unfortunately, Piercy opined, such men had the legacy of American, literary, male romance, "the strength of the American tradition of Huckleberry Finn escaping
down river from Aunt Polly, down through Hemingway where the bitch
louses up the man-to-man understanding, to draw upon in defense of [their]
arrogance."[21]

When all was said and done, Piercy charged, white, male, New Left leaders were enacting with women the very "marketplace masculinity" that their
revolution strictly opposed. The real basis of the white, male-led wings of
"the movement," according to Piercy, was "the largely unpaid, largely female
labor force that does the daily work."[22] Activist men, as Gitlin observed,
"were caught up short by the eruption of women's rage."[23] It was not just the

white race, as Cleaver had asserted, but the white, male New Left that had "lost its heroes." For many white, radical men, the 1970s would indeed see the "end of politics" rather than the beginning of a new stage. Some would turn to the counterculture of communes and dropping out and many others to the pursuit of self-making in often highly successful careers.

EARLY FEMINIST MEN

For a minority of white progressive men in the early 1970s, feminism did pose the possibility of a new political endeavor, one that would extend the explicit and implicit orientations to which SNCC had given new life—breaking with the ideals of national manhood and self-making masculinity, serving the interests of the oppressed, and giving fuller expression to feelings of vulnerability, love, and care. Some men who publicly embraced feminism as early as the 1970s did so by publishing feminist-inspired work, by participating in organized political activity that tried to accommodate gender change, and by enacting, and calling attention to, new codes of profeminist personal behavior.

The histories of such men, now fifty-five to sixty-five years old, often shared common elements. Three of the six men in our 1997 study who dared to publish feminist-inspired work in the early 1970s had experienced a heightened sense of marginality with respect to traditional masculine ideals. Paul remembered, "I've always been very woman-identified from the time I was a little boy. . . . I was terrible at sports. I had no male bonding. . . . By the mid-70s it was clear that my close friends were women." Daniel remembered feminism as "the first critique of gender roles that I had come across. . . and instead of taking that as an attack on me . . . there's a whole very oppressive narrative about what that role was, that when that was critiqued that seemed good to me."

Three of the men who were actively feminist in the early 1970s had also been long-term husbands or lovers to women who became feminist early on. Their exposure to critical gender analysis, in the context of long-standing, intimate relationships, gave them entry into feminist perspectives and politics. This entry often earned them approval from feminist partners and friends, thereby enhanced their self-esteem, and prompted them to continue profeminist activities. According to Richard, for example, he and Jenny "got a certain kind of malicious pleasure out of the extent to which I would adopt all these role reversals and how it would turn people around."

Three of the six men had also had close relationships to their mothers and considered themselves mother-identified. Ted, for example, speculated about the degree to which his early involvement in feminism might be explained by feminist psychoanalytic theory, which maintained that "especially in a household where the father is absent emotionally or physically . . . the mother cathects to the child, the male child in particular . . . and then the child must please her and of course he can never please her enough." According to Paul "insofar as I got involved in, originally, in the case of women, it comes through my mother identification, which was extremely powerful."

None of these men, however, became as actively feminist as Byron, whom I interviewed in 1999. Byron had helped run the first men's center, established in 1970, and had participated in a network of men who staged Men & Masculinity Conferences from 1975 on. He had also helped found the first and only national organization for profeminist men, the National Organization for Men Against Sexism (NOMAS). Like the early profeminist men in our 1997 study, Byron also began his political life with civil rights. Born and raised in Brooklyn, Byron was admitted to his top-choice graduate program at a university in the South in 1961, with a four-year fellowship offering him full tuition, room, and board. Byron's initial visit to the campus, however, would put an end to his dream of doing graduate work in that region. In the context of the expanding civil rights movement, Byron was appalled by the fact that the only black people he met on his trip were servants, and he was stunned to find that he himself was discriminated against for being a Jew. Convinced that "I wouldn't be able to survive there," Byron chucked his prestigious fellowship and went to his second-choice school, UC Berkeley, where he would participate in the civil rights struggle and would take important roles in the free speech movement and the protest against the Vietnam War. For Byron, as for the early feminist men we interviewed in our 1997 study, the investment in social justice that had informed his participation in civil rights, the student, and antiwar movements would be carried over into profeminist politics.

Byron's personal history, moreover, was similar to that of other early feminist men. Byron, for example, had also felt distanced from the masculinity of the dominating, self-made man early in his experience. Byron's father, although not successful at economic self-making, had been a salesman who was frequently away from home. He was resented by his wife, who felt victimized by his frequent absences, and by his son, who found him a distant and unsupportive parent. Like three of the men in our 1997 study, Byron developed a critical distance from traditional modes of male power early on, and, like three others, he developed an intense desire to please his mother—a desire all the more intense because she also verbally and physically abused him.

Byron also had a feminist mate in the early seventies and, most importantly, found ways to participate in feminist politics—by organizing a child-care center with another man and by co-developing a book with his wife that reviewed all the feminist writing available in English in 1971. The latter task opened Byron's eyes—"I was blown away by the information." It also involved him in feminist work for which he won female, feminist praise, and it led to a second book contract that provided him with even more access to feminist literature and to critical literature on men. Encouraged by his early feminist success, Byron turned his considerable organizing skills to the work of collaboratively running the first men's center. Once a spokesman for the antiwar movement, Bryon had become "committed to women's liberation" and had boldly entered into the next stage of "the revolution," a stage not entirely understood or supported by many of the men who had also participated in civil rights, the antiwar movement, and the New Left.

The "men's liberation" movement that split in the mid 1970s into profeminist and Men's Rights networks would also include many younger men. For these younger men, who were in college during the mid to late 1970s, the civil rights movement and Black Power were more distant, while the women's and gay liberation movements were current and influential. Nonetheless, the legacy of racial liberation movements often acted as preparation for participation in feminist and progay politics. Nick, for example, was in high school during most of the civil rights movement, during which time he regarded Martin Luther King Jr. as "a real hero." Although he initially rejected Black Power, he, too, was politicized by *The Autobiography of Malcolm X*, which a professor gave him to read in the mid-1970s.

As with many older men, it was this encounter with race liberation politics that produced "a sense of frustration at having been taught one thing and then seeing something else happening . . . there isn't equality, and there isn't equal opportunity, and there's institutionalized oppression." In the context of the women and gay liberation movements, however, this racial awakening helped Nick to see almost immediately that "it's not just in the South . . . and it's not just black people. It's working-class people and women and gay people. . . . And when I would hear that stuff it made sense to me." Younger men like Nick, moreover, unlike men some ten years older, were to have feminist teachers, both male and female, who gave them "strokes" for doing feminist analysis. This facilitated Nick's eventual participation in a men's group and in NOMAS.

WHITE "MEN'S LIBERATION"

Organized efforts to invent a new, implicitly white, masculine ideal emerged in a set of conditions very different from those surrounding efforts to reinvent ideals of black masculinities in the late 1960s and early 1970s. The attempts of

Black Power organizations to invent a new black masculine ideal had taken place in the context of an antiracist movement that men and women shared and that often compelled them to discuss the concrete practice of gender relations in the service of their shared higher cause. Formal attempts to construct a differently oriented, implicitly white, masculine ideal, in contrast, emerged as the larger movement in which white men and women had fully participated was on the wane. Indeed, efforts to transform white, straight masculinity expanded after what many white, leftist men came to see as "the end of politics"—at least for them. For these reasons, among others—not excluding the social and economic privilege of many white, activist, middle-class men—collective attempts by white men to reject a dominant masculine ideal were often loosely, and inconsistently, attached to an organized struggle for structural social change.

The networks that made up the early "men's liberation movement," for example, emphasized the reality of sexism and the necessity of a women's movement to combat it, but they also focused on inventing different modes of being men, on personal growth, and on the costs of dominant masculine ideals. Men died at higher rates than women, for example. Their jobs were often physically and emotionally demanding, forcing them to undervalue their families and their health. Men engaged in violence and high-risk behavior at higher rates than women and were taught to downplay or ignore their own pain.[24] Although some emphasis on structural social change would continue to inform the various networks of men who organized around inventing new masculine ideals, the focus on personal growth could become more dominant.

In the absence of a political movement that brought white men and women together, white men and women were not as engaged in public, political dialogue with each other as were black men and women. Thus, while white men and women certainly attempted to renegotiate the gender pact in living rooms, bedrooms, and places of work throughout the land, organized efforts aimed at changing white men's behavior tended to draw men away from women and, with a few exceptions, would eventually devote more energy to male/male relations than to renegotiating personal relations between women and men.

White, middle-class, straight-identified male activists were members of a privileged class as well, and many had enjoyed a good deal of cultural status in 1960s political circles. Their rather sudden encounter with sharp criticism and, at times, demonization by feminisms, by cultural nationalisms, and by the gay movement, as well, may help account for the fact that the various networks often identified as a white-led "men's movement" devoted a good deal of their attention to personal healing and to "reenchanting" (white, straight) manhood. The latter involved crafting a masculine ideal that might be seen as noble and moral and that might be experienced as something to feel good about once more.

This effort to reconstruct a noble ideal of white masculinity, of course, would often be interpreted, and sometimes functioned, as a form of resistance to feminism, but it had distinctly profeminist expressions as well. Many profeminist men, indeed, would eventually argue that some reenchantment of white masculinity was a necessary condition for male feminist political endeavor. According to the philosopher Harry Brod, a member of NOMAS for many years, "what enables men to do feminism effectively is a vision of men and of feminism in which their feminism is inseparably linked to their positive vision of themselves as men, which I take to be the basis of being 'male affirmative.'"[25] "If I do not have a positive attitude toward myself and others in the group through which I define my identity," Brod continued, "I will not be able to sustain effective action in favor of anyone else."[26]

"Men's liberation"—the term would fall out of favor by the mid-seventies—also employed many elements of male romance. Men's centers, for example, drew men away from women into a special, liminal place where men's center staff attempted to initiate them into a secondary masculine ideal. The process of taking on this revised model of manhood, as in other forms of male romance, was to be controlled by men, and, as in the Black Panther Party, it was to involve a conscious process of political reeducation. Byron, for example, believed that most men were "ill disposed to attend to women's messages about their behavior" and that women were also structuring feminism "so men could not succeed." He and his cohorts, therefore, tried to use their profeminist center's all-male drop-in evenings to "deliver the [feminist] message in a loving, fraternal way," thereby translating feminism into a language that could reach men's ears.

Unfortunately, however, the translation was often too close to the original to be effective. When center facilitators talked to drop-in groups of men about male–female relations, in particular, the focus was often upon repeating a female, feminist line. According to Byron, "every time a man wanted to raise an issue dealing with men and women's relations we all jumped to echo the [female feminist] party line. . . . I think men decided that there was no point to talking to [center men] about these issues because it was like talking to a women's group."

Men's consciousness-raising groups, another feature of early "men's liberation," would provide other, more autonomous, avenues to the transformation of masculine ideals. By 1973 there were reportedly three hundred men's consciousness-raising groups, mainly white and middle-class and involving men in their twenties to fifties.[27] Based on women's consciousness-raising strategies, these all-male groups also employed elements of male romance that were partially informed by feminist purposes. Many men joined consciousness-raising groups, for example, because they felt "guilty and

confused" and/or inspired by feminist women with whom they were in relationships or because they felt estranged from conventional white, middle-
class models of masculinity such as that of the self-made man. Such men felt
"dissatisfaction with ourselves, our jobs, our relationships with men and
women, and what we saw as our alienating futures."[28]

Like men's centers, consciousness-raising groups offered men protected
sites on which some of the traditional rules of masculinity could be safely
questioned without provoking the hostility of more conventional men. While
public meetings of men bent on examining their masculinist upbringing
elicited ridicule from the press, private consciousness-raising groups offered
a safe space, a forum in which "troubles and insecurities can be honestly
aired" and where a man could see that "his frustrations are not unique to him
alone."[29] Consciousness-raising groups, moreover, drew men away from
women, giving men a greater sense of control over their own change. Thus,
although groups often met in dwellings shared with female partners, men
might partially transform shared spaces into a male domestic realm or ritual
space with "turkey soup" and "jugs of wine and apple juice" supplied by fellow participants.[30]

Consciousness-raising groups also had their own behavior-modifying rituals for creating community among men. These rituals—like those of other
groups discussed in previous chapters—might require men to engage in emotionally risky behaviors, such as talking openly about feelings and experiences, paying "close attention to what another man is saying," asking "careful questions," confronting or fully empathizing with one another, holding
group criticisms, and learning to "offer our ideas with love and with the intention of improving our lives and not trashing other people."[31]

In contrast to what we know of most white, middle-class nineteenth-
century organizations, consciousness-raising groups more consistently challenged the dominant norms of masculinity. These norms, which were often
referred to, in monolithic fashion, as "the masculine role," included breadwinning, getting ahead, bringing home the bacon, winning and performing,
worshiping rationality, maintaining "cool," and stifling the softer feelings,
particularly those of vulnerability, compassion, and care. As with men's centers, these groups helped initiate men into a secondary masculine ideal, which
emphasized talking openly about feelings and experiences, showing empathy
and love for others, and thinking about and working on relationships. All of
these qualities were associated with SNCC and had been traditionally associated with women as well.

Although some participants testified to having spent a good deal of time
discussing relationships with women, they also reported movements within
their groups toward focusing more on the participants' relations to each other.

According to writer Anthony Astrachan's mid-1980s study, consciousness-raising meetings became get-togethers "'to talk about the things that matter in men's lives'—which in men's eyes often had little to do with either women or power."[32] In the words of another participant, the meetings on male-to-male relationships "have been among the most satisfying we have had."[33]

The satisfaction derived from finding spaces in which emotional connection with other men might be sustained was heightened, I believe, by the circumstances of the early 1970s for many white activist men. Friendship groups, sports, and fraternities had traditionally provided a means of having community with other males, but the civil rights, antiwar, and student movements had further encouraged strong bonds and the open expression of feeling among men in the course of political labor, thereby opening the possibility of more intense forms of male-to-male connection.

By the early seventies, however, when those movements had taken different shapes and/or were in decline, and when many women were focusing their attention upon themselves or upon their "sisters," male consciousness-raising groups may have helped to offset a loss of prior emotional connection for some older white, heterosexually identified, activist men. Finding communion with other men may well have offset some of the "powerful sense of loss and disorientation" that some older men experienced at finding themselves decentered from women's admiring attention.[34] Byron, for example, had found it "devastating" to hear such slogans as "a woman needs a man like a fish needs a bicycle."

Discussions of male–male relations also offered a greater sense of autonomy to men who wished to undergo change. Many of the men in consciousness-raising groups, for example, shared Byron's 1970s conviction that women "owned" the language of feelings, or had written the scripts for intimate male–female relationships. Many felt that relations with women must be worked out directly with female partners. There were few, if any, female, feminist scripts, however, for male-to-male relationships and little female, feminist investment in those relations. Working on their relations to each other may have allowed men to feel even more in charge of their own transformation and relatively free from women's mother-linked control.

Indeed, a focus on male-to-male relations, since it involved so little female, feminist intervention, may have facilitated the very capacity of some men to change at all. As philosopher Larry May has pointed out, "Criticism of male behavior will sometimes be more believable if it is issued by men rather than by women," for "men are afforded more trust than women not to be overly critical of the experiences of males and of masculinity more generally."[35] In working on their relations to each other, moreover, men sympathetic to feminism might also move in what they saw as feminist-approved directions, by, among other things, becoming more emotionally open. This openness, many men argued, was transferable to relationships with women and, especially, as it would turn out, to fathering relationships with children, as I suggest in chapter 6.

Consciousness-raising groups, however, were not entirely focused on the personal or on momentary respites from traditional (or female, feminist) scripts. In contrast to white nineteenth-century fraternal organizations, most men in consciousness-raising groups were not seeking momentary "solace" from the competitive, unfeeling masculinity of the workplace or from the burdens of national manhood and of its efforts to "stack the decks." Many were seeking to unlearn these masculine ideals and in many cases to alter the institutions and relations that sustained them. Inspired, in part, by the civil rights movement, Black Power, feminisms, and gay rights, men in consciousness-raising groups were often seeking alternative ways to be citizens and white males. Many supported the inclusion rather than the exclusion of "others," like women and men of color, in political and social power. Groups tended to see personal growth, moreover, as part of a larger politics. Nick's group, for example, had pushed men into experimenting with massages and group hugs, activities with which Nick never became comfortable, but all of this "fit into a larger political commitment, that the personal is political."

Nevertheless, in the absence of a larger movement for social justice in which white men were fully engaged, the link between the individual and the structural, the personal and the public, was often vaguely articulated: "We feel strongly that as men we need to see our problems as products of the larger society, and that ultimately our solutions can only come with a collective unity of men, women, minorities, gays, and working people." In the meantime, some groups focused on disseminating the feeling that there is "a new way to do things that isn't tied up in competitiveness and feeling better than others," while others held fast to the belief that "values" matter, and that "a change in any society is not first apparent in its overarching framework. It occurs much nearer the center—in the aspirations and attitudes of those who have created its framework."[36]

NOMAS: THE NATIONAL ORGANIZATION FOR MEN AGAINST SEXISM

Men's centers, men's consciousness-raising groups, and the activist networks that contributed to them and grew out of them were fundamental to the construction of an activist-oriented profeminist organization. This organization was to take shape in a series of conferences on men and masculinity that began in 1975 in Nashville, Tennessee. The first of these conferences was organized, with support from NOW, by a group of men taking a women's studies class at the University of Tennessee. At the third of these Men & Masculinity conferences in 1977, some participants, including Byron, began to promote the idea of a national, profeminist organization for men.

Despite the ongoing fears of some profeminist men that a national organization would involve hierarchy and would therefore reinforce dominant masculine norms, about thirty of the six hundred participants at the Boston conference in 1981 decided to go forward with the project. The organization they founded in 1982 was officially launched at a press conference in March 1983 and was named the National Organization for Changing Men (NOCM). (It would be renamed the National Organization for Men Against Sexism—NOMAS—in 1990. I shall refer to it as NOMAS in the pages that follow.) NOMAS held its first annual meeting at the eighth Men & Masculinity Conference in August of 1983, where it attracted some five hundred members. Mainly white and middle-class, though drawing some men of color, NOMAS was also 30 to 50 percent gay and bi-identified in its early days. (The number of participants in NOMAS conferences was to hover around four to five hundred until the early 1990s.)

NOMAS's draft statement of 1985 called for the rejection of the familiar limitations of the self-making masculine ideal—"excessive involvement with work, isolation from our children, discomfort in expressing emotions, lack of close friendships, excessive competition, and aggressiveness."[37] At the same time, the statement emphasized support for, and pride in, some elements of more traditional masculine ideals, such as independence and courage. NOMAS's statement, however, also strongly implied that a new model of manhood was to be based not just on a rejection of the more limiting components of the dominant masculine ideal, but on a struggle for structural social change as well. Thus, the statement supported women's struggle for equality, the creation of a gay affirmative society, and many other forms of progressive politics. The official goal of NOMAS was not just to change its members themselves or other men as individuals, but also society as a whole. As a national political organization, therefore, NOMAS signaled—much as Black Power had done—that inventing new ideals of masculinity was serious political activity for men. In contrast to Black Power, of course, NOMAS emphatically embraced profeminist politics and gay affirmation.

From the beginning, NOMAS made concerted efforts to combine political activism with an emphasis, in its conferences, on men's personal growth. NOMAS, for example, supported task groups and passed resolutions on gay rights, racism, men's violence, sexual harassment, pornography, and reproductive rights. In addition NOMAS staged its own "Campaign to End Homophobia" and supported many antirape projects and efforts to end domestic violence, such as "Brother Peace: An International Day of Men Taking Action to End Men's Violence." NOMAS also began the *Men's Studies Review*, a quarterly journal covering academic research and writings on men and masculinity, and it took on the task of organizing Men & Masculinity conferences. There men involved in profeminist political activism could meet, share information, and support each other in being feminist men.[38] One man remembered early conferences as a place where community "firebrands" came together to share strategies.

From the 1970s to the early 1990s, however, the primary focus of the Men & Masculinity conferences that NOMAS organized was on healing, support, and personal growth. Byron, for example, who had organized men in favor of the ERA, also led conference workshops on the ERA and sex harassment, but he remembers that while workshops on men's health and bodies regularly drew around forty-five participants (in conferences of some 350 men), his politically oriented workshops drew only three to seven. Anthony Astrachan, who wrote about Men and Masculinity conferences in the mid-1970s and 1980s, also observed that "the dominant flavors at an M & M conference . . . are psychotherapy and legacy of the counterculture."[39] The Men and Masculinity conferences that I myself attended in 1993, 1999, 2000, and 2001 also emphasized the personal.

To some extent, therefore, NOMAS Men & Masculinity conferences functioned much like men's centers and men consciousness-raising groups. They opened up a space in which men could come together to bond, to work out new modes of being men, and to do behavior-modifying emotion work that would facilitate their translation of new ideals into concrete practice. NOMAS also functioned to emphasize the difference between participants in NOMAS and participants in less activist networks and organizations. NOMAS opened up a space in which white, middle-class men, in particular, could establish, support, and protect a specifically activist feminist identity.[40]

From Byron's perspective, the emotion work at M & M conferences was chiefly designed to feed into and promote a more visible, public politics.[41] Conferences, according to Byron, were partially designed to bring men already involved in profeminist activism together, to nurture and support them, and to encourage them to "take care of themselves while working." Conferences, that is, were meant to renew and strengthen profeminist men so that they could return to their communities and work with female feminists and other sympathetic males, often in antirape, antipornography, and battered women's groups. Since the men at these national conferences were often men of marginal means, as Byron explained it, they needed "to get something from [the conferences] other than more obligations." Conferences also aimed at drawing not-yet-activist men into profeminist activities by meeting their needs for, or interest in, a noncompetitive community of supportive men, in personal healing and in personal change while also putting them in touch with activist men and activist projects.

However, Byron and a few other members of the NOMAS National Council had, from time to time, more far-reaching visions of what the ultimate goal of the organization could be. For Byron this goal was to lay the ground for a large umbrella movement in which gender justice was to be pursued alongside racial and economic justice, as well as gay justice and gay affirmation. In contrast to previous attempts at umbrella politics, however, such as those of the sixties "revolution," NOMAS's political project was to be grounded in the embrace of a reconstructed masculine ideal and in the personal work necessary to put that ideal into practice. As a national movement with large numbers of participants, indeed, NOMAS was to become the basis for a new New Left in which men, far from deriding feminism, made a feminist critique of society and progressive politics a central concern. For Byron, at least, NOMAS was to work toward healing the breach between leftist women and men that men's sexism and women's abandonment of the male Left had first opened up. The 1990s would see similar calls for an umbrella politics grounded in loving relation and in male self-transformation, as I shall suggest in chapter 10.

The goals of NOMAS were nothing if not transcendent, but like many political organizations with utopian goals, NOMAS could not evenly live up to them all. The complex and sometimes competing nature of its umbrella politics—healing and personal change for men and gender, sexual, race, and economic justice, as well as gay affirmation rather than merely gay tolerance—were, not surprisingly, difficult to sustain. NOMAS's efforts to incorporate more white working-class men and men of color into the organization, for example, were genuine, but they were not particularly effective in an ongoing way. And NOMAS, like most political groups, was beset by internal splits.

Men who emphasized the need to stop men's domination of, and sexual violence toward, women came together with men who emphasized socioeconomic structures of oppression and with men who emphasized men's sex-role victimization by dominant masculine ideals. Men who focused on serving men through therapy worked with men who were more interested in public activism. Men deeply invested in ideological purity met with men who emphasized the idea that reaching not-yet-activist or not-yet-feminist men required greater flexibility and an ability to meet men where they were. Some men left NOMAS over the years because they felt there was not enough emphasis on activism. Others left because they felt there was insufficient attention to male support.

These splits deepened in the nineties. In 1990, for example, members of the National Council voted to change the name of the organization from the

National Organization for Changing Men, with its intentional linguistic ambiguity—being *for* changing men and being for *changing* men—to the simpler slogan, National Organization for Men Against Sexism. The latter title placed less emphasis on being *for* men than on *changing* them and less emphasis on personal growth than on taking political stands. (*No más*, of course, is Spanish for "no more.") Some men left NOMAS over this change. A similar split over the degree to which the NOMAS's men's studies journal, then *Men's Studies Review*, should restrict itself to publishing manuscripts that endorsed the organization's feminist principles reduced the men's studies task force from 359 in 1992 to 130 in 1993 and 1994.

NOMAS, like many progressive organizations, also had few material resources. Those who kept the organization together were volunteers, all busy with their own work and projects. They were sometimes inexperienced in organizing and were unable from time to time to get the newsletter out, collect dues, or respond to mail in a timely fashion. Nationally speaking, moreover, activist feminism for men was only marginally appealing, as was the unglamorous work of organizing primarily white, middle-class men and the risky labor of bringing gay and straight men into comradely relation. As an organization for reinventing ideals of masculinity, NOMAS would be overshadowed by the mythopoetics (chapter 5), who were far less political, far less demanding of white men in respect to their power and privilege, and far less interested in the work of gay/straight male relations. One of NOMAS's major achievements, indeed, is that, despite these tensions and constraints, it has gone on with its work for almost thirty years. It has remained— against heavy odds—an important symbol for the possibility of "feminism as men's business" on a national scale.[42]

BROTHERS

As with many other organized efforts to reinvent masculine ideals, NOMAS devoted a good deal of energy to building more loving and open male-to-male relations. NOMAS was and is unique, however, in the way it has put loving relations between gay and straight men at its core. According to Byron, "There was no other place for straight men to meet other men in brotherhood that was open to gay men," and in this respect NOMAS constituted a politically significant frontier, not just for men but for the women they related to as well. As with other organized efforts to change relationships among men, NOMAS drew upon strategies familiar to male romance. Although women were and are welcome at M & M conferences and although women were and are powerful on the NOMAS National Council, the conferences I have attended have been overwhelmingly male. To some extent, Men & Masculinity conferences, like Men's Centers, drew men away from women into a world of men.

Like other men's networks and organizations, moreover, NOMAS created rules and exercises to draw participants into a "liminal" world where the usual rules of engagement were replaced by more communal and openly expressive behaviors. In 1999, 2000, and 2001, for example, the ground rules for conference attendance called for respecting other people's positions, for not interrupting, for giving all members equal opportunity to speak and be heard, for keeping criticism constructive and refraining from personal attack, and for processing disagreements in public rather than through gossip or grapevines or behind opponent's backs. These rules and the participants' enactment of them made many of the academic conferences, political groups, and even feminist events I have attended seem downright uncivil in comparison.

NOMAS also employed behavior-modifying rituals. The 2000 Conference in Colorado Springs, for example, began with a series of exercises that called on the men (and the handful of women) to solidify a sense of community. The group was divide into two concentric circles that were asked to stop every few minutes while the participants looked each other in the eyes in order to focus on the "humanity" of the person standing opposite them. This and similar group exercises had a distinctly bonding effect on me and, I imagine, on others. Indeed, the practice went a long way toward tempering my later impatience with some of the workshops.

NOMAS's work on gay–straight dynamics seemed especially forthright. Participants were called upon to behave in nonsexist, nonhomophobic, and nonracist ways. They were enjoined to be respectful of personal boundaries and needs and to refrain from unwelcome sexual overtures. They were also required to monitor any tendencies toward looksism, ageism, competitiveness, manipulativeness, aggressiveness, or neediness that might shame or exploit others.[43] In 1999 a straight and a gay man presented these rules to the participants in an entertaining fashion on opening night. Although NOMAS's work on gay/straight relations has not been without gay criticism, I personally know of no other contexts in which relations between men in general and between gay and straight men in particular are worked through at this level of concrete practice.

These strategies grounded a larger politics. For gay men NOMAS offered the possibility of meeting other profeminist gay men, establishing social and political community with straights, and combating homophobia and further affirming the positive nature of gay identity. (For some gay men, of course, the conference also presented an opportunity to cruise.) For straight men the political benefits were potentially higher. Fear and hatred of gays, and straight men's fear of feeling, or being seen as, homosexual, have always been key elements in enforcing tough, competitive, unfeeling behaviors and in deepening men's fear of the feminine within. Fear of the feminine encourages distance from the feminine in women and the need to prove heterosexual masculinity through controlling and dominating behavior. In adopting a gay affirmative politics, NOMAS did more than express an investment in social justice for gays. It also expressed an investment in changing straight men. If, as NOMAS recognized, homophobia was essential to enforcing straight men's adherence to dominant masculine ideals, this newfound freedom might make it possible to resist many other self-limiting masculine norms.

Straight men also stood to benefit from the example of profeminist gay men, who often modeled a more sensitive, more emotionally open manhood for their straight brothers. As I suggest in chapter 3, the Radical Faeries, who attended Men & Masculinity conferences for a time, were particularly valued for their interpersonal skills. Gay men also demonstrated the possibility of relying more on men and less on women for affirmation and for emotional support. As the philosopher Laurence Murdoch Thomas observed, men's greater emotional dependence on each other would reduce the burden that women now bear of having to affirm men's masculinity and of doing most of the emotion work in male–female relationships. In addition, relying more on men to fill emotional needs might alleviate men's fear of women's (and the mother's) emotional power and control.

A PROFEMINIST IMPASSE

Like other profeminist men's groups, NOMAS struggled with the issue of being "accountable" to female feminists. Alliance with feminist women, which Murrie called the "key dilemma" of the Australian profeminist men's group he studied, was made particularly difficult because of the ambivalent, suspicious, and sometimes hostile nature of some white female feminist response to men's various efforts to throw off the limitations of dominant masculine codes.[44] While often acknowledging the political usefulness of such "emotion work" for men, white heterosexual female feminists also expressed the (not unfounded) fear that even profeminist men might be focusing more on their own emotional expressivity or on intimacy with other men than on the problems they had in intimate relations with women. White feminists, from time to time, also expressed concern that men's "emotion work" might displace larger structural forms of fighting male domination and thereby end in securing men "the best of both worlds"—a fuller humanity *and* male privilege. This was hardly the romantic conclusion that female feminists had hoped for![45]

Ironically, however, some female feminist scepticism, while not without cause, did take such unrelenting forms at times that it often made alliance impossible and also discouraged the more activist forms of profeminist endeavor. Byron, for example, reported that he accepted the feminist critique of patriarchy and men's unearned privilege and wanted "to get with the program." That is, he wanted to work with female feminists in a collegial way and to confront problems together, but they were "suspicious of me and of men like me" and "I was hurt," he recalls: "Here I was really doing good work and was looked at with constant suspicion by many feminist and most feminist leaders like I was the enemy." Many female feminists, according to Byron, "were deeply, even jealously distrustful." If a man demonstrated that his politics reflected simple self-interest, "they trusted you and your motives," but "if you put forth moral motives, they appeared disbelieving." In the end Byron got tired of "being suspected." Since he then had joint custody of a teenage son and was in need of paid employment, he momentarily dropped out of being an activist, profeminist man. Two years later, however, Byron became involved in founding NOMAS.

Some profeminist men even identified "real" feminism with radical or cultural feminism that often identified men as the enemy. The Australian profeminist group, Men Against Sexual Assault (MASA), which Murrie studied, chose as potential allies the radical feminist women "who were often hostile or strongly critical" of even profeminist men. (Profeminist men, in my experience, sometimes replicate the harshness of judgment that dominant norms of masculinity prompt men in general to take with each other. In some cases, profeminist men turn this harshness against themselves, hence the choice of strongly critical women to work with.) These characteristics left the MASA participants "little space to negotiate and made the possibility of successful alliances less likely." Men found it "incredibly difficult to be critical of women full stop. Women held the high moral ground and then anything we did which they disliked it was, 'Fuck, I've made a mistake!'" Women supportive of MASA, in contrast, were often treated with suspicion. As one of Murrie's subjects put it: "I used to feel that a real feminist wouldn't actually believe that this was going to last for a second."[46] In the end MASA did little alliance work with female feminists.

In contrast to MASA, NOMAS chose to be "accountable" to female feminism. "Accountability," however, did not take the form, say, of consulting with a wide group of feminist organizations and then taking responsibility for one's decisions and actions. Accountability was chiefly expressed over the last few years as deference to the authority of the feminism represented by the female feminists who have been the most long-standing female members of the NOMAS National Council. This feminism, which was profoundly shaped by the battered women's movement, tended, not surprisingly, to emphasize women's victimization and men's responsibility for it and also insisted, as I was to observe at the 2000 and 2001 conferences, that NOMAS's female feminist leadership be taken as *the* authority on "feminism" itself. Deference to the authority of this feminism appeared to be deeply engrained in the culture of NOMAS and was sustained both by formal and informal rules of engagement and by long-standing loyalties to, and affection for, the individuals in question.

Disagreement with female feminist leadership, for example, was often cast by the women as a form of intimidating or of trying to dominate them, and few men or women publicly challenged these constructions in council meetings. Support of female feminist authority, moreover, was rewarded by a good deal of warmth, affection, and praise. This, too, functioned to keep open discussion at bay. Some men who had critical things to say or who simply wanted to engage in dialogue developed a sense of estrangement from their own public, profeminist identities. "I sometimes feel," a long-standing NOMAS member wrote, "if I say what I actually feel, I will be policed so carefully that I end up censoring myself."

The practice of deferring to female feminist authority and the impasse to which I believe it led seemed related to another unexpected discovery about M & M conferences. For all the emphasis given to personal relationships and growth, there were few sessions as a rule devoted to men and women's personal relationships (apart from those on sex and violence). Those that were offered were very sparsely attended. While there were several reasons for this lack of attention to male female dynamics, which I return to in chapter 7, one reason for the very evident disinterest in these encounters was surely the barely articulated fear that sessions devoted to open reflection upon the dynamics of men and women's intimate relationships might well tap into suppressed feelings of frustration with the gender dynamics of the organization itself.

The conference in 1999, for example, featured one workshop on men and women's personal relationships that strongly suggested this link. "He Said/She Said," which was to deal with interpersonal communication between women and men, initially drew only ten participants, half female and half male. As we were drawing our seats into a circle, however, the workshop received a sudden influx of seven more men—solely because the facilitator for a nearby workshop had not shown up. As the workshop began and the facilitator asked who wished to begin, I seized the opportunity to ask a question that was much on my mind: "What is it that profeminist men are not saying to feminist women?"

A current of electricity swept through the group and men spoke volubly for a few moments about "fear"—of "abandonment," of "dependency," of being "destroyed," of "being shot down for things done in good faith." While some younger men, in particular, felt they were not holding back and had nothing to disclose, other men owned up to "anger" at having been subjected to "shame," "scorn," and "humiliation," at feeling feminist women wanted things to happen on their own terms alone, and at the "all men are rapists" tenor of some feminist politics. One man, whose primary allegiance was to what was then called the "New Warrior Movement" maintained that men could not even work with women yet, and could not form political alliances with women, until they had further worked on, and with, themselves. "Wow," I thought, looking forward to the male–female dialogue that I was sure would now unfold. Within minutes, however, just as I thought to myself, "At last," the conversation turned to how men were relating to other men within the organization, and the question of what men were not saying to female feminists was quietly dropped. The session continued, but cross-gender dialogue did not. The men spoke—passionately—but mainly to each other.

Shortly before this conference, I was later to learn, the issue of men's deference to the authority of the feminist women on the NOMAS National Council, the tensions that this deference had produced, and the lack of open dialogue about these dynamics surfaced in a particularly dramatic way. A former member of the National Council e-mailed the membership, calling for an end to NOMAS as it now existed on the grounds that it had ceased to be an organization in which men's relation to men "was at its core." From the perspective of this council member, men now bent over backward "to receive the feminist stamp of approval" while "paying little attention to supporting other men." Members of the organization now emphasized ideological purity over nurturing and over maintenance of the organization, and the "gay/straight alliance work once at the heart of NOMAS seemed now decidedly in its periphery."

A storm of e-mails followed in which many men supported this position and some did not. While affirming the participation of women in the organization, many men expressed a desire to return to the early days in which NOMAS seemed a kind of "home," a place of safety, comfort, and nurturing, in which personal growth and men's relationships to each other were at the core and in which "a loving atmosphere and community" sustained commitments "to fighting sexism as a primary goal." Many of these men felt the organization now lacked this comfort and support and that the energy men had put into their relations with each other was now being diverted toward following the female leadership and "doing everything perfectly correctly." One woman who had newly joined the leadership council wrote that she herself was uncomfortable with "my role as being a member of the sex which men have to be 'accountable' to. . . . Further I am not comfortable with the kind of feminism that sees all men as victimizers. How can we possibly build a men's movement when all men's behavior is seen through that frame?" Her candid and reflective letter challenged NOMAS to engage in open dialogue around these issues and raised the possibility of reexamining what kinds of feminism would best serve the organization.

Those on the side of deferring to the authority of female feminist leaders accused their critics of finding NOMAS too feminist and of having problems with strong feminist women. This dialogue, however, was abruptly truncated when one of the men who insisted on deference to female feminist authority lapsed into ad hominem attacks. A second round of e-mails followed in which members devoted themselves to suggesting how to speak more forthrightly so that "hostilities do not build up and explode." Others, including Byron himself, pledged to try to pull the organization back together.

REVISIONING

The 2000 Men & Masculinity Conference in Colorado Springs represented an attempt to move beyond the impasse of 1999. Locating the conference in a city known for its support of organizations such as James Dobson's right-wing and antigay Focus on the Family and Colorado for Family Values gave the conference added motivation for constructing an activist emphasis. Among the activist-oriented sessions, a three-part workshop on how to reach out to unpoliticized but "kind hearted" men stood out for its originality and promise.

Ongoing tensions within NOMAS, however, played out through the activist emphasis (an emphasis that gave a lot more energy to this conference than I had seen in 1999). In two of the workshops I attended, for example, some female and male leaders insisted on the authority of NOMAS female feminist leadership in ways that seemed intended to silence criticism or to deflect the expression of alternative perspectives on the part of other participants. My extreme impatience with these moves was tempered only by the fact that I *had* looked in the eyes of several of those who took these positions and *had* in fact taken in their "humanity." I deplored their tactics but felt empathy for them at the same time. NOMAS was getting to me.

In the midst of the conference, Todd, a longtime NOMAS leader, offered a strong counterstatement to the emphasis in NOMAS on the "correct line." Todd's address told the story of his progress from hating himself for being male to a newfound ability to love himself and other men as well. His talk paid particular homage to the early Radical Faeries, who had "loved themselves while being profeminist." Todd also recalled that Gloria Steinem, whom he had invited to speak at the 1998 Men & Masculinity conference in New York, had reminded men of what they had to be proud of and of the role that healing, sustaining, and loving men played in inspiring them to activism.

Byron would echo this perspective in his own workshop on how to talk about sexual harassment to the unconvinced: "You have to love the brothers."

Todd expressed sadness at NOMAS's diminished capacity for carrying on this kind of work, owning up to his fear that this diminished capacity for loving men and enhancing their lives would make the organization "irrelevant." He ended the talk by offering a different model of feminism from that which had dominated the leadership over the last few years. Feminism, he suggested, offers "the politics of forgiveness." Of course, the forgiveness comes only after men have begun to reconstruct their own masculinities, but "feminism is about love." "Feminists love men enough to believe in change." There is no other way to change others than by changing ourselves, Todd continued, but we have to change with love: "Thirty-five years ago I hated you," he told the crowd of profeminist men; "Now I can say I love you."

Todd's address was one of the high points of the conference and was a striking contrast to the tone he had taken only five years earlier on a panel with the mythopoetic men's movement leader, Forest, which I take up in chapter 5. It was not clear, however, to what degree the speech had impact on the leadership. The Revisioning Session that followed the 2000 conference, NOMAS's twenty-fifth anniversary, involved a group of some thirty NOMAS members and conference participants. The session rigorously pursued an exercise in self-analysis, which was skillfully led by a female consultant.

The group, in which I also participated, listed the strengths and weaknesses of the organization, the opportunities and threats that faced it, and the organization's goals over the next ten years. Many of those present echoed Todd's emphasis on love and trust, on caring and heart, and on the acceptance of imperfection. Two of the organization's weaknesses, for example, were defined as its tendency to show impatience with "prereceptive" men and the insistence of some of its leadership on their own authority with respect to feminist issues. Such criticisms, however, were muted. To have pursued them more rigorously would have brought to the fore the divisions that already existed not only between men and men but between profeminist men and the female feminist leadership. The group focused instead on what political people, and often male political people, do best—planning for future action. The possibility of open dialogue between male and female feminists was dropped, or perhaps deferred, to an uncertain future.

CODA

NOMAS lives on despite the profeminist impasse with which it is plagued. For me, the utopian possibilities of the organization continue to hover like a translucent aura in and around its proceedings. I remember, for example, a particularly uplifting moment in 1993 during the first M & M conference that I attended. NOMAS had staged a march through the streets of San Francisco to the Federal Building, where it was sponsoring a demonstration that called for an end to the ban on gays and lesbians in the military. The march and demonstration were well attended, involving several hundred men. As I marched with the men through the city streets, they began a chant that I had never heard from men in all the many demonstrations I have attended: "Ho, ho! Ho, ho! Patriarchy has got to go. Ho, ho! Ho, ho! Patriarchy has got to go." As I listened and joined in I found myself filling with pleasure, respect, and affection for these men, who seemed like brothers—something I had never experienced in relation to a large group of men before. I felt for a moment what it might be like if I lived in a world in which these men were the majority, men who put social justice first, who truly cared about women's equality. I had a moment of being lifted up, of feeling weightless, happy— free at last!

Uneasily, however, I kept returning to the contrast between the freedom these men seemed to feel in this public expression of profeminist politics where dialogue and disagreement with feminist women were not required and how constricted some seemed when it came to discussing the sense of unfairness that they also felt in personal and political relationships with some feminist women. Behind this public voice, exuberant, unhesitating— how many men do any of us know who would wholeheartedly join in this chant?—there was a silence and behind that silence I suspect lay that "deeply internalized distrust" of women that Michael Messner finds in most "men's movements."[47] Behind that silence, I would guess, lay the anger that some profeminist men rightly feel for some feminist women, too, but that their devotion to profeminist politics and their need for feminist women's approval have long persuaded them, with sometimes paralyzing affect, to ignore, shelve, or brush aside. I shall return to this impasse in chapter 7.

NOTES

1. Timothy Beneke, *Proving Manhood: Reflections on Men and Sexism* (Berkeley: University of California Press, 1997), 31.

2. Cited in Cheryl Lynn Greenberg, ed., *A Circle of Trust: Remembering SNCC* (New Brunswick, N.J.: Rutgers University Press, 1998), 32, 33.

3. Cited in Greenberg, *Circle*, 34.

4. Todd Gitlin, *The Sixties: Years of Hope, Days of Rage* (New York: Bantam Books, 1987), 164.

5. Tom Hayden, "SNCC: The Qualities of Protest," *Studies on the Left* 5 (Winter 1965): 123, 119, 120, and Howard Zinn, *SNCC: The New Abolitionists* (Boston: Beacon Press, 1964), 327, cited in Gitlin, *Sixties,* 165.

6. Michael Kimmel, *Manhood in America: A Cultural History* (New York: Free Press, 1996), 267.

7. Todd Gitlin, *Sixties,* 349.

8. Judith Newton and Judith Stacey, "The Men We Left Behind Us, or Reading Our Br/others: Narratives around and about Feminism in the Lives and Works of White, Radical Academic Men," in *Sociology and Cultural Studies,* ed. Elizabeth Long (London: Blackwell's Press, 1997).

9. Maurice Isserman and Michael Kazin, *America Divided: The Civil War of the 1960s* (New York: Oxford, 2000), 178.

10. Gitlin, *Sixties,* 389, 403, 401, 417.

11. Gitlin, *Sixties,* 411–13.

12. Ruth Rosen, *The World Split Open: How the Modern Women's Movement Changed America* (New York: Viking, 2000), 140.

13. Cited in Isserman and Kazin, *America,* 179 and in Rosen, *World,* 108.

14. Cited in Rosen, *World,* 111.

15. Cited in Rosen, *World,* 113, 114, 124.

16. Rosen, *World,* 126, 128, 130; Gitlin, *Sixties,* 371.

17. Kimberly Springer, "The Interstitial Politics of Black Feminist Organization," *Meridians: Feminism, Race, and Transnationalism* 1, no. 2 (March 2001); Benita Roth, "The Making of the Vanguard Center: Black Feminist Emergence in the 1960s and 1970s," in *Still Lifting, Still Climbing: Contemporary African American Women's Activism,* ed. Kimberly Springer (New York: NYU Press, 1999), 73.

18. Rosen, *World,* 129, 134, 135; Gitlin, *Sixties, 374.*

19. Marge Piercy, "The Grand Coolie Damn," in *Sisterhood Is Powerful: An Anthology of Writings from the Women's Liberation Movement,* ed. Robin Morgan (New York: Vintage, 1970), 424.

20. Piercy, "Coolie Damn," 426, 434, 433, 430.

21. Piercy, "Coolie Damn," 434.

22. Piercy, "Coolie Damn," 424.

23. Gitlin, *Sixties,* 371.

24. See Michael A. Messner, *Politics of Masculinities: Men in Movements* (Thousand Oaks, Calif.: Sage Publications, 1997), 6.

25. Harry Brod, "To Be a Man or Not to Be a Man—That Is the Feminist Question," in *Men Doing Feminism,* ed. Tom Digby (New York: Routledge, 1998), 198.

26. Brod, "To Be a Man," 199.

27. Barbara J. Katz, "A Quiet March for Liberation Begins," in *Men and Masculinity,* ed. Joseph H. Pleck and Jack Sawyer (Englewood Cliffs, N.J.: Prentice-Hall, 1974), 152, 153; Pleck and Sawyer, introduction to *Men,* ed. Pleck and Sawyer, 2.

28. Michael Weiss, "Unlearning" in Pleck and Sawyer, *Men,* 166; "A Men's Group Experience," in *Men,* 159.

29. Jack Nichols, *Men's Liberation: A New Definition of Masculinity* (New York: Penguin Books, 1975), 315, 317.

30. Katz, "A Quiet March," in Pleck and Sawyer, *Men,* 154; "A Men's Group Experience," in *Men,* 150.

31. "A Men's Group Experience," in Pleck and Sawyer, *Men,* 161.

32. Anthony Astrachan, *How Men Feel: Their Response to Women's Demands for Equality and Power* (Garden City, N.Y.: Anchor Press, 1986), 290.

33. "A Men's Group Experience," in Pleck and Sawyer, *Men,* 161.

34. Ruth Rosen, *World,* 140.

35. Larry May, "A Progressive Male Standpoint," in *Men Doing Feminism,* 348–49.

36. "A Men's Group Experience," in Pleck and Sawyer, *Men,* 161; Nichols, *Men's Liberation,* 319.

37. Astrachan, *How Men Feel,* 295.

38. Program for Building Bridges for A Multicultural Men's Community: 18th National Conference on Men & Masculinity, San Francisco, 8–11 July 1993.

39. Astrachan, *How Men Feel,* 296.

40. See Linzi Murrie, *Feminism as "Men's Business": The Possibilities and Limitations of Profeminist Politics in Men against Sexual Assault,* Dissertation, University of Queensland, 2002, 175, 193–94. He finds similar elements among the participants in the Australian profeminist men's group, Men Against Sexual Assault (MASA), which he studied.

41. This was also the case in MASA.

42. From Murrie, *Feminism.*

43. Program for Building Bridges, 12–13.

44. See Murrie, *Feminism,* 178.

45. Lynne Segal, *Slow Motion: Changing Masculinities, Changing Men* (London: Virago, 1990), 284–91; Messner, *Politics,* 38–42.

46. Murrie, *Feminism,* 178.

47. Messner, *Politics,* xiv.

5

Iron and Ironing Johns

Being Born Again in the Mythopoetic Movement

> Women can change the embryo to a boy, but only men can change the boy to
> a man. Initiators say that boys need a second birth, this time a birth from men.
>
> —Robert Bly, *Iron John,* 1990.[1]

IN NEED OF MIRACLES

The early 1990s were marked by cultural anxiety over dominant versions of
what it meant to be a man in U.S. terms, as the effects of global restructuring
noticeably hit even white male members of the middle class. By the late
1980s, for example, corporate downsizing, a decline in real wages, and the
growing necessity of two incomes to sustain a middle-class life had significantly eroded traditional definitions of manhood grounded in primary breadwinning and authority as head of the house. The continued entry of women
into the labor force, the consequent decentering of men at work and at home,
high divorce rates, custody struggles, the modest integration of men and
women of color into middle-class jobs, and the continuing criticism of white,
straight, middle-class masculinity by identity movements on every front further contributed to a growing impression that being straight, white, middle-
class, and male had lost material as well as moral authority. By the late 1980s,
indeed, newspapers were announcing that white men no longer led "the
march to prosperity," and by the early 1990s news journals were observing,
in articles with titles like "Saving the Male" and "A White Male Lament,"
that "it's hard to feel heroic when you're the one everyone rebels against."
White men, according to more ominous accounts, were also "disaffected" and
suffering from "paranoia." One white, male journalist was moved to reflect

that "if I try to discuss issues of race and feminism—admittedly in bumbling ways—I hear comment such as 'You can't understand because you're not one of us,' or, 'It's well-to-do white men like you who run the country and cause our problems.'" "We wonder," he continued, "if we wouldn't like some zeal in our lives to discover a cause."[2]

One response to this sense of concern over the fate of white, middle-class, straight men was the media-hyped development of the Angry White Male whose "cause" was to take back the privilege and authority that had once been his—not by challenging corporate policies, to be sure, but by targeting the advances of white women and especially men and women of color.[3] I return to this figure in chapter 6. Another response, however, was to cast white, middle-class, male transformation as itself a higher "cause," one that offered new modes of heroism to those whom "everyone rebels against." Thus, in the early 1990s Hollywood produced a rash of films in which white men were shot, stricken with disease, or made to relive childhood traumas in order to emerge–born again—as more whole and tender, if not less privileged, human beings. Films like *Regarding Henry, The Doctor, and The Prince of Tides* suggested that recovery from self-making masculine ideals might in itself constitute a form of heroic journey, although they implied that white, middle-class men might well require some kind of miracle, or at least radical intervention, to undertake this quest.

This view of white, middle-class, male change was not the property of Hollywood alone. It was also in the early 1990s that a sympathetic male therapist informed a friend and colleague of mine that men her age (fifty and older) could only change if life "had crushed them." Older white men's privilege and socialization, he implied, went too deep for them to change for less pressing reasons. The liberal and spiritual mythopoetics and the conservative, Christian Promise Keepers would both provide less painful entries into the "miracle" of recovery from some traditional masculine ideals. (I return to the Promise Keepers in chapters 8 and 9.)

IRON JOHN

By 1991, when the mythopoetics were discovered in a major way by mainstream media, Mythopoetic men's groups had reportedly involved some fifty thousand to a hundred thousand men in weekend retreats. These retreats drew men into the woods with other men, prompted them to form temporary worlds away from women, and persuaded them to engage in some unusual forms of male activity. Eschewing the customary rites of white male romance in U.S. literature and film—fishing, hunting, or drinking—these weekends with "the guys" had promoted the far less customary practices (at least for white men) of drumming, chanting, dancing, and reciting poetry, and, in addition, crying, hugging, and talking intimately about personal matters, such as the wounding experience of having distant or unloving fathers. By 1992 a rash of reports were estimating that there were some fifteen hundred of these groups in the United States, and they were citing the work of poet Robert Bly, Jungian analyst James Hillman, performer and writer Michael Meade, and mythologist Joseph Campbell as foundational.[4]

The mythopoetics received intense media scrutiny, and often ridicule, between 1991 and 1994 (at which point Promise Keepers appeared writ large on the media scene) after Bill Moyers aired a PBS documentary in January 1990 on Robert Bly and his all male retreats. By June of that year, twenty-seven thousand copies of the video, *A Gathering of Men*, had been sold, and by November 1991 Bly's *Iron John: A Book for Men* had been on the *New York Times* bestseller list for forty weeks.[5] Despite, or perhaps because of, the movement's apparent appeal, many mainstream media men seemed eager to dismiss it as not worth taking seriously.

The mythopoetics, for example, were portrayed as a "sort of summer camp for man scouts," as a movement with no "real ideas," a group of "men with problems" or as a gathering of "spoiled middle-class white people who wish to consolidate their assorted emotional problems into a single addiction: addiction to group therapy." A writer for *Christianity Today* dismissed the movement as a purveyor of "stag spirituality," noting that there was neither male nor female in Christ and that gender was irrelevant to Christians. *The American Spectator*, taking a somewhat lower road, maintained that the mythopoetics were bent upon turning a "bunch of patheticos into a loving, hugging band of drum-bangers, poem-shouters, and Dad-haters."[6] Clearly the "men's movement" had hit some nerves.

A more sympathetic reporter, however, would confess that although "there seemed a patent foolishness in the rituals . . . the drumming and dancing" and "though the men around the fire had seemed at times ridiculous . . . they were ridiculous and real." "What men seem to want, he continued, "are more forums in which they can talk directly to one another, a kind of recovery program for victims of errant masculinity, a sort of Men's Anonymous."[7] The sales figures for *Iron John*—it had sold half a million copies by November of 1991—suggested that more than a few men were intrigued by the notion of a "men's anonymous" and that many were privately reading this "men's movement" bible than ever cared or dared to expose themselves by attending a "wild man weekend."

Although the mythopoetics were not given a great deal of media attention until 1991, at which point they were (incorrectly) identified as "the men's

movement," they had actually emerged in the early 1980s partially in response to a sense that the existing networks or groups bent on transforming
masculine ideals needed a more appealing program.[8] According to the sociologist Bob Blauner "in focusing on sexism and men's role as oppressors of
women, children, and the entire planet" many men's liberation activists
"found themselves feeling guilty about being men."[9] The profeminist National Organization for Men Against Sexism (NOMAS), as I observe in chapter 4, had tended to deal with the problem of men's guilt with respect to
women—and men's unspoken sense of feminism's sometimes impossible
terms—by focusing most of its conference energies on personal growth and
on producing compassion and care in relations between men, while also promoting antisexist, antiracist, and progay activism.

Mythopoetic leaders, however, while officially sympathetic to feminism,
distanced mythopoetic gatherings from female feminist influence not just by
avoiding discussion of male/female relations but also by maintaining all-male
groups and by deemphasizing antisexist politics as well. According to the sociologist Julie Bettie, who interviewed participants in one mythopoetic men's
group in 1992, discussions focused on "'men's issues' such as war, violence,
work, isolation, men's role historically, men not living up to masculine ideals,
and fathering sons (not parenting but *fathering*, and not children but *sons*)."[10]

From the perspective of the mythopoetic leader Robert Bly, indeed, some
men had taken feminist and other calls for a more sensitive masculinity to an
extreme. According to Bly, the political movements and feminisms of the
1960s and 1970s had contributed to producing more sensitive men, but these
"sixties/seventies men" struck Bly as incomplete: "There's something won-
derful about this development—I mean the practice of welcoming their own
'feminine' consciousness and nurturing it—this is important—and yet I had
the sense that there was something wrong."[11] The "something wrong," Bly
observed, was that the new, more sensitive man, while he was "a nice boy
who pleases not only his mother but also the young women he is living with,"
was neither "happy" nor energetic: "You quickly notice the lack of energy in
them." Many of the women who had "graduated" from the sixties, in contrast,
struck Bly as "strong," "life-giving," and as "positively radia[ting]) energy."[12]

Bly's solution to the relatively languid state of these post-sixties new men
was to invoke a "third possibility"—not the traditional masculine ideal of the
dominating patriarch or of the self-made man, not the alternative masculine
ideal of the "soft male" who had developed his "feminine side" (nor of the "san-
itized, hairless, shallow man" produced by corporations), but the third ideal of
the "deep male" who could say what he wanted and stick by it. This energy, Bly
emphasized, was not the same as "macho energy" but was "forceful action un-
dertaken, not with cruelty but with resolve."[13] The point was not to dominate

women but to hold one's own with them, especially the most critical, and, in so doing, to hold one's own with the motherly power they often represented.

Like those who joined NOMAS, the men who were attracted by the mythopoetic promise of masculine rebirth were mainly white, middle- or upper-middle-class and between thirty-five and sixty years old. (Bly felt that the need for a new map of manhood did not hit men until they were thirty-two or thirty-five years of age.) In some contrast to the demography of the early NOMAS, however, most mythopoetics were also self-identified as heterosexual.[14] According to the sociologist Michael Schwalbe, perhaps one-fourth of the mythopoetics he studied had some interest in erotic contact with men, but, in the main, Schwalbe felt, mythopoetics were heterosexual and "wanted others to know it."[15] Men of color and working-class men among them, moreover, were even fewer in number. Schwalbe observed that, although some mythopoetics talked about making the movement racially and economically more diverse, they were generally stumped about how to go about it or simply refused to feel guilty about the fact that race and class were not their issues. Out of some seven hundred men at the October 19, 1991, First International Men's Conference in Austin, Andrew Ferguson claimed to have seen only two black men.[16]

The movement's centers, according to the cultural critic Fred Pfeil, were located in enclaves of white counterculture in the twin cities of Minnesota, Austin, Santa Fe, Denver, Boulder (where the Promise Keepers would begin), the Bay Area and other sites of the Pacific Northwest (where Radical Faerie networks had also developed).[17] Although the counterculture had not embraced gender equality, it had held out the possibility of men's being freed from the breadwinner role, and, with its late-sixties cultivation of long hair and beads, it had offered a softer, more androgynous masculine ideal to men. Contact with countercultural traditions was one reason for mythopoetic men's tending to be critical of, or alienated from, the self-making masculine ideal before they joined.

Some studies, moreover, have suggested that men involved in mythopoetic networks were men for whom self-making had not worked well—because of personal vulnerabilities or misfortunes, because of records as draft resisters, or because of their own aversion to the values of the self-making masculine ideal. Bly himself, for example, had hidden out in a run-down farmhouse for many years rather than push his career as a poet, and participants in the mythopoetic men's group that Bettie studied in 1992 "revealed a discomfort with having a masculinity they perceived as marginalized in some way, at times related to prestige and class status."[18] The participants, for example, included Keith, who described himself as an "unsuccessful author," and Dave, a butcher, who felt that because of his job he was not living up to a masculine ideal (a consequence of his record as a draft resister).

Dave described the other participants in his group as having opted for low-status kinds of professions and as feeling social stigma as a result. One served meat at a deli counter, another "works for a newspaper," one was a probation officer who "supervises juvenile delinquents who pick up garbage along the freeway," and another "in his 40's is just starting a career as a massage thera-pist. He previously owned a pet store."[19] In 2000, moreover, I interviewed Sam, a man who had begun participating in mythopoetic men's groups after having gone through bankruptcy and losing his professional license. He was currently teaching part-time. Schwalbe also reports that three-quarters of the mythopoet-ics he studied came from working-class backgrounds. Although they had steady jobs and earned above the national median, many had gravitated toward help-ing professions, which rewarded nurturing and were, therefore, marginal with respect to the emphasis on ruggedness in working-class masculine ideals.[20]

Many of the mythopoetics in Schwalbe's wise and empathic study had had distant or angry fathers and had felt alienated from dominant forms of mas-culinity in their youth. Schwalbe estimated that a third of the men he studied had fathers who been "alcoholic or abusive in some way."[21] Mythopoetics, by and large, had also been "nice" boys who were good to their mothers and who had grown up to be sensitive, nurturing, and eager to please others. Bob Blauner was to claim that many, like himself, had been "mama's boys," boys and men whose intense involvement with their mothers had run up against the cultural rule that one could not be a mama's boy and a "real man" at the same time.[22] Bly, indeed, described himself as having loved his alcoholic father un-til he was three or four years old, at which point he agreed to "be on mother's side" and to become her helper instead of a companion to his dad.[23]

Late in life, however, Bly had come to the conclusion that he must recon-cile himself with his father and rewrite "the contract" with his mother, by rec-ognizing that he had helped her as much as he could and that he must now find a place "in the masculine world."[24] Having specialized in giving semi-nars on matriarchies and on "the goddess" to women, Bly began to work with men, holding his first all-male retreat at the Lama Commune in New Mexico in 1981, two years after the First Spiritual Conference for Radical Faeries in nearby Arizona. Bly's personal history in many ways would inform, and be reflected in, the movement with which he came to be associated, for the mythopoetics would focus on men's relations to their fathers and would sup-press talk of men's relation to mothers and to other women. Sam, for exam-ple, reported that his groups had focused on "self-esteem, absent fathers, mother issues a little bit," but that he felt that it was "still tough for me to get to mother issues after all this work."

The majority of the men whom Bettie and Schwalbe studied were also sympathetic to feminism, another indication of their alienation from dominant, self-making masculine codes. Their often painful personal histories, their distance from their fathers, their identification with their mothers, and/or their generally liberal politics had made them empathize with those who were victimized or oppressed. Many had been in relationships with feminists, had been sensitive to feminist criticism, and had had close contact with its cultural feminist forms, that often named men as "the enemy," categorized all men as potentially violent, and made no exceptions for "nice guys" like themselves.[25]

Eager to please women and seemingly vulnerable to cultural feminist critique, many mythopoetics felt, nonetheless, that they had been called upon to meet contradictory feminist demands. They often suspected, for example, that women themselves were ambivalent about whether men were to be protectors and breadwinners or not. Many mythopoetics, according to Schwalbe, felt confused, "wounded" by feminist condemnations, and stuck in the category "man." They had no choice, they felt, but to try to "redeem" the category, and, like some men in NOMAS, to remake man as a "moral identity," even to celebrate elements of masculinity for its value to them. According to Keith, "one of the things I am looking for is a positive gender image. . . . I want to feel good about being a *man*."[26]

Many studies of the mythopoetics suggest that a large proportion of participants had also been involved in 12-step recovery or other forms of therapy and self-help. Two reporters attending the October 19, 1991, First International Men's Conference: A Journey Toward Conscious Manhood, in Austin, claimed that of the 765 men at the conference 70 to 90 percent of the attendants had been in 12-step recovery. Schwalbe estimated that one-third of the men in the local group he studied had been in 12-step recovery, usually as children of alcoholics, "sex addicts," "co-dependents" or as survivors of abuse.[27] Many of the men joining the mythopoetics, then, were already open to group work, confession, ritual, and to seeking help from forces that they deemed more powerful than themselves. Finally, many of the men in Schwalbe's study came from religious or church-going families, some from fundamentalist ones. Disliking moral dogma, however, they did not want a church. What they did want to experience was "a sense of mystery and wonderment about their connections to the universe and each other."[28]

It was the vulnerability of these men, their marginality to self-making masculine ideals, their nice-guy attitudes and behaviors, their past sensitivity to feminist criticism, their proximity to countercultural enclaves, their inclination toward self-help therapies, and their desire for "mystery and wonderment," not their desire to dominate females, that must explain the heightened emphasis that the movement gave to familiar elements of male romance. These elements included going off with other men, establishing liminal communities, and making use of rituals, symbols, male mentors, and higher, transforming male powers to work the miracle of being born again into a "higher" white, middle-class, largely heterosexual masculine ideal.

Transforming higher powers, moreover, were easily at hand. "Deep" masculinity, according to Bly, was at once a psychic potential that already existed in men and a "being who can exist and thrive for centuries outside the human psyche."[29] Bly imagined this figure as a "large, primitive being covered with hair down to his feet," a "Wildman," whose other incarnations in folklore, religion, and mythology included the Greek god Pan, the Roman god Dionysus, the Indian goddess Shiva, the Old Testament figure of Esau, the New Testament figure of John the Baptist and at times Christ, and the medieval myth of the Wildman: "When a contemporary man looks to his psyche, he may, if conditions are right, find under the water of his soul, lying in an area no one has visited for a long time, an ancient hairy man."[30] Radical Faerie lore had named both Pan and Dionysus as early prototypes of gay personhood, but Bly did not take up this thread.[31]

According to Bly, social and religious forces in the West, most particularly the asceticism of early Christianity, had put an end to the cultural power of this Wildman figure, although Bly noted that the dreams of both men and women in recent decades suggested a hunger for "a new figure, a religious figure, but a hairy one, in touch with God, sex, with spirit and earth"—a "sort of hairy Christ."[32] This hirsute holy man was represented in Bly's *Iron John* by the title character, who was derived from a fairy tale that went like this:

> *When Iron John was found lying at the bottom of a pond, the king of the kingdom had him dredged up and imprisoned in a cage. He then gave the key of the cage to the queen who placed it beneath her pillow for safekeeping. When a golden ball belonging to the young prince of the kingdom rolled into the Iron John's cage, Iron John persuaded the boy to steal the key from under his mother's pillow and to exchange it for the golden ball. Once freed from his cage, Iron John initiated the boy into vibrant manhood, and in the end the prince married and received a treasure.*[33]

Iron John, it would appear, represented a masculine higher power that helped the prince achieve the "miracle" of breaking free from his mother. Only after this break, Bly's fairy tale suggested, was adult male life, requiring a domestic, heterosexual relation with a woman, really possible.

GATHERINGS OF MEN

Like many other organized efforts to reinvent masculine ideals, the mythopoetics created "a temporary world governed by special rules of interaction." In contrast to black cultural nationalists and white profeminists, however, mythopoetics employed more radical modes of intervening in, or cutting men off, from their everyday lives and most especially from women. Like Radical Faeries, mythopoetic men quite literally went off together into the uncharted "territory" of the desert or the woods, where drumming and chanting (which received much media ridicule) further distanced them from the ordinary so that initiation into a differently constructed masculine ideal could take place.[34] Like Harry Hay, Bly believed that men could change only in "ritual space."[35]

Despite the fact that mythopoetics tended to believe that there was a true, inner, and gendered self, with divine or mystical sources, and that this true self was a guide to moral judgment, they also believed that change was possible. On the one hand, according to Schwalbe, there was no need to "prove" a masculinity that was already given, but, on the other, men who felt they were not as good or as powerful as they liked might enter into their psyches in a kind of heroic journey to the frontier. There they might tap into male "archetypes," potential identities or energies, that were stronger and more powerful than their individual selves and, in this way, they might take on what they saw as a "higher" masculine ideal.[36]

In some respects Bly's "deep" masculinity resembled Hay's "third gender" identity in that it combined and balanced qualities contained in different male figures, or archetypes, such as the king, the warrior, the magician, and the lover. The latter, in particular, was associated with qualities like gentleness, expressivity, affection, nurturing, and concern with relationships. These traditionally feminine traits, however, that were lovingly embraced as the "sissy boy" within by Radical Faeries, were redefined in mythopoetic thinking as part of the "deep" masculine. Since in a masculinist and misogynistic culture, men's displays of tender emotion, shows of affection, and concern for relationships were devalued, defining these characteristics as part of a deep masculine gave participants permission to be the sensitive men they already were. At the same time this strategy moved men "from the margin to the center of their gender category," loosening their identification with the feminine.[37]

As in many of the cultures David Gilmore studied, movement into this secondary masculine ideal involved ritual and risk. Aside from drumming, chanting, dancing, and giving blessings, participants were often encouraged to make personal statements about something "shameful, tragic, or emotionally disturbing about their lives."[38] Just as Hay had emphasized the importance of marginality and pain in the production of male "gay consciousness," so Bly had been convinced by his own anthropological and mythological readings that initiation into manhood, and adulthood generally, required some form of wounding: "No one gets to adulthood without a wound that goes to the core." This wound, according to Bly, if it was received at the right time and in the right company," might function as a "male womb," opening men "to the soul and spirit world" and rebirthing the male subject this time by men.[39]

In mythopoetic rituals, indeed, a secondary or calculated wounding took place, in that men were urged to confront prior emotional suffering and pain, much of it in relation to distant or unloving fathers or in relation to the failure of older men to welcome younger men into "the male world." Failure to confront this prior wounding, Bly believed, could lead to the "road" of depression and numbness, as it had for him, or to the "road" of "infantile grandiosity," as practiced, for example, by "junk-bond dealers, high rollers, and the owners of private jets."[40]

As in other networks that focused on inventing new masculine ideals, father figures played a central role in the process of masculine change. The Radical Faeries, for example, had tried to compensate for the fact that gay boys often lose their father's "favor," by creating new of rites of initiation in the 1970s. The journals of the "men's liberation movement," according to Bob Blauner, had also been filled with articles about "'finding our fathers,' the need to heal the father son relation, and above all stories about a particular man's father pain."[41] Attention to father loss, however, reached its apogee in the mythopoetics.

Bly, for example, was of the opinion that, quite apart from their personal relations with their fathers, "sixties-seventies men," in rejecting "the establishment"—the government, the military, and the self-made masculine ideal—had symbolically killed their fathers and that they were now grieving the absence of respected father-figures.[42] (Perhaps some also grieved the loss of political movements that had compensated for their patricide.) The mythopoetics, however, supplied a way of explaining the distant relations between fathers and sons as the product of impersonal social forces and may thereby have rendered the experience of having symbolically killed the father, or of having an actual distant or abusive one, less personal and potentially easier to bear.

According to Bly, it was industrialization that brought about a break between father and sons. Sons who had worked alongside fathers as farmers or craftsmen gained an inner knowledge of what it meant to be a man, a kind of "cellular confidence" in their very being, that few men seem to have today: "There's no sense in idealizing preindustrial culture, yet we know that today many fathers now work thirty or fifty miles from the house, and by the time they return at night the children are often in bed, and they themselves are too tired to do active fathering."[43]

Talking about distant fathers, Schwalbe suggested, as part of a shared cultural experience, provided participants with a therapeutic outlet for painful feelings while promoting a healing sense of community among men. In acknowledging the wounding nature of their own relations to their fathers, moreover, mythopoetic men also encountered some of the ways in which dominant masculine ideals hurt men as well as women. Finally, sharing information about neglectful or abusive fathers also provided inspiration to participants for trying to do a better job in their own lives and thereby gave them a basis for feeling good about themselves as well.[44]

In repeatedly revisiting the figure of the distant or unloving father, mythopoetics also shared in processes that female feminists had themselves engaged in. Feminists, themselves, according to the philosopher Rosa Braidotti, had had to revisit and "work through" a "stock of cumulated images, concepts, and representations" that acted as "regulatory fictions" on their own identities.[45] Dominant ideals, as female feminists can attest, have power over those who also dislike and resist them. Mythopoetic men, as Schwalbe has observed, were trying to resist the dehumanizing and dominating affects of capitalism, of unrelenting competition, and of hegemonic masculine ideals. They were trying to gain insight into themselves and to create deeper emotional connections with other men, in order to affirm their worth as human beings and to create more meaningful lives.

In the mythopoetics, I believe, the figure of the distant, unloving father and the related figure of the career-obsessed, competitive, rationalistic, emotionally repressed, controlling self-made man were repeatedly revisited—not, for the most part, in the service of a fantasized return to them, but as part of a process of disengaging from them and from their hold. These often painful, processes of repetition have understandably prompted scholars writing about the transformation of masculine ideals to reach for descriptive terms such as "the long and winding road." Yet lengthy processes of repetition may have been necessary strategies for dealing with self-transformations that did not operate on the level of "willful political choice" alone, but on the level of tenacious, often unconscious structures and desires. The mythopoetics might be read as taking time, made necessary by the power of dominant ideals and by men's unsurprising resistances to change, for turning melancholy into grieving and for devising, as the philosopher Rosi Braidotti put it, "adequate burial ceremonies for the dead."[46]

As in nineteenth-century fraternal orders, mythopoetic leaders also offered participants a species of surrogate fathers to help with the task of masculine rebirth. Bly, for example, emphasized the importance of finding a "mentor," a "male mother," or a "substitute father who could reveal a "male mode of feeling."[47] Bly, moreover, made himself available for that role. Pfeil accurately describes Bly as a kind of "wacky oracle," whose blend of folk and fairy tale, confession, poem, and rambling address had, in its very lack of fixity and its formlessness, a distinct "wisdom effect" that conveyed the message that there is "*something* wrong with normative white heterosexual masculinity" but failed to couple it with "any clear statement or diagnosis of what that something is."[48] Nonetheless Bly's "wisdom effect" clearly operated to suggest that he had higher powers to heal and transform.

As in other movements focused on reinventing or reforming masculine ideals, brotherly love, of an almost religious intensity, was also paramount: "I feel there's so much love in this room right now it hurts"; "I think what I get out of the gatherings is an assembly of people, not necessarily just male, but an assembly of people that is a family I never had. It's uncritical, it's supportive, and it's nurturing of the way I am." Sam also felt that his men's group was the most meaningful experience he had had since being in a fraternity and that it was "the family I never had."

Loving brothers, as well as male mothers, it would appear, were important agents of transformation, though the work they did was relevant to more than men's relations to each other. Mythopoetic ritual addressed, albeit indirectly, men's relations to mothers and other women. Both caring fathers and loving brothers, for example, may have helped to supply what the philosopher Martha Nussbaum described as a common human, and indeed primate, need—"the need to be held and comforted," "a felt need for the removal of painful or invasive stimuli, and for the restoration of a blissful or undisturbed condition." This need for being held and comforted, according to Nussbaum, begins in our helpless infancy and is met, if one is lucky, by one's caretakers, who supply what Nussbaum, citing the psychoanalyst D. W. Winnicott, called "holding," a combination of nutrition, sensitive care, and the creation of a "facilitating environment."[49]

In an infant's life, caretakers who supply this "holding" are perceived of as "the agents of this restoration of the world" and take on central emotional importance. The infant itself, moreover, experiences their restorative agency as a "process of transformation" through which the infant's own state of being is altered. Longing for this early caretaker and its ministrations continues throughout the rest of human life and is inscribed as the desire for a "second coming of that shift toward bliss, and for an object that can be its vehicle."[50] Since in U.S. culture, as I argue in chapter 1, it has characteristically been women who supplied this "facilitating environment" to the young, and since gender ideology also defined females as those fated to serve men, men have often turned toward women to recapture this sense of bliss.

This was a habit of mind and heart that feminisms initially disrupted for many men, most especially those who were drawn to the mythopoetics. In calling upon men or male figures—rather than hypercritical or unreliably nurturing women—to provide the longed-for comfort and care, mythopoetics addressed both the wounding experience of distant dads and the wounding experience of some feminist women as well. In the context of often painful life histories, such fatherly and brotherly comfort and care might indeed feel, if not like a "miracle" or "second coming," then at the least like an assurance that, as Nussbuam put it, the "world was worth living in" again.[51]

In the mythopoetic "family," however, women might be present in some ghostly way, but, by all reports, they were not frequently discussed. Feminism, meanwhile, was seen as a perspective men must agree with but not openly share.[52] By officially supporting feminism while generally avoiding it as a topic to be discussed, mythopoetics "solved" the problem that had plagued NOMAS and reduced its numbers: the problem of feeling accountable to feminisms that were sometimes controlling and supercritical as well. In rendering feminism an "untouchable subject, an unspeakable tongue," mythopoetics also asserted control over the meaning of their own identity as men—for cultural feminisms had not just attacked "men's innate goodness," according to Schwalbe, they had also challenged men for control of the meanings of men, "'man,' masculinity and patriarchy" themselves.[53] This desire to take charge of masculine change was surely one explanation for the fact that mythopoetic leaders sometimes urged participants not to tell women too much about what "[they had] heard, felt, and learned that day."[54]

At the same time, the mythopoetics also offered men a species of redemption from the harshest forms of feminist critique. In mythopoetic, Jungian-based philosophy, for example, all things are good and evil and all humans have a "shadow side." Men, therefore, were no worse than women. Indeed, since facing up to the shadow was a potential source of "goodness, strength, and growth," while lacking or denying the shadow was harmful, mythopoetic men might be better and more heroic than those "strong" feminist women, who often appeared to deny that they had a "shadow side" at all.[55] These mythopoetic strategies, of course, did little to promote critical reflection upon the power relations between women and men or upon ideas and institutions that sustained them, leaving mythopoetics open to critical observations to the effect that they operated on the level of therapy alone. More unfortunately, perhaps, as the next section will discuss, the strategies also proved incomplete as therapy.

THE RETURN OF MOTHER

While NOMAS maintained political task groups and made political resolutions aimed at undoing sexism, racism, and homophobia, the mythopoetics put more emphasis on the political nature of individual personal change. Feminists, of course, had done this as well, but the point of feminist assertions that the "personal is political" had been to establish the relation between the personal and larger structural formations and inequalities. The mythopoetics, in contrast, tended to emphasize the political nature of personal alteration without an accompanying emphasis on structural transformation. In the words of Keith:

> [We were] working things out for ourselves. Trying to end some of our own confusion about gender roles or about violence in this sort of way rather than doing a lot of outreach, rather than having some kind of political agenda. Ahm, it was introspective experience. . . . The movement isn't really political. Ahm, I think that it really is about personal transformation.[56]

Dave felt that "real social change happens from micro to macro," and still another participant, Terry, explained, "Whereas the women's movement was outer, it was about how women were treated in the workplace and home, the men's movement is inner, dealing with spirit and soul."[57] Schwalbe also reported that the mythopoetics he studied were not anxious to take on discomfiting perspectives. They seemed blind, for example, to feminist criticism of institutional and structural forms of gender inequality. As men who were fairly comfortable in material terms, they were reluctant to challenge the economic status quo, although they did reject some of the more dehumanizing effects of an economic system that requires unrelenting competition, a focus on economic self-making, and the suppression of tender feeling.[58]

By 1992, however, some mythopoetic leaders were actively promoting a larger politics that would ally men and women in caring for Mother Earth and that would thereby return women and mothers to the mythopoetic family circle, thereby healing the split between women and men. I was to hear an account of these politics at an April 4, 1992, forum on "the Men's Movement," that featured Forest, a spokesman for the mythopoetics; Todd, who belonged to NOMAS; Joseph, a professor, who was sympathetic to NOMAS and to the mythopoetics both; and Annie, a leftist, female feminist historian. Held at UC Berkeley, the event drew large numbers of men involved in mythopoetic types of groups as well as large numbers of female feminist students and faculty and variously assorted non-mythopoetic profeminist men. The forum, which had been scheduled to run from 3:30 to 6:00 p.m., was to last a full four hours.

Staged as an encounter between different perspectives on the "men's movement," the forum initially threw some of the differences between NOMAS and the mythopoetics into high relief, although it would also suggest, far more subtly, some of the ways in which these two networks overlapped. The male panelists, for example, established dramatic stylistic differences among themselves from the very beginning. The clean shaven, close-cropped Todd had chosen to wear a suit and a buttoned-down shirt, although this was not characteristic of Men & Masculinity Conference dress. Joseph, in contrast, sported a mustache and moderately long grey hair and wore a silken, wine-colored shirt open at the neck. Forest, finally, whose tan set off his crinkly blue eyes and collar-length white hair and beard, was attired in an open-collared, multi-color striped shirt, which he wore with an amulet and a belt of many colors.

I read in a brochure I picked up outside that Forest was involved in something called a Kokopelli Traveling Lodge, which advertised itself as a touring group that specialized in men and gender and that featured "stories, drums poetry, lectures, songs, masks and other ceremonial arts" as well as "soul gatherings and rituals." The group's namesake, Kokopelli, a humpbacked flute player who originated in Mexico among indigenous peoples, represented "earthy wisdom, music, and a sense of play." Forest might have been playful in other contexts, but at Berkeley that day he would seem vulnerable and belabored.

The juxtaposition of styles was carried through in the presentations. Todd, the NOMAS spokesman, delivered a lengthy, analytical, and sharp critique of the mythopoetic movement as constituting a backlash against, or at least a retreat from, feminism, one that validated men's sense of powerlessness only to give them new ways of having power. Todd also argued that the mythopoetics involved too much separation from women (rather than too little, as Bly had maintained) and asserted that, rather than taking off for the woods in order to become more compassionate and caring, the mythopoetics would do better to learn these capacities at home—through shared parenting of children. (Many men, of course, were doing just that, as I remark in chapter 6.) "Ironing Johns," rather than Iron John, were the key to masculine rebirth.

Todd's lengthy presentation, however, was interrupted near the end by an unhappy choir of male voices. One man accused the NOMAS spokesman of delivering a "Rambo-like presentation." Another called out, "You're over time," and still another complained, "I'm feeling oppressed by this presentation." "*I'm* not feeling oppressed," a young woman cried from the back of the room, while the man sitting next to me, who seemed to be identified with the mythopoetics, kept murmuring the word "control," "control." Forest spoke next (and at just as great a length as Todd—several young women were to point this out), but he began by dramatically, if temporarily, discharging the tension in the room. Announcing that it was Earth Day and that he wanted to "clear the air," Forest then demonstrated what I imagined it meant to create a traveling lodge, a "container for play and sacred work," a "ritual space," by calling on one of his companions to play what looked to be a three-cylinder clay pipe.

There was indeed a noticeable shift of mood during this musical interlude —somewhat similar to the effect of an opening hymn in church. In this congregation, however, the assembly, and young women in particular, would punctuate the service with challenging remarks, not quite the version of call and response most likely to encourage the speaker. Thus, after Forest thanked the musician for his performance and for his work as a fireman, a young woman called out, "He's a fire person. There are women firefighters." Forest countered, "There are fire*women* and there are *fire persons*. But this man before you is a fire*man*," but then he appeared somewhat to collapse: "I'm in a foreign forest," he murmured. His distress, which seemed puzzling to many young women, given the large number of his followers in the room, brought another female retort, "You've got friends here, baby."

Forest began to speak, then, in a quiet and distinctly nonlinear way, about men's changing consciousness, about how men and women collude in building a sexist system (with men getting all the blame), about how feminist women engaged in shaming men, about how poetry was necessary to dismantle sexism, about how feminism must draw the circle differently so the men were included, and about how men must get beyond self-loathing and shame. As he spoke, another follower began softly drumming. This drumming, Forest suggested, shifting his tack, was like the heartbeat of the mother in the womb. "We honor women consistently," Forest asserted, offering to teach any woman who wanted to learn how to drum, insisting that feminism was "in his bones," and pointing out that Bly himself organized a Great Mother Conference every year. Forest then read a poem on the Great Mother that I found hard to follow but that seemed to emphasize forgiveness and blessing. I began to wonder whose.

In the seventies, Forest continued, the focus of the men's movement was on men and women; in the eighties, the focus was on fathers and sons, and in the nineties the focus would be on the "threat to earth," on eco-masculinity, on moving past the "warrior masculinity" to being "husbandmen of the earth." Men and women both, according to Forest, would collectively build this movement together. Forest, indeed, was already engaged in alliance building between women and men—a project, he explained, that emphasized giving counsel, singing lullabies, cradling, comforting, and affirming beauty, joy, and celebration.

These were attractive images indeed, and the forum by now felt distinctly like church. It was not clear, however, how men and women were to get to this place of alliance without skipping over a number of less soothing conversations—about the traditional dynamics of male–female relations, about sexism and inequity. Why, for example, did this place of alliance seem to feature ("the mother's"? women's?) blessing and forgiveness while men organized mother conferences, taught women how to drum, and husbanded the earth? As the historian Annie would wryly observe in her comments on the panel, we need to look at "gender difference and inequality before getting to alliance with the earth."

In the long discussion that followed, several men involved with the mythopoetic movement rose to testify, some breaking down in tears, about the difference the movement had made in their lives. A machinist and recovering alcoholic spoke of learning to love his children and of being with men "in a different place." Another man testified to teaching the disabled, another to working with fire victims, another to visiting prisoners, and still another to sitting with crack babies. An ex–Green Beret spoke of learning to bond with people who were racially unlike himself. Forest also pointed out that there were gay men in the leadership and that men hugged and kissed: "You'd think we were women." All of this suggested that the mythopoetics did indeed heal men and that they promoted compassionate and nurturing attitudes and behaviors and perhaps more resolute and vibrant ones as well, although these particular men seemed pretty fragile to me. Not one man, however, had talked about how compassion and nurturing had changed, or even entered into, his relationship with an actual female. Cross-gender alliance, at this point, began to seem a long way off.

I left the forum feeling no little skepticism about mythopoetic politics, and not just along gender lines. What structural changes, for example, did "eco-masculinity" stand for? I also left, however, feeling empathy for these men and slightly guilty as well. These men *were* sensitive and compassionate, and I, as a feminist, was supposed to want this, wasn't I? I had thought I did, but if these were the sensitive new men Bly was talking about, I had to agree that, even after mythopoetic initiation, there was something "incomplete." Was it that these men lacked resolve or "energy," as Bly had claimed? I, for one, had been feeling positively robust, as if I were "radiating energy" in their company, like one of those post-sixties women Bly had described. Was it a class division I was picking up on? Was I divided from them by my relative immersion in the masculinist culture of academe?

Bly had written that the mythopoetic men's movement spoke best to those who had opened the "grief door into their own childhood." I was certainly a member of that tribe.[59] Had my own long therapy worked better than theirs? Was it that I was free from the burden of having to prove manhood—or womanhood either, for that matter? Was it that I felt sustained, even into the nineties, by a feminist political community and a higher cause? Or was it as Bob Blauner was to suggest, in an essay on the "men's movement" that year, that—for all the father work these men had ostensibly accomplished—their feelings about their mothers, women, and feminism had never been worked through except on the level of fairy tale and symbol? Did the protection of Mother Earth stand in for actually encountering their feelings of dependency on, and rage toward, mothers and the women who in some way stood in for or represented them? Was it that their failure to confront the mother wound, exacerbated by the feminist wound, had left them in a state of continuing anxiety and vulnerability, that bled through in their self-presentations and in their relation to the world at large?

According to Blauner, it was "only by working through our relationships with our mothers (with whom our father feelings are also inextricably intertwined) that we can be become more responsible as adults and responsive to the women in our lives and to the changes brought about by the feminist movement." Blauner's hope was that by reclaiming love and closeness to their mothers, by confronting the deeply suppressed and inchoate tangle of love, desire, anger, and anxiety in which men's relations to their mothers, and therefore to women and feminism, were enmeshed, that men "might find more humanistic ways of being men, and perhaps even graduate from the state of 'perpetual adolescence' that so many of us seem to remain in."[60] The mythopoetics, of course, were already subject to sharp criticism for having "addicted" themselves to group therapy, but was the problem that a different therapy was needed and not less? Child care and ironing, at any rate, seemed unlikely in themselves to put things right.

NOTES

1. Robert Bly, *Iron John: A Book about Men* (New York: Addison-Wesley, 1990), 16.

2. Lester C. Thurow, "Average White Male No Longer Leads the March to Prosperity," *Los Angeles Times*, 20 October 1985, 3; Andrea Stuart, "Saving the Male," *New Statesman and Society* 5, no. 194 (20 March 1992): 38; Donald A. Clement, "A White-Male Lament," *Newsweek*, 2 July 1990, 8; David Gates, "White Male Paranoia," *Newsweek*, 29 March, 1993, 48.

3. See, for example, Joyce Millman, "Revenge of the Angry White Male," *San Francisco Examiner,* 29 August 1993.

4. Erik Hedegaard, "The Men's Movement Is Here, but Where Is It Taking Us?" *McCall's*, November 1991, 98; William H. Willimon, "Stag Spirituality: What Do Drums, Earthly Masculinity, and Gender Quotas Have to Do with the Gospel?" *Christianity Today* 34, no. 7 (1990): 26.

5. David Gelman, "Making It All Feel Better," *Newsweek*, 26 November 1990, 66.

6. Mark Lawson, "The 'Wild Man' Mystique," *World Press Review* 38, no. 12 (December 1991): 40; "Men in Trouble," *Fortune* 124, no. 13 (December 1991): 184; Joe Queenan, "Three Days of the Con Job," *Gentleman's Quarterly* (March 1992): 215, 214; Willomon, "Stag Spirituality," 26; Andrew Ferguson, "America's New Man," *American Spectator* 25, no. 1 (January 1992): 26.

7. Trip Gabriel, "The Call of the Wildmen," *New York Times Magazine*, 14 October 1990, 47.

8. See Erik Hedegaard, "The Men's Movement Is Here, but Where Is It Taking Us?" *McCall's,* November 1991, 98.

9. Robert Blauner, "The Men's Movement and Its Analysis of the Male Malaise, or Men on the Move? But Why? and Where To?" unpublished paper, 1992, 4.

10. Julie Haase, "Reinventing Masculinity: The Politics of Gender Identity in the Mythopoetic 'Men's Movement,'" unpublished paper, 1992, 38.

11. Bly, *Iron John,* 2.

12. Bly, *Iron John*, 2, 3.

13. Bly, *Iron John*, 4, 6, 4, 8.

14. Michael Schwalbe, *Unlocking the Iron Cage: The Men's Movement, Gender, Politics, and American Culture* (New York: Oxford, 1996), 19.

15. Schwalbe, *Iron,* 198, 197.

16. Schwalbe, *Iron,* 206, 208; Andrew Ferguson, "America's New Man," *American Spectator* 25, no. 1 (January 1992): 28.

17. Fred Pfeil, *White Guys: Studies in Postmodern Domination and Difference* (London: Verso, 1995), 208.

18. Lane Morrow, "The Child Is the Father of the Man," *Time,* 19 August 1991, 52 (3 pages); Hasse, "Reinventing Masculinity," 27–28.

19. Haase, "Reinventing Masculinity," 27–28.

20. Schwalbe, *Iron*, 29.

21. Schwalbe, *Iron*, 19.

22. Schwalbe, *Iron*, 20; Blauner, "The Men's Movement," 19.

23. Robert Bly, interview with Terry Gross, National Public Radio, 12 May 1992.

24. Bly, interview with Terry Gross.

25. Schwalbe, *Iron*, 25.

26. Schwalbe, *Iron,* 64, 112, 110, 102, 213; Bettie, "Reinventing Masculinity," 29.

27. Ferguson, "America's New Man," 33; Queenan, "Three Days," 214; Schwalbe, *Iron*, 23.

28. Schwalbe, *Iron*, 28.

29. Bly, *Iron John*, 36.

30. Bly, *Iron John*, 6, 238–49, 6.

31. Bly, *Iron John*, 241, 247.

32. Bly, *Iron John*, 249.

33. Bly, *Iron John*, 1–28.

34. Schwalbe, *Iron,* 81.

35. "A Gathering of Men," produced by Betsy McCarthy, directed by Wayne Ewing, a production of Public Affairs Television, Inc. New York: Mystic Fire Video [1990?]; Bly, *Iron John*, 49.

36. Schwalbe, *Iron*, 65, 67, 63.

37. Schwalbe, *Iron*, 58. I am also indebted to Michael Schwalbe's written comments on this chapter.

38. Schwalbe, *Iron*, 75.

39. Bly, *Iron John,* 219, 209, 216.

40. Bly, *Iron John*, 31–2, 34–35.

41. Blauner, "Men's Movement," 12–13.

42. Blauner, "The Men's Movement," 13. Bly, interview with Terry Gross.

43. Bly, *Iron John,* 19.

44. Blauner, "The Men's Movement," 17; Schwalbe, *Iron,* 78.

45. Rosi Braidotti, "Revisiting Male Thanatica," *differences: A Journal of Feminist Cultural Studies* 6, 2–3 (Summer–Fall 1994): 199. All references in this paragraph are to this essay.

46. Schwalbe, *Iron*, 75; Braidotti, "Revisiting Male Thanatica," 199. R. W. Connell, "Long and Winding Road: An Outsider's View of U.S. Masculinity and Feminism," in *Masculinity Studies & Feminist Theory*, ed. Judith Kegan Gardiner (New York: Columbia University Press, 2002), 193.

47. Bly, "A Gathering of Men."

48. Pfeil, *White Guys,* 193, 194, 195.

49. Martha C. Nussbaum, *Upheavals of Thought: The Intelligence of Emotions* (Cambridge: Cambridge University Press, 2001), 186, 183, 185–86.

50. Nussbaum, *Upheavals,* 184.

51. Nussbaum, *Upheavals*, 184, 186, 187.

52. Pfeil, *White Guys,* 190.

53. Pfeil, *White Guys,* 190; Schwalbe, *Iron,* 134.

54. Schwalbe, *Iron,* 135; Pfeil, *White Guys,* 197.

55. Schwalbe, *Iron,* 56, 57.

56. Haase, "Reinventing Masculinity," 24.

57. Haase, "Reinventing Masculinity," 25.

58. Schwalbe, *Iron*, 188, 239.

59. Bly, *Iron John*, 236.

60. Blauner, "The Men's Movement," 22.

6

Fathers of Themselves

The shift to active fathering . . . may turn out to be the most profound of all the changes in men that reflect the changes women have been making.

—Anthony Astrachan, *How Men Feel*, 1986[1]

SOME WOUNDED SONS MOVE ON

The more vulnerable, nurturing, and emotionally expressive masculine ideals that black cultural nationalists, Radical Faeries, the men of NOMAS, and the mythopoetics came to extol were partially produced by men "getting on the bus" with other men. Almost by definition, they were not precisely the ideals that feminist women would have chosen for them. (This historical stubbornness on the part of men—wanting to set terms for their own change—is surely one source of the vague but persistent feminist conviction that men "can never get it right.") That men in heterosexually oriented networks *have* set terms of their own for developing and practicing more expressive, more tender, and more nurturing masculine ideals has much to do with the fact that loving relations with children—rather than, say, intimacy with women or other men—appear to have been the area of greatest interest and emotional growth. This turn (or return) to nurturing fatherhood, moreover, was embraced by large numbers of men who had never participated in an organized effort to transform ideals of masculinity.

In the late 1960s and 1970s, as previous chapters have detailed, groups consciously informed by the project of reinventing masculine ideals had focused upon rejecting many of the values of self-making masculinity and upon

157

(variously) generating more altruistic, caring, vulnerable, and/or emotionally connected models of manhood. These models were often enacted through forms of community-oriented political activity, through building brotherly relationships between men, and/or through forms of mourning over lost, distant, and unloving dads. In the mid-1970s and early 1980s, however, spokesmen for black nationalisms and for largely white profeminist networks alike not only embraced loving fatherhood as a major form of personal development for men, but also speculated that it might be the most rewarding avenue of all for developing more open and emotionally expressive masculine ideals.

Writing in 1974 the co-editors of an early profeminist anthology, *Men and Masculinity*, speculated that

> of all the areas in which men are beginning to examine themselves and go beyond the limits of the traditional masculine role perhaps the one to bear the most sweet fruit will be our relations with children. . . . For some of us being with children and joining the immediacy of their emotional life may be a route toward reclaiming the spontaneous emotional awareness which our own masculine training drove into hiding so long ago.[2]

In 1982 the much-cited black nationalist writer Jawanza Kunjufu also named loving fatherhood as a central means to redefining manhood, so as to reject "male seasoning," a dehumanizing training process designed to "make you a skeleton, with no feelings and compassion for your children, women or brothers." As a counter to "male seasoning," Kunjufu proposed rites-of-passage programs that would mentor young boys and provide "the intimacy our boys should have received from their fathers."[3] At the same time, these programs would provide rites of passage for adult men, too, by engaging them in the rehumanizing process of practicing more tender and compassionate attitudes and behaviors. Nationalist writers of the 1980s and 1990s would continue this theme.

Advocates of "generative fathering" in the 1990s—largely white academics in family science, psychology, and sociology—also emphasized the role of fathering in men's personal change. They defined the generative father as a man who took on housework and physical and emotional care of children not as "a reluctant personal sacrifice of privilege for the sake of social justice" but as an essential part of his own personal growth. They argued that involving men in parenting on those grounds might be a more pragmatic course for transforming men's lives within families than the "painful emotional work" required by many organized efforts to transform models of masculinity. Involving men in generative fathering would also be more effective in changing men than the defense-provoking strategies of some feminist demands for male reform: "People are less likely to change from a position of imposed guilt and defensiveness" than from a "personal vision of a better way and a sense of empowerment."[4] African-American advocates of generative fathering, moreover, extended its social significance by also pointing to the ways in which the emphasis of generative fathering upon "agency over victimhood" fostered "empowerment through love and nurturing as opposed to devitalization through cynicism and bitterness." This personal development in turn could lead to forms of family and community involvement that promote resilience in children as surely as they could "reclaim neighborhoods."[5]

There were good reasons why love for children, rather than intimacy with women, say, or with other men, became the primary site for exploring, encouraging, and celebrating greater nurturing and feeling on the part of many heterosexual males. One is that for many men producing a more humane, less emotionally constricted masculinity was more safely accomplished with children than with female adults or other men. Intimacy with children, for example, did not so easily evoke the uneasiness over homosexuality that often haunted men's intimacy with each other.[6] Loving relationships with one's children might also circumvent the anxiety that many heterosexual men experienced at the notion of becoming more intimate emotionally with female domestic partners or with wives. Women in domestic relationships with men could already evoke the fantasy and fear of merging with the comforting preoedipal mom, a desire that might be accompanied by anxious fantasies of resubmission to the early mother's power and control.[7] For many U.S. men, in particular, such fantasies might threaten a troubling loss of masculine identity altogether, an identity often forged in compulsive acts of separation from women and the feminine.

Feminisms, which boldly demanded that men change and on the terms that women set as well, further threatened some men's (already fragile) sense of control over their own identities. In the 1970s and 1980s, in particular, this undoubtedly intensified the yearning, anxiety, and anger that many men already experienced as an underlying part of their intimate relations with women. Close relationships with children, in contrast, so long as they seemed chosen rather than imposed, not only gave many men a less threatening opportunity for emotional growth than relationships with adult female partners, but also offered men the possibility of feeling in charge of their own change. Children, for example, did not "own" the language of adult–child interaction as women, and especially feminist women, appeared to "own" the language of male/female relations.

For the activist sons of the 1960s, moreover, nurturing fatherhood might have provided one form of recovery not only from their rejection of traditional father figures and authorities but from the wounding decline of the New Left and Black Power movements. The latter, in representing alternative ideals to those of traditional, or less radical, father figures, had in some ways taken the fathers' place. For men who had participated in the mythopoetics' mourning over lost, distant, or unloving dads, becoming a father oneself might have provided a means of moving on. In lovingly fathering a child, and a male child in particular, some men might cease to be grieving sons and become the longed for fathers of themselves.

At the same time, nurturing fatherhood, particularly of the hands-on the-dirty-diaper form, also spoke to feminist demands, providing many men with a gratifying sense of having responded to women's calls for change. Fathering was, and remains, an arena in which men's self-interest *has* undeniably inter-sected with feminist politics. Autobiographical literature, moreover, suggested that many men did engage in more child care than before, though sometimes at the insistence of their female partners, and often at some cost to their sense of entitlement as men. The turn to shared parenting, finally, was also driven by the effects of global and domestic restructuring. Between 1973 and 1988, as inflation drove up the price of housing, transportation, education, and health care, and as real median incomes in the United States stalled, the rising cost of the American dream pushed women into the labor force in ever higher num-bers. Thus, in 1970, 29 percent of women with children under five worked in the labor force, but in 1988 the number had risen to 51 percent, a change with significant impact on gender relations at work and in the home.

The turn to fathering, however, was to be replete with ironies and contra-dictions for men and women both. On the one hand, involved fathering opened a road to personal change that was less threatening to men than that of brotherhood or greater intimacy with women and that did produce new ca-pacities for tenderness and care. On the other hand, involved fathering might also contribute to subtle forms of gender conflict and revenge. The turn to fa-thering, indeed, was at once the most promising avenue for male transforma-tion and the example par excellence of men's ambivalence and deep-seated conflict about gender change.

THE NEW FATHER

One of the earliest signs of a general turn to involved fathering was the flurry of attention to what was called "the new father" in the early 1980s, a category most often confined in media accounts, although not in life, to a white, middle-class professional with a working wife. These young urban profes-sionals, newly designated "Parenting Urban Professionals" (or "Puppies" rather than Yuppies) were said to take part in childbirth classes, to coach their wives in childbirth, and even to cut the umbilical cord.[8] This new father, moreover, did not want to stop there: "He wants to look after his child, interview the baby sitter, and on his lunch break, take Johnny for his DPT shot."[9] A series of books on *How to Father, Pregnant Fathers,* and *Father Power* appeared, as new fathers duly became new marketing opportunities. Parenting classes for "fathers only" became available, and catalogues entitled "Me and My Dad" offered *The Father's Almanac* and extra-tall models of the Jogger stroller for those over six foot three.[10] Although new fathers discovered, to their dismay, that they, too, must now wrestle with the child-vs.-career conflicts that "working mothers" were already struggling with, studies were asserting by 1986 that there had been a 15-to-20 percent increase in the amount of time that men spent with their children.

The degree to which men actually put hands-on fathering into action, however—by taking on the day-to-day chores of feeding, changing, and bathing children and of managing their schedules as well—is open to considerable debate. Some men, like political scientist Isaac Balbus, who has documented and theorized his feminist fathering in the early 1980s, did appear to have taken on a full share.[11] Richard, another academic, profeminist man whom I interviewed in the early 1990s, reported, "I always understood that I had primary child-care responsibility. We shared it, to be honest, fifty-fifty." He recalled watching his wife leave for work at 8:00 a.m. every other day while he watched from the window, washing the dishes.

Several studies of men's involvement in child care have nonetheless indicated that many men overassessed their involvement, used their male privilege to avoid the more distasteful aspects of child care, and emphasized play. Even Paul, a profeminist father I interviewed in the 1990s as well, recalled that although he was the only father on the playground in the late 1970s, it was only on weekends. He did not give up his weekday time for the children. One study in the late eighties, indeed, claimed that although 74 percent of the men interviewed said they shared child care equally with the mother, only 13 percent actually did. A recent summary of scholarly work on child care and housework by the sociologist Scott Coltrane reported that although men in dual-career families did increase the hours they spent doing housework from 11 percent of the total in the mid-1970s to 28 percent in the mid-1990s, their involvement in child care rose more moderately, from 20 percent to 33 percent of the total during the same period. Women in dual-career households, therefore, were still performing two-thirds of the child care in the middle nineties.[12]

Most accounts of the new father gave less emphasis to the rate at which devoted dads changed dirty diapers and wiped up drool than to the emotional rewards men experienced in forging a greater connection with their children.[13] Like many a new mother, new fathers felt overcome "by the incredible wonder of it all." One book on the new father, *The Birth of the Father*, indeed, offered "engrossment" as a special term for referring to "the sense of absorption, pre-occupation and interest new fathers feel for their newborns."[14] Some studies suggested that men who were willing to share parenting in the 1980s already had strong motherly feelings. Balbus, for example, was a motherly man, as was Richard, who had grown up "in a touchy-feely home," where he had helped care for his sick mother. Fatherly connection, however, appears to have had much broader appeal. In 1986, for example, the psychologist Samuel Osherson spoke of the "tremendous yearning in men to have more connection with their children" and speculated that suburbanization had "created a generation of men who felt exiled" from home.[15] Fatherly yearning, moreover, also surfaced at a time when women's increasing entry into the labor market, their feminist-inspired focus on self-development, and their increasingly critical conscious-ness of traditional gender roles had dislodged white men, in particular, as pri-mary breadwinners and as the focus of women's emotional energies. For many men in the 1980s, involved fatherhood may have functioned as another com-pensation for these emotional and material dislocations.

Fatherly "engrossment," however, did not always lead to motherly delight, and although shared parenting in the 1980s might draw men and women to-gether in an absorbing common project, it had features that women found de-centering to themselves in turn. In a study of white, middle-class, dual-income Bay Area families in the early 1980s, for example, psychologist Diane Ehrensaft noted that fathers willing to share parenting did have strong motherly tendencies and, although generally "hungry" for intimacy and for merging with another being, found it "safer" to open up with children than with the women they lived with. According to one father, "There is a close-ness with my daughter that I have nowhere else. I don't have to get through any barriers with her, like I do with my wife."[16]

According to another, "My son doesn't stay angry at me for more than the situation lasts, and I can't stay angry with him. . . . That's different if my wife and I get angry with each other. It's much more threatening." In contrast to the ease and safety that men experienced in opening up to their children, opening up to a female partner appeared to activate fears of being engulfed or rejected.[17] In the lives of the men Ehrensaft interviewed, indeed, shared par-enting not only meant an expected transfer of attention from wife to child, but the expression of a playfulness, openness, and emotional intensity with chil-dren that men had never shown their wives at all. Wives, moreover, were quite conscious of the gap. According to one woman, "My husband is more childish with Valerie than with me. I wish he would be able to do it with me." According to another, "Bernard's very outgoing with our daughter, much less with me. He feels safer to do this with her because she's his kid. Old ways die harder with a wife than with parenting." Several women were also embarrassed to admit that they noticed the little, material gestures or, more accurately, the absence of them: "He does not and never has brought me little presents, and he's more apt to do that for our son."[18]

While the women Ehrensaft interviewed often took pleasure in their husband's attention to the child and welcomed shared child care and increased autonomy with respect to their children, some also felt that they had lost a good deal in the bargain. In a world where women were still largely invisible and lacking social and economic power, they felt they had sacrificed some of the emotional power they had felt in being the indispensable wife and mother, the primary source of emotional provision in the home. In the words of a writer for the *New York Times* in 1986, "That is the price I pay for sharing her equally with him. Women who do all the parenting, or who share it with paid helpers, have a special power that I have relinquished. It is the power of being everything to the child."[19] Fathers, in contrast, though they might express envy of their wives' parenting abilities, did not report feeling like odd men out in Ehrensaft's study, although Balbus reports, and many female feminists would confirm, that fathers did feel jealous if their child preferred the mother. Balbus, for example, records his "gut wrenching" jealousy over his wife's breast feeding: "This was exactly as I had feared: Shayla loved Dotty more than me. . . . You can't beat the breast."[20]

Involved fathering, moreover, inevitably gave men a potential power over women that some found tempting to enjoy. Several fathers in Ehrensaft's study mentioned their delight in their greater centrality to the child: "Carole is a little jealous of Aaron's greater attachment to me. She keeps it under wraps, but she's jealous. *I* love it, I absolutely love it."[21] Although Ehrensaft suggested that these men were not callous or gloating but merely oblivious to everything but their own "engrossment" with their child, more skeptical readings are possible. As one divorced father confessed to me in the late 1990s, "Involved fathering is a weapon men use against women too." This was a reading that many second-wave feminists arrived at on their own after encountering what they saw as overly aggressive forms of committed fatherhood in action. "They've gone too far!" one of my white feminist colleagues pronounced in the early 1980s, after the involved father of her young child insisted on taking a year-long turn at being resident parent while the two were in a commuting relationship. I had the same dark feelings when my daughter's super-committed dad sometimes pushed me out of the way in his haste to comfort her first when she was hurt.

Writing in the 1980s, Ehrensaft was uncertain whether the greater openness and spontaneity that men practiced with their children would function as a "corrective emotional experience" that would spill over into relationships with women or whether it would become a permanent "escape hatch" from greater male/female intimacy. In the 1980s, her interviews suggested that the new openness men experienced was more often turned to "the world" or "people" than to female partners. Women in shared parenting relationships, meanwhile, feeling guilty for giving the child less attention than the traditional norms of motherhood required, often compensated by including children in every possible family moment. This posed the possibility, Ehrensaft suggested, that shared parenting for men and women might become a way of working on a common project while studiously avoiding emotional connection with each other.[22]

Ironically, of course, the 1980s also marked a high point of feminist optimism about the potential contribution of involved fathering to gender reconciliation. If men were to act as primary parents of infant children, it was theorized, boys might identify merging and overwhelming forms of power with fathers and mothers both, rather than with mothers and women alone. This would decrease boys' psychic preparation for unconsciously fearing women as a special category of person who represented threats to masculine identity, while it would increase their ability to reconcile nurturing and emotional expressivity with being proper boys and men. Girls, in contrast, might be less prone to associate dependence with being feminine. Boys and girls both, thereby, might be better prepared to practice gender identities less at odds with each other in terms of the need for, and the fear of, intimate emotional connection. This longed-for outcome, however, would take place slowly, as involved fathering produced new generations of daughters and sons. In the meantime, the new fathering may have contributed as much to gender struggle as to gender reconciliation, with mothers and fathers both vying for first place in their children's hearts.[23]

THE NEWLY ANGRY DAD

The decade of the "new" father, almost always identified as white and middle-class, was accompanied by an increase in the divorce rate. This increase was fed by changes in women's work roles, by women's greater economic independence of men, by the development of no-fault divorce laws, by women's increased sensitivity to the inequities of traditional gender arrangements, and by men's sense of having lost ground on both the economic and the home fronts. Although divorce rates began rising as early as the 1840s, they reached an all-time high between 1980 and 1985, before leveling off in the later 1980s. In 1975, for example, 18 percent of white women and 22 percent of black women were divorced, but by 1985 the numbers had risen to 27 and 31 percent, respectively.[24]

At the same time, instances of female-headed households were rising. In 1970 black women headed about 28 percent of black households, but in 1987 the figure was around 42 percent. Single white females headed only 9 percent of white households in 1970 and 12 percent in 1987, but in 1970 most white female heads of household had been widowed (47 percent) with only about 25 percent divorced, and around 9 percent single. In 1987 most white female heads of house were divorced (about 42 percent).[25]

Although most female heads of white households were working or lower class, the number of professional, middle-class white women who opted for single motherhood did rise. Lesbians, moreover, were in the vanguard of this shift. In the mid to late seventies, according to sociologist Judith Stacey, many lesbians, inspired by the legacy of the sexual revolution, by feminist assertions of female autonomy, and by the "Black Matriarchs" who had been turned into political martyrs by Daniel Patrick Moynihan's mid-sixties attack, began to seek custody of children whom they had conceived in partnerships with men. They also actively chose having children on their own—whether through artificial insemination or through adopting children with female partners.[26]

In the early eighties, too, a modest number of white, heterosexual feminists, then in their forties, hastily began last-minute families as well, sometimes with male partners and sometimes without. It was in the 1980s, for example, when several of my lesbian friends were on their second child, that I began my own campaign to have one, too. Although marriage was not a necessary (and, at this point, not a likely) first step, I preferred sharing this profound experience with someone I could trust. Thus, I asked my gay ex-husband and best friend to enter into a parenting relationship with me, something that he proved quite willing to do. Our attempt to conceive a child failed, and ultimately I was to have my child in marriage, but this had not been my original, or most desired, plan. It had simply made sense, in the flush of eighties feminism and in the waning moments of a biological ticking clock, to pursue my motherly yearning without waiting for a standard-issue "Mr. Right."

It was not surprising, in this era of deliberately chosen single motherhoods, that articles on the "new father" were interleaved with those on newly angry dads. In the context of the material and emotional decentering of non-elite men, and in the context of a climate that had opened up the vision of recentering oneself in devoted fatherhood, the possibility that access to one's children might be cut off as well—by custody arrangements that automatically favored women or by women themselves who did not look with favor on their ex-husband's visitation rights—was painful and obviously hard to take.

For all these reasons—and because relations with children offered an arena in which women were highly vulnerable to being hurt—it was not surprising that the set of policy issues that men most often organized around as fathers were not those that would have secured father-friendly work environments or paternal leave. Instead, the policy changes men most eagerly pursued were those that limited women's control over offspring—beings whom men and women both often regarded as extensions of themselves. Thus, mandatory joint child custody (which some feminists had also favored), lower child-support payments, and the right to intervene in women's decisions to abort or put their children up for adoption became the central issues for father's rights organizations. In 1982, by one estimate, there were already three hundred father's rights organizations, with ten thousand members, in the United States, Europe, and Australia. In the United States, such groups had helped pass new or revised joint custody legislation in twenty-four states.[27]

As if mirroring women's newly fluid and unconventional modes of mothering, father's rights legislation multiply expanded the traditional meanings of fatherhood as well. Father's rights groups, for example, rejected a definition of fatherhood mainly based on economic provision, complaining that women who insisted on child support but who refused fathers visitations with their children were trying to "severe all but the economic ties between father and child."[28] Middle-class men, according to these groups, "yearned" for the role of nurturer even after divorce.[29] New forms of fatherhood, like new forms of motherhood, peppered the news. Among the newly constructed categories of fathers seeking visitation, joint, or sole custody, for example, were "nonbiological," "nonadopting," "unmarried," "de facto," "estranged," "casual," spermatic, and "emotional"—both straight and gay.[30] Fathers, moreover, were seeking custody of children adopted by other families, of fetuses, and of in-vitro embryos as well. In the interest of reducing women's control over children, father's rights groups proved quite willing to depart from traditional definitions of fatherhood.

Like new fathers, newly angry dads were fueled by a contradictory mix of emotions and desires. Advocates of father's rights might be motivated by a desire to overcome the limits of "the male role" through a "new fatherhood" based on nurturing and the greater expression of tender emotion, by the pain of being separated from their children in divorce, by anger at child custody laws that assumed, in the 1970s, that moms were the more capable parent, and by rage at women and feminisms both. If, on the one hand, therefore, fathers' rights organizations combined "feminism's language of equal rights with the vocabulary of male nurturance to fight for change," on the other the very language of equal rights that father's rights groups employed might be used to justify traditional forms of unequal parenting and male privilege.[31]

According to one study of two Canadian father's rights organizations, most men sought joint rather than sole custody, often as a means to avoid child support payments. While anxious to maintain access to children, information about them, and decision-making power, many men did not interpret joint custody as meaning equal physical and primary child-care responsibilities.[32] Although the number of single fathers increased from 10 percent in 1980 to 15 percent in 1991, proving that more men were willing to take responsibility for raising children, most men in the groups studied wanted equal status as parents but not equal responsibilities—a continuation, despite the multiplication of noneconomic fatherhoods, of their predivorce role as "the traditional father who exercises his power and control."[33]

In the 1990s, moreover, in the context of the increasingly dramatic erosion of the ideal of national manhood, which had been based on the white, middle-class father's traditional breadwinning role, many father's rights organizations wed themselves to a new conversation around fatherhood that contradicted the previous emphases of father's rights organizations on love and care and on the multiplicity of fathering modes. This new version of the (implicitly) white father, the "good [enough] family man," rejected the new, more nurturing father as not properly a father at all. It reemphasized the importance of men's competition and economic provision for their families, stressed the superiority of biological fatherhood, and asserted that white fathers must be returned to the home, "as they are."[34]

This was not for the good of women, who were criticized for their selfishness in pursuing work and careers, but for the sake of the children and the nation as a whole. National manhood, that is, was resurrected in the "good [enough and implicitly white] family man," whose mission was to control the social disorder that selfish working women and an implicitly black "fatherlessness" had created. Newly angry dads, whose public image often seemed more defensive or spiteful than powerful or noble, had been offered a more heroic and more commanding cultural role.

FROM WARRIOR SON TO FATHER OF A KINGDOM

It was in 1965, the year of the Watts riot and of Patrick Moynihan's report on "The Negro Family: The Case for National Action," that black fatherhood and family life became the object once more of intensified national scrutiny. Taking its key from the social science of the 1950s and 1960s, which had emphasized the importance of a traditional division of gender roles, the report argued that growing divorce rates, a rise in female-headed families, and burgeoning welfare rolls were a sign of the "deterioration of the fabric of Negro society." All of this, the report contended, had hit black men harder psychologically than black women in that it had undermined men's ability to take their rightful position as family head. The solution was both to get black men jobs and to restore the black man, and especially the father, to his rightful place as head of household.[35]

The report's reading of current data, in the words of a contemporary, was "over dramatic."[36] Although by 1965 one-quarter of black marriages could be expected to dissolve, one-quarter of all black births were illegitimate, and one-quarter of black families were headed by a single female, the majority of black households continued to be two-parent and often extended units as before, with hardworking fathers, stepfathers, uncles, and other male figures contributing to the family's survival and well-being.[37] One common model of the black father, which remained invisible for the most part within mainstream culture, was that of the proud, hardworking, often stern, sometimes tender man.

The Black Panther Huey Newton, for example, recalled that his father worked "two and sometimes three jobs at once. . . . We could not understand how he did it—never a day to rest or relax—and never a complaint." Another Panther, David Hilliard, also remembered that "no one worked harder than my father. Idleness was anathema to him. . . . Work was his whole life." In a recent anthology on black fathers, literary critic Henry Louis Gates Jr. reported that "Daddy worked all the time, every day but Sunday. Two jobs— twice a day, in and out, eat and work, work and eat." Houston A. Baker, also a literary critic, recalled his hardworking father's injunction to "Be a man!" There was "no time or space for sentimentality, tears, flabby biceps, fear, or illness in the stark image of American conquest my father set before himself."[38] The prevailing image of black fathers in mainstream culture, nonetheless, remained that of the failed, delinquent, abandoning man.

The continuing focus on the "dysfunctional" nature of black family life diverted attention from the fact that economic and social forces, informed by racism, denied black men and women full citizenship and full belonging to the national family. According to literary critic Marlon Ross, the "gap" in U.S. conceptions of the citizen, whereby white men were citizens but black men were not, was displaced onto, and justified by, the purported "absence" of most black men from the home. The focus on "restoring" the black patriarchal family may also have functioned, Ross suggested, as a form of displaced anxiety over white feminism, over white women's entry into the workforce, their increasing economic independence of men, and the high divorce rates—all signs of white men's inability to "discipline" their own women as national manhood required. It was through an assault upon the black family that the establishment sought to reassert "the patriarchal model of the [white] *bourgeois* family as the cornerstone for U.S. social, economic, and political

progress." This focus on the irresponsible, absent, or disappearing black father, finally, appeared in the context of Black Power that insisted on the "progressive protective presence of Black men."[39]

The media and some Black Power leaders most often represented this "protective presence" in the figure of a young, urban, warrior-like, heterosexual,
largely nondomestic, lower-class male. Elements of a differently constituted
protective masculine ideal, however, were also implicit in the Black Power
Movement—in Newton's serve-the-people philosophy, in Black Panther
community programs, in Karenga's Kawaida doctrine, and in Malcolm X
himself as benevolent patriarch.[40] This differently constituted ideal, that of
the loving, domestically invested, in-charge husband and father, would most
fully emerge after the destruction of Black Power in the late 1970s. In the
context of this significant political loss, many cultural nationalist writers
would seek new models of resistance and new ideals of the black (implicitly
male) citizen and activist—ideals that would not require community members
to relate to activists "by picking up the gun."[41] In the work of many cultural
nationalists, living out this ideal became a central condition for manhood and
political leadership both. Thus, according to Na'im Akbar in 1990, "You are
prepared to lead a big community when you learn to lead a little community.
You must first be a king in your personal kingdom. If you can't rule the kingdom at your feet, you can't lead a bigger kingdom."[42] Rites-of-passage programs would become central to this father-based politics.

Rites-of-passage programs began as early as 1964 with Maulana Karenga's
Simba or Young Lions Program, which was grounded, like many programs to
follow, on an African-inspired value system called Kawaida, or Nguzo Saba,
which emphasized unity, self-determination, collective work, responsibility,
cooperative economics, creativity, and faith.[43] Jawanza Kunjufu was also a
proponent of rites-of-passage programs that he saw, in the early 1980s, as a
means to counter forces undermining black values. *The Conspiracy to Destroy Black Boys,* his short, three-volume series, would sell a million copies
by 1993. In this series Kunjufu called on all black men to "become responsible for giving direction to at least one male child," preferably by means of
programs and organizations designed to protect and develop them. In calling
on black men to mentor boys in an intimate and loving way—one of Kunjufu's central images of fathering is that of "bringing your son to your
chest"—Kunjufu offered adult black men a means of expressing or recasting
themselves as well.[44] Black men, that is, would teach themselves, along with
black boys, to embrace a masculine idea that enshrined fathering and familial commitment as well as tender emotion.

Like many male, black nationalist writers to follow, Kunjufu criticized core
values of the ideals of self-making masculinity and of national manhood as

well, ideals that identified citizenship with the white, the middle-class, and male. Kunjufu, for example, described his proposed program as similar to that of the Boy Scouts, with the exception that it did not support the status quo of "European-American male supremacy." Rather, it would equip African-American boys to understand why African-Americans were oppressed, and, while training boys for mainstream employment, would educate them "to remove the injustices of racism, capitalism, sexism, and to fuel liberation and the maximization of human potential."[45] This was not quite the set of family values, perhaps, that white mainstream leaders had in mind for "dysfunctional" black dads.

By 1986 Karenga's Simba program had been adopted in fifteen cities, Nathan and Julia Hare had written their own book on rites of passage, *Bringing the Black Boy to Manhood*,[46] and Kunjufu's second volume appeared with his own detailed rites-of-passage programs for boys at various stages of development. In the meantime the idea of training men for fatherhood had spread. By 1982 Charles Ballard, a social worker who had abandoned his own child and his child's mother at eighteen years of age, had had a subsequent conversion experience while in jail, had eventually adopted and raised his son while working two jobs, and had formed what became the National Institute for Restored Fatherhood and Family Development. The goal of this successful grassroots organization was to motivate young fathers to legitimate, and provide for, their children and to learn parenting skills while finishing their education and finding employment.[47]

In 1984 and 1985 the National Urban League's conventions also initiated a "male responsibility campaign" to help meet the problem of teenage pregnancies and impoverished single-mother households.[48] Meanwhile, the number of single black fathers rose from 180,000 in 1980 to 339,000 in 1989, a sign that men were involving themselves in fathering on their own. While devoted black fathers continued to be largely invisible in mainstream media, magazines for black readers like *Ebony* were publishing accounts about black Mr. Moms and "Black Patriarchs," both "The Other Side of the Black Father Myth."[49]

Cultural nationalist writers, moreover, like Na'im Akbar and Haki Madhubuti, were defining responsible fathering as a crucial step in the passage from emotional boyhood to manhood and emphasizing love, quality time, listening, building a child's self-love and self-esteem, being slow to criticize, practicing nonviolence, and, not incidentally, taking an equal share of housework as the crucial elements of what fatherhood should mean.[50] This turn to nurturing fatherhood was also prominently featured at the Million Man March, at which Akbar, Kunjufu, and Madhubuti all spoke. By 1995, indeed, according to journalist Donna Britt, middle-class black fathers seemed "al-

most as kid-immersed" as their wives and were far more physically affectionate with their children than their own fathers had been. In some ways,
Britt wrote, "black men have never been better fathers."[51]

In late 1990s, rites-of-passage or manhood development programs were continuing to multiply across the nation. Of the forty manhood development programs that Roderick J. Watt surveyed in the early 1990s, for example, the median duration was four years.[52] On the one hand, these programs trained boys
to succeed in the white mainstream, by schooling them in math and science and
by exposing boys to career opportunities. Many manhood development programs, however, also retained a criticism of the economic individualism and
materialism of Euro-American masculine ideals and made a point of socializing black boys into a model of manhood based on the principles of Nguzo Saba
instead—with its emphasis on collectivity and commitment to community.

According to one proponent of rites-of-passage programs in the 1990s,
African-American values of communalism, spiritualism, acceptance of diversity, and the maximization of interpersonal harmony directly challenged the
value system of the dominant culture (and dominant masculine ideals). The
latter, according to this participant, were based on individualism, materialism,
a single standard for views and behaviors, and a mode of self-expression
based on measurable accomplishments such as one's job, social status, and
educational achievement.[53] In the frequent identification of alternative values
with Africa, as opposed to dominant U.S. culture, moreover, the programs
maintained a critique of the moral authority of the white mainstream—a
moral authority that a good deal of white family values rhetoric would seek
to restore.

BLACK FAMILY VALUES

African-American rites-of-passage programs also embodied models of the
family different from those that had traditionally been claimed as dominant in
the United States. Since the men who most often performed parental roles in
rites-of-passage programs were not married, not related by blood, and not the
children's source of economic support, for example, the programs embodied
an extended rather than nuclear family. As lawyer Dorothy Roberts put it, "If
we want to imagine nurturing fatherhood, decoupled from the patriarchal
economic model, we might begin by looking to Black fathers."[54] Rites-of-
passage programs emphasized the importance of "giving back" to the community as well. They also consciously linked the well-being of family with a
struggle for racial justice and emphasized the role of familial love in creating
larger social change.

It is unclear, nonetheless, to what degree the "do for self" emphasis of rites-of-passage programs translated into structural forms of transformation. According to Watts, the manhood development organizations that he interviewed were concerned with transforming African-American communities but were not thinking in terms of changing institutions dominated by European Americans, perhaps on the understandable grounds that powerful whites would not support an egalitarian world. Words like "oppression," for example, did not turn up in Watts's eighty-thousand-word data base, while the word "racism" appeared only once. As many black feminists have pointed out, moreover, the families constituted by rites-of-passage programs were not only male led but almost exclusively male. Watts found only two women associated with the forty programs he studied.[55]

Girls and daughters, therefore, were also marginalized in these efforts. Black fathering and mentoring organizations had justified their marginalization on the grounds that black girls and women far outstripped black boys in graduating from high school, attending college, and getting advanced degrees. Many black women, however, incisively pointed out that this focus on boys overlooked the difficulties that black girls also had in making their own way through schools and into careers. Thus, when Detroit funded several schools exclusively for black boys in 1991, they met with resistance from black women, who succeeded in getting the schools to admit girls as well. The schools, however, remained predominantly male.[56]

It is significant that "high quality" gender relations were often one of the programs' announced goals, although it was not always clear what "high quality" consisted of. While many 1990s programs, like Kunjufu's 1980s model, made a point of training boys to do housework and to take on domestic responsibilities as a matter of course, they also assumed men's leadership in bringing up boys, both blamed and did not blame black mothers for doing a poor job, and, in often defining their goal as that of providing a cadre of black male leaders, tended to define black community politics as a male affair. According to Barbara Ransby and Tracye Matthews, this identification of community politics as male not only failed to acknowledge black women's historic role in social activism and community leadership, but also obscured the degree to which grassroots activism and daily organization and struggle, often carried on by women, had been the backbone of the SNCC, the Mississippi Freedom Democratic Party and, in a different way, the Black Panther Party as well.[57]

If rites-of-passage programs were not precisely the form of black fathering and black family life that members of the white establishment had had in mind, they were not, in very different ways, what many black feminists had been looking for, either. Black men and women's debates over parenting were only one part of a larger set of conversations over black gender relations generally and over the workings of race, gender, sex, and class in U.S. culture. I will turn to these important conversations in chapter 7.

FROM "ANGRY WHITE MALE" TO GOOD [ENOUGH] FAMILY MAN

By the late 1980s, as I remark in chapter 5, corporate downsizing, a decline in real wages, and the necessity of two incomes to sustain a middle-class life had visibly hit even white male members of the middle class, for whom they undermined the likelihood of living out a traditional manhood based on primary breadwinning and authority as head of household. Changing gender relations at work and in the home, as well as the modest inclusion of men and women of color in middle-class jobs, deeply challenged old ideals of national manhood based on white middle-class men's self-interest, economic success, and domestic control.

By the late 1980s mainstream media had begun to represent the effects of this unexpected loss in the figure of the initially "anxious" and then "angry" white male. (Ellen Goodman was to joke that calling white men "anxious" was a sure-fire way to make them "angry."[58]) Media representations of white men's anxiety, however, often focused on the economic. According to a 1988 article in the *Los Angeles Times*, the median white male's income, adjusted for inflation, declined by 22 percent between 1976 and 1984, even though the GNP had risen by 26 percent. Women would represent two-thirds of the labor force growth in the years to come, with minority males and immigrants of unspecified gender accounting for much of the rest. White, non-Hispanic, U.S.-born men would represent only 9.3 percent of labor force growth. As the title put it: "Average White Male No Longer Leads the March to Progress."[59]

Reports on this version of what Lauren Berlant once called a "traumatized" national citizen" might acknowledge that the new workforce would consist largely of women and minority and/or immigrant men doing low-paid labor.[60] They might also acknowledge that white men made up 39 percent of the population but accounted for 77 percent of Congress, 92 percent of state governors, 70 percent of tenured professors, and more than 82 percent of the folks who made more than $265 million a year.[61] Nonetheless, media constructions of anxious white men suggested good reason for white male alarm, while subtly noting at times that white men expressed their anger at affirmative action programs but not at corporations, whose profit-making strategies had actually stripped white men and other workers of employment and status: "Get Set: Here They Come! The 21st Century Work Force Is Taking Shape Now. White, U.S. Born Men Are a Minority."[62]

Between 1985 and 1996 the "average" white male became the "angry" white male, playing at "white male politics," being "left out," "disaffected," taking "revenge," steeped in "paranoia," bearing "the white man's burden," and engaged in "struggle" for jobs, sometimes as a "gypsy" scholar. He was given to "fear" of "rampant female power" and was "forgotten" in workplace diversity schemes. His "rage" swept America as he engaged in "backlash" by becoming "bedfellows" with Republicans. And then, at the end of 1995, the angry white male was discovered, somewhat dubiously perhaps, to have been a "myth." Voting polls reported that 70 percent of white male voters asserted that they were *not* angry. In terms of political influence, moreover, "angry white males," or AWM, had given way to SHF, or soft-hearted females, who were largely responsible for reelecting Clinton. "Soccer moms," as Ellen Goodman observed, had become the "group du jour," nearly running over AWM in their Dodge Caravans.[63] By 1996, however, whether angry or not, white, middle-class men had already been offered a more palatable cultural role—that of the "good [enough] family man."[64]

The rise of the "good [enough] family man," the white father as cultural hero, was closely tied to the emergence of white "family values" as a subject of national, and deeply political, concern and debate. Profamily movements erupted into public visibility in the 1970s and early 1980s as a form of reaction by conservative religious groups against many forms of sixties politics and cultural change. These included the sexual revolution, feminism, and gay liberation, which, as Judith Stacey put it, were viewed not without cause as antifamily and antimotherhood.[65] The secular New Right, which was seeking to expand its mass base, made common cause with Christian Right activists on issues of abortion, gay rights, and the Equal Rights Amendment (ERA). This focus on the family, of course, not only expanded the voting base of the New Right but also provided a way of thinking about social problems that tended to obscure critical reflection upon the effects of free market policies—which were benefiting the elite at the expense of the middle class as well as the poor.

White conservative evangelical attention to family values, however, was not marked by a particular focus on fathering. A more central family issue in the 1970s was to respond to the feminist movement by reasserting the necessity of women's "submission" to their husbands and the justness of men's traditional headship in the home. Larry Christenson's 1970 *The Christian Family*, for example, began with a chart depicting the vertical hierarchy of God, men, women, and children—the book is nothing if not clear—and devoted most of its attention to the meaning of women's submission and to the role of men as heads of household and as providers for, and protectors of, the household.[66]

Within the context of this gender hierarchy, the book did give men primary authority over children—women's authority over children being secondary and derived—and both mother and fathers were instructed to engage in "hugging love."[67] Nonetheless, *The Christian Family* was not much concerned with what would become the "new," more tender dad. Fathers should not be "part-time nursemaid so that they will be as 'emotionally enriched' as mothers." Male physiology and psychology "aren't geared to it." A father's relation to his children "can't be built mainly around child-caring experiences. If it is, he's a substitute mother—not a father." In a book that heartily endorsed "really hard spanking" (always with a paddle rather than with the bare hand), fathers seemed chiefly distinguished by the fact that they had primary responsibility for discipline. Mothers, like SHF, were too soft-hearted.[68]

White fatherhood, moreover, had not played a particularly central role in Reagan's rhetoric about a return to "traditional values" and to "family, work and neighborhood" or to his celebration of the family as "the fundamental unit of American life" and his vague promise to give serious consideration to strengthening it.[69] A focus on fathers, of course, was most famously launched by Dan Quayle, in a 1992 law-and-order speech tailored to a conservative Bush constituency in California. During this speech, Quayle accused the fictional television character Murphy Brown, played by Candace Bergen, of "mocking the importance of fathers by bearing a child alone and calling it just another lifestyle choice."[70] Nonetheless, the 1990s focus on the father, according to Stacey, stemmed mainly from centrist to liberal Democrats and was developed in the context of anxiety over the political efficacy of Republican family-values rhetoric.

LOST DADS

The central force behind this second wave of family values, according to Stacey, was an "interlocking network of scholarly and policy institutes, think tanks, and commissions" that began mobilizing to forge a national coalition on family values that rapidly shaped the family ideology and politics of the Clinton administration."[71] Central to these efforts were the Institute of American Values, an initially small, home-based operation, codirected by David Blankenhorn and Barbara Dafoe Whitehead and cosponsored by research offshoots of the Council on Families in America, jointly chaired by David Popenoe and Jean Bethke Elshtain. According to David Popenoe, "Most of us are neo liberal. . . . New Democrats affiliated with the Progressive Policy Institute. We try to keep to the middle of the road." Stacey characterized these networks as "waging a cultural crusade, one modeled explicitly on the anti-smoking campaign, to restore the privileged status of lifelong, heterosexual marriage."[72]

The campaign for intact two-parent families as well as the beginning emphasis on the "good[enough] family man" was partially fueled by concern over the dramatic increase of working mothers, by high divorce rates, and by growing urban and female poverty. Along with inventive policy changes such as raising the tax exemption for dependents, creating a non-poverty working wage, and making the workplace family-friendly, however, the Progressive Policy Institute also recommended making divorce more difficult and insisted that sociologists had agreed upon the crucial significance of two-parent biological families.[73]

When David Popenoe published an op-ed entitled "Two Person Families Are Better" in 1992, followed by Barbara Dafoe Whitehead's "Dan Quayle Was Right" in 1993, several female feminist sociologists pointedly challenged this liberal/conservative "consensus," questioning the methodology of the studies cited, arguing that "job and wage structures, not family structures account for most of our country's poverty" and pointing out that the fastest-growing poverty group in America since 1979 has been married-couple families with children. They also emphasized the importance of child-friendly policies such as reducing unemployment rates, providing universal health care, revitalizing public education, and enforcing comparable worth standards of pay equity so that single women as well as men might earn a livable family wage.[74]

Informed by the contentious spirit of this cultural skirmish, the two books on fathering that emerged from these networks in 1995 and 1996, David Blankenhorn's *Fatherless America: Confronting Our Most Urgent Social Problem* and David Popenoe's *Life without Father: Compelling New Evidence that Fatherhood and Marriage Are Indispensable for the Good of Children and Society*, contested not only female feminist revisions of traditional gender roles but also those that men themselves had taken on in producing new, more generative dads.[75] Thus, two years after Ellen Goodman observed that our socially approved images of fatherhood are "emotional, not financial. They are about love not money," *Fatherless America* set out to rescue the breadwinning dad.[76]

Citing a host of feminist-informed academic works on how dominant definitions of masculinity, which equated manhood with primary breadwinning, competition, and economic success, have historically cut men off from their children's lives, the book registered scorn for the notion that a father should work less to be with their children more. The book then praised the competitive, rule-oriented, "goal-driven" nature of breadwinning, along with the "aggression" and "competition" that it necessitated: "Most important, the provider role permits men to serve their families through competition with other men. In this sense, the ideal of paternal bread winning encultures male aggression by directing it toward a prosocial purpose." The book failed to consider whether the economy would even permit this return to the man as breadwinner model, but it did redirect white, middle-class men to another set of grounds on which to feel deprived. The problem was not "the economy, Stupid," or even affirmative action; it was feminist-inspired efforts to encourage gender change.[77]

Popenoe based a similar argument against the new father on "innate biological propensities," which he admitted did not determine behavior but which he cited nonetheless as justification for a return to a familiar sexual division of labor. Men were biologically "much harder to train and motivate" for child care than women. Fortunately, for those dads who hated those early morning feedings, men's biology did not suit them for infant care: "The parenting of young infants is not a 'natural' activity for males." Although Popenoe maintained that men's attachment to their children might and must be "culturally fostered," the project of creating a more nurturing dad turned out to be a dangerous proposition—especially for women.[78] Many men, Popenoe threatened, might avoid marrying and having children altogether if they had to engage in "'unnatural' nurturing and care taking roles," for men's "innate biological propensities" disinclined them to marry, too. Since married women who neglected this warning might find that their marriages "have a high likelihood of breakup," it was better for women, after all, to basically go with the masculine flow.[79] As Blankenhorn put it, the best plan was to "endeavor, however imperfectly, to incorporate men as they are into family life."[80] So much for new fathers and new men.

The primary argument for restoring unrenovated fathers to the home, however, had little to do with female desire for men-as-they-were but much to do with what were imagined to be the needs of children and of the nation as a whole. Since, according to *Fatherless America,* "fatherlessness is the most harmful demographic trend of this generation . . . the engine driving our most urgent social problems from adolescent pregnancy to child sexual abuse to domestic violence against women," the "good [enough] family man" might become a national hero once again, not through attempts at structural change, but through a private and relatively effortless mode of going home.[81]

What gave this new/old father a good deal of its mainstream cultural appeal—and the notion that fatherlessness was the primary cause of social disorder became a form of gospel in the mid 1990s—was in part men's anger over economic and domestic decline and in part their need for a more positive self-image than that of the resentful divorced dad or angry white male. The cultural power of the "good [enough] family man," however, was also bolstered by revived images of the hapless black single mother and the disorder-producing absent, black dad, for the Los Angeles uprising of 1992 had provoked a new surge of liberal and conservative writing on the "deviancy" of implicitly black "fatherless" households.[82]

While never as punitive as some pieces that were published at this time, neither *Fatherless America* nor *Life without Father* mentioned black families or fathers who were not lower-class. Lower-class families, moreover, were mentioned only in relation to fatherlessness, poverty, and low marriage rates. There was no mention in either book of black rites-of-passage programs or other forms of black male mentoring and no mention of nonresidential fathers who played an important role in children's lives. (In Blankenhorn, one should note, fatherless families included those in which children lived with stepfathers and in which children spent half their time with fathers in joint custody arrangements.) Failure to acknowledge successful forms of black fathering solidified the identification of good-enough fatherhood with white, middle-class men, while effectively reviving the tradition of a national manhood based on white male control of black family disorder.

The late twentieth-century (re)turn to fathering, therefore, was full of contradictions. On the one hand, conversations about proper fathering were used to reassert traditional forms of male authority, to individualize problems that required collective social solutions, to scapegoat lower-class black families, and to obscure the very economic and social injustices that were at the heart of the perceived "crisis" over masculinity.[83] On the other hand, ideals of nurturing and involved fathering did engage men in more sensitive and caring attitudes and practices, did rescue "at risk" boys, and if, my profeminist male students are any indication, did generate male offspring who were better prepared for being close to others, including women, than older men had been at their age.

Some version of these tensions and contradictions, moreover, was present in almost every national conversation about fathers, fathering movement, or organization. In this area, in particular, seemingly conservative movements such as Promise Keepers were often, unevenly, more "liberal" than most. (I shall return to this topic in chapter 8.) Perhaps it was the very contradictions of involved fathering, the wide range of needs and purposes it might serve, and the ease with which it might seem to support women's demands for change, while renewing forms of men's control, that explain its popularity in the 1980s and 1990s.

The ambiguities and contradictions of men's efforts to reconstruct ideals of fathering and fatherhood, nonetheless, should help challenge overly hasty conclusions to the effect that invocations of fatherhood and family values are merely well-rehearsed modes for enforcing patriarchy—a challenge all the more meaningful in the context of gay fathering and "gay family values." That "traditional family values" at the Million Man March were sometimes defined so as to include the equal partnership of men and women and that nurturing fatherhood seemed, at times, to require that fathers join antiracist political organizations must also complicate our understanding of men's efforts to be "fathers of themselves." The ideals and practices of fatherhood, like those of male romance, are open to continuing reconstruction and to a range of political uses, a topic to which I shall return in chapter 8.

NOTES

1. Anthony Astrachan, *How Men Feel: Their Response to Women's Demands for Equality and Power* (Garden City, N.Y.: Anchor Press, 1986), 231.

2. Jack Sawyer, "Men and Children," in *Men and Masculinity*, ed. Joseph H. Pleck and Jack Sawyer (Englewood Cliffs, N.J.: Prentice-Hall, 1974), 53. On "generative fathering," see Alan J. Hawkins and David C. Collahite, eds., *Generative Fathering: Beyond Deficit Perspectives* (Thousand Oaks, Calif.: Sage Publications, 1997); on nurturing fathering, see Ralph La Rossa, *The Modernization of Fatherhood: A Social and Political History* (Chicago: University of Chicago Press, 1997); Larry May and Robert A. Strikwerda, "Fatherhood and Nurturance," in *Rethinking Masculinity: Philosophical Explorations in Light of Feminism*, 2nd ed., ed. Larry May, Robert Strikwerda, and Patrick D. Hopkins (Boulder, Colo.: Rowman & Littlefield, 1996), 193–210; and Robert L. Griswold, *Fatherhood in America: A History* (New York: Basic Books, 1993).

3. Jawanza Kunjufu, *Countering the Conspiracy to Destroy Black Boys* (Chicago: African-American Images, 1985), 1: 24, 33.

4. Alan J. Hawkins, Shawn L. Christiansen, Kathryn Pond Sargent, and E. Jeffrey Hill, "Rethinking Father's Involvement in Child Care," *Journal of Family Issues* 14, no. 4 (December 1993): 542; Alan J. Hawkins and David C. Dollahite, "Beyond the Role-Inadequacy Perspective of Fathering," in *Generative Fathering,* 12.

5. William D. Allen and Michael Connor, "An African American Perspective on Generative Fathering," in *Generative Fathering,* 65, 69, 68.

6. On the therapeutic nature of fathering, see Hawkins et al., "Rethinking Fathers' Involvement," 531–49.

7. Scott Coltrane made a similar point in *Family Man: Fatherhood, Housework, and Gender Equity* (New York: Oxford University Press, 1996), 232.

8. Desson Howe, "Families: Sometimes Father Knows Best," *Washington Post* 25 September 1984: C5.

9. Howe, "Families," C5.

10. Patricia Dibsie, "Father-and-Baby Classes Bridge the Gap," *The San Diego Union–Tribune*, 30 June 1987: D-1; Glenn Collins, "Fathers Get Their Own Catalogues," *New York Times*, 22 December 1986: B, 20.

11. Isaac Balbus, *Emotional Rescue: The Theory and Practice of a Feminist Father* (New York: Routledge, 1998), 25.

12. Evan Thomas with Pat Wingert, Patricia King, Nonny Abbott, and Jeanne Gordon, "The Reluctant Father," *Newsweek*, 19 December 1988, 64; Scott Coltrane, "Research on Household Labor," paper delivered at UC Davis, March 2000.

13. Robert Joseph Taylor, Linda M. Chatters, M. Belinda Tucker, and Edith Lewis, "Developments in Research on Black Families: A Decade Review," *Journal of Marriage and the Family* 52 (November 1990): 996.

14. Susan Perry, "Personal Observations at Core: Books Examines the Father–Infant Bond," *Los Angeles Times*, 4 December 1985, 5, 1.

15. Smart, "The New Father," D5.

16. Diane Ehrensaft, *Parenting Together: Men and Women Sharing the Care of Their Children* (Urbana: University of Illinois Press, 1990), 143, 144.

17. Ehrensaft, *Parenting,* 148, 146.

18. Ehrensaft, *Parenting,* 149, 145, 152.

19. Joanne Kates, "Hers" (column), *New York Times,* 9 October 1986, cited in Ehrensaft, *Parenting,* 154.

20. Balbus, *Emotional Rescue,* 79, 78.

21. Ehrensaft, *Parenting,* 155.

22. Ehrensaft, *Parenting*, 159, 160, 164.

23. Works by two early theorists are Dorothy Dinnerstein, *The Mermaid and the Minotaur: Sexual Arrangements and Human Malaise* (New York: Harper & Row, 1976), and Nancy Chodorow, *The Reproduction of Mothering: Psychoanalysis and the Sociology of Gender* (Berkeley: University of California Press, 1978). See also Balbus, *Emotional Rescue*, 18–19.

24. Judith Stacey, *Brave New Families: Stories of Domestic Upheaval in Late Twentieth Century America* (New York: Basic Books, 1990), 9, 15. See also Jeremiah Cotton, "The Declining Relative Economic Status of Black Families," *Review of Black Political Economy* 18, 1 (Summer 1989): 75; Ronald F. Levant, "The Crisis of Connection between Men and Women," *Journal of Men's Studies* 5, no. 1 (August 1999): 3–4.

25. Cotton, "Declining," 75.

26. Judith Stacey, *In the Name of the Family: Rethinking Family Values in the Postmodern Age* (Boston: Beacon Press, 1996), 110.

27. Catherine Foster, "Plea for Fathers' Rights: Divorced but Still a Dad," *The Christian Science Monitor*, 6 July 1982, Focus 2.

28. David Hopps, "For Some Fathers, This Is a Day without Joy or Justice," *Los Angeles Times*, 17 June 1984, IV, 5.

29. Eric Bailey, "State Continues as Custody Battlefield," *Los Angeles Times*, 6 September 1993, A3.

30. Jennifer A. Kingson, "Courts Expand the Rights of Unmarried Fathers," *New York Times,* 28 October, 1988, B9; Elizabeth Kolbert, "Fathers Rights on Adoption Are Expanded," *New York Times*, 11 July 1990, B1; Dianne Klein, "More Than Mere Biology, *Los Angeles Times*, 21 June 1992, A 26; Dan Morain, "Casual Fathers Win More Control in Adoption Cases," *Los Angeles Times*, 23 October 1984, I, 5; Pat Spallone, "Fathers Day," *New Statesman and Society*, 15 September 1989,15; "AIDS Looms as an Issue in Visits by Fathers," *New York Times*, 5 October 1986, 33; "'Nonbiological' Fathers," *Wall Street Journal*, 30 June 1993, B2.

31. Robert L. Griswold, *Fatherhood,* 261–63.

32. Carl Bertoia and Janice Drakich, "The Fathers' Rights Movement: Contradictions in Rhetoric and Practice," *Journal of Family Issues* 14, no. 4 (December 1993): 603.

33. Bertoia and Drakich, "The Fathers' Rights Movement," 613.

34. David Blankenhorn, *Fatherless America: Confronting Our Most Urgent Social Problem* (New York: Basic Books, 1995), 117.

35. *The Negro Family: The Case for National Action* (Washington, D.C.: U.S. Government Printing Office, 1965), 5.

36. Franklin, *Ensuring Inequality*, 163.

37. Andrew Billingsley, *Climbing Jacob's Ladder: The Enduring Legacy of African-American Families* (New York: Simon & Schuster, 1992), 36.

38. Huey Newton, *Revolutionary Suicide* (New York: Harcourt Brace, 1973), 41; David Hilliard and Lewis Cole, *The Autobiography of David Hilliard and the Story of the Black Panther Party* (Boston: Little, Brown and Company, 1993), 22; Henry Louis Gates Jr., "Playing Hardball" in *Speak My Name: Black Men on Masculinity and the American Dream*, ed. Don Belton (Boston: Beacon Press, 1995), 73; Houston A. Baker, "On the Distinction of 'Jr.'" in *Speak My Name,* 80.

39. Marlon Ross, "In Search of Black Masculinities," *Feminist Studies* 24, no. 3 (Fall 1998): 602–603.

40. bell hooks, "Malcolm X: The Longed-for Feminist Manhood," in *Outlaw Culture: Resisting Representations* (New York: Routledge, 1994).

41. Huey P. Newton, "On the Defection of Eldridge Cleaver from the Black Panther Party and the Defection of the Black Panther Party from the Black Community: April 17, 1971," in *To Die for the People: The Writings of Huey P. Newton* (New York: Random House, 1972), 51.

42. Na'im Akbar, *Visions for Black Men* (Tallahassee, Fla.: Mind Productions, 1991), 15.

43. See chapter 2 for a fuller account of Kawaida.

44. Jawanza Kunjufu, *Countering the Conspiracy to Destroy Black Boys,* vol. 1 (Chicago: African American Images, 1985), 27, 24.

45. Kunjufu, *Countering,* 1: 27, 33

46. Nathan Hare and Julia Hare, *Bringing the Black Boy to Manhood* (San Francisco: Black Think Tank, 1985).

47. Charles Augustus Ballard, "Prodigal Dad: How We Bring Fathers Home to their Children," *Policy Review* 71 (Winter 1995): 66.

48. Luix Overbea, "Family and Jobs Are Top Priorities for Urban League in '85," *The Christian Science Monitor*, 19 July 1985, 4.

49. "They Call Them Mr. Mom," *Ebony*, June 1991. 52; "Present and Accounted For: The Other Side of the Black Father Myth," *Ebony,* June 1992, 54.

50. Na'im Akbar, *Visions for Black Men* (Tallahassee, Fla.: Mind Productions, 1991), 13–15; Haki R. Madhubuti, *Black Men: Obsolete, Single, Dangerous? Afrikan American Families in Transition: Essays in Discovery, Solution and Hope* (Chicago: Third World Press, 1990), 189–90.

51. Donna Britt, "Devoted Dads Defy the Bum Rap," *Washington Post*, 13 June, 1995, A 22.

52. Roderick J. Watts, "Community Action through Manhood Development: A Look at Concepts and Concerns from the Frontline," *American Journal of Community Psychology* 21, no. 3 (June 1993): 333.

53. Craig C. Brookins, "Promoting Ethnic Identity Development in African-American Youth: The Role of Rites of Passage," *Journal of Black Psychology* 22, no. 3 (August 1996): 397.

54. Dorothy Roberts, "The Absent Black Father," in *Lost Fathers: The Politics of Fatherlessness in America*, ed. Cynthia R. Daniels (New York: St. Martin's Press, 1998), 153.

55. Watts, "Community Action," 25.

56. Elaine Ray, "All–Male Black Schools Put On Hold in Detroit: Girls Will Be Admitted after Court Challenge," *Boston Globe,* 1 September, 1991, A16.

57. Barbara Ransby and Tracye Matthews, "Black Popular Culture and the Transcendence of Patriarchal Illusions," in *Words of Fire: An Anthology of African-American Feminist Thought*, ed. Beverly Guy-Sheftall (New York: New Press, 1995), 529.

58. Ellen Goodman, "Anxiety Binds Soccer Moms, Angry Males," *The Tampa Tribune,* 13 November 1996, 17.

59. Lester C. Thurow, "Average White Male No Longer Leads the March to Prosperity," *Los Angeles Times*, 20 October 1985: 3.

60. Lauren Berlant, *The Queen of America Goes to Washington City: Essays on Sex and Citizenship* (Durham, N.C.: Duke University Press, 1997), 1.

61. David Gates, "White Male Paranoia," *Newsweek*, 29 March 1993, 48.

62. Janice Castro, "Get Set: Here They Come! The 21st Century Work Force Is Taking Shape Now. White, U.S. Born Men Are a Minority." *Time* 136, no. 19 (Fall 1990): 50–51.

63. Howard Fineman, "Playing White Male Politics," *Newsweek*, 28 October 1991, 27; Charlene Marmer Solomon, "Are White Males Being Left Out?" *Personnel Journal* 70, no. 11 (November 1991): 88; Thomas B. Edsall, "Disaffected," *The Washington Post*, 3 June 1992, A15; Joyce Millman, "Revenge of the Angry White Male," *San Francisco Examiner,* 29 August 1993, D1; Gates, "White Male Paranoia," 48; "The White Man's Burden," *Harper's Magazine,* July 1993, 18; Jim Newton, "White Male Applicants Struggle for LAPD Jobs," *Los Angeles Times*, 25 August 1993, A1; Robert Weissberg, "The Gypsy Scholars," *Forbes,* May 1993, 138; "White Male Fear," *The Economist* 330, no. 7848 (January 1994), A34; Glenn Rifkin, "Workplace Diversity: The Forgotten White Male," *Harvard Business Review* 72, no. 4 (July–August 1994): 8; Herbert Stein, "Male Rage Sweeps America," *Wall Street Journal*, 9 February 1995, A14; Carl Mollins, "A White Male Backlash," *Maclean's* 108, no. 12 (March 1995): 22; "The GOP's New Bedfellows," *U.S. News & World Report* 118, no. 16 (April 1995): 72; Charles Krauthammer, "Myth of the Angry White Male, *Washington Post*, 26 May, 1995, A27; "Election Offers a New 'Showdown at Gender Gap,'" *Los Angeles Times*, 26 May 1996, 1; Ellen Goodman, "Anxiety Binds Soccer Moms, Angry Males," *Tampa Tribune*, 13 November 1996, 17.

64. "The Good Family Man" is the title of a chapter in David Blankenhorn's *Fatherless America: Confronting Our Most Urgent Social Problem* (New York: Basic Books, 1995), 201.

65. See Stacey, *In the Name of the Family*, 52–82, and Judith Stacey, "Scents, Scholars and Stigma: The Revisionist Campaign for Family Values," *Social Text,* 1994.

66. Larry Christenson, *The Christian Family* (Minneapolis, Minn.: Bethany House Publishers, 1970), 17.

67. Christenson, *Christian Family*, 122.

68. Christenson, *Christian Family*, 122, 44, 107.

69. E. J. Dionne Jr., "Family and Ethics Are Bywords in '86 Races," *New York Times*, 28 September 1986, 1; Don Irwin, "Reagan Stresses Family Values while Hart Laments Iran Scandal," *Los Angeles Times*, 21 December 1986, 30.

70. Michael Kranish, "Swipe at Murphy Snarls White House," *Boston Globe*, 21 May 1992, 1.

71. See Stacey, *In the Name*, 54.

72. Stacey, *In the Name*, 54, 55.

73. Elaine Ciulla Kamarck and William A. Galston, "Putting Children First: A Progressive Family Policy for the 1990s" (Progressive Policy Institute, 1993), 7.

74. David Popenoe, "The Controversial Truth: Two Parent Families Are Better," *New York Times*, 26 December 1992, N13, L21; Barbara Dafoe Whitehead, "Dan Quayle Was Right," *Atlantic* 271, no. 4 (April 1993): 47–84; Stephanie Coontz, "Dan Quayle Is Still Wrong: Reflections on the 'Two-Parent Paradigm,'" *Washington Post*, 9 May 1993, C5; Judith Stacey, "Nostalgia For Family Can't Undo Cutback Era," *New York Times* 16 January 1993, sec. 1, 20; Arlene Skolnick and Jerome Skolnick, "Love Conquers All," *New York Times*, 16 January 1993, sec. 1, 20.

75. Blankenhorn, *Fatherless America*; David Popenoe, *Life without Father: Compelling New Evidence that Fatherhood and Marriage Are Indispensable for the Good of Children and Society* (New York: Free Press, 1996).

76. Ellen Goodman, "Upping the Ante on Fathers," *Washington Post*, 31 October 1993, A23.

77. Blankenhorn, *Fatherless America*, 113, 116.

78. David Popenoe, "Parental Androgyny," *Society* 30, no. 6 (September–October 1993): 9, 7, 9.

79. Popenoe, "Parental Androgyny," 10, 9, 10.

80. Blankenhorn, *Fatherless America*, 117.

81. Blankenhorn, *Fatherless America*, 1.

82. See, for example, Daniel Patrick Moynihan, "Defining Deviancy Down," *The American Scholar* (Winter 1993): 17–30.

83. For a trenchant analysis of these tendencies, see Judith Stacey, *In the Name of the Family*.

7

Reinventing the Husband

> The most important change in men's position, as they experience it is a
> loss of centrality, a decline in the extent to which they are the center of at-
> tention.
>
> —William A. Goode, "Why Men Resist"[1]

ANOTHER MISSING REVOLUTION?

The emergence of black rites-of-passage programs in the 1960s, the birth of
the "new" father in the 1970s, the development of fathering movements in the
1980s, the acceleration of new scholarship on fatherhood in the 1990s, and
the torrent of media work devoted in the same decade to the necessity of turning "absent," "reluctant," and "deadbeat dads" into "good family men" were
not accompanied by any sustained meditations on the part of men about improving or reforming the male mate. Organizations such as the National Fatherhood Initiative, the Fatherhood Project, the National Association for Fathers, the National Institute for Responsible Fathers and Family
Development, the Father's Center, the Institute for Responsible Fatherhood
and Revitalization, Fathers United, Fathers Behind Bars, the American Fathers Coalition, and Dad and Me inspired no similar proliferation of centers,
coalitions, unions, associations, or national initiatives bent on improving men
in their roles as domestic partners or as husbands. There was no National Institute for Committed Husbands, or Male Partnering Project, or Responsible
Mates United. Nor did the wave of publication on fathers—*Fatherhood in
America, Fatherless America, Life without Father, Black Fatherhood, Generative Fathering*—give way to any succeeding swell of scholarship on the

male spouse. There was no *Husbandhood in America*, no *Generative Part-nering*, no *Black Men as Mates*.

There was, in the late 1990s, of course, an abundance of magazine litera-ture on male partners and husbands, but, by and large, it was addressed to women and reflected the degree to which male partnering had *not* generally been perceived of as an area in which men had changed much or reformed. A survey I conducted in 1999, involving 559 magazine articles published be-tween 1988 and 1998 in the white- and African-American–focused publica-tions carried by my local library, revealed that two-thirds of the essays dealt with bad husbands, the negative qualities of male mates, or how to improve the implicitly faulty spouses that women might already have. At the grimmest end of the spectrum, there were forty-eight articles devoted to addicted hus-bands and to partners who killed, raped, committed incest, or otherwise en-gaged in child and spousal abuse. There were fourteen on husbands who con-trolled or dominated their wives, including eleven on domestic partners who refused to share expenses or to pay taxes, and thirteen on male mates who sabotaged their partners' diets or who refused to have sex with fat or frumpy wives. Men's domination and control of women, therefore, were continuing concerns.

There were a whopping seventy articles on unfaithful husbands, twenty-one of which focused on famous unfaithful husbands such as the then presi-dent of the United States. (The Clinton/Lewinsky affair was beginning to un-fold at the time the survey was made, and in the context of this literature Clinton appeared downright symptomatic—a poster boy for husbands behav-ing badly.) Thirty-three other articles were devoted to male mates who were inattentive or preoccupied with work or hobbies, and there were an additional twenty-two articles giving details about the sexual secrets women *wished* their husbands knew. Clearly, male intimacy, in one way or another, was a major issue. An additional twenty-three essays were devoted to a miscella-neous array of annoying traits that husbands were wont to exhibit, and 145 ar-ticles offered advice on how to change or improve the husband you have— "Get good raw material," a friend once advised me, "and then work with it." Many of these articles were devoted to tips on persuading men to do more child care or housework or to getting past male defensiveness about, or re-sistance to, requests for change.

Perhaps not unexpectedly, there were seventeen articles in the survey on women killing their spouses and thirteen on women who took revenge, six of the latter devoted to Lorena Bobbitt's infamous cut-and-run act with her hus-band's penis. There were an additional seventy-five essays in the survey that focused on the effects of divorce, child custody laws, and working wives on men, and seven essays, obviously aimed at men, on how to avoid marriage altogether. Some of these essays clearly focused on men's victimization and drew some of their insights from men's rights literature, which I shall return to later in this chapter.

Out of 559 articles, there were only thirty-two on new or improved forms of husbanding, and twenty-three of those dealt mainly with husbands who were good dads. That left a lonely nine articles that focused on new, improved mates, all nine of which were devoted to husbands who were supportive of working wives. Negative articles on husbands, overall—not counting the seventy-five essays devoted to the ill effects of marriage upon men—were seven times more numerous than articles on how husbands have changed for the better, and when negative articles were added to those focused on how to upgrade the partner you have, the ratio was twelve to one. As far as this magazine literature was concerned, male partnering had not been much of a growth area for men.

Marriage to men, however, was not without support. The thirteen articles on how to find and keep a husband, the twenty-four on keeping him in good health, and the thirty on keys to good marriage suggested a continuing investment in intimate male–female partnership of the domestic kind. Divorce rates in the United States might have stood at 41 percent, but remarriage and countless other forms of male–female partnerships were flourishing, including some between lesbians and gay men.[2] There were nonmarried domestic partnerships, partners who commuted or lived together part-time, and even some collectives, my own favorite form of domestic arrangement. Despite the bad press, intimate male–female relations still spoke to multiple and complex desires.

Men as individuals, of course, certainly had thought about and worked on their domestic relationships with women—in day-to-day negotiations, in individual or couples therapy, and in marriage or relationship weekends and encounters, although, according to one popular therapist, men often entered these treatments at the insistence of female partners. (One of the men I dragged into couples therapy spent most of the sessions staring at the ceiling. "Are you with us, Bill [not his name]?" the female therapist would gently prod.) Self-help literature on long-term relationships also abounded, but it, too, was addressed more to women than to men and tended to define men's interest in relationships in terms of sex.

Thus in the year 2000 the relationship literature listed on Amazon.com specifically addressed to heterosexual men often focused on *How to Give Her Absolute Pleasure, A Lifetime of Sex,* and *Satisfaction Guaranteed,* while the literature explicitly addressed to heterosexual women offered sex manuals as well but tended more toward titles such as *Love Advice for Women, Undefended Love,* and *What Mama Couldn't Tell Us about Love.* (Advice on how

to get out of relationships with men who were abusive or unable to love—
Breaking Free, Ditch that Jerk—was also a major category.) Finally, my own
experience of the many books addressed to both partners, such as *How to
Change Your Spouse and Save Your Marriage, Make Up, Don't Break Up,* and
Practical Miracles for Mars and Venus, was that women bought and read
them and then optimistically passed them on to their male mates. I was not
the only relation-minded female to watch her purchases gathering dust on her
partner's bedside table.

Given many men's individual resistances to "working on the relationship,"
it might make sense that networks organized by men did little work in this
area as well, although it initially struck me as curious that the organization
most responsive to feminism appeared to have made so little headway on this
topic in organizational terms. Thus, the National Organization of Men
Against Sexism (NOMAS), which actively embraced profeminist politics,
appeared to have had little to say about men and women's intimate relationships over the last eighteen years. Men's rights spokesmen, in contrast—who
claimed to be profeminist but who often focused upon the ways in which
women and feminism colluded in making personal relations, marriage, and,
indeed, the world itself oppressive to males—had had a great deal to say
about the dynamics of domestic, heterosexual relations. The solutions these
authors proposed for improving men as domestic partners, however, left a lot
to be desired. Promise Keepers, moreover, which as an organization had almost never addressed the issue of gender equality in the public sphere and
whose conservative evangelical participants seem to have had the least personal contact with self-identified feminists, had been the most active group of
all in directly working on men's partnering skills. I return to Promise Keepers in chapter 8.

Only the recent work of some black male activists and intellectuals seemed
to make any sense at all. Having vigorously engaged in public dialogue with
black feminists for many years about issues of sexism and about the dynamics of personal relations in the public and domestic spheres, cultural nationalist writers and profeminist black intellectuals had been taking up these issues with some frequency. Indeed, it was a striking feature of the magazine
literature on husbands and male partners that nearly three-quarters of the literature appeared in magazines directed at a middle-class African-American
reading public (426 out of 559). In a similar informal survey of popular work
on fatherhood, black-authored articles constituted less than half the total.

These numbers, I would suggest, should not be read as an indication that
relationships between middle-class blacks are completely different from
those between middle-class whites. Surprisingly, in fact, given the differences
in economic and social privilege, black middle-class men and women ap-

peared to be confronting dynamics that played out in white, middle-class relationships as well. Institutionalized forms of racism, however, intensified the difficulties of middle-class black domestic relations and intimate male–female relations of all kinds, while a "higher cause," a shared investment in antiracist politics, made alliance between black men and women and "working on the relationship" a matter of survival for them both. It was not surprising, then, that black activist-intellectuals, male and female, did seem to be talking more openly about their relationships in public dialogue than were whites. In the process, I would argue, they constituted something of a relationship frontier. I will return to this significant trend somewhat later in this chapter.

A DANGLING CONVERSATION

The sustained public discussion of gender relations by politicized African-American women and men was particularly striking in the context of the fact that publications dating from early 1970s "men's liberation," which had been dominantly white and middle-class, produced relatively little on the topic of intimate male–female relations. It was all the more remarkable given the fact that many white, heterosexual, middle-class men reported joining consciousness-raising groups in the first place out of feelings of guilt and confusion over their relations with suddenly feminist female partners. I was one of those women who became feminist with startling rapidity in the early 1970s, and although I appear to be among a minority of early white feminists who have *no* memories of feminist struggle with their mates during those years, even my already feminist, largely gay-identified first husband briefly joined such a group—largely, I believe, out of solidarity with the women's movement and with me.

Early reports on 1970s consciousness raising groups, however, as I observe in chapter 4, often noted that an initial emphasis on talking about relations with women rapidly gave way to a focus on the limitations of what was then called "the male role," to the exploration of men's relations with each other, to mourning men's relation to distant, wounding, or abusive fathers, and to renewed interest in their own fathering as a mode of personal transformation. This was an understandable shift in many ways, it being hard for anyone, let alone traditionally trained white men, to sustain a group based on guilt and self-criticism for very long. Indeed, some early male profeminist leaders, like Byron, who appears in chapter 4, encouraged this turn in other men, sensing that they would not stay profeminist for very long if there were nothing more "in" it for them than sustained criticism of their personal behavior toward women and calls upon them to give up privilege and power.

Freedom from a "male role" that called for compulsive devotion to bread-winning, competition, and other forms of proving manhood, including the suppression of tender feeling and vulnerability, was one of the gains that feminism might be construed as offering white, middle-class men. Emphasizing this gain, Byron had reasoned, would help secure men's interest in, and loyalty to, other, less comfortable forms of feminist politics. That some classic anthologies of men's liberation writing that did include reflections upon women's oppression gave rather slim coverage to men's and women's intimate, domestic relations may have had something to do with this profeminist logic. In Joseph H. Pleck and Jack Sawyer's 1974 *Men and Masculinity,* for example, only one article out of thirty-one focused on intimate relations between women and men. In Deborah S. David and Robert Brannon's 1976 *The Forty-Nine Percent Majority*, there was one short essay out of thirty-six, and in John Snodgrass's 1977 *For Men against Sexism*, there were none out of thirty-two.[3]

MEN'S RIGHTS: THE SHADOW SIDE OF "THE MEN'S MOVEMENT"

Men's rights was a spinoff from Men's Liberation, with which it shared a focus upon the way in which men were limited or damaged by the "male role." Although some men's rights advocates were initially associated with profeminist networks, they would give more emphasis to conditions that they saw as proof of men's "oppression," such as men's shorter life span and men's violence toward each other, than did men who became associated with the profeminist NOMAS in a lasting way.[4] (Many profeminist writers, in contrast, referred to such conditions as the "costs of being on top.") Men's rights took formal shape in organizations such as the 1971 Coalition of American Divorce Reform Elements. The latter gave birth to the 1973 Men's Rights Association, which aimed to reduce what it saw as discrimination against men in divorce, custody, and marriage laws. The Men's Rights Association was followed by an international men's organization, Men's Equality Now International, which shared the same agenda. By 1977 men were organizing in other small groups devoted to men's rights issues such as Men's Rights, Incorporated, and the 1980 Coalition of Free Men. In 1980 these organizations joined with several father's rights organizations to form the National Congress of Men, whose premise was "preserving the Promise of Fatherhood." Father's rights were the most successful rallying point for men's rights networks and promoted the 1980s boom in father's rights organizations.[5]

Men's rights networks made a practice of taunting the profeminist NOMAS for its "joyless" engagement with "guilt," but it was Astrachan's obser-

vation in 1986 that the profeminist wing of the movement had done "too little with their guilt and even less with their anger to move very far toward
men's liberation." Anger, in particular, struck Astrachan as a crucial emotion
to recognize and grapple with: "Denial of anger at women makes it harder to
love the target of that anger, to love the 'class enemy,' to love the people we
must love to keep ourselves and our society going."[6] Anger at women, however, may be said to have been the specialty of men's rights organizations and
literature.

From the mid-1970s on, the leading spokesmen of men's rights networks
produced a series of books that devoted a good deal of attention to the topic
of men's oppression and men's rights and to implicitly white, middle-class,
domestic relations between women and men. Representative books included
Herb Goldberg's 1977 *The Hazards of Being Male: Surviving the Myth of
Masculine Privilege;* Warren Farrell's 1986 *Why Men Are the Way They Are:
The Male–Female Dynamic*; and Aaron R. Kipnis's 1991 *Knights without Armor: A Practical Guide for Men in Quest of the Masculine Soul.*[7] Perhaps, the
anger at feminism and women that men's rights advocates were determined
to express enabled them to speak more freely about the dynamics of men and
women's intimate relations than did profeminist men. Certainly, in emphasizing the ways in which men, not women, were victims, men's rights groups
had little favor to lose with many female feminists by delving into the troubled waters of domestic relationships.

Men's rights authors like Goldberg, Farrell, and Kipnis tended to agree that
emotional dependence on women, a need to be at the center of women's attention, and a fear of not being able to survive without them were central features of men's domestic relationships with women. Psychiatrist Herb Goldberg, for example, following the belief that "adult emotions cannot be
understood without understanding their history in infancy and childhood," located men's dependency on female domestic partners in men's desire to replicate their "relationship of primitive dependency" on their mothers: "like the
baby from whom the breast is unexpectedly removed, they rage and despair
when this source of comfort is withdrawn."[8] All infants must separate from
the primary parent to some extent in order to view themselves and the parent
as separate persons, the hope being, according to philosopher Martha Nussbaum, that child and parent will enter into a "subtle interplay" of dependence
and autonomy.[9] Dominant U.S. forms of boy and man culture in 1977, however, as Goldberg observed, required more stringent forms of separation from
the mother and the feminine. At five or six years of age, according to Goldberg, boys were called upon to "disown" the feminine components of themselves and to be "all boy." As part of that defeminizing process, boys were socialized to adopt a "supermale" posture of, among other things,

overcontrolling emotion, construing females as weak, and expressing cruelty toward men who were effeminate in behavior or who were constructed as effeminate because they were homosexual.[10]

Women in domestic relations with men, Goldberg argued, could not help evoking men's unconscious memories of the early mother and the seductiveness of their infantile dependency upon her. These memories were further strengthened by the fact that women in domestic relationships often took on mothering functions as well, such as feeding, taking care of clothing, and caring for children and the house. Men in first marriages, in particular, Goldberg argued, had a tendency to become progressively "more childlike, dependent, and helpless in their interaction with their wives" or female partners.[11] This unconscious identification of domestic female partners with the mother, however, not only evoked the comforts of the mother's care and of the infant boy's dependence on it, but it could also bring to the surface the infant's buried rage at the mother figure who controlled and sometimes denied the infant and child's desires. Dominant norms of masculinity that required self-sufficiency and independence, as well as separation from the feminine, significantly contributed to the anxiety and anger that this projection of the mother onto the wife involved.

It was these multiply enforced fears of being dependent on, and being controlled by, women in domestic situations, Goldberg wrote, that helped explain men's fear of "commitment" to intimate relationships with women—a phenomenon familiar to cross-race readers of women's magazines and self-help manuals. According to Goldberg, however, simply challenging men to overcome their fear only fed men's need to "prove" their manhood by conquering or rising above their gut reactions of "panic and resistance."[12] Instead of understanding the source and nature of these emotions, and possibly coming to terms with them as well, men felt compelled to meet the challenge of living up to expectations of intimacy that were "not congruent with [their] early training." In their extreme efforts to hold themselves together under these circumstances, men might strike out at women or fall into self-alienating patterns. Some men heavily repressed their anger, but a repressed rage often then manifested itself indirectly in the form of "emotional detachment, interpersonal withdrawal, [and] passivity in relationship to women," an outcome that further compounded men's hidden anger by making them feel like the spoilers, the selfish ones, the heavies.[13]

Clearly, as Goldberg observed, a women's movement organized around female demands that men acknowledge the oppressive nature of their performance in a vast range of traditional behaviors, from being closed down emotionally to resisting criticism to being complicit with or actively perpetuating structural inequalities of many kinds, tapped into something more than men's anxiety and anger at the thought of losing control over "the system." The women's movement, in refocusing many heterosexual women's emotional energies onto themselves and their sisters, may have evoked some men's buried sense of loss over the early mother and may have augmented whatever buried shame, fury, and resentment already lodged in the mother-related feelings that some men projected onto women in domestic relations.

As Goldberg also observed, men often responded to feminist demands as they responded to the demands of their partners at home, by angrily striking back or by trying to please women, thereby burying rage and resentment, perhaps turning inward, and becoming detached. For some, this detachment might take the form of refusing to discuss personal relationships at all or of avoiding discussion of the dynamics between men and women in public political situations. *I Don't Want to Talk about It* was the well-chosen title of a book about largely white, middle-class men.[14] How often have white feminists of my generation heard that same sentiment subtly, or not so subtly, expressed?

LOSING OUT

Several autobiographical accounts of the way in which white, profeminist men responded to feminism early on were to anticipate or recall Goldberg's analysis of men's dependence on women in domestic situations. Anthony Astrachan, for example, was to observe in 1986 that while the emphasis of white liberal feminism upon women's right to enter the labor force did raise fears of women's ending elite "male control of the system," it raised other fears as well—the fear, for example, that "a woman who works, especially a woman who takes her work seriously, will change into a being who will not want or not be able to love us, to take care of us."[15] S. M. Miller, an early member of NOMAS, was one of the few white, profeminist men who wrote about this experience in the 1970s. In his refreshingly revealing essay, "The Making of a Confused, Middle-Age Husband," first published in 1971, Miller confessed that the fear of no longer having family life arranged around their needs played a significant role in men's reluctance to make changes in the organization of family life.

One of high-achieving men's greater fears, according to Miller, was that family life would cease to be organized around the requirements of their work and success.[16] Despite the ways in which even white, middle-class men might find breadwinning oppressive or stultifying in the 1970s, success in one's career still constituted the dominant form of performing, and thereby sustaining, a sense of proper masculine identity in this culture. Organizing family life around men's work, therefore, functioned as something more than a rational investment in the economic well-being of the family and as something more than a form of pressure upon breadwinning males. It also functioned as a way of centering the family upon masculine identity and ego needs. As philosopher Victor Seidler put it, "we come to identify ourselves as men very much with what we *do*."[17] Even for men who continued what Barbara Ehrenreich has named a "male revolt," a criticism, or refusal, of the burdens of being primary provider, the threat of losing the ego support that came with that role often produced a threatening form of gender anxiety.[18]

Miller also acknowledged the degree to which many men resisted greater involvement in housework and child care on these grounds. Of the early morning feeding times in which he was prevailed upon to participate, he recalled the following: "I resented that degree of involvement; it seemed to interfere terribly with the work I desperately wanted to achieve."[19] Like several of the officially profeminist men I myself have lived with, Miller maintained "useful incompetences" with respect to housework and child care, finding that "failure is its own reward."[20] For Miller's family in the late sixties, as with mine in the early eighties, the ideal was that of equality and sharing but the practice was "'lapsed egalitarianism,'" a daily drifting from the faith. To Miller, indeed, it seemed that "families that openly embrace both bourgeois and sexist values don't live very differently from us."[21]

Miller also reflected upon what I shall call male-defensive collapse, a habit of taking requests for change as a species of assault upon the very selfhood of the man in question, and the production, through various forms of anger, passivity, and denial, of an atmosphere in which it is simply easier, after a while, to accommodate than to pursue the desire for alteration.[22] As for intimacy, Miller touched on the issue with a telling brevity: "I am rather inaccessible, to say the least. I work against this tendency but don't do notably well."[23] Miller's memories of his early struggles with feminism in his domestic life often read like illustrations of Goldberg's claims that feminism evoked deep-rooted patterns of dependence on, and anger at, women, and that men sometimes responded by suppressing rage and becoming distant and withdrawn.

Seidler also comments on a tendency toward emotional detachment in himself and other men, identifying it both as a method of exercising control in relationships and as something men often cannot control in themselves. On the one hand, for example, "we find ourselves automatically withholding our love, more or less as a way of asserting our control in relationships, making sure that others love us more openly than we can love them. Our diffidence becomes a source of power." On the other hand, "the denial of our emotions and feelings, which is such an integral part of a masculinity so tied to a morality of reason, weakens our capacity to love."[24] Both of these explanations ring true. Seidler's mode of addressing this problem was, among other things, to do emotion work in therapy.

THE SHADOW SIDE OF THE WOMEN'S MOVEMENT

Goldberg's attempts to get at the psychic roots of men's domestic difficulties with women should not be read as mere attempts to naturalize them by reducing them to psychic structures, to argue that women or mothers were at fault, or to suggest that change was not possible. Goldberg made none of those arguments and, indeed, emphasized the role of men's socialization and their capacity to change through therapy. Nor is there a point to insisting, if one is a feminist, that Goldberg's findings must be tainted because they came from a spokesman for men's rights. Would that life were that simple! Indeed, for all my disagreement with men's rights visions of the power relations of the world, I have to attest that men's rights advocates were often astute, not only in analyzing some of the recurrent dynamics in men's and women's domestic relationships but also in illuminating the "shadow side" of the largely white women's movement. Several suggested, rightly, that many feminisms had oversimplified the category "men," and especially the category of white, middle-class men, by casting the latter as uniform "bad guys." Men's rights authors pointed out that some feminisms constructed "men" as "the enemy" and as biologically propelled to violence against women. Feminists of many stripes sometimes made little space for critiques of feminism on the part of white men who would have liked to be counted as feminist allies. The "I can hit you but you can't hit me back because I'm a girl" ethic *was* in force at times.[25] Feminists could also confront men at times with the "damned if you do and damned if you don't" conundrum with respect to a range of things from paying for dinner to doing gender scholarship. As one of the men my colleague interviewed in the 1990s put it, "It was easier to be damned if you didn't."

If, to white female feminists, white men have often appeared to be stuck in infantile fears of dependency on mother and mother's control, something of the "kid" entered into some early, and some long-standing female feminist attitudes and behaviors as well. It entered into the expectation, for example, that men would change precisely on female feminist terms, in the failure at times to recognize progressive change if it was not the change that the feminists in question were looking for, and in the unwarranted assumption that feminist women were always less powerful than men. Gender inequality is rampant and deep, but it does not operate evenly across the globe or across the United States. There have been situations, for example, NOMAS being a prime example, in which white feminists have exercised considerable control.

THE SHADOW SIDE OF MEN'S RIGHTS

Men's rights, however, had its own shadow side, both with respect to how it saw power relations in the world at large and with respect to the solution it proposed for reinventing intimate relations between women and men. Although officially in favor of women's liberation, much men's rights literature embraced a politics that, while promoting men's welfare, obscured the systematic ways in which women were oppressed. Indeed, it tended to argue that men, not women, were the real victims. Men's oppression by women, for example, according to Warren Farrell's 1986 *Why Men Are the Way They Are,* was inherent in marriage itself, because men and women as a whole had opposite primary fantasies and because marriage satisfied women's fantasies but not those of men. In this books' cartoon-like and economically dated version of gender difference and desire, men's primary fantasy was to have sexual access to "a number of beautiful women," while women's primary fantasy was "a relationship with one man who either provides economic security or is on his way to doing so." Marriage, which meant that women got their fantasy while men gave up theirs, was thus inherently unequal and primarily disadvantaged men.[26]

It was the same story in the public sphere as well. Often ignoring differences between women's power over men's emotions and psychology and the structural power that men maintained in their control of the economy, political office, and the institutions of violence, not to mention the home, men's rights politics often asserted that men were as oppressed as women—or more. Citing the admittedly real costs to men of having to go to battle, of being assigned, historically speaking, the primary breadwinner role, and of being encouraged to neglect their health, men's rights literature was often silent about the fact that elite men controlled the institutions that imposed these costs upon other men.

Men's rights literature often conflated female support for men's being assigned the tasks of breadwinning and battle with decision-making power. The assertion that "men do not cause wars by fighting in wars, any more than women cause wars by raising the boys who fight in wars" begged the question of what group—that is, elite men—overwhelmingly controlled international affairs and the military.[27] While men's rights' literature was incisive about the links between men's dependence upon and fear of women and the way in which feminist politics had deepened both, its vision of the world, in which women's emotional power outweighed men's control of social and economic structures, seemed immersed in the very fantasy about the mother's all-controlling power that men's rights authors often astutely described in other men. Given this fantasy version of women's all-controlling power, it

was not unexpected, perhaps, that men's rights solutions to male–female relations had less to do with men's facing and taking responsibility for their
feelings and behaviors or with negotiating and compromising than with asserting their right to do what they wanted despite what women might desire.

Herb Goldberg's preferred solution to men's emotional bind was, not unexpectedly, therapy, and there was and is a lot to be said for therapy as a mode
of facilitating personal change. There was some logic to Goldberg's observation that he had never seen a person grow in constructive ways when motivated by "guilt, shame, or self-hate." There was also logic to his belief that
constructive growth for men, by which Goldberg seemed to mean the rejection of "externally imposed, predefined 'masculine' roles," would "stem from
openly avowed, unashamed, self-oriented motivations."[28] As a white person
committed to antiracist struggle, for example, I happen to believe that guilt,
though perhaps not shame, can be a useful emotion and a positive force for
personal and social change. I must also admit, however, that guilt has not
been the primary motivation for my social activism. A far more powerful
force for me has been a sense of identity with a higher goal and with a community of others pursuing a more just society. Passionate commitment to social justice may become a form of self-orientation, a form of acting for the
self as well as for others.

Goldberg, however, writing from the perspective of the me-focused late
1970s, and of men's rights' versions of the world, rejected the influence of
such larger motivations when he maintained that men should not reject
"'masculine' roles" for ideological or political reasons but simply because
they were painful and self-destructive.[29] Indeed, it would appear that men
should not reject traditional masculine behaviors for the purpose of having
better relationships, either. Men needed to act out of their "right and need to
develop and to grow, to be total and fluid, and to have no less than a state of
total well-being." In terms of sexual relations, for example, this translated as
the recommendation to "forget all the old imperatives regarding male obligations to satisfy the female. . . . Instead focus on your own responses and plea-
sures."[30] That's enough to provoke most of the heterosexual women I know
best to run right out for a copy of *Breaking Free* or *Ditch That Jerk.*

Aside from the fact that it reinforced the individualistic ethic of the self-
making masculine ideal, which men's rights spokesmen also set out to criticize, another problem with this solution, at least for anyone who maintained
official loyalty to gender justice, was that men charting their own way, most
particularly if motivated by no larger goal than that of their own "right and
need to develop and grow," often ended up fortifying their own privilege and
power. As the sociologist Bob Connell astutely observed, men in all-male
groups might seek to advance their *own* interests — as in learning to become

more expressive, better fathers, and the like—but it was difficult for men to organize in any large-scale way against sexism, for "the project of social justice in gender relations is directed *against* the interest they share."[31] While I see a more positive role for male solidarity than this, NOMAS being a prime example, men's rights literature, unfortunately, has often presented a case history of the phenomenon Connell described.

CAN WE TALK?

One male rights author was to renegotiate his position, perhaps under the influence of a feminist partner (or so I was fond of imagining). Aaron Kipnis and Elizabeth Herron's *Gender War, Gender Peace* (later entitled *What Women and Men Really Want,* a play on Goldberg's *What Men Really Want*) returned us to a version of the world in which I thought I lived, a world in which there was no doubt that many men "in our culture have had more political and economic power than [most] women," but in which women have "incredible power to create and sustain the relationships that make up the fabric of our culture." This was a world that wounded men, too, and in which most violence was committed against men by other men, but it was a world in which "clearly, men create much of their own suffering."[32]

Also refreshing was the way in which Kipnis's anger at feminism and at women, in this book, did not give rise to knee-jerk attempts to deny men's responsibilities for the construction of systems of inequality that harmed them as well as women. The demand that men take "real responsibility for destructive past behaviors" on the collective and individual, public and domestic levels made a significant break, not just with the "no guilt" emphasis of some men's rights literature but also with its tendency to emphasize male fragility to the point that men slipped quietly off various hooks.[33] "Criticism rarely undoes fragility," Farrell had warned us in 1986, anticipating John Gray's *Men Are from Mars, Women Are from Venus*.[34] Gray observed, for example, that when a woman attempted to change a man, he received the message that she thought he was broken. This hurt a man and made him very defensive. Gray's advice then was to "let go of *trying* to change him in any way." Share your feelings with him but don't ask him to change and trust him to grow on his own.[35] The sad thing about Gray's advice is that it can indeed "work" in getting men to feel better about themselves and perhaps even to change in moderate ways (although I have not had a lot of luck with this approach), but it does not work as a sustained strategy. Such behavior can lead to and perpetuate a sense of scorn for men, based on the feeling that they have fallen short of becoming full adults. For feminists, moreover, especially those who participated in sixties and seventies politics organized around the rigorous demand for individual and social change, the thought of political alliance, let alone intimate relationship, on these terms is difficult to take. One secret appeal of Promise Keepers, to some feminist women at least, is the non-whining, non-self-pitying, tone of its address: "Grow up! Act like men!"

Gender War, Gender Peace, however, took a more negotiated approach than had men's rights literature in the past. Although emphasizing the immobilizing effects of shame—"shame makes you feel that *who* you are is wrong"—and the importance of support in helping to actualize "the inherent good in men," Kipnis and Herron insisted that men make efforts to take responsibility for their "part in the war between the sexes." Kipnis also suggested, however, how easily such efforts induced a sense of shame in men, thereby producing a form of what I have called male-defensive collapse:

> It was easy to talk about our anger, somewhat more difficult to talk about our fears and our grief, but it felt significantly harder to consider taking responsibility for things being the way they are. Over the years, as I have worked with thousands of men, a primary issue that keeps presenting itself is men's struggle to recover from a deep, personal, and collective sense of shame.[36]

Much self-abuse, violence, and abuse of women, Kipnis observed, had stemmed from the fear of women's power to shame: "Women do have good cause to fear us."[37]

In their rejection of Goldberg's individualist "you do your thing, I'll do my thing" ethic and the often whining "I'm more oppressed than you" ethic of Farrell, Kipnis and Herron attempted to recapture something of the more communal orientations of the 1960s in which many forms of political transformation came together and in which working on personal relations (though not necessarily gender relations) emerged as a form of politics along with sit-ins and demonstrations. Recalling the "peace and justice" coalitions of the late 1960s, Herron and Kipnis's gender, peace, and justice politics embraced a general concern about destruction of the environment, about violence (ethnic cleansing, the systematic rape of women in war), and about what the British social critic Anthony Giddens called "productionism," or production for the sake of producing.

Herron and Kipnis also called for a transformation of masculine identity as a central part of a larger conversion of global, capitalist values:

> The dying myth of masculinity was primarily concerned with material success and the acquisition of power at any cost. The new myth defines success according to the capacity to father our children, nurture the earth, achieve balanced partnerships with women, and direct our institutions in a manner that empowers everyone around us while increasing our own well-being."[38]

Herron and Kipnis thus emphasized the link between polarization and aggression in personal relationships and those in national and global relations as well. Their call for individuals to "create more compassionate communities that support each sex for its unique value" was of a piece with the construction of a larger and more compassionate social order.[39]

Gender War, Gender Peace was indeed one of several books published in the 1990s that called for a wider politics of structural change based on renegotiating the pact between women and men and on giving value to, and working on, relationships of all kinds. I will return to these politics in chapter 10.

One of the authors' mechanisms for healing the breach between (implicitly white, middle-class) women and men was the use of gender retreats, during which Herron and Kipnis took men and women both into the woods. Using many of the strategies of male romance, such as safe space, ritual, confession, and behavior-modifying activities, such retreats also required male participants —shades of Promise Keepers and the Million Man March—to apologize to women on behalf of men and to promise future responsibility, accountability, and the making of amends. On these occasions, however, women were required to apologize, too.[40] Unfortunately, white, middle-class men and women did not appear to have been gripped by these retreats in an ongoing way. By the year 2000, by which time I had intended to attend one of these retreats myself, Herron and Kipnis were no longer running them in California, where they and I live, and the retreat they had planned for Michigan over Labor Day weekend, which I dutifully signed up for, was ultimately canceled because of low registration. "Can we talk?" Apparently, "No, not now, not yet." As in NOMAS, the question and the answer appeared to be the same.

THE PERSONAL AS REVOLUTIONARY

For progressive, white, middle-class men and women, talking out gender issues has not been a matter of survival. Both race and class privilege and the absence of a unified political movement directly involving them have contributed to a certain willingness on the part of many white, especially older, feminist and profeminist men to just let things pass, at least in public contexts. For politicized black men and women, however, even men and women of the middle class, the pressure to keep up the fight against racial and economic inequalities has kept the issue of male–female gender dynamics on the table as a matter of pressing political and public concern.

In some ways, black activist men were prepared, as white activist men were not, to understand the meaning of the phrase "the personal is political." The black feminist writing that emerged in the late 1960s and early 1970s in the context of the Black Power movement drew, like that of white feminists, upon the language of political revolution in its call for changes in personal relationships between women and men. As writer Toni Cade (later Toni Cade Bambara) put it in her 1970 anthology, *The Black Woman,* "revolution . . . begins with the self, in the self."[41] Such language spoke to black male activists, not only in its evocation of shared revolutionary goals, but also in its assumption that the personal and familial were inextricably tied to a capacity for political resistance. The language of black feminisms, that is, drew on a shared understanding of the historically close relation between black families, community well-being, and antiracist struggle.

Black activist women also shared with black activist men a long-standing consciousness of the ways in which oppressive economic and social conditions had shaped black family life in general and male–female relations in particular. There was some agreement in the 1970s, for example, that white dominant culture equated manhood with primary breadwinning and economic self-making while also creating, in the words of activist Frances Beal, "a situation, where the Black man found it impossible to find meaningful or productive employment." There was some shared acknowledgment that black women might find employment in "the white man's kitchen" and therefore might become "sole breadwinner of the family." While many reversals of mainstream gender ideals were endorsed by black feminists, the limitations imposed on black men's earning power were not.

If black men understood that the personal was the political, however, they did not always agree with black women about what a revolutionary personal life should look like. Many black activist men found it hard, for example, to perceive black middle-class women as disadvantaged with respect to black males as a whole or with respect to themselves. This was one, though not the only, reason, that male Black Power leadership revived earlier traditions of thinking about black liberation struggles in terms of the economic and social liberation of black men. Even though black women overall were on the bottom of the economic ladder, some Black Power leaders sustained a view of the world in which black women had more power than black men both in public and within the home. If black men needed to change, some reasoned, it was in the direction of taking more, rather than less, power vis-à-vis women.

While many black feminists found Black Power a "necessary and vitalizing force" that led black men to "strengthening of their masculinity," Black Power also appeared to them to have led to "an airing of [men's] egos" and to further justifications for Moynihan's patriarchal and polarizing observations about the baleful effects of matriarchy. Some Black Power leaders, indeed, in (unevenly) focusing on issues of manhood, in emphasizing the leadership of men, and in often trying to cast women in secondary roles, seemed to attempt to reverse the dynamics of many actual black households in which nonsubmissive women customarily worked outside the home and in which family life was not necessarily organized around men's work or ego needs.

Between 1970 and 1979, however, black male activists, like white, were to undergo a process of political decentering as internal rifts splintered the Black Power movement from within and as FBI and CIA Cointelpro agents infiltrated Black Power organizations. Although the Black Panther Party continued operations until it closed its last school in 1982, by 1976 *Ebony* magazine was already mourning the passage of black radicalism. Many white, middle-class male activists, of course, also declined from political prominence in the 1970s, but many regained status through their relative power and privilege, some turning to highly successful careers. When black male activists ceased to command national attention as spokesmen for the Black Power movement, many could not count on this cushioning effect.

The production and publication of novels, anthologies, and scholarship by black women in the 1970s and 1980s and the fact that the white-led women's movement provided a large crossover audience for black women writers further obscured some black male activists, who complained that they could no longer find publishers for their work. For example, like many white feminists I know, I had regularly taught work by black men in the late 1960s—Malcolm X, Eldridge Cleaver, Leroi Jones, Ishmael Reed—with zero reflection on their gender politics, I might add. With the beginnings of the women's movement and women's studies, however, I began to focus on the trove of production by black women writers—Toni Cade Bambara, Toni Morrison, Alice Walker, Sonia Sanchez, Audre Lorde, and many others. It was difficult to keep up.

While Black Power leaders were fading from view as nationally recognized activists and authors, they were often finding themselves in an uncomfortable spotlight as recipients of black feminist critique. Michelle Wallace's 1978 *Black Macho and the Myth of the Superwoman,* for example, although it criticized both women and men, did contain provocative lines such as: "Come 1966 the black man had two pressing tasks before him: a white woman in every bed and a black woman under every heel."[42] Meanwhile Ntozake Shange's *For Colored Girls Who Have Considered Suicide/When the Rainbow Is Enuf,* which, according to some reviewers, emphasized the untrustworthiness of men, was enjoying great commercial success. The publicity that both women enjoyed ultimately prompted public male response. One sociologist, Robert Staples, for example, responded to both Wallace and Shange in the pages of *The Black Scholar* in 1979, prompting a vigorous set of responses to his article in turn.

TALKING ABOUT IT

The frankness of the 1979 *Black Scholar* exchange has no parallel I know of among white middle-class activist/intellectuals on the subject of gender relations. Its candid character owed a good deal to the fact that, as Audrey Lorde put it, dialogue between black men and women was "necessary for survival."[43] With economic restructuring and rollbacks in affirmative action and public spending programs, conditions for non-middle-class black communities were growing worse. (Unemployment rates for blacks in the late 1970s, for example, were twice that of whites, and for black youth the rate was 40 percent.[44]) A shared and pressing higher cause, concrete concerns about organizing a unified movement, the necessity for dialogue across a geographically scattered community all helped account for the public nature of the debate. In addition, black male activist/intellectuals lacking, in the words of Julianne Malveaux, "a media certified spokesperson" were naturally feeling "some frustration and a need to respond."[45]

Given the very different situations of black activist/ intellectuals from those of their white counterparts, it is striking how many themes in black activist male writing on male–female relations in the late 1970s overlapped with those in white male activist reports. Robert Staples's initial response to Wallace and Shange, for example, gave particular emphasis to men's fear of being decentered by feminism and thereby losing the "holding environment" that women, replacing the mother, were expected to provide. Referring to *For Colored Girls*, Staples wrote, "At the end of the play, what I find unsettling, was Shange's invitation to black women to love themselves. This seems to me no less than an extension of the culture of Narcissism. She does not mention compassion for misguided black men or a love of child, family and community."[46] Black feminists writing in response to Staples were also quick to isolate this theme. Audre Lorde, for example, responded like this: "Here we have an intelligent black man believing—or at least saying—that a call to black women to love ourselves (and no one said 'only') is a denial or, a threat, to his male identity."[47]

Black feminisms, like white feminisms, also seemed to deepen men's already existing anxieties about and resistance to, women's power and control, prompting threats of withdrawal or refusal to commit. Staples, for example—and we should keep in mind that he was writing this over twenty years ago—both mentioned and reenacted this pattern: The middle-class black male "screens out the strong black woman beforehand in his choice of mates": "Women, to a large extent, are victimized by the fact that the very same characteristics they need to obtain career mobility (aggressive, strong achievement drive) are the ones which make it difficult to attract and hold a man."[48] In the context of the fact that black middle-class women outnumbered black middle-class men in 1979, such threats of male withdrawal were particularly pointed.[49]

Staples also spoke for many black male intellectuals and activists in finding it difficult to entertain criticism, most especially the charge of acting in sexist ways. Since black men did not "control the system," he argued, "the problem of defining what is sexist behavior among black men" on the "institutional level" was that "most black men do not have the power to force women into subordinate roles."[50] Not all black men writing in response to this agreed. Kalamu ya Salaam was to counter that "African American men have adopted a sexist outlook." Sexism was embedded in institutions, Salaam argued, and black men acted out sexist behaviors that the controllers of society condoned.

By the 1990s black therapists like Audrey B. Chapman, Derek S. Hopson, and Darlene Powell Hopson were reporting that a similar set of dynamics operated in ordinary, middle-class heterosexual, black lives—male fear of abandonment or decentering, a desire for women's attention coupled with fear of women's control, and difficulty in hearing requests for change as something other than an assault on masculine identity, as well as a protective withdrawal or refusal to commit. Chapman, for example, repeated the observation made in Kunjufu's 1982 book *The Conspiracy to Destroy Black Boys*, that the tradition of "raising their daughters and loving their sons" tended to consolidate an already present but unconscious sense that women were self-sufficient and powerful and that men lacked self-confidence and a sense of responsibility toward others: "The women learn that controlling their environment is a must if they are to take care of themselves and their families. And the men learn to fight this control with every means at their disposal."[51] For black men, of course, the fear of being controlled by women was also determined by their experience of being denied control over their economic, racial, and psychic lives by a racist culture.[52]

Rather than blaming black women for men's responses, however, Chapman carefully noted the role of racism and economic exclusion in laying burdens on women: "Historically, black women have been forced to be the caretakers of the family because black men have not been able economically to play the role of breadwinner and father-protector." Women, therefore, lived a life of self-sacrifice, refrained from meeting their own physical and emotional needs, and were praised or blamed for what happened with their children.[53]

The style of loving that many black men had taken up, according to Chapman, was a "style designed to control women"—"a style full of anger and hostility that gets masked as macho behavior."[54] Like Goldberg, Chapman and the Hopsons both cited some of the most familiar ways in which this need to control women might be expressed, through suppressing vulnerability and neediness, refusing commitment, avoiding intimacy, and suppressing tender feeling: "Some Black men deliberately maintain distance from the women with whom they become involved. We call them 'Ice Men' because they are mysterious about their activities, guarded about their feelings, and extremely reluctant to explore emotional issues."[55] Men might also play the field, disappear, and in the worst cases verbally and physically abuse women.

The Hopsons also reflected upon male-defensive-collapse or the tendency of men to be wounded to the very core by requests for change, a tendency also produced in black men by the fact that they lived in a black-shaming culture. Thus, black men were "extremely sensitive to perceived threats against their manhood and often bristle if they feel they are being criticized or ordered around."[56] Finally, while noting that sharing was the custom in some black households, the Hopsons cited their clinical experience with "traditional men [who] expect women to carry more of the daily load, even if they both work full time."[57] Without equating white and black domestic experience and without wanting to diminish the particular pains of the fact that black relationships were carried on in a racist culture, it bears saying, nonetheless, that male domination, lack of intimacy, male-defensive-collapse, and the unequal sharing of household chores had been precisely the major themes of magazine articles on black *and* white husbands over the last ten years.

REBIRTHING THE BLACK MALE SUBJECT

Although there has been some disagreement over the degree to which black men and women have openly and effectively discussed gender relations, the 1980s and 1990s were regularly punctuated by sustained interchanges between black intellectuals over gender, race, sexuality, and class.[58] There were, for example, sustained debates over Alice Walker's novel *The Color Purple* (1982), the film version of the novel (1986), the Clarence Thomas and Anita Hill hearings (1991), Sherharazade Ali's *The Black Man's Guide to Black Women* (1992), Orlando Patterson's "Backlash: The Crisis of Gender Relations among African Americans" (1993), the trial of O. J. Simpson (1994–1995), and the movie version of Terry McMillan's *Waiting to Exhale* (1995). Activists and intellectuals also published anthologies on the subject of black gender relations, such as Nathan and Julia Hare's *Crisis in Black Sexual Politics* (1989), Devon W. Carbado's *Black Men on Race, Gender and Sexuality* (1999), Rudolph P. Byrd and Beverly Guy-Sheftall's *Traps: African American Men on Gender and Sexuality* (2001), and Johnnetta Betsch Cole and Beverly Guy-Sheftall's *Gender Talk: The Struggle for Women's Equality in African American Communities* (2003).[59]

Whatever these interchanges are called, they and the anthologies represented sustained, critical attention to gender relations in the context of the power relations of gender, race, sex, and class that shaped our public and domestic worlds. Individual contributions to the exchanges, in particular, were sometimes angry and even demonizing (most particularly with respect to feminisms), but more were finely analytical and at the same time passion-filled. Indeed, some of these meditations were among the most illuminating I had read on the nature of power relations and politics in the United States. They were teaching texts, not just for black readership but for all of those with an interest in how to understand our common world. The prominence of gender as an analytical category and of talk about gender relations on the personal and larger political levels was far more sustained in these pieces than in any of the debates over social issues that I encountered in the 1990s in the conversations of some groups and e-mail lists associated with the white, cultural Left. Taking gender seriously seemed a hallmark of black public intellectuals in the 1990s, and that is partly what I mean about black men and women constituting a relationship frontier.

The 1990s, in particular, saw a continuing but now more intense emphasis on the importance of "working on the [black] relationship" as a key to antiracist alliance between women and men. The Hopsons' plan for achieving strong personal relations, for example, recommended the staples of marriage manuals—cooperation, negotiation, confronting conflict, and compromise—but also advocated a shared sense of mission that was larger than the relationship itself: "In the Afrocentric world view, we live not only for ourselves, but for others."[60] It was a continuing, not necessarily Afrocentric, political imperative, a shared higher cause, a deepening sense of despair over the social situation of African-Americans, and the development and flowering of black feminist thought that sustained the conscious refashioning of black activist masculinity in the 1990s.

In that decade and in the early years of the new millennium, for example, a series of black male activists and intellectuals, straight and gay, called on black men to embrace feminist political positions. (Even the Million Man March had its share of speakers condemning the "sin" of sexism.) Luke Charles Harris, a professor of politics and law, for example, enjoined black men to embrace feminism by addressing the problems stemming from patriarchal relations between black men and women, such as violence in the home, sexual harassment in the workplace, and "unwarranted demands" on black women "to express racial loyalty by passively accepting sexist attitudes and behaviors."[61] Central to this politics, for Harris, was the disclaiming of homophobia and the expansion of a vision of leadership so as to embrace women, gay, lesbian, and bisexual black Americans.[62]

Law professor Devon W. Carbado, noting in 1999 that "there is not yet a self-consciously defined black male feminist community," urged black men "to embrace and assert a feminist political identity," which should not attempt to "replicate female feminism" or to encroach on feminist safe spaces. Rather, male feminism should include self-criticism by black men of the way in which "social, patriarchal codes of manhood are enacted and naturalized in their every day interactions with other men and with women." Noting that "sexual privilege is one of the few privileges that straight Black men *know* they have," even though heterosexual black men continue to be regarded as deviant (as potential rapists) or irresponsible (as jobless fathers of children out of wedlock), Carbado also challenged heterosexual black men to "dismantle male heterosexual privilege."[63]

At times profeminist black intellectuals attempted to facilitate this embrace of feminism by giving emphasis to the feminist sympathies of black male role models from the past. The literary critic Gary Lemons, for example, called for reclaiming the history of black male support of woman suffrage. Reviving the pro-woman legacy of such men as Frederick Douglass and W. E. B. Dubois, who "'moved' incisively," if unevenly at times, "to empower themselves as *black men* in feminist terms," Lemons argued, could "be a powerful means to engage contemporary black men in dialogue about the viability of a feminist movement focused on the liberation of all black people."[64]

Theologian Rufus Burrow Jr. and literary critic bell hooks, by the same token, documented a shift in the thinking of Malcolm X toward the end of his life toward greater acknowledgment of women's role in political leadership. The move Malcolm X made from "a sexist, misogynist standpoint to one where he endorsed efforts at gender equality was so powerful. It can serve as an example for many men today, particularly black men."[65] Carbado's anthology, moreover, included Huey Newton's famous essay on the need for alliance with the women's and gay liberation movements.

Another radical approach to masculine transformation was offered by literary critic Michael Awkward, who borrowed from literary critic Hortense Spillers the idea that the "African-American male has been touched by the *mother, handed* by her in ways that he cannot escape" and that the black American male "embodies the *only* community of males that has had the specific occasion to learn *who* the female is within itself. It is the heritage of the *mother* that the African-American male must regain as an aspect of his own personhood—the power of 'yes" to the 'female' within."[66] What such a project would involve was not entirely clear, although Awkward noted that it would not include dependence on women for a second birth.

In calling on black men to embrace the mother and the feminine within, however, Awkward challenged the notion that a boy's "need" to separate from the mother and the feminine was natural or irreversible. Instead, he suggested that this "need" was largely a socially constructed one, a "need" that could be dismantled through conscious effort. Consciously embracing the mother and the feminine within might loosen the destructive hold of dominant forms of male socialization in the United States and might begin to redefine the dominant meaning of masculinity in this culture—something of benefit to all men and women. The bare call to begin such exploration and to couple it with feminist politics—to make claiming the feminine a "means by which black men can participate usefully in and contribute productively to the black feminist project"—took us beyond men's rights and the mythopoetics. In his plain speech, Awkward took us beyond some white profeminist men as well. Drawing on a long legacy of open debate, Awkward wrote in fairly direct terms about black men and women's relationships in the academy and about the limits and shortcomings of black feminisms that posited black men as "always already damned and unredeemable even when they appear to take black women's writing seriously."[67] Here Awkward built upon the legacy of some black female feminists themselves.

Bell hooks and the cultural critic Cornel West, for example, in their cowritten book *Breaking Bread: Insurgent Black Intellectual Life,* maintained in 1991 that renegotiating the bond between women and men remained "the crucial work in gender relations which has not been done." Central to this work was the renegotiation of black masculinity, but, just as radically, hooks proposed a change for black feminist women as well: "We as Black women must also undergo a conversion experience so that we can appreciate and affirm those Black men."[68] According to hooks, "Feminist thinkers cannot demand that men change, then refuse to extend full positive acknowledgment when men rethink sexism and alter their behavior accordingly."[69] The call for men to think through and embrace their relation to the mother and to the feminine within, coupled with a call for female feminist rethinking and rebirth, might be key to a vision in which "feminism," rather than past forms of male romance, might represent "a fruitful and potentially nonoppressive means of figuratively birthing twice the black male subject."[70]

NOTES

1. William J. Goode, "Why Men Resist," in *Men's Lives*, ed. Michael S. Kimmel and Michael A. Messner (New York: Macmillan, 1989), 50.

2. "Divorce Rates," www.divorcereform.org/rates.html.

3. Joseph H. Pleck, and Jack Sawyer, eds. *Men and Masculinity* (Englewood Cliffs, N.J.: Prentice-Hall, 1974); Deborah S. David, and Robert Brannon, *The Forty-Nine Percent Majority: The Male Sex Role* (Reading, Mass.: Addison-Wesley, 1976); Jon Snodgrass, ed., *For Men against Sexism* (Albion, Calif.: Times Change Press, 1977).

4. M. E. Kann, "The Costs of Being on Top," *Journal of the National Association for Women Deans, Administrators & Counselors* 49 (1986): 29–37.

5. Michael A. Messner, *Politics of Masculinities: Men in Movements* (Thousand Oaks, Calif.: Sage Publications, Inc. 1997), 42, 44. Kenneth Clatterbaugh, *Contemporary Perspectives on Masculinity: Men, Women, and Politics in Modern Society* (Boulder, Colo.: Westview Press, 1990), 62–63.

6. Herb Goldberg, *The Hazards of Being Male: Surviving the Myth of Masculine Privilege* (New York: Signet, 1977), 5; Anthony Astrachan, *How Men Feel: Their Response to Women's Demands for Equality and Power* (New York: Anchor Books, 1986), 303.

7. Warren Farrell, *Why Men Are the Way They Are: The Male–Female Dynamic* (New York: Berkley Books, 1986); Aaron R. Kipnis, *Knights without Armor: A Practical Guide for Men in Quest of the Masculine Soul* (Los Angeles: Jeremy P. Tarcher, 1991).

8. Goldberg, *Hazards*, 12. Martha C. Nussbaum, *Upheavals of Thought: The Intelligence of Emotions* (Cambridge: Cambridge University Press, 2001), 178.

9. Nussbaum, *Upheavals*, 232.

10. Goldberg, *Hazards*, 86, 87, 15, 55.

11. Goldberg, *Hazards*, 146.

12. Goldberg, *Hazards*, 142.

13. Goldberg, *Hazards*, 143, 5–6, 143.

14. Terrence Real, *I Don't Want to Talk about It: Overcoming the Secret Legacy of Male Depression* (New York: Fireside, 1998).

15. Anthony Astrachan, *How Men Feel: Their Response to Women's Demands for Equality and Power* (Garden City, N.Y.: Anchor Press, 1986), 207.

16. S. M. Miller, "The Making of a Confused Middle-Aged Husband," in Pleck and Sawyer, *Men and Masculinity*, 51.

17. Victor J. Seidler, *Recreating Sexual Politics: Men, Feminism and Politics* (New York: Routledge, 1991), 73.

18. Barbara Ehrenreich, *The Hearts of Men: American Dreams and the Flight from Commitment* (Garden City, N.Y.: Anchor Books, 1983).

19. Miller, "Making," 46.

20. Miller, "Making," 47, 48.

21. Miller, "Making," 46.

22. Miller, "Making," 49, 52.

23. Miller, "Making," 47.

24. Seidler, *Recreating*, 83.

25. M. Adams, "Child of the Glacier," *American Man Magazine*, cited in Kipnis, *Knights*, 67.

26. Farrell, *Why Men*, 150.

27. Farrell, *Why Men*, 361.

28. Goldberg, *Hazards*, 5, 183.

29. Goldberg, *Hazards*, 183.

30. Goldberg, *Hazards*, 184, 40.

31. R. W. Connell, *Masculinities* (Berkeley: University of California Press, 1995), 236.

32. Aaron Kipnis and Elizabeth Herron, *Gender War, Gender Peace: The Quest for Love between Women and Men* (New York: Morrow, 1994), 147, 97, 100.

33. Kipnis and Herron, *Gender War,* 158.

34. Farrell, *Why Men,* xxvii; John Gray, *Men Are from Mars, Women Are from Venus: A Practical Guide for Improving Communication and Getting What You Want in Your Relationships* (New York: HarperCollins, 1992).

35. Gray, *Men Are from Mars,* 147, 140.

36. Kipnis and Herron, *Gender War,* 156.

37. Kipnis and Herron, *Gender War,* 158.

38. Kipnis and Herron, *Gender War,* 116.

39. Kipnis and Herron, *Gender War,* 28.

40. Kipnis and Herron, *Gender War,* 180, 175.

41. Toni Cade, "On the Issue of Roles," in *The Black Woman: An Anthology,* ed. Toni Cade (New York: Signet, 1970), 109.

42. Wallace, *Black Macho,* 32.

43. Audre Lorde, "Feminist and Black Liberation: The Great American Disease," *The Black Scholar* (March–April 1979), 19.

44. Wallace, *Black Macho,* 53.

45. Julianne Malveaux, "Political and Historical Aspects of Black Male/Female Relationships: The Sexual Politics of Black People: Angry Black Women, Angry Black Men," *The Black Scholar* (March–April 1979), 33.

46. Robert Staples, "The Myth of Black Macho: A Response to Angry Black Feminists," *The Black Scholar* (March–April 1979), 26.

47. Lorde, "Feminist," 18.

48. Staples, "Myth," 28, 29.

49. In 1979 there were 732,000 more black women than black men in the 24-to-44-year-old group. Diane Weathers, Diane Camper, Verne Smith, Brenda Russell, Sylvester Monroe, "A New Black Struggle," *Newsweek,* 27 August 1979, 58.

50. Staples, "Myth," 27.

51. Chapman, *Entitled,* 27.

52. Chapman, *Entitled,* 76.

53. Chapman, *Entitled, 27, 28.*

54. Chapman, *Entitled,* 76.

55. Chapman, *Entitled,* 86.

56. Derek S. Hopson and Darlene Powell Hopson, *Friends, Lovers, and Soul Mates: A Guide to Better Relationships between Black Men and Women* (New York: Simon & Schuster, 1994), 23.

57. Hopson and Hopson, *Friends,* 23, 182.

58. Orlando Patterson, "Backlash: The Crisis of Gender Relations among African Americans," *Transition* 62 (1993): 7; Rita S. Williams, "Strangers in the Night," *Transition* 62 (1995): 131; bell hooks, "Feminist Transformation," *Transition* 62 (1995): 93.

59. Nathan Hare and Julia Hare, eds., *Crisis in Black Sexual Politics* (San Francisco: Black Think Tank, 1989); Devon W. Carbado, ed., *Black Men on Race, Gender, and Sexuality: A Critical Reader* (New York: New York University Press, 1999);

Rudolph P. Byrd and Beverly Guy-Sheftall, eds., *Traps: African American Men on Gender and Sexuality* (Bloomington: Indiana University Press, 2001); Johnnetta Betsch Cole and Beverly Guy-Sheftall, *Gender Talk: The Struggle for Equality in African American Communities* (New York: Ballantine Books, 2003).

60. Hopson and Hopson, *Friends*, 218, 219.

61. Luke Charles Harris, "The Challenge and Possibility for Black Males to Embrace Feminism," in *Black Men on Race, Gender, and Sexuality Critical Reader,* ed. Devon W. Carbado (New York: New York University Press, 1999), 384.

62. Harris, "Challenge," 386.

63. Devon W. Carbado, "Epilogue: Straight Out of the Closet: Men, Feminism, and Male Heterosexual Privilege," in *Black Men*, 421, 417, 420, 442.

64. Gary Lemons, "A New Response to 'Angry Black (Anti)Feminists': Reclaiming Feminist Forefathers, Becoming Womanist Sons," in *Men Doing Feminism*, ed. Tom Digby (New York: Routledge, 1998), 280, 281.

65. bell hooks, "Malcolm X: The Longed-for Feminist Manhood," in *Outlaw Culture: Resisting Representations* (New York: Routledge, 1994), 195; Rufus Burrow Jr., "Some African American Males' Perspectives on the Black Woman," in Carbado, ed., *Black Men,* 396–99.

66. Michael Awkward, "A Black Man's Place in Black Feminist Criticism," in *Men Doing Feminism*, ed. Tom Digby (New York: Routledge, 1998), 157.

67. Awkward, "A Black Man's Place," 153.

68. bell hooks and Cornell West, *Breaking Bread: Insurgent Black Intellectual Life* (Boston: South End Press, 1991), 126.

69. bell hooks, "Malcolm X," 195.

70. Awkward, "A Black Man's Place," 162.

8

Doing the Work of Love

Promise Keepers on Work, Marriage, and Fathering

> My identity is no longer based upon what I do, who I know, or what I own—
> but now is based upon *whose* I am. I no longer have anything to prove.
>
> —Rodney L. Cooper, *Double Bind: Escaping the
> Contradictory Demands of Manhood.*[1]

"IRON JESUS"

On October 1–3, 1993, at a lodge and conference center in Lacy, Washington, a young seminarian working for his doctorate at San Francisco Theological Seminary held a retreat for Christian men that would become the basis for his doctoral dissertation on "Iron Jesus: Lessons from the Mytho-Poetic Men's Movement for Christian Men: A Retreat Design Exploring Masculine Identity and Spirituality." Noting, on the one hand, that men were absent in large numbers from the church and, on the other, that men were trying to find their spiritual identity through ritual and fairy tales, the seminarian proposed to make Jesus rather than Bly's "Wildman" the center of a weekend retreat for men. Jesus, after all, was also the son of a distant Father, had entered the wilderness (with the hirsute John the Baptist), and had himself burst from the water as the "new wild man." According to the seminarian, however, Jesus's wildness was expressed in more structural concerns than the mythopoetics had seemed to raise. It was expressed in detaching oneself from capitalist values and in embracing radical discipleship to the poor.[2]

The retreat also proposed to deal with issues that the mythopoetics had raised for men, but it evidently differed from the mythopoetics by focusing more on women and on mothers. Thus, remote fathers, initiation rites, warrior

213

experience, work, sexual performance, male friendship, and male spirituality would constitute some of the topics, while separation from mothers and women would constitute others. The retreat, I gather, was a moderate success. Although the churches had failed to advertise it much, last-minute phone calls rounded up some twenty-one men who engaged, among other things, in talking about Jesus and masculinity, discussing archetypes, and watching both *The Good, the Bad, and the Ugly* and *The Last Temptation of Christ.*

By 1993, however, a far more massive experiment in Christian male romance had already begun, with fifty thousand men attending Promise Keepers' third annual conference at the University of Colorado. Like black cultural nationalists, the Radical Faeries, NOMAS, the mythopoetics, and the young seminarian, as well, conservative evangelicals had launched their own organized efforts to construct a "new" masculine ideal. The Promise Keepers organization, in a now familiar story, was initiated by Bill McCartney, then football coach at the University of Colorado. McCartney had first dreamed of "filling a stadium with Christian men" on a three-hour car ride to a Fellowship of Christian Athletes in Pueblo, Colorado, in March 1990, a mere two months after Moyers's documentary on Bly's gathering of men. Later that year seventy-two men began to pray and fast about this concept, and in July 1991 forty-two hundred men attended a single rally.[3]

By 1996 twenty-two conferences had brought out over a million participants, and in 1997, in addition to drawing 638,297 men to its nineteen regional conferences, Promise Keepers staged a Million Man gathering in Washington, D.C. Attendance at Promise Keepers conferences has subsequently declined, from a high of 1.1 million in 1996 to less than half that number. There were only 306,700 participants in 1999 and 194,000 in 2000. In 1999, however, Promise Keepers events were estimated to have involved over 3.2 million participants, and by the year 2000 the organization claimed to have reached five million men.[4] These numbers seemed to include men who returned year after year, but they easily established Promise Keepers as the largest organized effort to transform masculine ideals in the United States.

Like mythopoetics, Promise Keepers in the mid-1990s were mainly white, although participation by men of color ranged from 5 percent in Oakland in 1995 to 14 percent at the 1997 Stand in the Gap Assembly in Washington, D.C., to a reported 20-some percent at a conference in Los Angeles. In contrast to mythopoetic leadership, however, the leadership of Promise Keepers was racially mixed, with one-third of the staff, almost one-third of the roster of speakers, and one-fourth of the board of directors being men of color in 1999.[5] As with the mythopoetics, Promise Keepers were largely middle-class as well. Like the mythopoetics, moreover, Promise Keepers were mainly thirty to sixty years old, although Promise Keepers in the main seemed younger overall. Thirty-one percent at the Stand in the Gap Assembly were in their thirties, for example, and another 30 percent were in their forties. (The age of the Promise Keepers may have contributed to some degree to their distance from 1960s politics and countercultures. Many were too young to have been born the first time in the 1960s.)

Although, like many evangelical groups, Promise Keepers saw homosexuality as a sin, in the spirit of its "love the sinner" rhetoric it did invite gay men to attend conferences (to the chagrin of more conservative religious groups). The organization patently geared itself, however, toward men whose heterosexuality was taken as a given. Eighty percent of those attending the Stand in the Gap Assembly, for example, were married, and 77 percent had children. In contrast to the liberal mythopoetics, 61 percent of Promise Keepers participants rated themselves as conservative to very conservative (48 percent conservative, 13 percent very conservative). Thirty percent rated themselves as moderate to very liberal (22 percent moderate, 6 percent liberal, 6 percent very liberal). A whopping 90 percent described themselves as "born again," that is, as having accepted Jesus as their personal savior.[6]

In the mid-1990s, several accounts of the movement, written by progressives who watch the Right, claimed that Promise Keepers' central political vision was to take the nation for Jesus—a prospect that sent chills down the spine of those, including me, who opposed the fusion of church and state.[7] My own research, however, suggested that this was not the vision that Promise Keepers centrally presented to its conference participants. It was not the public face of Promise Keepers, no matter what ambitions along that line some of its leaders might have entertained, and it was not the central meaning that Promise Keepers conferences enforced for the men who participated in them. A far more central vision, according to my interviews and participant observation, was defined by Promise Keepers' gender project—producing a less career-focused and more compassionate and caring Christian masculinity, that, while retaining many conservative elements of evangelical thought, was distinctly more liberal than some conservative, evangelical masculine codes.

I based my interpretations of Promise Keepers on my participant observation at Promise Keepers events, on my reading, and on my interviews with Promise Keepers participants and staff. Between 1995 and 1999, for example, I attended seven two-day Promise Keepers conferences and the Stand in the Gap Assembly and also listened to tapes from three conferences that I did not attend. At a minimum I read twenty-five Promise Keepers–related publications, including eleven official Promise Keepers books and study guides, eight books by men who had spoken at Promise Keepers conferences, and six by men who were Promise Keepers directors at some point. Over the years I either heard or read works by fifty-two of the men on Promise Keepers' 1998 list of speakers (which included 109 men), plus two men who were not listed but who had spoken at conferences.

Between 1995 and 1999 I also interviewed a half-dozen Promise Keepers staff and fifty-five Promise Keepers participants. Of those fifty-five, I talked with twenty-four at greatest length, in sessions averaging from forty minutes to two and a half hours. Sixteen of the sessions took place at Promise Keepers conferences and two on airplanes on the way to conferences. I also conducted six interviews in Promise Keepers' homes or places of employment. Twelve of the twenty-four men were white and middle-class; of whom eleven were in their thirties and forties and one was in his fifties. Six lived in California, four in the Bible Belt, and two more in Western and Southwestern states. Twelve of the twenty-four were men of color—eight African-Americans, one Latino, one Asian-American, and two Native American men. Ten of this group were in their thirties and forties and two in their fifties. Four lived in California, two in the Middle West, two in the East, one in a Southern state, one in the Bible Belt, and two in Western states other than California. I base most of my observations on these twenty-four interviews, although the shorter interviews, which did not cover as many topics, support the general conclusions I draw here.

None of the twenty-four men I interviewed at length saw the organization as political in the sense of promoting a political party, platform, or wing. Only three of the twenty-four identified themselves unambiguously with the Religious Right, and these three were white men living in the Bible Belt. John, a middle-class white man living in northern California, was more typical of the white men I interviewed in that he identified as a political and religious conservative in "a lot of ways" and agreed with Promise Keepers' rejection of abortion and homosexuality, though he felt that "homosexuality was not more or less serious than a lot of other conduct." He did *not* identify, however, with the Religious Right. Although he listened on the radio to James Dobson—a conservative Christian, family psychologist who was an active proponent of the Religious Right—he felt certain that Dobson would find him "a flaming liberal." John did not see Promise Keepers as "political," that is, as identified with a political platform, party, or wing. For John, as for the other eleven white Promise Keepers I spoke with at greatest length, the focus of Promise Keepers was on strengthening faith, on fellowship with other Christian men, and on becoming better husbands and fathers.

None of the twelve men of color I interviewed at length identified with the Religious Right. James, a middle-class African-American man living in southern California, was typical of this group. James also felt that Promise Keepers was important for its impact on faith and on men's relations to women and to children. (Like John, he saw homosexuality as a sin "like adultery" but felt it best to let "homosexuals be.") While he did not see Promise Keepers as political and did not identify with the Religious Right, he was typical of all the men of color I interviewed in putting primary emphasis on Promise Keepers' race reconciliation project. Promise Keepers, for example, represented the possibility of "coming together" across race and of combating racism at work and in church. Promise Keepers, he hoped, might also act as a revitalizing force with respect to the black inner-city community, most particularly with respect to those men who felt "you can't make a difference so why try?" Evoking the patterns of black cultural nationalist attempts to recreate masculine ideals, more Promise Keepers of color saw the issue of masculine transformation as potentially bound to structural social transformation than did Promise Keepers who were white.

BORN AGAIN

As with mythopoetics, those who participated in Promise Keepers conferences were already somewhat marginal with respect to dominant masculine ideals before they joined. Some of the fifty-five Promise Keepers I spoke with had distant fathers, identified with their mothers, were emotionally vulnerable, had been discriminated against as men of color, and/or had been downsized, often several times, in their careers, but it was not these factors that they cited as distinguishing them most from more traditional men. What made three-quarters of the men I interviewed at length feel somewhat distant from dominant masculine codes was the commitment they had made to being an evangelical Christian or "born again." James, for example, noted that black Christian men were stereotyped as "marshmallows" although, in his opinion, "it takes a real man to stand up and be ethical" and to "say no to crack." Stephen, a young, earnest, white, and well-built Promise Keeper from Northern California, felt that "being macho's easy, but being born again, well. . . ."[8]

Ideally, being "born again" means taking one's identity from being saved by Christ, and in Promise Keepers rhetoric, this meant rejecting the need to prove manhood. In the words of the 1996 publication, *Double Bind: Escaping the Contradictory Demands of Manhood,* written by the organization's then National Director of Education, the black psychologist Rodney L. Cooper, "a man who is secure in his identity in Christ recognizes he has all the approval he will ever need."[9] White men and men of color both echoed this perception. Glenn, for example, a white man living in Northern California, reported that before he became an evangelical Christian he had felt the need to "prove" himself through his work and income. After his conversion, however, he realized that "you can't prove yourself to God." He now drove the old car while his wife drove the new one—a situation that, before his conversion, would have made him anxious about what others would think.

Ed, a white man living in a Western state, confided that he no longer looked to his running skills to give him confidence, and Don, another white man living in the Southwest, confessed that he had given up womanizing as a mode of proving himself as a man. Dwight, a black man living in southern California, felt that men became more "self-assured" as Christians, and Luis, a Latino living in the South, told me that he was "macho," a man's man, before his conversion and that "all that changed." "A real man," he concluded, was not about conquest but about "being a friend." Being a real man meant asking, "What can I do for you?"

As in Black Power, the Radical Faeries, the profeminist NOMAS, and the mythopoetics, Promise Keepers offered a set of values clearly alternative to those of the ideal of the self-made man, although the identification of these alternatives varied from one author to another. In *What Makes a Man?* a 1993 official Promise Keepers Study Guide, for example, authors Stephen Griffith and Bill Deckard emphasized assertiveness, self-control, independence, self-confidence, and stability as central values for Christian men. They somewhat complicated common understandings of these qualities, however, by warning against taking one's identity as a man from one's career.[10] Cooper's 1996 *Double Bind*, however, was pointed in its criticism of self-making ideals. Echoing refrains from black cultural nationalist and white "men's liberation" writers both, Cooper evoked a "male mystique" that defined men as successful only if they were characterized by "autonomy," "efficiency," "intense self-interest," "disconnectedness and emotionlessness."[11] "The masculine code," Cooper continued, "may grant him status and power; it may push him higher up the ladder, but in exchange, the man gives up his compassion, empathy, sensitivity and joy." The world becomes an arena in which "to compete and win."[12]

Masculinity, within this context, was identified with economic success and material goals, while workaholism was "an addiction that our society not only tolerates but applauds," causing some men to "'feel like my role is just to feed the machine.'" Most men, nonetheless, chose to compete, only to learn that their previous successes "[did] not count." Men must succeed today.[13] *The Making of a Godly Man,* an official 1997 Promise Keepers Study Guide by John Trent, paid less attention to the role of economic pressures, but it was also critical of individualistic ideals: "In today's culture, men are told from their earliest days on the playground, to the athletic fields of their youth, to the working world they labor in daily, that rugged individualism is what counts. We don't need others."[14]

In contrast to the more radical young seminarian, however, whose Iron Jesus called on men to eschew capitalist values and dedicate their lives to the poor, the Promise Keepers conferences I attended and most of the official Promise Keepers books I read had little to say about economic injustice or poverty as structural, social issues, although some talks and publications on racism tended toward this focus.[15] (I turn to these in chapter 9.) In this respect Promise Keepers, like the mythopoetics, might be said to have reinforced the economic status quo by directing men's attention to the personal. Promise Keepers, nonetheless, did directly call upon men to adopt values and practices that ran counter to standard corporate notions of how to get ahead. Trent's manual, for example, urged men to resist manipulating company figures under pressure from upper management—a timely message from the perspective of the days of Enron and many other corporate scandals.[16]

Six of the twelve white Promise Keepers reported putting these values and practices into action in some detail. Matthew, for example, another white, middle-class, thirty-nine-year-old from the same church as John, testified to not feeling competitive. He noted that he tended not to be "very competitive over splitting commissions. . . . I think that God brings my commissions my way and it's for Him. I also try if I can, to be aware of people around me so that if they're hurting or if they're struggling, I can be an encouragement to them."

Matthew also felt that the influence of being an evangelical and a Promise Keeper at work expressed itself in his telling the truth, in his being ethical, deferring to others, not thinking too highly of himself, looking for ways to serve, not gossiping, and making coffee as "a common courtesy." Promise Keepers' ethic of moral purity also made some Promise Keepers a source of support and sympathy for women at their places of employment. Matthew's wife, Sarah, testified that the sexual harassment at work drove Matthew "nuts," while Ed reported that he had privately spoken out against sexual harassment in his office and that his best friend at work was a woman who belonged to NOW.

The men of color I interviewed, in contrast, lacking the relative privilege of the white, middle-class men, tended to emphasize the racial discrimination and structural inequities that they faced in places of employment, not excluding churches. Being an evangelical Christian and a Promise Keeper, they suggested, functioned as a source of strength in these contexts and as an antidote to anger and despair. Anthony, for example, a black man living in the Middle West, had struggled with racism in his line of work and felt that Promise Keepers had "revitalized him," while Jerome, a black man living in Southern California, felt that Promise Keepers in particular gave him "strength" and that "things are so screwed up you can't lose by turning to God."

Promise Keepers' leadership, moreover, has also acted in some fairly uncorporate ways. The board of directors, for example, decided to drop entrance fees for its stadium events in 1998, in the interest of attracting more poor men and men of color. This decision, according to one member of the board, put the board on the "hot seat," provoking a "barrage" of criticism—"what kind of board of directors is this?"—along with some suggestions that the members of the board should be promptly fired. The decision also proved fairly devastating to the Promise Keepers budget, which had been heavily sustained by conference fees of some sixty dollars a head. Promise Keepers funds, for example, dropped from $87 million in 1996 to $41 million in 1999, after fees were dropped in 1998.[17] In 2000, the Promise Keepers leadership reinstituted conference fees at the request, they explained, of many participants. The decision may also have been prompted by continuing financial duress, for in 2000 Promise Keepers announced that it was closing down all eight of its regional offices.

Like black cultural nationalists, Radical Faeries, NOMAS, and the mythopoetics, Promise Keepers also proposed a more sensitive and caring masculine ideal. Indeed, Promise Keepers spokesmen, at times, seemed more at home with traits traditionally defined as feminine than did the mythopoetics, although this differed from author to author. Authors such as Stu Weber and Ed Cole, who have spoken at Promise Keepers conferences but were not writing official Promise Keepers guides, emphasized the idea that men should be "tender yet tough" in their 1992 and 1993 publications.[18] Gary Oliver's *Real Men Have Feelings Too*, an official Promise Keepers guide, defined such traits as gentleness, compassion, tenderness, meekness, and sensitivity, as "human" rather than feminine traits and as traits best exemplified by Jesus.[19] Trent's 1996 official Promise Keepers guide followed the mythopoetic Robert Bly in defining as not "unmasculine" such conditions as being broken (or wounded), crying in public, looking to another man for help, and nonsexual closeness with another man.[20]

Cooper, however, writing his own book but using the title Promise Keepers Director of Education, went much further in embracing traits that he identified as being associated with women. Although the back cover of Cooper's book, like Bly's *Iron John*, suggested that men could have it all by being "aggressive and take charge" while also being "sensitive and caring, and considerate," Cooper actually proposed a more relational and more expressive set of masculine ideals. Like cultural nationalist Jawanza Kunjufu, Cooper cited Herb Goldberg, along with Aaron Kipnis, on how the equation of masculinity with economic autonomy and intense self-interest put men in a "MAN box" and gave them three rules: do not trust, do not feel, and do not talk.[21]

A boy might learn "compassion, nurturing, and kindness and so on" from women but from the time he turned six he "must disown that part of himself that had been shaped by his mother" and must live "as an incomplete person, alienated from that part of himself that is key for developing intimate relationships."[22] As with mythopoetics, Cooper called for more sensitive and expressive masculine codes. Cooper, for example, characterized Jesus as a man who chose to sacrifice himself rather than fight back because that was the greater good. A man like Jesus was not stuck in the hero image. He has "absolutely nothing to prove and "does not always have to fight or win." Jesus was not searching for an identity and could therefore "connect with all of his emotions," even the negative ones. Jesus touched and allowed himself to touch. Jesus felt deeply and wept openly.[23]

As with the mythopoetics, therefore, Promise Keepers also identified emotional capacities traditionally identified with the feminine as part of a masculine or sometimes of a simply human ideal, often giving men permission to be the sensitive men they already were. Cooper's weeping Jesus, however, was at some distance from Bly's more masculinized "hairy" Christ and from earlier evangelical takes on masculinity as well. *The Christian Family*, for example, which was still in print some twenty-nine years after its initial appearance in 1970, associated masculinity with restless activity, hard labor, economic burden, and toil. It also maintained that it was foolish to urge men to do housework and child care: "Male physiology and psychology aren't geared to it."[24]

IRONING JOHNS

Like earlier networks, then, Promise Keepers was critical of a dominant ideal of masculinity that made individualism, overwork, competition, making it, being tough, and being in control the measure of what it meant to be a citizen and a man in U.S. terms. Like earlier networks Promise Keepers also embraced more sensitive and caring masculine attitudes and behaviors. Only Promise Keepers, however, echoing themes from black cultural nationalism and the Million Man March, called on mixed-race audiences to make devotion to family the basis for a new, heterosexual, masculine ideal. Indeed, rather than organizing family life around the gender project of their work, Promise Keepers men were to organize their careers around the needs of family. As the Asian-American minister Dan Chun put it in Los Angeles in 1998, "long hours may not be the best thing for women and children." Families need "quality and quantity time."[25] "Success," in the words of the white minister John Maxwell, becomes "having those close to me love and respect me."[26]

Only Promise Keepers, moreover, actually urged heterosexual men to put the emotional needs of women and children first rather than expecting a focus on their own. Men were not decentered in this rhetoric, of course, but they were recentered as those who must devote their lives to others. Thus, Promise Keepers exactly reversed the individualistic, self-pitying tendencies of much men's rights literature, and, in contrast to the profeminist NOMAS, which had little to say at its conferences about the dynamics of men's and women's intimate relations, put male–female relations at the center of its conference activities. Promise Keepers accomplished these significant moves, of course, at certain costs. While completely eschewing men's rights versions of the world, in which it was women who ostensibly controlled and oppressed men, Promise Keepers also rejected NOMAS's emphasis on men's patriarchal privileges in the public sphere. Promise Keepers, indeed, had almost nothing to say about sexism or women themselves in relation to the public. I shall return to these erasures later in this chapter.

It was not unusual for Promise Keepers conference talks on marriage to begin with an account of the speakers' past focus on himself. In Seattle in 1997, for example, Gary Smalley, once a youth minister and now the white president of Today's Family and an author of books on love and marriage, recalled how two years into his troubled marriage everything had been centered on *his* needs. Attending a Christian conference, however, had made him aware of "how self-centered I had been," a realization that prompted him to stage a mock death of this self-focused being and to set about becoming different. Smalley, who continued to celebrate this death and resurrection on the eighth of June every year, brought his talk at the Seattle conference to a close by providing cards so that a stadium full of men could list what forms of self-centering *they* were prepared to relinquish on the spot. Buckets were then passed out, as symbolic "caskets," and men dropped their cards in.[27]

That Promise Keepers conferences repeatedly called on men to "love selflessly," "serve," "sacrifice," and "give" to their wives and children, was clearly an application of the Christian ideal of mercy modeled on the sacrifice of Christ. Mercy is giving *more* than is deserved. Christians are to go the *second* mile and give the *cloak* as well as the coat. Promise Keepers, however, was the only mass men's organization to have applied this principle to men's behavior in the home. Marriage was not a fifty-fifty proposition, according to Dan Chun. Promise Keepers were to go in with a "60/40" attitude.[28]

Chun was one of the few Promise Keepers speakers to suggest, sensibly enough, that this attitude should also apply to wives, but in general, Promise Keepers participants were told to give *more* than women. According to the African-American minister Larry Jackson in 1998, "it is my responsibility to give only and not to take."[29] At times, out-serving your wife took an oddly masculinist turn, as when in Los Angeles in 1996 the African-American minister Wellington Boone urged men not to let their wives "out-serve" them and then recalled ironing his wife's clothes until she burst into tears. "You're out-loving me," she cried. Most other speakers, however, avoided this competitive edge.[30]

Loving selflessly, in Promise Keepers terms, began with cutting hours at work—a practice that seven of the white Promise Keepers I interviewed had adopted. Three of the white men living in the Bible Belt did not report cutting hours, reflecting what I felt was their closer alignment with traditional head-of-household status. Of the men of color I interviewed, only one reported cutting hours, a reflection, I surmised, that men of color often felt beset by racist barriers to advancement and that, for even black middle-class men, cutting hours at work was riskier than it would be for a white man.

Don, a white, middle-class southwesterner in his forties who worked in sales, was one of the most dramatic cases of white men who cut their hours at work. Don had been a "workaholic" until his first Promise Keepers conference in 1995, staying at the office until 9:00 o'clock at night and striving to impress his coworkers by exceeding his quota of sales. After his first conference, however, Don's behavior had begun to change. He became less obsessed with his job and with "manipulating" customers. He subsequently married, and, in order to spend more time with his wife, began to leave work at 4:00 in the afternoon. Matthew, also in sales, reported that he made a point of being home for dinner, although that was "a very productive time" for him at work. His wife, Sarah, meanwhile, told me of a Promise Keepers friend, who chose to leave a big law firm for a job with less money and fewer hours: "He will never be a partner but he made a choice to be with his family." Promise Keepers, according to Sarah, "gives men permission" to prioritize their families over their careers.

Time at home, moreover, was to include a version of the working woman's "second shift." Promise Keepers participants were repeatedly told that they, too, had a "second job" that precluded their sitting down in front of the television with a beer when they got home. "Put down the remote control," Dan Chun urged participants at Los Angeles in 1998: "Look to see what is to be done." African-American speakers like Larry Jackson were often particularly emphatic about this message: "The dishes in the dishwasher—yours! The dirty carpet—yours! The baby's diapers—yours! The dirty house—it's your fault! That's not women's work. That's your work."[31] Promise Keepers appeared to get the message, for 90 percent of those interviewed at the 1997 Stand in the Gap Assembly agreed that housework and child care should be shared. Sixty percent had wives who worked outside the home.

What Promise Keepers husbands actually did at home, of course, was another matter, as was the case with some of the leftist, ostensibly profeminist men, with whom I myself have lived. My interviews with Promise Keepers and their wives suggested that the division of labor in Promise Keepers households, as in most U.S. households described in the literature, was a modified form of the traditional. Husbands, for example, almost always did car maintenance and yard work, although many also mopped, vacuumed, cleaned, and occasionally cooked. As in most studied households, wives organized the household labor and kept the job lists, although, as Sarah put it, Matthew "will do anything . . . he wants to meet my expectations." Husbands also reported spending more time on child care than on housework, as was the national norm. Promise Keepers, in short, seemed to embrace the national principle of shared household labor and child care, along with the tendency to assign women primary responsibility for both.[32]

What *was* unusual about Promise Keepers ideals, however, was that men were urged to assume a good deal of the emotion work that women are used to performing. Men, that is, were to plan their intimate relationships as they planned their work, and they were to pursue intimacy on the terms that women have said they needed. This was a distinct break with the men's rights focus, which still expressed a good deal of anger at women for wanting men to be intimate on women's terms. Taking some of their cues from a survey of conservative evangelical women, Promise Keepers spokesmen spelled out the relation work required of men—nonsexual affection, conversation, honesty, and commitment—in some detail. It was Promise Keepers men, not women, who were to be "the initiators of love, grace, warmth, peace," and it was men, not women, who were to be "the first to apologize," according to John Maxwell.[33] Other forms of love work that Promise Keepers were regularly enjoined to perform were talking about their feelings, showing their vulnerabilities, demonstrating that they cared, being gentle, being selfless, having date nights with their wives, and being willing to enter into couples therapy.

Promise Keepers were particularly emphatic about training men to confess their faults, take responsibility for their actions, ask forgiveness, and undergo change, a welcome antidote to what I have called male defensive collapse—the tendency of many men to take women's requests for change as a species of assault upon their very being. It was not at all uncommon for Promise Keepers men to be called on to repeat such words as "I was wrong, I am sorry, please forgive me" en masse and to be told that they might have to go home and ask forgiveness for having been a "jerk." It seemed clear, moreover, that the semi-public confession, apology, and behavior-modifying rituals that took place at Promise Keepers stadium events were not meant to function as a substitute for change at home. Promise Keepers participants at these events were strongly encouraged to join or form small "accountability" groups in their local churches, and ten of the twelve whites and four of the men of color I talked to mentioned that they had.

A mixture of Bible study, consciousness raising, and group therapy, these groups met once a week, sometimes over breakfast, often working through one of the Promise Keepers' guides for men, which offered Bible verses, prayers, questions for discussion, and projects to complete.[34] Promise Keepers' 1994 small group guide to strategies for a successful marriage, for example, written by white minister E. Glenn Wagner, then the Promise Keepers Vice President of National Ministries, provided a questionnaire aimed at uncovering whether individual men were "workaholic." It also called on men to examine themselves in relation to a list of marriage "breakers": hardness of heart, excess baggage, unresolved conflicts, and unreasonable demands. Sections on "communication," "explicit action," "sacrificial giving," "forgiveness," "complete acceptance," "commitment," "praise," and "romance and fun" explained and listed possible forms of activity for each.[35] The discipline of reading this guide in the context of a men's accountability group was undoubtedly aimed at preventing this marriage manual from gathering dust on the bedside table.

I interviewed only six Promise Keepers wives, and though the numbers are not significant, the interviews suggested that Promise Keepers did have at least two kinds of impact on men's behaviors in the home. Five of the women reported that Promise Keepers either changed men for the better or gave them further encouragement in being the good men that they always were. Caroline, a white woman in her thirties who attended the Dallas conference as a volunteer, for example, claimed that her husband became completely different after four years in a Promise Keepers' men's group. He now listened to her, she reported, spent more time with the family, and shared his feelings with male friends. "My husband used to be so angry," she continued. "Now he's found content." Bernice, a black woman in Los Angeles, talked of how her husband was more responsible to her and to the community, of how he was more loving and affectionate. She expressed pride in seeing him take a leadership role in church and in the family. Of course, she also reported that she sat on the board of directors in her church, which worked as a collective, and that, in general, "I've always been a leader."

Sarah, in contrast, felt that there was no difference in Matthew after he joined a Promise Keepers' small group: "He was already thinking these things." She felt, that, in general, the evangelical Christian men they knew were used to giving "a lot of respect to family" and to putting the needs of wives and children "high on the list." A lot of evangelical men were not "self-centered." They're "looking for ways to serve other people." Of course, there were exceptions, and she did not find the same qualities in non-evangelical Christian men. Her view was that Promise Keepers enforced these qualities by giving evangelical Christian men further permission to be different from the norm.

Another white, middle-class woman, Janet, living in the Bible Belt, had grown children and a full-time professional career. She also testified that while Promise Keepers had made her husband more attentive to devotions, it had not changed him with respect to their relationship. The real change had come with David's conversion to evangelical Christianity some years back. It was then that the "whole nature of our relationship changed." David was "like a new person." He wanted to be sure that he wasn't "selfish in any way." He became more "honest" while before he might not have been "totally open." He grew more considerate of people with problems. Janet described their division of household labor as "at least 50/50" and maintained that "he gives more than I do. . . . I couldn't ask for more." Only one woman, Alice, also white and middle-class, reported that she was still "waiting" for significant change to take place. Her husband, I noted, was not a member of an accountability group.

Promise Keepers, of course, was vulnerable to the charge that it extracted a high price for this reaffirmed or reinvented spouse, and the movement was regularly accused by many female feminists and male progressives of covertly, or baldly, substituting one form of traditional masculine power for another. Servant/leadership in the home, that is, was to compensate for a diminished sense of power and control in the public sphere. That Promise Keepers publications and speakers touted men's "servant/leadership" cannot be denied. Indeed, the evocation of such leadership might have played a central role in containing the anxiety or "gender vertigo" that the demand for commitment, confessing faults, talking about the relationship, and other forms of intimacy with women often entailed for men.[36] But it was far from clear that "servant/leadership" operated as simply or as uniformly as many critics asserted or too hastily assumed.[37]

Promise Keepers publications and conference talks, for example, interpreted biblical injunctions about male leadership in both conservative and liberal ways, with most conference interpretations increasingly emphasizing leadership as a form of servanthood and responsibility. In Dallas in 1995, Dennis Rainey, the white president of Family Life, the family ministry of Campus Crusade for Christ, urged Promise Keepers to "lead like a servant," while in Los Angeles the next year Wellington Boone spoke of giving women a "reason" to "submit."[38] Over the years, however, the multiple changes wrought by conference speakers on the theme of men's "servant/leadership" gravitated toward the "servant" end of the spectrum, while "leadership" was increasingly defined as "spiritual."

At the Stand in the Gap Assembly in 1997, for example, Pastor Evans wrestled mightily to give his fatal lines—urging men not to "ask" for their leadership role at home but to "*take* it back"— a different twist. Men were to be "spiritual leaders," and since God Himself had enjoined men to take spiritual responsibility for their families, this was not a role for which they had to "ask." (Unfortunately for Pastor Evans, only one other account of Promise Keepers, so far as I know, picked up on this subtle shift.[39]) The following year, in Fresno, the African-American pastor Bishop George McKinney described the Promise Keepers husband as the "chief servant," and in Los Angeles Dan Chun repeated the same theme: "You as head of the family are to give way more than anyone else.". . . [You are] "the head servant."[40]

At the same time, perhaps in response to rumors or reports that some Promise Keepers husbands had taken leadership to mean domination and even physical abuse, and in further response to NOW's caricature of Promise Keepers as an organization devoted to encouraging both, Promise Keepers began a strong antiviolence and antidomination message. Thus, speakers at the 1997 Assembly called for "no more abuse or abandonment" and urged husbands not to act like a "despot" or a "boss." According to George McKinney in Fresno the next year, God did not empower men to "dominate," to act "macho," or to be a "despot."[41] Dan Chun also explained that being head of household did not mean "top down authority."[42] Finally, in Stockton in 1999 Dennis Rainey called upon a newly working-class crowd to stop abusing, kicking, and cursing while assuring the noticeably hushed stadium that Christ welcomes all "no matter what you've done."[43]

It was clear, moreover, that Promise Keepers leadership often exercised a liberalizing influence on many of its speakers. Some speakers, such as Paul Reis and Dennis Rainey, were far more traditional in their own publications or in interviews than were in conference talks. By the same token, some publications by Promise Keepers officials were more liberal than conference rhetoric. Wagner's official Promise Keepers guide on *Strategies for a Successful Marriage*, for example, argued that "the macho idea that men must make all the decisions, or have the final say, is not what marriage is about. Marriage is about a vibrant partnership."[44]

My ethnographic work with Promise Keepers suggested that there was considerable regional variation in how men's servant/leadership was interpreted. Thus, in the Bible Belt, three-quarters of the men I interviewed *did* claim to be the head of house and to make final decisions, although they acknowledged that since becoming Promise Keepers they actually listened, or believed in listening, to what their wives said! Don, who lived in the Southwest, also defined himself as head of house. He and his wife had attended an evangelical marriage workshop, one which was not affiliated with Promise Keepers, and, with his blessing, the workshop leader had tutored his reluctant wife in how to "submit." The exception among the Bible Belt men was David, for whom Promise Keepers did not mean being "head of house or being the leader" but being "true" and "responsible." He had not been the leader in his marriage. Indeed, Janet had needed to make the decisions about the children, who were hers. A lot of this was because "we both worked." Basically, "We felt our way along."

Six of the seven white men living in the West, however, reported that they and their wives acted as a "team." Ed, for example, who had obviously discussed Promise Keepers with his best friend at work, the woman who belonged to NOW, observed that although NOW feared that Promise Keepers encouraged domination, he didn't find that was what he wanted. He didn't want leadership. He wanted a "partner" instead, although he also aspired to be like Jesus washing the apostles' feet, laying down his life, and giving "everything." Sarah and Matthew reported that they had long discussions when they had different opinions. Although they had agreed that if a really difficult decision had to be made, Matthew would make it, according to Matthew this "may have happened only once." Sarah, in contrast, could recall no instance in which he "unilaterally decided."

John reported that although the "ultimate responsibility" for decisions lay with the husband, his and his wife's decisions were "consensual." He recalled only one time that he made a decision over his wife's head when, on a shopping trip with his wife, he decided to buy a jacket for his son. He stuck with his decision, over his wife's objection, because he had been heavily persuaded by her to participate in the shopping venture in the first place. "If you want me to go shopping with you," he had told her, "you have to let me make some of the decisions." For the men I interviewed in the West, men's leadership seemed more mythic than actual.[45]

Of the men of color I interviewed at length, five emphasized the equality of their marriages, past and present. Millman, a black man living in the East, reported that Promise Keepers had improved his marriage and that he and his wife made decisions together. Clarence, another black man living in the East, also described his marriage as one in which he and his wife shared decision-making power. Both men reported doing laundry and dishes, cleaning, and occasionally switching roles. Luis and Bill, an Asian-American man living in Southern California, also saw their marriages as a partnership. Five other men described blended arrangements in which they felt they were head of the house but in which their wives had "input."

James, for example, liked the idea of being head of the house, but he felt that this didn't mean he and his wife had not been "partners." Both in the domestic and public realms, James felt, "Women can lead too." The two Native American men, Tony and Jack, focused on the way in which Promise Keepers had increased their and other men's responsibility toward, and respect for, their wives. They did not do more dishes, they pointed out, and they were not "henpecked" but they and other Native men were giving more to women and going "over half way." In many of these men, it was clear, racism, which had made advancement in the world difficult, had deepened an investment in feeling they were the heads of their family. At the same time, these same men felt that their wives had been "partners" and that "women can lead too."

WORKING MIRACLES

It seemed ironic to me at first that the men's organization that had been the subject of the most sustained feminist criticism had had such apparent success in getting its participants to admit faults, apologize, and make efforts to change. Not only that, but Promise Keepers had put men's and women's intimate relations at the heart of its conference activities, had regularly urged men to put women and children at the emotional center of their lives, and had called upon men to take responsibility, not just for household chores and child care, but for working on the relationship as well. A feminist, family therapist who works in a family clinic testified that of all the men he had worked with over the last fifteen years, those allied with Promise Keepers had tried hardest to improve their relations with their wives and families.

What accounted for Promise Keepers' apparent success in getting men to change with respect to intimate relations with women in the home? Multiple dynamics, I came to conclude, had been at work. Despite the fact, for example, that men's servant/leadership appeared to be compatible with the practice of various forms of partnership in the home, the mere evocation of servant/leadership, with its assurances that men, not women, did (or should) have ultimate control, might have sustained not only the willingness but the very ability of some Promise Keepers husbands to be more open, more vulnerable, more humble, more giving, and more intimate with their wives. Even mythic evocations of men's servant/leadership might have limited the anxiety that often attended men's domestic relationships with women and that informed their protective strategies of distance and control.

Let me be clear that I am far from recommending servant/leadership. I, and most of the women I know best, would find even mythic evocations of men's leadership personally intolerable and also dangerous in their larger social implications. It did seem clear, however, that in some evangelical households the evocation of men's servant/leadership had helped produce more loving, more responsible, and even more egalitarian mates. One had only to read some other highly popular evangelical texts on familial relations—those that justified women's submissive role with handy charts, those that claimed that men were psychologically and physiologically unfit for washing dishing and feeding

babies—to see that in many ways Promise Keepers had liberalized conservative evangelical masculine ideals. Indeed, that the Southern Baptist Church
declared in 1998 that St. Paul's use of the word "submit" *really did mean submit*, seemed a direct response to Promise Keepers' liberalizing tendencies.[46]

Most Promise Keepers I interviewed, moreover, were too young to have
been in intimate relations with women who suddenly shifted gears in the
1970s—by throwing traditional gender divisions into question and by suddenly refusing to remain the motherly, self-sacrificing figures they had been.
Even older Promise Keepers did not mention having undergone the sense of
surprise, vertigo, and/or wounding of men who were involved with early feminists, nor did they feel accountable to cultural feminist points of view. This
may also help to explain why the Promise Keepers conferences I attended
were marked by a surprising absence of anger and resentment towards
women. Even feminism was spoken of in kindly ways.

Promise Keepers' success, as arguably the largest organization designed to
reinvent the husband on this globe, also had much to do with the fact that it
had no vision of the world that would require men to address the inequalities
of gender in the public sphere. As one self-identified feminist Promise Keeper
put it, "Promise Keepers has never apologized for sexism." Promise Keepers'
silence on sexism, moreover, was all the more striking given the fact that
Promise Keepers *were* called upon to repair the damaged public solidarities of
race, as I relate in chapter 9. That Promise Keepers men were urged to extend
the million little moments of compassion and care—which they were called
upon to practice within the family—to larger, public circles of caring where
men of other races were concerned was, in itself, a dramatic alteration of national manhood as traditionally imagined. However, the extension of this care
to women in the public sphere was never made. An earnest, often touching
"love work" in the home, but national manhood in the world outside—these
were the terms of the renegotiated pact that Promise Keepers so far offered.

Like other organized efforts to invent new masculine ideals, Promise Keepers conferences draw upon familiar elements of male romance. Conferences
began, for example, by creating ritual space—a space that was, first of all, a
space away from women. The exceptions here were women volunteers, who
remained outside the stadium for the most part, and female press, who were
very few in number. The temporary world of the mythopoetic network, however, drew men away from ordinary guy activities, playing up the way "deep"
masculinity broke from traditional masculine codes, a strategy that provoked
media ridicule and helped to keep the networks small. Promise Keepers, in
contrast, emphasized masculine change in the context of reaffirming some familiar emblems of U.S. man and boy culture.

Promise Keepers conferences, as is well known, were staged in sports are-
nas, and Christian athletes were often introduced early in the program, as if
to normalize the link between Christianity and widely recognized forms of
being masculine. In the spirit of the surroundings men often tossed balls, flew
paper planes, and engaged in playful competition over what sections could
give the loudest cheer: "We love Jesus, yes we do. We love Jesus, how bout
you?" Promise Keepers men, therefore, were literally surrounded with the
signs and symbols of a familiar element of dominant masculine ideals, an interest in sports and competition. At the same time, sports activities were sites
on which men were most open to emotion, to intimacy with men, and to
cross-race harmony. As Pastor Evans put it in 1995, the Raider's uniform
hides the color of a man's skin.

The first evening of the seven conferences I attended, however, was devoted to further transforming this ritual space from that of innocent boys-will-
be-boys playfulness to an intense ritual moment of giving oneself to Jesus and
thereby taking on a secondary masculine ideal. Speeches of welcome, joking,
the introduction of Christian athletes, music, hymns, collective prayers, and
videos of men discussing their own personal transformations in Jesus gradually established distance from the initial moments of playfulness and were
followed by an impassioned talk that sometimes recalled the speaker's own
heroic journey from a life of drugs, drinking, crime, and violence to being
born again. Like the mythopoetics, Promise Keepers assumed that true masculinity was both eternally given and an identity to be striven for.

As in nineteenth-century fraternal organizations, Promise Keepers conferences initiated men into this secondary masculine ideal though a series of ritual activities that compelled them to take the "risk" of touching other men
and of revealing their innermost thoughts. Thus, Promise Keepers were regularly exhorted to take hands, hug, confess, pray together, ask forgiveness of
each other, and form small groups. As media coverage repeatedly documented, Promise Keepers men cried openly.

As in mythopoetic and Radical Faerie gatherings, male transformation in
Promise Keepers came about through male agency, but in Promise Keepers
this agency was embedded in the familiar and culturally powerful narrative of
Christianity. Wounded sons with distant fathers, along with the redeeming
near-death trauma of nineteenth-century fraternal rituals, were displaced in
Promise Keepers by the wounding, traumatic death, and resurrection of a divine and transcendent Son, who rose from His death to change all others and
to reconcile them to a Father who was all powerful but loving, too.

This narrative of divine male figures giving birth to the masculine soul was
delivered at Promise Keepers conferences by ministers in established Christian

churches or by Christian counselors, figures with far greater cultural capital, in an overwhelmingly Christian nation, than the "wacky oracles" of the mythopoetic movement with their long hair and drums, or the controversial and marginalized leaders of black nationalisms. Mainstream media reports on Promise Keepers, for example, maintained a far more respectful attitude toward Promise Keepers gatherings than was the case in their reporting on the mythopoetics.

Promise Keepers gatherings also drew on a long U.S. tradition of evangelical meetings and of belief in the possibility of sudden and dramatic transformation—as expressed in conversion itself, in taking Jesus as Lord and Savior. They drew as well on traditions of faith healing—traditions visually enacted in countless living rooms through evangelical television shows—and on belief in the presence of the Holy Spirit or Comforter. This presence had often been dramatically enacted in the expressive style of Pentecostal and charismatic worship and, most particularly, in the practice of glossolalia, or speaking in tongues. In Promise Keepers, however, belief in the Comforter was harnessed to the work of getting men through "gender vertigo" as they partially undid masculinity by confessing failure, acknowledging vulnerability, hugging and talking intimately with other men, choosing to make family more central than career, and vowing to be more loving and responsible in their relations with women and with children. Belief in the presence of the Holy Spirit, according to one profeminist, evangelical journalist I interviewed, was what made it possible to stand up against "the sick values of the world," including "the sad rule of the fist": "You can't resist without the Comforter."

Just as importantly, however, was that in Promise Keepers' constructions of Christianity many of the functions that mothers and women have performed for men were taken on by God the Father and by Jesus the Son. Both male figures were seen as loving men unconditionally, and both, being seen as divine, were imagined to be inexhaustible in that love. Men might depend on Them as they might not depend on mortal figures, male or female. That God the Father and God the Son provided a "holding environment," much as good-enough mothers did, seemed to release Promise Keepers from some of men's usual anger at women over issues of emotional dependency and fear of women's emotional control. Belief in this love, that is, seemed to alleviate what the psychologist Ronald F. Levant had called men's sense of "destructive entitlement" with regard to women.[47]

In Promise Keepers contexts, moreover, it was God the Father and God the Son, along with their male spokesmen, who called on men to be different, who became the voice of women and of quasi-feminist demand by insisting that men acknowledge fault, treat women less selfishly, be more intimate, and embrace the feminine within. God and Jesus became the voices, calling on men to renegotiate the pact with women for the sake of a higher cause. If, as the philosopher Larry May observed, "criticism of male behavior will sometimes be more believable if it is issued by men [or male figures] rather than by women," it was even more effective to translate female, and even vaguely feminist, demands into the voice of male figures who were perceived of as divine.[48] Promise Keepers, finally, like most of the networks organized around the transformation of masculine ideals, also offered forgiveness of the past, but where many men's rights spokesmen "forgave" men by effectively transferring their "guilt" to women, Promise Keepers insisted that the guilt of men was real. Guilt, however, did not mean "shame," for "Christ welcomes all— no matter what you've done."[49]

The power of Promise Keepers' belief appeared to give many Promise Keepers a sense of "energy" and "resolve" that mythopoetics sometimes seemed to lack. Although, out of the fifty-five men I spoke with, I encountered perhaps half a dozen Promise Keepers of intense emotional vulnerability, they were far outnumbered by men whose belief appeared to function as a source of considerable vitality and direction in their lives. This was true even for men of color, who were exposed on a daily basis to the poverty, suffering, and, in their own words, the "apathy" of inner city or of reservation life. Promise Keepers conferences, moreover, were characteristically bracing in their address to men. Promise Keepers sons, in contrast to mythopoetic ones, for example, were not invited to dwell upon past wounds. Indeed, they were exhorted to "grow up" on the spot, or, in conference rhetoric, to "act like men."

Promise Keepers, in short, took strategies employed by black cultural nationalists, white Radical Faeries, white profeminists, and mythopoetics and blended them with a version of the well-established and culturally powerful belief system of evangelical Christianity, in which mothering was transposed onto divine male figures. In so doing, Promise Keepers raised male romance to a powerful new level, appearing to provide men, indeed, with the miraculous intervention in and conversion of masculinity that Hollywood had weakly fantasized in the 1990s and with the second birth that Bly hoped to accomplish through fairy tales and poetry. It was not just the provision of a sometimes mythic leadership or the erasure of women from the public sphere but also the cultural power of Promise Keepers' belief system, as well as the born-again masculinity on which Promise Keepers went to work, that helped explain its apparent efficacy in transforming men's ideals of masculinity and even their attitudes and behaviors with respect to women in the domestic sphere.

FROM HOMO ECONOMICUS TO THE GODLY FAMILY MAN

Although Promise Keepers was often assumed to be the most conservative articulation of fatherhood on the contemporary scene, it both accepted and revised the father scripts of the past, sometimes attending to problems that more liberal versions of the "new father" had not anticipated or taken on. In 1995, for example, the year I first began attending conferences, some Promise Keepers speakers followed the mythopoetic movement's lead in calling on men to mourn the loss of their fathers, to vent grief, and in so doing to become the healed healers of society. A far more dominant father discourse in 1995 and 1996 conferences, however, was the centrist emphasis of Popenoe and Blankenhorn on "fatherlessness." In Los Angeles in 1996, the white minister Joseph Stowell, citing Popenoe, repeated the familiar argument that fatherlessness is to blame for crime, premarital sex, depression in women, and children in poverty. In Fresno in 1998, the year of the Clinton/Lewinsky scandal and the year in which Hawaii considered, and eventually passed, a constitutional amendment against same-sex marriage, the African-American minister George McKinney offered a reprise of the same theme. He called on Promise Keepers fathers to enter "a holy war against evil"—the evil being a "major attack on families," whereby the meaning of family was "perverted," marriage was mocked, and promiscuity and lying became a way of life.[50]

Promise Keepers, however, in contrast to the author of *Fatherless America,* whose non-transformative philosophy was that we would do best to "incorporate men as they [were] into family life," called its men to the hard work of masculine transformation. Thus, while assuming economic provision as a taken-for-granted form of paternal activity and while evoking an essential, God-determined plan for being a godly dad, Promise Keepers gave a good deal of emphasis to reducing men's investment in career and to expanding their capacity for fatherly, as well as husbandly, nurturing and love. "Get off the fast track," the white counselor Ken Canfield urged Promise Keepers in 1995, "get on the father track."[51] In Los Angeles in 1996, Stowell admonished men for giving their "hearts" to their careers when "heart" was the "provision kids want from us." Kids want a father's "time" and "attention."[52] In Los Angeles the following year the Latino preacher Isaac Canales evoked the image of children asking, "When are you going to be part of our lives?"[53] In Promise Keepers, Homo Economicus gave way to the godly father and family man.

Where *Fatherless America* rejected the "new father" as feminized, Promise Keepers generally embraced something very like the new dad. Promise Keeper fathers were regularly urged to stop judging and give mercy, to hug and kiss their children, to say "I love you," to ask forgiveness, and to follow Jesus in giving their children unconditional love.[54] The Los Angeles conference in 1996, while a high point in this regard, was nonetheless typical. After Stowell's talk on the importance of fatherly time, attention, and love, Promise Keepers sons were brought into the stadium en masse (they had been attending their own break-out groups) and urged to run toward the platform in a great stream while Promise Keeper men were asked to stand and to repeat the following phrases over and over in a loud roar: "You have our hearts"; "We are proud of you"; "We have been wrong"; "We repent for not having given your our hearts"; "We love you"; "You will never be alone"; "We will stand by your side." It was a moment of such intensity that it brought tears to the eyes not just of participants but of mainstream media men as well.

Promise Keepers also seemed far more relaxed about gender roles in parenting than did the ostensibly centrist *Fatherless America*, which maintained that fathers had a specific and gendered contribution to make to their children, in early childhood in particular. Cooper, in contrast, juxtaposed "the *motherly man*—showing tenderness and compassion when someone is hurt"—to the "*fatherly man*—showing strength and setting boundaries when needed," but then called upon men to be both. Blending the New Testament with the values of an East African tribe, Cooper cited Paul's letter to the Thessalonians: "We were gentle among you, like a mother caring for her little children." He also cited Walter Trobisch's *All a Man Can Be* on a carving by the Kiga tribe: "The carving is a symbol of the God who takes care of human beings with the tender care of a mother."[55]

Promise Keepers subtly guided its men to make the transfer from child to wife that scholars of generative fathering had hoped to see. Canales, for example, in Los Angeles in 1997, spoke of the greater humility with which men were to take on in relation to their families: The Lord has called them to "get down on [their] knees and shine Jesus' shoes." Humility with respect to Jesus became, in turn, humility with respect to one's children, as Canales described having apologized to his son after punishing him harder than he deserved. Humility toward one's children, in turn, became a capacity for acknowledging fault in front of wives: "Let's not go back home as fools. . . . Let's not go back home and say 'I'm back!' It's going to take something more. . . . We might have to go back home and apologize for being jerks."[56] Promise Keepers, however, put caring for wives before caring for children and urged men to bring home those little presents—a red rose in Stockton in 1999—which the wives of some new fathers had felt they missed.

Following the emphases of Afrocentric writing on fatherhood and the emphases of those who espoused the "generative" dad, Promise Keepers also embraced shared child care as central to fatherhood. Child care, for example, was included in what Promise Keepers were admonished to regard as their "second job," and nine of the twelve white men I interviewed most at length shared child care to some degree. Of the men of color who reported having children, all five reported doing child care. Another five men were involved in mentoring projects with boys who were not blood related. Promise Keepers men, however, did not split child care fifty-fifty and were under no illusion that they did.

After having had children, and long before Promise Keepers arrived on the scene, the majority of white Promise Keepers wives had opted to work less than full-time to be home with the children. Child-care arrangements, moreover, sounded similar to those of many men who "help" with child care rather than taking a full share.[57] Matthew, for example, did a traditional 75 percent of the disciplining, listened to the children as they practiced their music lessons, and drove them to sporting events. John bathed the children, and he and his wife split putting them to bed. On weekends, they divided the child care between them. Mark, who had a highly paid, full-time working wife, seriously considered staying home with their first child, but he, like many men, did not do so in the end.[58]

STAGING THE NATION

As with black cultural nationalisms and the "good [enough] family man," Promise Keepers also made fathering the basis on which men were invited to lay claim to leadership and indeed possession of the public sphere. It was men who had a generational sense, according to Ken Canfield, "men who must guide, shape, and direct the next generation."[59] In identifying men as the leaders and protectors of the next generation, of course, Promise Keepers conferences affirmed long traditions of American national manhood that had symbolically tied the founding of the nation to male protection and that had implicitly identified the citizen as male, but not simply male—rather, a property-holding, heterosexual, familied, and white one. Vietnam, however, and the emergence of identity politics, with its celebration of race, gender, and sexual difference and with its demands for expanded citizenship, too, undermined the easy equation of U.S. citizens with white male protectors as they undermined automatic support for national missions in which white elite men were in control. Postmodern conceptions of identity as fluid and multiple, moreover, had raised questions about the very notion of *a* model citizen or national mission or even one national identity. Much of Promise Keepers' cultural resonance, I would suggest, stemmed from its development of a national identity that emblematically resolved some of the tensions between the abstract figure of the (implicitly white, male) citizen and the economic, social, and cultural limitations of its applications to, in this case, straight, nonwhite men.

In casting men, a.k.a. citizens, as fathers of families rather than as economically competitive individuals, for example, Promise Keepers deemphasized the unfriendly and unequal relations of the marketplace. In shifting the focus of men's attention to a site of officially collective and harmonious relations, the family, Promise Keepers also directed their attention away from such conflict-laden and racially divisive developments as, for example, the backlash against affirmative action on the part of "angry, white males." Home, after all, was a place in which all Promise Keepers participants were invited to be loving fathers and to feel equal with all other right-thinking men (no matter how compromised by real arrangements Promise Keepers' affirmation of men's leadership might be).

The family, moreover, was presumed to be private, natural, and God-given and to operate separately from economic and political affairs. Thus, all (implicitly) heterosexual men, regardless of economic and social location, might be alike in being good family men. Since Promise Keepers was surely the only organization in the 1990s in which literally millions of white, middle-class men were regularly instructed by men of color about how to be good fathers, citizenship became a cross-race and, implicitly, cross-class affair.

Because family units have historically served men of color as a means of survival and protection in a racist world, Promise Keepers' family-man rhetoric was understandably appealing to them on this level as well. The Nation of Islam and other black nationalisms, indeed, spoke a similar language. Men were leaders of family first, then leaders of community. Although Promise Keepers' message to men of color—"Christ, not culture"—directly challenged nationalist priorities such as separatism and Afrocentricity, Promise Keepers also rivaled cultural nationalisms in positing an imagined nation in which men of color were citizens, too. Thus, in grounding masculinity in family rather than career, in affirming men's equal role as fathers in the home, and in casting family men as citizens and representatives of the nation, Promise Keepers constructed a new national manhood that spoke to the angry white male and to the enraged man of color both. This national manhood, however, like many others, omitted women and gay men.

NOTES

1. Rodney L. Cooper, *Double Bind: Escaping the Contradictory Demands of Manhood* (Grand Rapids, Mich.: Zondervan Publishing House, 1996), 27.
2. Richard P. Morse, "Iron Jesus: Lessons from the Mytho-Poetic Men's Movement for Christian Men. A Retreat Design Exploring Masculine Identity and Spirituality" (Doctor of Ministry, San Francisco Theological Seminary, 1993).

3. From a Promise Keepers "Fact Sheet," 21 May 1999, www.promisekeepers .org/fact.htm.

4. Promise Keepers History, www.promisekeepers.org/genr/genr12.htm (accessed 1 January 2004).

5. These figures were based on counting the speakers and board members listed in brochures (early brochures featured pictures of the speakers) and on Promise Keepers website.

6. Richard Morin and Scott Wilson, "Men Were Driven to 'Confess Their Sins,'" *Washington Post*, 5 October 1997, A1, A19.

7. Introduction, nn 2 and 3.

8. On the feminization of U.S. evangelical Protestantism in the United States, see John P. Bartkowski, "Breaking Walls, Raising Fences: Masculinity, Intimacy, and Accountability among the Promise Keepers," in *Promise Keepers and the New Masculinity: Private Lives and Public Morality*, ed. Rhys H. Williams (Lanham, Md.: Lexington Books, 2001), 44.

9. Cooper, *Double Bind*, 82.

10. Stephen Griffith and Bill Deckard, *What Makes a Man?* Study Guide (Colorado Springs, Colo.: NavPress Publishing Group, 1993), 85.

11. Cooper, *Double Bind*, 9.

12. Cooper, *Double Bind*, 10, 47.

13. Cooper, *Double Bind*, 53, 57, 48.

14. John Trent, *The Making of a Godly Man: A Guide to Help Men Live Out the Seven Promises* (Colorado Springs, Colo.: Focus on the Family Publishing, 1997), 13.

15. See Raleigh Washington and Glen Kehrein, *Break Down the Walls: Experiencing Biblical Reconciliation and Unity in the Body of Christ* (Chicago: Moody Press, 1997), 139, 146, 151; Rodney L. Cooper, *We Stand Together: Reconciling Men of Different Color* (Chicago: Moody Press, 1995).

16. Trent, *Making*, 92–93.

17. From a Promise Keepers, "Fact Sheet," www.promisekeepers.org/fact.htm (accessed 21 May 1999).

18. Edwin Louis Cole, *Real Man* (Nashville, Tenn.: Thomas Nelson, 1992), 36; Stu Weber, *Tender Warrior: God's Intention for a Man* (Sisters, Ore.: Multnomah Books, 1993). On the complexity of Promise Keepers' masculine ideals, see Bartkowski, "Breaking Down," 35–37.

19. Gary Oliver, *Real Men Have Feelings Too* (Chicago: Moody Press, 1993) 61–62, 65–66, cited in Bartkowski, "Breaking," 37.

20. Trent, *Making*, 10, 37, 38.

21. Cooper, *Double Bind*, 9, 106, 107.

22. Cooper, *Double Bind*, 37, 38.

23. Cooper, *Double Bind*, 82, 158, 132, 131.

24. Larry Christenson, *The Christian Family* (Minneapolis, Minn.: Bethany House, 1970), 44.

25. Dan Chun, address delivered at Promise Keepers Men's Conference, "Living a Legacy," Los Angeles, 22–23 May 1998.

26. John Maxwell, address delivered at Promise Keepers Men's Conference, "Making of a Godly Man," Fresno, 27–28 June 1997.

27. Gary Smalley, "The Influence of a Godly Man," address delivered at Promise Keepers Men's Conference, "The Making of a Godly Man," Seattle, 23–24 May 1997.

28. Chun, 1997.

29. Larry Jackson, "Living a Legacy on the HomeFront," address delivered at Promise Keepers Men's Conference, "Live a Legacy," Sacramento, 9–10 October 1998.

30. Wellington Boone, "Becoming a Man of God's Word," address delivered at Promise Keepers Men's Conference, "Raise the Standard," Oakland, 29–30 September 1995.

31. Chun, 1997; Jackson, 1998. According to sociologist Scott Coltrane, women performed two or three times as much housework as men nationally in 2000. Women also performed three times as much routine (cooking, cleaning) as opposed to occasional (car service, yard work) labor as men and most often assumed the manager role. Only a third of women found this division unfair, however. See "Research on Household Labor: Modeling and Measuring the Social Embeddedness of Routine Family Work," *Journal of Marriage and the Family* 62 (2000): 1208–33.

32. According to Coltrane, by the late 1990s the average co-resident father was three-fourths as available to his children as the mother was, "Fathering: Paradoxes, Contradictions, and Dilemmas," in Marilyn Coleman and Lawrence H. Ganong, eds., *Handbook of Contemporary Families: Considering the Past, Contemplating the Future* (Thousand Oaks, Calif.: Sage, 2004). See also Scott Coltrane, *Family Man: Fatherhood, Housework, and Gender Equity* (New York: Oxford University Press, 1996), 53, 54.

33. Maxwell, 1997.

34. In the accountability groups that John P. Bartkowski studied, "highly private topics," such as dilemmas with wives, children, colleagues, and friends, were discussed, and the groups were blatantly confessional and cathartic, "Breaking," 43.

35. E. Glenn Wagner with Dietrich Gruen, *Strategies for a Successful Marriage: A Study Guide for Men* (Colorado Springs, Colo.: NavPress, 1994), 51–63, 67–69, 70–71, 79.

36. I take this helpful concept from R. W. Connell, *Masculinities* (Berkeley: University of California Press, 1995), 137: "To undo masculinity is to court a loss of personality structure that may be quite terrifying: a kind of gender vertigo."

37. For studies that emphasize the diversity of Promise Keepers' interpretations of the servant/leader concept, see Rhys H. Williams, "Promise Keepers: A Comment on Religion and Social Movements," 5; Jon P. Bloch, "The New and Improved Clint Eastwood: Change and Persistence in Promise Keepers Self–Help Literature," 23; Bartkowski, "Breaking,"41; and William H. Lockhart, "'We Are One Life,' but Not of One Gender Ideology: Unity, Ambiguity, and the Promise Keepers," 85, in Williams, *Promise Keepers*.

38. Boone, 1995; Dennis Rainey, "Raising the Standard in Our Marriages," address delivered at Promise Keepers Men's Conference, "Raise the Standard," Dallas, 27–28 October 1995.

39. Tony Evans, address delivered at the Promise Keepers Stand in the Gap Assembly, Washington, D.C., 4 October 1997.

40. George McKinney, "Living a Legacy on the Homefront," address delivered at Promise Keepers Men's Conference, "Live a Legacy," Fresno, California, 5–6 June 1998); Chun, 1997.

41. McKinney, 1998.

42. Chun, 1997.

43. Dennis Rainey, "Being the Spiritual Leader of Your Home," address delivered at Promise Keepers Men's Conference, "Choose This Day," Stockton, 10–11 September 1999.

44. Wagner, *Strategies*, 59.

45. Judith Stacey made a similar argument about the servant/leadership practiced by some of the evangelical couples she interviewed in the Silicon Valley in the mid-1980s. Stacey suggested that feminist evangelical writing had had considerable impact on evangelical thinking that defined servanthood as service, emphasized loving teamwork between married couples, and called on women to yield only if the disagreement was irreconcilable. Stacey called this "patriarchy in the last instance." *Brave New Families: Stories of Domestic Upheaval in Late Twentieth Century America* (New York: Basic Books, 1990), 133, 142–143.

46. Contrast Promise Keepers' rhetoric to that of Pat Robertson: "I know this is painful for the ladies to hear, but if you get married you have accepted the headship of a man, your husband. Christ is the head of the household and the husband's head of the wife and that's just the way it is." Cited in "Feminazis versus Machonazis," *The Freedom Writer*, May 1995, ifas@crocker.com.

47. Ronald F. Levant, "Nonrelational Sexuality in Men," in *Men and Sex: New Psychological Perspectives*, ed. Ronald F. Levant and Gary R. Brooks (New York: John Wiley & Sons, 1997), 21.

48. Larry May, "A Progressive Male Standpoint," *Men Doing Feminism*, 349.

49. Rainey, 1999.

50. George McKinney, "Living a Legacy on the Homefront," address delivered at Promise Keeper Men's Conference, "Live a Legacy," Fresno, California, 5 June 1998.

51. Ken Canfield, "Raising the Standard for Our Children," address delivered at Promise Keeper Men's Conference, "Raise the Standard," Oakland, 30 September 1995.

52. Stowell, "Turning Your Heart," 1996.

53. Isaac Canales, "The Influence of a Godly Man," address delivered at Promise Keeper Men's Conference, "The Making of a Godly Man," Los Angeles, 23 May 1997.

54. John Trent, "Turning Your Heart toward Your Children," address delivered at Promise Keeper Men's Conference, "Break Down the Walls," Oakland, 29 June 1996; Gary Smalley, "The Influence of a Godly Man," address delivered at Promise Keeper Men's Conference, "The Making of a Godly Man," Seattle, 1997; Stowell, "Turning Your Heart," 1996; Canales, "The Influence," 1997.

55. Cooper, *Double Bind*, 129.

56. Canales, "Influence."

57. According to Coltrane, fathers share less of the "responsibility for the planning, scheduling, emotional management, housework, and other maintenance activities associated with raising children," "Fathering," 6.

58. See Coltrane, *Family Man*, 75.

59. Canfield, "Raising the Standard."

9

Beyond a Focus on the Family

Love Work as Race Reconciliation

Because most people ask, "What's the bottom line, what's the minimum I have to put out to achieve reconciliation?" we believe marriage is a realistic analogy. Commitment and hard work, crucial to marital success, are essential for solid personal relationships with members of other races.

—Raleigh Washington and Glen Kehrein, *Breaking Down Walls*[1]

BEYOND A FOCUS ON THE FAMILY

So much critical attention in the 1990s was focused on the gender politics of the Promise Keepers and its relation to the politically organized religious right that Promise Keepers' most original contribution to contemporary culture was all but overlooked. Promise Keepers was redefining conservative Christian masculinity so as to make antiracism a defining feature of being a "godly man." The identification of manhood with an antiracist stance was not new to black religious and political traditions, from which the mixed-race leadership of Promise Keepers certainly borrowed. Resistance to slavery, for example, was firmly identified in black abolitionist writing with being "a man." The civil rights movement, the Black Panthers, and 1970s black cultural nationalisms, as well, linked manhood to antiracist struggle. Similar definitions of manhood have been entertained by white abolitionists and other progressive men, both secular and religious, throughout much of U.S. history.

Promise Keepers, however, was the only contemporary men's organization to call on hundreds of thousands of 61 percent conservative, largely white, heterosexual, middle-class men to embrace antiracism as a central feature of a masculine ideal. Whatever legitimate criticisms might be made of the gender and sexual politics that complicated this progressive move, it represented a stunning intervention into dominant cultural notions of what it meant to be a "man" in U.S. terms. Promise Keepers' antiracist manhood, of course, was a pointed reversal of white supremacist definitions of masculinity that had been a consistent feature of the extreme religious right, but it also presented an alternative to the more subtly racist masculinities exhibited by spokesmen for a range of political positions, who felt free to scapegoat inner-city men of color as the source of the nation's ills. Promise Keepers' antiracist manhood, indeed, in coupling manhood with taking an active stand against men's own racist attitudes and behaviors, represented an intervention into everyday performances of masculinities as well. No other white-dominated organization that I know made antiracism so central to masculine ideals while managing to sustain a large mass base.

That Promise Keepers took the considerable risk of asking its white, mainly conservative, clientele to take this project on (and many white Promise Keepers proved resistant) owed much to the passion of its leaders in relation to this issue. Bill McCartney, for example, the founder and once president of Promise Keepers and former football coach for the University of Colorado, worked in the cross-race area of college football, recruited heavily in poor minority areas, and became grandfather to two interracial grandchildren born of his daughters' relationships with former Colorado football players. All were important factors in his commitment to racial issues. Indeed, the three high-placed staff I interviewed at length testified to McCartney's passion about continuing this racial work. "He will never let it die," one staffer proclaimed to me.

McCartney's persistence was all the more impressive given the hostile responses that Promise Keepers' race reconciliation project consistently evoked. Many white participants registered resistance to Promise Keepers' racial reconciliation project in letters of protest to the organization. Indeed, "hate mail and caustic letters" attended the race reconciliation project almost from the beginning. McCartney, for example, ended the initial Promise Keepers's conference in Boulder, Colorado, on July 31, 1991, by telling the four thousand mainly white participants: "Men . . . next year . . . we expect a sell out. But I believe if we fail to gather a fair representation of *all* of God's people, God will not join us." To this, one early letter writer was to sputter, "God did not state in scriptures, 'Go ye therefore and eradicate racism.'"[2]

The anger expressed by some white Promise Keepers toward the reconciliation project, or toward some of its harder-hitting rhetoric, was not difficult, of course, to understand. Most of Promise Keepers' conservative white participants, prior to attending a Promise Keepers conference, had little history of hearing that a stand against racism was a defining element of what it meant to be a man. Men of color had their issues, too. If for participants of color it was not new to hear that "being a man" entailed an antiracist stance, many testified that it *was* unusual to be asked to atone for their racism toward each other or for bitterness toward whites. As Dwight, an African-American man living in Southern California, put it, "Blacks don't criticize themselves." There was good reason, then, why Promise Keepers conferences generally took their participants through a series of sessions involving acknowledgment of fault, expressions of remorse, and dedication to and exercises in the practice of new attitudes and behaviors within the family, where feelings of love, remorse, and longing for connection were easier to tap, before introducing the sessions on race.

The success of Promise Keepers conferences in getting participants to imagine themselves as potentially better men at home had much to do with the organization's ability to get hundreds of thousands of men to pay sixty dollars a conference, year after year, for a stern lecture on the need for biracial brotherly love. The psychology here was very much like the psychology embraced by many profeminist men, who asserted (with some reason) that men who were invited to feel good about themselves as men were more likely to take on political missions involving self-sacrifice than those who felt dismissed as oppressive or even angry white males or as enraged and irresponsible men of color.

Of course reenchanting masculinity in the home ran the considerable risk of merely affirming men's sense that they were now fine, thank you, and could otherwise continue as they were, but this was not the avenue along which Promise Keepers attempted to lead its participants. Indeed, Promise Keepers' most original contribution to contemporary culture lay in its attempts to move participants, through a "focus on the family," through contemporary fixations on the role of fathers in salvaging the nation, and through its own attempts to reinvent the husband, toward a wider-ranging conception of social good. Promise Keepers' originality lay in its attempts to expand domestic "love work" into an antiracist project.

As happens with any organization, Promise Keepers' articulation of its project changed over time. From 1995 on, for example, when I first began attending Promise Keepers stadium events, conferences were marked by highly orchestrated emphases on embracing difference. Thus, conferences characteristically included black and Latino music, bilingual prayers, videos of men in mixed-race situations and relations, a generous representation of blacks, Latinos, Asian-Americans and some Native Americans among the speakers (of six speakers in Los Angeles in 1996, only two were white), and variations of the Promise Keepers logo of three hands or three bodies—white, brown, and black. All of these created ritual space in which the Christian and national community looked and sounded cross-racial. (Attendance by men of color, according to Promise Keepers' records, has varied from 6 percent to 14 percent at the Stand in the Gap Assembly to a reported 25 percent at a conference in Los Angeles, although critics of Promise Keepers are skeptical.[3]) The sports arena setting, moreover, in which men typically did enter a cross-racial community and root for mixed-race teams, reinforced the message. Men of color were citizens. They also represented the nation.

The Promise Keepers conferences I attended in 1995 staged racial difference chiefly as a matter of skin color and cultural variation. Conference patter about cultural difference leaned heavily toward metaphors of culinary or linguistic exploration—sampling tacos, for example, saying the Lord's Prayer in Spanish, wondering whether Moses gave Aaron a high five. Racism was defined as a matter of attitude, by and large, rather than as structural inequality. As attitude, its resolution could be imagined as individual and then ritually performed. In Oakland, where there were enough men of color in attendance to make this feasible, attendees were urged to cross the aisles, embrace a man of a different race, and to repeat the words, "I have failed you; things are going to be different." The moment was moving and impressive, but the assumed mutuality of racism symbolically canceled out the structural inequalities of race and white domination.

In 1996, however, in a significant discursive shift—owing in large part, I believe, to the greater influence of men of color in the Promise Keepers leadership—the racial mission of Promise Keepers was somewhat differently defined. If in 1995, for example, Promise Keepers men were invited to an unrealistic *mutual* forgiveness, in 1996 white brothers were forgiven and then urged to give up privilege for the sake of racial justice. "Give it up," the African-American minister Raleigh Washington urged white listeners in Los Angeles that year. "Give it up so the walls may come down." In a particularly striking segment of the program, a mixed-race group of ministers and Christian counselors prayed, one by one, for forgiveness of themselves and implicitly of their ethnicity or race. Men of their own ethnic or racial group were urged to stand when the prayer touched something in their heart.

The white president of Promise Keepers, then Randy Phillips, prayed for what seemed to be ten or fifteen minutes to be forgiven for the sin of apathy and distance. He prayed to be forgiven for the sin of failing to see how his advantages were the product of historical racism and how the sins of the fathers had become "economic benefit" for whites. He prayed to be forgiven for neglecting the inner city and for participating "in political power which was harmful to brothers of color." He prayed to be forgiven for seeing racism in spiritual terms only and for being patronizing to men of color. He prayed,

"Don't let my culture dictate my heart." White men rose, but rather slowly it seemed to me, confirming Phillips's earlier observation that the Promise Keepers' emphasis on race had been vigorously resisted among some white conference participants.

Race reconciliation, moreover, went beyond the usual black-and-white division and evoked self-criticism on the part of men of color, too, for bitterness toward whites but also, this time, for crimes against each other. Wellington Boone significantly did *not* pray for black forgiveness but, after duly forgiving Phillips and, implicitly white men as a whole, called for another great awakening. Like the Pentecostal Azusa Street revival, which began with a mixed-race congregation in Los Angeles almost a century ago, the next revival movement, racial reconciliation, with its beginning there in the Coliseum of South Central Los Angeles, would sweep the nation. It was no accident, of course, that Promise Keepers' first conference in 1996 was scheduled for the same month and housed near the site of the Los Angeles uprising four years before. Finally, as a practical means of "breaking the back of racism," conference participants were urged to enter into a "committed relation" with a man of another race/ethnicity and to attend the next year's Stand in the Gap Assembly together.

The 1996 conference in Los Angeles, in particular, according to one member of the Promise Keepers Board, produced a torrent of letters from white Promise Keepers complaining of being made to feel guilty, of being hit on the head, of not knowing what to do. "We've said we're sorry," one letter opined. More than one member of the Promise Keepers Board speculated that the declining attendance at stadium events in 1997 had been a result of white disenchantment. Although an alternative explanation of that decline was that participants had saved up their time and money to attend the Stand in the Gap Assembly, attendance at Promise Keepers events remained at less than half its 1966 high of just over one million in the years that followed. White resistance, moreover, was ongoing. One spokesman told me in 1998 that several clergy who attempted to instigate race reconciliation in their churches after having attended a Promise Keepers Clergy Conference were subsequently fired. He also reported that potential corporate sponsors offered to help fund the Promise Keepers organization on the condition that it drop the racial reconciliation effort. To their credit, the Promise Keepers board was not deterred. As one staff member put it, race reconciliation was "part of Promise Keepers' DNA." In 1998, however, it appeared that the rhetoric of racial reconciliation had been fine tuned. In Sacramento that year, the session on race focused almost entirely on entering into committed relations with men of other races or ethnicities and on the steps required. Another change was that race sessions across the nation were entrusted to fewer speakers than before. Whereas talks on family, for example, were farmed out to sixteen different speakers in the nineteen stadium events that year, five of the talks on race were delivered by Raleigh Washington, then Promise Keepers' vice president for reconciliation, whose oft-repeated motto was "No guilt, just understanding." (The African-American minister Bishop Porter, then head of the Promise Keepers board, also delivered one of the talks on race.)

In Sacramento in 1998, for example, Washington drew upon a 1994 book, *Breaking Down Walls,* which he had coauthored with the white minister Glen Kehrein, to make an explicit statement about what had already been implicit in the structure of Promise Keepers conferences since 1995: The love work that Promise Keepers had called on men to perform in domestic settings was the same work required for relations of racial reconciliation. In a wonderfully crafted talk that began and ended with anecdotes about love across race lines—one about Washington's own mixed-race family and the other about a white friend of Washington's in the racially divided social world of the civil rights era—Raleigh delivered the basic Promise Keepers message on race: "Love has everything to do with it." A committed cross-race relation, Raleigh implied, was like a marriage. It required hard work, and "divorce [was] not an option."

Although sessions on race often produced the most powerful sermonizing at Promise Keepers conferences—and many of these men could really preach!—conference sermons and exercises in hugging, praying, expressing regret, asking forgiveness, and promising to change were just a prelude to the emotion work that Promise Keepers were encouraged to engage in at home. As with marriage, the Promise Keepers organization, with its usual attention to detail, developed workbooks that guided accountability groups in dealing with race reconciliation. The most thoroughgoing of these workbooks was also written by Washington and Kehrein and was based on their *Breaking Down Walls.* Here, they repeated their eight guidelines for entering into a committed relation with a man of another race/ethnicity: being called to reconciliation, entering into a committed relation, practicing intentionality and sincerity, learning sensitivity, and taking on sacrifice, empowerment, and interdependence.[4]

Each section began with a pertinent anecdote about race relations. Then the principle was broken down into parts that included scripture readings, prayers, explanations, and questions to answer. At the end of the book there were guidelines for group leaders, suggestions for books and videos on race—including such classics as *Yo Soy Chicano, Eyes on the Prize,* and *Bury My Heart at Wounded Knee,* as well as a 1991 University of Illinois publication, described as "secular and technical," *The Anti-Chinese Movement in California.* There were also short "sensitivity building" sections on how to communicate with different racial groups and a series of lists suggesting further actions that individuals, groups, churches, and communities might undertake. The latter run the gamut from asking someone of another race or ethnicity to dinner, to entering into a committed relation, to going on city prayer walks, developing ethnic leadership for churches in changing neighborhoods, submitting to minority leadership if white, including different worship styles, and meeting the needs of the community in relation to hunger and oppression by volunteering for inner-city ministries.[5]

THE POLITICS OF RECONCILIATION

"Reconciliation" as an evangelical Christian concept was usually derived from St. Paul's letters to the Corinthians, in which he reminded Christians that "all things are of God, who hath reconciled us to himself by Jesus Christ, and hath given to us the ministry of reconciliation."[6] Reconciliation in this passage had been interpreted to mean including all groups regardless of race, nationality, ethnicity, class, religious tradition or status within the church. As such, it had been read as a statement about evangelism and relations within evangelical Christian circles. In this sense, reconciliation had been a feature of some evangelical Christian practice throughout much of the twentieth century.

Racial reconciliation, for example, was a central feature of the 1906 Azusa Street revival that was often said to have begun the Pentecostal movement. Centered in Los Angeles and led by a black minister, William J. Seymour, and a mixed-race leadership, the interracial congregation embraced, wept, and prayed together, believing that "the dissolution of racial barriers was the surest sign of the Spirit's Pentecostal presence." Ultimately, the Azusa Street revival was dissolved, in the face of white resistance to interracial fellowship, and a rival, predominantly white Pentecostal denomination, Assemblies of God, was formed.[7] The Church of God in Christ, however, which became the largest black Pentecostal denomination, continued to emphasize race reconciliation, "creating a new community in Christian brotherhood" as the "surest mark of divine power" and often combined this emphasis with ministry to the poor. Aimee Semple McPherson, founder of the International Church of the Foursquare Gospel and the most famous of the Pentecostal leaders in the 1920s and 1930s, continued the tradition of racial reconciliation, as do some forms of Pentecostalism worldwide today.[8]

Reconciliation, however, had also been interpreted more broadly to mean that Christians were called upon to fight racism outside the church as well. Cecil "Chip" Murray, the African-American senior pastor at the First African

Methodist Episcopal Church of Los Angeles, used this wider interpretation in a 1993 interview with *Christianity Today*: "Calling sinners to repentance means also calling societies and structures to repentance—economic, social, educational, corporate, political, religious structures."[9] It was this broader understanding of reconciliation that entered into some post-sixties evangelical activism, as some evangelicals who had participated in the civil rights movement or had been touched by it sought out ways to "live their faith" in relation to issues of racism and economic justice.

The African-American minister John M. Perkins was central to this development. In the early 1960s Perkins began a form of "holistic ministry" in Mendenhall, Mississippi, that combined efforts at "winning black folks to Jesus" with efforts to improve their economic situation. Perkins joined the civil rights movement "with a vengeance" and was almost beaten to death in a Mississippi jail cell. While in jail, he made a bargain with God that if he survived he "would preach a gospel that could reconcile black and white," and that is what he went on to do. Perkins's ministry emphasized three principles: "relocation," or intentional living among the poor, which was seen as vital to creating personal stakes in the development of poor neighborhoods; "reconciliation," or using love to break through racial, ethnic, and economic barriers; and "redistribution," or addressing issues of "social action and economic development." The last of these principles called for using one's skills and resources to empower poor communities by ministering to their "felt needs" and working with them to create jobs, schools, health centers, and legal clinics and to promote home ownership and economic development.[10]

In the 1970s, Perkins planted a similar effort in Jackson, Mississippi, which, with help from Billy Graham's crusade, became the Voice of Calvary Ministries. Perkins then established the Christian Community Development Association (CCDA) as an umbrella for a series of grassroots efforts that, inspired by Mendenhall, combined evangelical ministry with community outreach and development and a struggle against institutionalized racism. In 1994 there were 180 churches and ministries in the CCDA network.[11] By the early 1980s, however, cultural and racial divisions had emerged in Jackson, and the interracial Voice of Calvary Fellowship began a series of meetings to address these splits. The meetings were painful, and many parishioners left the fellowship altogether, but Perkins felt that the exercise in talking problems through had "solidified the purpose of the work in Mississippi."[12] From that time forward, intentional efforts to air feelings and establish solid, personal relationships became a part of the reconciliation mix.

It was Perkins who inspired Glen Kehrein, a young white minister—"too theologically conservative to be a liberal, too socially liberal to be a conservative" —to enter into inner-city outreach work for Circle Church, a cross-racial church on Chicago's Westside in 1971. When the biracial Circle Church ministry dissolved in cultural conflict and racial tension in 1976, Kehrein, too, became convinced "that racial reconciliation among Christians requires solid relationships" and that without "solid, committed relationships building the vision was more like building on sand."[13]

Thus, when Kehrein and Washington began their own cross-race collaboration, combining a "spiritual and a social ministry" in 1984, they also developed strategies for creating committed interracial relationships. These were to encourage racial understanding and acceptance, but they were also seen as necessary foundations for sustaining the very work of interracial ministry and community outreach and development.[14] Kehrein and Washington themselves, for example, began to hold regular "conflict-resolving 'summits'" at the local Pancake House once a month and found that confronting each other and expressing disagreements was crucial to their work and to taming the "knee-jerk reaction to cut and run."[15] Washington and Kehrein then extended this practice to their mixed-race congregation (70 percent black and 30 percent white) through a strategy called "fudge ripple Sundays." On these Sundays, four times a year, black and white parishioners met separately to talk out issues. They were then brought together for a two-hour meeting in which they reported back from their groups, aired grievances, and tried to resolve conflicts. The goal was to prevent blowups before they happened, and the expectation was that there would be pain. Fudge ripple ice cream and Oreos were served to sweeten the proceedings and to represent the racial reconciliation goal.[16]

Perkins, Kehrein, and Washington, along with several other men involved in CCDA—Noel Castellano, Charles Blake, and Edward Spees, to name three—have been on the Promise Keepers list of conference speakers. Washington, as I have noted, was the Promise Keepers vice president for reconciliation and then executive vice president for global ministries. These men, in turn, were part of a still larger network of spiritually based social activists who attempted to live their faith by serving the inner city. At one end of the spectrum this network included members of the all-male Promise Keepers, who maintained conservative positions on abortion and homosexuality. On the other end it included ecumenical, cross-gender groups such as the Christian Call to Renewal, which identified itself as beyond left and right but stood for an end to poverty, for an end to white domination, for gender equality, and for gay civil rights.[17] The lines, moreover, were not so neatly drawn as one might suppose. Some members of the progressive Call—much to my initial astonishment—identified as feminists and Promise Keepers both, while a high-placed member of Promise Keepers staff expressed keen interest in forging official ties with the Call.

A more recent wave of racial reconciliation emerged in mainstream evangelical circles after the Los Angeles uprising of 1992 and after the 1993 publication of a hard-hitting book, *The Coming Race Wars? A Cry for Reconciliation,* written by William Pannell, an African-American professor of preaching and practical theology at Fuller Theological Seminar in Pasadena. The book angrily documented the continuing racism and economic oppression of inner-city blacks—most particularly black men, although Pannell saw sexism as a sin and apologized for his gender-exclusive focus. The book's message was that "we're going to have to take some rather courageous and extraordinary steps to avoid race war. The first step is sincere repentance of racism."[18]

If the city had any hope, Pannell believed, it lay with the church: "It is not that the future of the city depends solely on the church, but rather the glue that holds so much of the city together, certainly in black communities, is the church." Calling for inner-city coalitions of Protestants, Catholics, and Jews, Pannell also called for a revival of specifically Christian and evangelical efforts to make reconciliation the "well spring for evangelistic effort and social activism." For Pannell one key to this effort was the hard work of building personal relationships, which required "confrontation, getting beyond mere words to true feelings and attitudes." Such work, he argued, "must become the preoccupation for the church's leadership. Unless it does, the church will be mute before the ravages of ongoing racial and ethnic animosity." Pannell, it should be noted, vigorously chastised white, evangelical churches for fleeing the city and taking refuge in gated communities and suburbs. "Free at last!" he quipped.[19]

Pannell's book was not well received in *Christianity Today*—Pannell had suggested in *The Coming Race War* that the journal be renamed *Suburban Christianity Today.* African-American evangelical leaders, however, praised the book as "prophetic," "courageous," "insightful," and "powerful."[20] This may have prompted the journal to commission a piece by Andres Tapia, who interviewed forty-one African-American and largely evangelical leaders about what they wanted their white evangelical brothers and sisters to hear. Called "The Myth of Racial Progress" and featuring black religious leaders from a spectrum of political positions, Tapia's essay conveyed a wealth of black anger at white "dominance and arrogance" as well as at betrayal and rejection.[21]

Cheryl J. Sanders, for example, associate professor of Christian ethics at Howard University and associate pastor of leadership development at Third Street Church of God, Washington, D.C., remarked, "If we were practicing reconciliation, affirmative action, and level playing fields in our churches it would challenge our society's dominant racist values and would give Christians something to preach to others." Spencer Perkins, son of John Perkins and editor of *Urban Family Magazine,* also warned whites that "black Christians are no more interested in working toward racial reconciliation than white Christians. Blacks are interested in eliminating racial injustice, in confronting racism and ensuring that the playing field is level."[22]

Clearly, Pannell's book did become an occasion for dialogue about racism among evangelicals, as Tapia had hoped it would do in his own review of the book for *Christian Century.* In 1994 and 1995, for example, one after another mainstream evangelical organization apologized publicly for its racism and embraced "racial reconciliation" as a project. These moves, of course, may also have been inspired, and/or provoked, by Promise Keepers' highly publicized mass-based work on race reconciliation, which had begun in 1991. Thus, in October of 1994 the all-white Pentecostal Fellowship of North America disbanded and formed a new multiethnic organization, the Pentecostal Charismatic Churches of North America, with an African-American minister, Bishop Ithiel Clemmons of the predominantly black Church of God in Christ as its elected head.[23] In 1995 the National Association of Evangelicals devoted part of its annual convention to challenging members on racial issues, and in June of that same year the Southern Baptist convention (historically white until the civil rights era) officially apologized to African-Americans for "condoning and/or perpetuating individual and systemic racism in our lifetime," and stated, "We genuinely repent of racism of which we have been guilty, whether consciously or unconsciously."[24]

This embrace of racial reconciliation by a cross-section of white evangelical churches, had impact on more secular circles as well. In January of 1997, for example, the conservative and overtly politicized Christian Coalition launched its own "Samaritan Project" that included proposals for economic empowerment zones, scholarship programs for low-income children, and a $500 tax credit for those who donated time and money to poverty-fighting organizations. Ralph Reed, invoking Martin Luther King, vowed to make race reconciliation "the center piece of [the Christian Coalition's] agenda."[25] Six months later President Clinton announced his own year-long initiative on race relations and "racial healing," and four days after that Newt Gingrich sketched out his ten-point program to promote racial healing and black achievement.[26] The latter included a curious statement to the effect that "obsessing on race will not allow us to move beyond race" and an even stranger strategy for encouraging black achievement by ending all "Federal affirmative action programs that give any kind of preference on the basis of race, sex, or national origin."[27] Clearly, racial reconciliation projects were allied with very disparate political objectives.

THE LIMITS OF RECONCILIATION

Although no one attending Promise Keepers conferences for very long could question the passion and sincerity of the racially mixed speakers when they spoke of wanting racial reconciliation, the meanings and possible effects of its work must be weighed within contexts and relationships of power that intentions, no matter how worthy or passionate, do not control. Critical and sympathetic observers of the Religious Right, for example, frequently noted that black and Latino communities were a potential source of moral and political alliance for conservative white evangelicals. A higher percentage of evangelicals were found among blacks than among whites, and a substantial percentage of black evangelicals classified themselves as "conservatives."[28] Some black clergy, like Pannell himself, were socially liberal on race but adopted antigay positions.

White evangelicals leaders, moreover, stressed this mobilizing potential. The biggest failure of the Religious Right, according to Richard D. Land, director of the Christian Life Commission of the Southern Baptist Church in 1993, lay in its failure to reach out to African-Americans and Hispanics: "It seems to me that we share with African American churches and with Hispanic culture a lot of common ground on what we would call traditional-values issues. This outreach should be one of the highest priorities of evangelicals in the last decade of the twentieth century."[29]

The embrace of racial reconciliation by the right-wing Christian Coalition, with its history of supporting tax relief for the rich and cutbacks for the poor, also raised the possibility that racial reconciliation could become still another way of courting voters of color for the Right or a means of convincing swing voters that conservative social and economic policies were not racist.[30] Ralph Reed himself noted that the racial record of the Christian Right could hamper its fight against abortion and out-of-wedlock births. After the election results of November 1998, moreover, in which black voters helped elect three Democratic southern governors, increased Republican efforts to woo black and other voters of color were certainly on the agenda.

On another front, the rapid growth of Islam raised fears among many Christians, whites, and conservatives that it could become the dominant religion in U.S. urban areas by 2020. The events of September 11, 2001, of course, have consolidated an already existing tendency in the United States to identify Muslims as terrorists and has cast an even more sinister light, from nationalist perspectives, upon the growth of Islam in inner cities. Certainly one function of race reconciliation was to keep black men, in particular, within the Christian fold—a fold still dominated by whites and white-centered in its understanding of race relations and racial progress. Moreover, the resemblance of some Promise Keepers rhetoric to that of the Nation of Islam, with its emphasis upon male leadership and pride, gave Promise Keepers a crucial role to play.[31]

Other critics, taking note of the massive networks that Promise Keepers helped to build, feared that Promise Keepers' emphasis upon racial and denominational reconciliation would simply serve to mobilize more men for the purposes of global Christianizing goals. The 1999 conference at Stockton, for example, did little to put the latter anxieties to rest, seeming more intensely focused on "revival" and on massive conversions than any of the other seven conferences I have attended. Even for someone like myself, who was an evangelical in her youth, the multiple references to the anarchy of the present day, the fear that Christians would "have no voice," the repeated theme of "bold leadership," and the call both to "hear" and to "obey" were deeply unsettling in current contexts, when many leaders of, and candidates for, the politically organized Religious Right did indeed support the notion that only Christians should make policy and lead the nation.[32]

Promise Keepers' antiracist work, moreover, while it drew upon traditions of socially liberal racial reconciliation efforts, focused upon that part of racial reconciliation that called for entering a committed relation with men of different race/ethnicities. Despite the Los Angeles conference in 1996, Promise Keepers conferences did not consistently embrace a need for structural change. Although seeing oppressed others as persons whom one cares for was crucial in the abolitionist and civil rights movements, if sympathy is not coupled with a social vision that criticizes structures of oppression and gives value to changing them, committed relation work could function much as corporate efforts to ensure harmonious diversity in the workplace do. That is, such efforts might reconcile individuals to each other while hiding from view the very real structural inequalities that sustain institutionalized racism and create ongoing bitterness and despair. This was why overtly progressive faith groups like the Call to Renewal emphasized the phrase "no reconciliation without justice."

Untoward racial consequences might be accompanied by regressive consequences with respect to sexuality and gender. Although Promise Keepers' "love the sinner" rhetoric with respect to gays was less harsh than the "condemn the sinner" rhetoric of many leaders on the Religious Right, such as Falwell and Robertson, Promise Keepers had yet to follow more liberal evangelicals, such as those in the Call to Renewal, in extending love for the "sinner" to endorsing gay civil rights. This rhetoric inevitably contributed to a climate in which discrimination and violence against gays were flourishing.[33] In laying claim to leadership of the antiracist struggle, a cross-race male community, despite the nobility of its purpose, could also strengthen the exclusion of women from citizenship and render gender inequality even less visible as an issue that should engage male hearts and minds.

From a distance, at least, Promise Keepers' race reconciliation project might also evoke what Robyn Weigman described as a central U.S. drama: the bonding of a white man with a man of color and their romantic flight from civilization into each other's arms. As Weigman argued, the negative possibilities of this narrative were multiple. In such narratives the man of color might function largely to assist in the white man's redemption and rebirth or the cross-racial pair might bond through gender to reestablish black liberation as a "male quest narrative," thereby begetting the American nation once again as male.[34] Certainly these narratives had been enacted many times in U.S. literature and in Hollywood films, for example, *The Apostle*, in which people of color witnessed and validated the white hero's rebirth. As with most narratives, however, other readings were also possible.

LOVE WORK AS RACE RECONCILIATION

It would have been unwise in the nineties to discount the possibility that racial discourse and perhaps racial politics might be shifting, or to assume that evangelicals of color were ripe for takeover, or that they had no agendas of their own. The presiding bishop of the Church of God in Christ, L. H. Ford, did not attend the Memphis meeting at which the Pentecostal Fellowship was formed, and many men of color remained suspicious about the motives and record of white evangelical efforts at antiracist work. The ministers of color who were willing to work with whites on racial reconciliation, moreover, had agendas that sometimes differed from those of their white counterparts. While some white leaders of the new Pentecostal fellowship, like Jack Hayford, for example, expressed skepticism about engaging in political activity together, black evangelicals like Charles Blake spoke not only of cooperation with white churches but of pressing the inner-city problem and seeking their support in pushing for federal and state action to meet the needs of the poor.[35] Both Hayford and Blake had been on the Promise Keepers speakers list.

It is too easy, moreover, for secular progressives to dismiss relation work as unpolitical, unnecessary, or as a plot to keep the workers happy. I know because I did as much myself. When I first began to research Promise Keepers and attend its conferences in 1995, I made a point of asking whoever on the staff would listen whether Promise Keepers planned to push beyond this focus on personal relationship to something more structural and, by implication, more serious and important as well. I was impatient, suspicious, and embroiled in the "yes, but . . ." impulse of many feminists and progressives when one of our "others" makes a promising move.

It took a good three years for me to understand, largely through my own experience in working to create a cross-race alliance, how far relationships of friendship, conflict resolution, dialogue, loyalty, love, and trust could go. It took a good three years to understand how great a distance such emotion work *must* go if cross-race coalitions are to be formed and if they are going to change anything at all. I came to understand that Promise Keepers had chosen what it could do in this regard without losing its mass base. The "yes but" impulse faded when I reflected that there was no other group currently sending hundreds of thousands of men back to their local churches and communities with the message that godly manhood meant shouldering the burden of antiracist work.

My interviews with Promise Keepers men suggested two things at once. The first was that the greatest division between white Promise Keepers and Promise Keepers of color lay in the emphasis that each gave to race reconciliation work. The second was that, despite this difference, Promise Keepers had had some progressive effects. Only six of the white men I interviewed at greatest length raised the issue of race reconciliation in their account of the impact that Promise Keepers had had on them as men. The six included only one of the four men I interviewed from the Bible Belt. This was David, who reported that he had been "different" in regard to race from most of his peers. He had grown up with a black nanny and her child, and he and his brother, upset that the former were confined to the back of the bus and to the theater balcony, began sitting with them at an early age. Promise Keepers, nonetheless, had made a difference in how judgmental he was with respect to race and this, he confided, had been "a big deal for me."

The five men from the West who brought up race reconciliation felt that Promise Keepers had increased their sensitivity to these issues. Neal, for example, a white clergyman living in Northern California, was shocked at what he heard from a pastor of color at the Promise Keepers Atlanta Conference for Clergymen in 1996 and came to see that he had been blind to many injustices before this. Living as he did in a very white town, however, he was unsure of how to address race issues in his immediate environment. Don, who lived in the Southwest, had never thought of himself as a racist until he attended a Promise Keepers conference. He then began to see that his family had had a history of racial prejudice and that he himself had held blacks responsible for national decline. Some of these feelings still remained, he noted, but now he tried "to get past them." Although he did not want to see race become the "dominant" theme in Promise Keepers conferences, he noted that he did now have a "Hispanic" friend and that he felt that racism had to be addressed on the level of "feeling." Ed, living in a Western state, had felt "hammered" about race at his second Promise Keepers conference, but he had been encouraged by Promise Keepers' emphasis on moving beyond, though not forgetting, the past. He was the only white Promise Keeper I interviewed at

length who was directly involved in outreach efforts. Indeed, he was often the
only "catalyst" and organizer for race reconciliation efforts at his church that
focused on reaching out to a "Hispanic" church in another part of town.

Every one of the twelve men of color I interviewed at greatest length gave
central emphasis to race reconciliation as the reason he had become involved
with Promise Keepers or had attended Promise Keepers functions. Although
aware that many men of color regarded Promise Keepers as a conservative
"white man's thing," these men had all seen hope in its practices. Three of the
men of color were pastors who had been invited to speak at a Promise Keepers conference, and all had been wary of Promise Keepers at first. Luis, for
example, felt that in 1993 and 1994 Promise Keepers had been practicing a
kind of "affirmative action" but had not been really listening to clergymen of
color. Then, according to Luis, something had "broken" and the "clique had
busted up." Now he felt Promise Keepers officials "heard him out."

Clarence, an African-American clergyman, had watched Promise Keepers
from the first year and felt that the relations of "support and responsibility" he
had seen of late were "phenomenally" important. Although he said that one
couldn't "overcome one hundred years of suspicion with a hug," he did feel that
genuine friendship was the beginning of understanding another's needs and that
it could lead to "genuine, structural, systematic change." The Native American
men I interviewed commented that Promise Keepers had not just asked them to
"dress up for dignitaries," but had delivered resources. In Promise Keepers' approach to the Native community they felt the organization had "proved they
were real." Bill, an Asian-American man living in southern California, was also
convinced that "social justice comes out of sensitivity" and mentioned that he
himself was now learning more about Native American men.

It was not clear in 1999 where Promise Keepers' racial work would go, nor
was it entirely clear what effects the racial reconciliation project was having beyond its effects on individuals. Some clergy of color whose ministries were already involved in race reconciliation and community development projects testified that Promise Keepers' work on race had produced dramatic
transformations. According to one Asian-American clergyman whom I briefly
interviewed in 1999, men returned from conferences wanting to be "intentional"
about antiracist work. "I never thought I'd live to see the day," he said, his face
lighting with emotion. For him the issue of race had finally been "jump-started"
in the church. Two white clergy whom I also briefly interviewed in 1999, however, ministered to churches that were mainly white or harmoniously, if marginally, mixed-race. Promise Keepers conferences, in the absence of references to
structural inequality, had seemed to leave them wondering what there was to do.

A website survey of 949 participants that Promise Keepers conducted in November 1998 suggested similar uncertainties. While 75 percent of the partici-

pants strongly disagreed with the statement that racial reconciliation was already an accomplished fact in the United States, only about 20 percent were in a committed relation with a man of a different racial group and only 29 percent felt their church was doing all it could. Still, between 40 and 50 percent wanted more workshops, more examples, and more local forums on the issue of reconciliation. It was one of the continuing contradictions of this organization that its heartfelt race reconciliation efforts went hand in hand with a new version of national manhood in which heterosexual men were still the primary citizens and in which women and gays were erased from the public sphere. At the very least, however, Promise Keepers appeared to be creating a core of earnest and, for the most part, "good-hearted" men who had begun to think of antiracism as central to their understanding of what it meant to be a godly man.

NOTES

1. Raleigh Washington and Glen Kehrein, *Breaking Down Walls: A Model for Reconciliation in an Age of Racial Strife* (Chicago: Moody Press, 1993), 117. My chapter title alludes to J. Michael Clark's *Doing the Work of Love: Men & Commitment in Same-Sex Couples* (Harriman, Tenn.: Men's Studies Press, 1999).

2. Bill McCartney with David Halbrook, *Sold Out: Becoming Man Enough to Make a Difference* (Nashville, Tenn.: Word Publishing, 1997), 177.

3. See Frederick Clarkson, "Righteous Brothers," *In These Times*, 5 August 1996.

4. Raleigh Washington and Glen Kehrein, *Break Down the Walls: Experiencing Biblical Reconciliation and Unity in the Body of Christ* (Chicago: Moody Press, 0000), 23.

5. Washington and Kehrein, *Breaking Down Walls*, 187–89.

6. 2 Corinthians 5: 18.

7. Harvey Cox, *Fire from Heaven: The Rise of Pentecostals Spirituality and the Reshaping of Religion in the Twenty–First Century* (Reading, Mass.: Addison-Wesley, 1995), 46–65, 63.

8. Cox, *Fire*, 72, 123–28.

9. Andres Tapia, "The Myth of Racial Progress," *Christianity Today,* 4 October 1993, 20.

10. John Perkins with Jo Kadlecek, *Resurrecting Hope: Powerful Stories of How God Is Moving to Reach Our Cities* (Ventura, Calif.: Regal Books, 1995), 18, 19, 20–23.

11. Joe Maxwell, "Racial Healing in the Land of Lynching," *Christianity Today*, 10 January 1994, 26.

12. Perkins, *Resurrecting*, 32–35.

13. Washington and Kehrein, *Breaking*, 72, 77.

14. Washington and Kehrein, *Breaking*, 90.

15. Washington and Kehrein, *Breaking*, 117.

16. Washington and Kehrein, *Breaking*, 131–32.

17. "The Cry for Renewal: Biblical Faith and Spiritual Politics, May 23, 1995." http://calltorenewal.com/about–us/index.cfm/action/history/htm (accessed 1 January 2004). The Call to Renewal was founded in February 1996 as an alternative to the Religious Right and in response to "welfare reform." Although it does not support gay marriage or abortion, it does stand for gay civil rights and for dialogue around abortion. It has been very active with respect to poverty and racism on the level of community involvement and on the level of public policy. I take up the work of one of its leaders, Jim Wallis, in chapter 10.

18. William Pannell, *The Coming Race Wars? A Cry for Reconciliation* (Grand Rapids, Mich.: Zondervan, 1993), 51, 20.

19. Pannell, *Coming*, 118, 140, 139.

20. James Wilson, book review, "The Coming Race Wars? A Cry for Reconciliation," *Christianity Today,* 9, 16 August 1993, 61–63; Pannell, *Coming*, 113.

21. Andres Tapia, book review, "The Coming Race Wars? A Cry for Reconciliation," *Christian Century* 110, no. 33 (November 17, 1993): 1172; Tapia, "Myth," 18.

22. Tapia, "Myth," 26, 18, 23.

23. Larry B. Stammer, "Black, White Pentecostals Unite in One Association," *Los Angeles Times*, 20 October 1994, B8.

24. Helen Lee, "Racial Reconciliation Tops NAE's Agenda," *Christianity Today,* 3 April 1995, 97; Timothy C. Morgan, "Racist No More? Black Leaders Ask," *Christianity Today,* 14 August 1995, 53.

25. Sam Fulwood III, "Christian Coalition Courts Minorities," *Los Angeles Times*, 31 January 1997, A22.

26. James Bennet, "Clinton Plans Moves Aimed to Improve Nation's Race Relations," *New York Times*, 5 June 1997, A22.

27. Steven A. Holmes, "Gingrich Outlines Program on Nation's Race Relations," *New York Times,* 19 June 1997, A12.

28. See Corwin Smidt, "Evangelical Voting Patterns: 1976–1988," in *No Longer Exiles: The New Religious Right in American Politics*, ed. Michael Cromartie (Washington, D.C.: Ethics and Public Policy Center, 1993), 108.

29. Richard D. Land, "Comment," *No Longer,* 84.

30. Ann Monroe, "Race to the Right," *Mother Jones*, May/June 1997, 36.

31. Carla Power and Allison Samuels, "Battling For Souls," *Newsweek,* 30 October 1995, 46–48.

32. Bill McCarthy, "Understanding the Times and Knowing What to Do about It," address delivered at Promise Keepers Men's Conference, "Choose This Day," Stockton, California, 10–11 September 1999.

33. See "Curing Homophobia and Other Conservative Pathologies," *tikkun* 8, no. 5 (September/October, 1993), 9, on how "the legitimation of a soft, nurturing, empathetic capacity in men can be a central part of the strategy to undermine conservative politics and to weaken the homophobia that is central to it."

34. Robyn Weigman, "Fiedler and Sons," in *Race and the Subject of Masculinities,* ed. Harry Stecopoulos and Michael Uebel (Durham, N.C.: Duke University Press, 1997), 66, 45, 50.

35. Stammer, "Black, White," B8.

10

The Politics of Feeling

Emotion is central to the transformation of individual identities. It is emotion that creates the movement culture and persuades individuals to risk their lives for the movement. . . . Emotion is the conduit through which self-interest moves toward consonance with collective interests.

—Belinda Robnett, *How Long? How Long? African-American Women in the Struggle for Civil Rights*

THE POLITICS OF FEELING

Mass gatherings of men, ritually atoning for past mistreatment of women, children, and other men, pledging themselves to forswear "the altar of machismo" for devotion to lives of greater responsibility, selflessness, compassion, and care, were not isolated phenomena at the end of the twentieth century. Indeed, men's organized efforts to construct masculine ideals that were less individualistic, less competitive, less materialistic, and more compatible with vulnerability and tenderness appear to have paved the way for what I call a "politics of feeling" that made love, working on relationships, and often male self-transformation the foundation for new political alliances and renewed efforts at larger structural change. In the late 1980s and the 1990s, for example, at least a dozen publications called for a version of this politics. Among them were J. Michael Clark's *A Place to Start: Toward an Unapologetic Gay Liberation* (1989); bell hooks and Cornell West's *Breaking Bread: Insurgent Black Intellectual Life* (1991); Lawrence A. Chickering's *Beyond Left and Right: Breaking the Political Stalemate* (1993); Anthony Giddens's *Beyond Left and Right: The Future of Radical Politics*

(1994); and Jim Wallis's *The Soul of Politics: Beyond "Religious Right" and Secular Left"* 1994).[1] These were followed by Wallis's *Who Speaks for God? An Alternative to the Religious Right—A New Politics of Compassion, Community, and Civility* (1996); Michael Lerner's *The Politics of Meaning: Restoring Hope and Possibility in an Age of Cynicism* (1996); Clark's *Doing the Work of Love: Men & Commitment in Same-Sex Couples* (1999); and, most recently, by David Nimmons's *The Soul Beneath the Skin: The Unseen Hearts and Habits of Gay Men* (2002).[2]

Central to this literature was the belief, so familiar from 1960s politics and from religious traditions, that solutions to current social crises must be grounded in a new ethos—"a sense of values beyond the self and a commitment to the larger good," "a perspective broader than our defended ghettos," "a life of serving others."[3] Almost universally fond of three-part phrases, the authors variously summarized this new ethic as "service and risk and sacrifice"; "*compassion, community, and civility*"; "courage, compassion and prophetic judgement"; "protection, conservation, and solidarity"; and "love, care, compassion, and kindness."[4]

Adopting this ethos, these books argued, would involve a significant transformation of personal and cultural values, a "conversion," "a turning of consciousness and intention" from "preoccupation with the self and toward some larger identity," a "shifting [of] society's discourse—from one of selfishness and cynicism to one of idealism and caring": "We are meant for something far beyond ourselves and our own selfish concerns."[5] Wallis, hooks, and West grounded their versions of the politics of feeling in Christianity, but hooks and West reassured their more secular readers that "Christians have no monopoly on the joys that come from service and those of you who are part of secular culture can also enjoy this sense of enrichment" through a "commitment to a life of service."[6] Lerner, who is Jewish, also saw a close relation between his evocation of an "ethical and spiritual framework that gives our lives some higher purpose" and familiar traditions of religion, philosophy, and movements for social justice. Most recently, Nimmons described the "intentional communities" forged by gay men as "following practices espoused by the great spiritual traditions," although "'what is different about what we do comes up from the grassroots, not down from a central religious authority.'"[7]

This politics, moreover, was to be anchored in the repair of "*damaged solidarities*" on the level of individual, familial, and community relationships. For others the politics of feeling was to "close the enormous gap that exists between the personal and the political," by expanding "our circle of caring," by building on "millions of little moments of caring on an individual level," and by promoting thereby "broad affiliative networks" and "wider and wider circles of loyalty."[8] Ideas and language such as these, of course, had been common in the work of Harry Hay and in that of some black cultural nationalists as well.

Basic to this politics of feeling was the conviction that community provided "a sense of belonging that every human being needs" and that this sense of belonging was key to sustaining the "resistance" necessary for political change. Hooks and West observed that "Black people in particular, and progressive people in general, are alienated and estranged from communities that would sustain and support us. We are often homeless." The political "home," however, that hooks and West envisioned for the future was a transfigured domestic space, an egalitarian and inclusive sphere where "love and the sweet communion of shared spirit" could flourish without "sexist domination."[9]

For most of these authors this turn to a politics that emphasized service, compassion, and community was prompted by a sense that economic and social problems were overwhelming— indeed, out of control—that prior solutions were inadequate, and that a radical renewal of political energy was required. For British social theorist Anthony Giddens, the very pursuit of human knowledge and of "controlled intervention" into society and nature had itself become a source of "unpredictability" and of "manufactured uncertainty." "Controlled intervention" had degraded the environment, increased poverty and homelessness, widened the gap between elites and both the middle class and the poor, eroded familial and communal ties and responsibilities, and promoted violence, along with many other signs of anxiety and social distress. This "runaway world" of "dislocation" and "uncertainty" was dominated by "rampant industrialism," a compulsive commitment to what Giddens calls "productivism," in which the mechanisms of economic development "substitute for personal growth, for the goal of living a happy life in harmony with others," and in which consumerism becomes "the standard-bearer for moral meaning" or, rather, a "substitute for such meaning."[10]

Writing from a U.S. context, hooks and West observed that black communities were in a "state of siege' that was linked not only "to drug addiction but also to the consolidation of corporate power as we know it," to the "redistribution of wealth from bottom to the top," and to the ways in which "a culture and society centered on the market, preoccupied with consumption, erode structures of feeling, community, tradition." These economic and social dislocations, moreover, had been accompanied by an "intensification of internalized racism" that followed shortly upon the civil rights and the Black Power Movements, producing a "feeling as though 'the world had really come to an end' in the sense that a hope had died that racial justice would become the norm."[11]

A new politics adequate to the times, most authors agreed, would involve a shift away from "individualism" as expressed in the pursuit of economic self-interest and career, in consumerist behavior, and in a reliance on external rewards, such as money, status, or power, "to improve one's standing relative to others." The politics of feeling, therefore, continued that critique of competition and materialism that most of the groups I studied articulated in some form or another. For Chickering, "increasing individualism and people's related dependence on publicly recognized rewards as affirmations of self worth are the major causes of modern social problems." For Nimmons, "capitalism is completely interwoven into most of the ways gay men now connect."[12]

There was a striking division, however, between authors who did and did not see the runaway nature of the world and the me-first ethic of individualism as tied to a "new global regime" of "unregulated international finance markets and multi national corporations" and to a "revived confidence in laissez faire."[13] Chickering, for example, saw the advance of something called advanced individual consciousness as "responsible for the enormous problems that socialists mistakenly attribute to capitalism." Others, like Giddens, Lerner, Wallis, hooks, West, and Clark, believed with NOMAS that individualism was deeply rooted in the practices of an unregulated global economy and in a free market ideology that held that "our collective well-being is best served when everyone pursues his or her own narrow self-interest without regard to the well-being of others" and when the economy is left to run itself.[14]

While productivity and corporate profits were going up, Jim Wallis observed, "employees' wage and job security [were] going down." Thus, from 1979 to 1993 the economy grew by 35 percent, but in 1993 the median household income was less than it had been in 1979, adjusted for inflation. Between 1983 and 1989, moreover, the top 1 percent captured 62 percent of newly created wealth.[15] This growing division of rich and middle-class and poor, hooks and West pointed out, took place on a global scale. The scarcity of resources that free market ideology had imposed upon the majority of the world's population, moreover, only worked to intensify the competitive ethos. Because "one half of one percent of America owns 22 percent of the wealth, one percent owns 32 percent, and the bottom 45 percent of the population has 20 percent of the wealth," the bottom 45 percent found itself in "competition and conflict," "struggling over crumbs."[16]

Strategies for resolving social problems often divided along similar lines. To Chickering, for example, "self governance" was the answer. With respect to public services such as schools and housing, self governance would yoke government funding with provisions for local control and would thereby involve participation from the bottom up: "The day of self governance is coming and when it arrives, the crisis in politics will be over."[17] Wallis shared with Chickering an emphasis on government responsibility and community control and called for community-based development projects that would allow poor people access and opportunity to use their own assets. For Wallis, however, there must also be more thoroughgoing structural change—the elimination of "corporate welfare," the institution of corporate "'accountabilities' as the requirement for doing business in our communities and our country," and the payment of rewards to community-minded entrepreneurs. Workers must participate in decision-making and ownership of corporations, and when economic sacrifices were required CEO salaries and benefits must also be cut.[18]

Most importantly, for Wallis, the global economy and its dysfunctions must become objects of national scrutiny, and the "purchased silence" about the growing economic divisions in U.S. life must be broken through. For Lerner and Giddens, and for Wallis as well, there must be a "new bottom line" according to which institutions or social practices would be judged productive not because of the wealth and power that they produce but according to whether they fostered "ethically, spiritually, ecologically and psychologically sensitive and caring human beings."[19]

Despite profound differences with regard to the role of economic systems and ideologies, nonetheless, almost all of these authors tended to agree that a single focus on the strategies historically identified as conservative, liberal, or Left was now inadequate. Jim Wallis, for example, faulted the liberal/Left for continuing to take refuge in the support of the welfare state and in failing to acknowledge the importance of rebuilding relationships, family, and other forms of community. Clark was critical of a gay male subculture that "in the decade immediately following liberation unwittingly fell prey to a heterosexist conditioning which resulted in a frequently dehumanizing, sexually competitive, and ultimately isolating ghetto experience." Bell hooks also took progressive circles to task for dismissing talk of love as "naive," while "outside those circles people openly acknowledge that they are consumed by self-hatred, who feel worthless, who want a way out." If leaders of progressive movements "refuse to address the anguish and pain of [these people's] lives, they will never be motivated to consider personal and political recovery. Any political movement that can effectively address these needs of the spirit in the context of liberation struggle will succeed."[20]

At the same time, according to Jim Wallis, conservatives talk endlessly about personal morality and responsibility but deny "the reality of structural injustice and social oppression." To call for individual self-improvement and a return to family values while "ignoring the pernicious effects of poverty, racism and sexism is to continue blaming the victim." The Right also supported tax relief for the rich and welfare for corporations, while failing to acknowledge the way in which an ethic of selfishness rooted in free market ideology threatened the familial relations that it saw as a cure for social ills. Instead, the Right blamed social crises on liberal programs or on various "others," such as the poor, especially the African-American poor, feminists, and homosexuals.[21]

MEN FOR A POLITICS OF FEELING

The economic and social problems that the politics of feeling addressed, and the strategies that they proposed, implied that dominant ideals of masculinity, along with men's actual attitudes and behaviors, must be changed—an idea that had characterized the work of many of the groups I studied. In Giddens, for example, global restructuring and the "runaway world" that it had ironically produced were seen as the responsibility, by and large, of elite males, while the values that sustained global restructuring were seen as deeply tied to dominant understandings of masculinity. As Giddens put it, "An orientation to productivism [or compulsive production] has long been primarily a phenomenon of the masculinized public domain."[22] The further entry of women into the marketplace, of course, meant that these values became more widely shared, but in the 1990s they were still not central to any widely shared understanding about what it meant to be a proper woman in U.S. or British terms. If no one could say, therefore, whether or not these traditionally masculine ideals would become dominant for both sexes in the time to come—in "a world in which men no longer value economic success in the way they once did and where they live more for love and emotional communication—the least one can say is that this would look very different from the present one." For Giddens, as for Hay and NOMAS, changing dominant ideals of masculinity was fundamental to changing the production-oriented nature of the world.[23]

The call for an ethic of love and care also implied a reconstruction of other widespread and powerful masculine norms that taught young boys that it was unmanly to express fear, vulnerability, and tender emotion. Critics of the women's movement in the 1990s, of course, were fond of accusing feminists, and nonfeminist working women as well, of having abandoned an ethic of selflessness and nurturing where men and even children were concerned. But while it was true that women working one job in the labor market and another job at home had attempted to share more of their uneven burdens with their men, squeezing emotions, care, and responsibility to the margins of one's social life did not define norms of being womanly in U.S. terms.

The politics of compassion and care, moreover, implicitly and explicitly called on men not just to feel more tenderly but actually to perform the labor of putting sensitivity into action, just as Hay, NOMAS, and Promise Keepers insisted men do. Men, like women, were to initiate, work on, and maintain caring relations in virtually every sphere of life—from that of the family to that of the workplace, the community, and politics in general. Such work was in a different category of effort from that of crying in public or being a "sensitive new age guy." "Love work" was a form of labor, and it was not the labor that U.S. men, by and large, had been called upon to perform.

Giddens, for example, gave special emphasis to what he called a "pact between the sexes," arguing that such a pact was "key to the retrieval of other forms of solidarity." While this pact between women and men would have to involve a "mutual emotional realignment of the sexes," Giddens emphasized the understanding that women's "claim to autonomy and equality is irreversible" and that men must, in the future, take on a much larger share of the tasks associated with the care of others.[24] For Wallis "to assume the shared responsibilities of nurturing and caring for children is a revolutionary change in a patriarchal society." Such change does not come easily, but "gender equality is essential to political transformation."[25]

For hooks, as well, renegotiating the pact between women and men was crucial to political resistance. Hooks reaffirmed what she saw as a "critical breakthrough" in Afrocentric black nationalism in which political figures like Haki Madhabuti had tried to "confront the reality of sexism" and to inform black men that they "can no longer expect black women to go out and work all day and come home and 'service' their needs, either their domestic needs or their sexual needs."[26] For hooks, as for other proponents of a politics of feeling, the personal and political were intertwined.

Most versions of the politics of feeling also called upon their readers to engage in more civil and less polarized forms of political debate, issuing a challenge that certainly spoke to politicized middle-class men and women both, for politicized women were no strangers to polarized and conflictual public discussion. To follow Lerner in reaching the (reluctant) conclusion that one's political enemies were "sometimes more insightful on other issues than are one's best friends" would be a hard lesson for politicized men and for women as well. As Chickering put it, "People on all sides of every issue talk as if they know everything and when it is obvious that they (and we) know very little." Nonetheless, the injunction to listen to the ideas of erstwhile "others," even when they had been "deeply wrong" on many things, weighed heavily upon the gender that was still required to pretend that it had an answer to every question, a chicken for every pot, and no need to ask directions as it entered the millennium.

The call to forge alliance across difference, central to most forms of the politics of feeling, as well, posed a particular challenge to politicized, heterosexual, white men. Feminist women, at least, had had to encounter racial and sexual difference and had engaged in fragile coalition building within feminist communities over some thirty years. Politicized heterosexual men of color had been called upon, in vigorous and persistent ways, to deal with gender and sexual difference in the context of race liberation struggles that they shared with women and gay men. Gay men had at least been challenged to build similar bridges across race and gender lines with respect to projects for combating AIDS and securing gay civil rights. Politicized white heterosexual men, however, while they had certainly entered into coalitions and had worked to cross race, gender, and sexual divides, had had no large-scale movement over the prior twenty years that had urgently hailed them to do this work (although organizations like NOMAS and Promise Keepers did call upon white men to make antiracism central to their ideals of masculinity). Indeed, as Robert Reid-Pharr observed in *Black, Gay, Man,* some white progressive men seemed to feel that the real danger to progressive community came not from the Right but from feminists, gay activists, and Afrocentrists.[27] The politics of feeling, in positing a new basis for a cross-race and cross-gender movement, proposed to fill a political void.

The very modesty of the goals that some forms of the politics of feeling embraced seemed to require another departure from traditional masculine ideals, at least for men whose gender identities in the past were wed to images of themselves as heroic political actors or leaders. In Giddens, for example, "utopian realism," "damage control," and "repair," not revolutionary change, were the salient terms. In Lerner the concept of "wounded healers" took the place of the *machers* or radical male activists of the sixties past, whose "fantasies of being fully healthy and actualized" led many of those leaders "to be insufficiently attentive to ways in which their behaviors [were] insensitive or hurtful to others." In hooks and West, as well, progressive politics was identified with patience and forgiveness more than with political purity or revolutionary rigor: "If we are serious about acknowledging and affirming other people's humanity, then we are committed to trusting and believing that they are forever in process. Growth, development, and maturation happen in stages."[28]

Hooks applied this principle to feminist women as well as to men, stressing the need to refrain from putting men in a "no-win situation" by asking for change and then dismissing change that came too rapidly or that garnered rewards for men. Rather than requiring men's perfect alignment with feminist points of view, hooks maintained, there needed to be focus upon friendship: "a commitment to the process of change and convergence which opens up the possibility of love, renewal, and reconciliation." This commitment to patience and to forgiveness was surely central to what hooks meant when she maintained, with Paulo Freire, that "there can be no revolution without love."[29]

WOUNDED HEALERS

These articulations of a politics of feeling, I have argued, were prepared for and made possible, to some degree, by the organized efforts to transform masculine ideals that I have reflected upon in these pages. Indeed, Giddens cited "men's movements" that critique dominant forms of masculinity as the potential equivalents of "peace movements—trying to help put an end to the undeclared war of men against women."[30] Within U.S. contexts, however, it was often men and women on the margins who most directly and fully articulated the transformation of masculinity as central to these politics. In the work of profeminist black men and women, gay and straight, as I suggest in chapter 7, a willingness to work on issues of gender and sexuality in men and women both and a willingness to name the transformation of masculine ideals as a central goal was driven by the "higher cause" of antiracist politics and by the need for political alliance.

A similar higher cause and a similar marginality with respect to dominant masculine ideals may explain why some white gay male writers have also been motivated to articulate a politics of feeling that names the transformation of masculinity as a central project. Two contemporary examples from this category are gay liberation theologian J. Michael Clark, in *A Place to Start (1998)* and *Doing the Work of Love: Men & Commitment in Same-Sex Couples* (1999), and activist David Nimmons, in *The Soul Beneath the Skin: Tthe Unseen Hearts and Habits of Gay Men* (2002). I will turn to these both in some detail.

Like other articulations of the politics of feeling, these books share two of the most central preoccupations of men's organized efforts to transform masculinity over the last half century—the critique of self-making, aggressive, and violent masculine norms and the production of more vulnerable and caring masculine attitude and behaviors. As with the work of Giddens, Lerner, Wallis, and hooks and West, these books also link the personal and the larger political. They propose that the transformation of masculine ideals and of men's actual feelings and practices could lead to a new national life that might include "more freely loving, publicly altruistic men." They speculate that the habits of such men might "shift the most deeply held values of the majority culture," helping to produce a new politics based on community and care, and thereby "[sweetening] the shared life or our planet."[31] Clark, moreover, would extend these politics to include structural economic change.

Nimmons begins *Soul Beneath the Skin,* for example, by emphasizing the ways in which many gay men already practice less violent and more caring forms of masculinity than are the national norm. He devotes one chapter to the lower level of violence in gay, as opposed to heterosexual, male public life and another chapter to the higher rate of volunteerism and care- taking activities among gay men. A 1994 study in San Francisco, he tells us, reported that in a sampling of central gay neighborhoods, 54 percent of the population had cared for other men ill with AIDS. In another study of twenty-three thousand people living in Milwaukee, Philadelphia, and San Francisco, gays (the sample seems to include women) gave 61 percent more time to volunteer work for nonprofit groups than did the heterosexuals. "Perhaps," Nimmons ventures, "queer men have held on to values of neighborliness, volunteerism, and mutual assistance more than most any other group of men one can name. Call it a victory for traditional values."[32]

Nimmons also sees a form of creativity in gay men when it comes to constructing new forms of beloved community, family, friendship, and personal intimacy. Among the most prominent of these "affectional innovations" is friendship. Drawing on the work of the sociologist Peter Nardi in *Gay Men's Friendships*, Nimmons argues that gay men are likely to have more close friends than heterosexual men do, that gays rank friendship higher, create friendships around emotional bonds rather than around activities, and engage "more deeply and fully . . . touching more, discussing more intimate and emotional topics."[33] Gay men's friendships are also more likely to involve a wider range of functions and intimacies: "We live our lives awash in complex stews of house mates, friendship networks, care teams, communal houses, and play partners." Such "social interventions" may not translate well in all their particulars—I myself would fall apart in the three and more–way sexual and romantic relationships that Nimmons describes—but innovations such as these give permission to the less venturous for finding new, personally appropriate, forms of relation-making and happiness in our own existence.[34]

Clark also sees a visionary potential in gay men—and in lesbians as well. (Nimmons consciously chooses not to discuss lesbians in *Soul* on the grounds that lesbian cultures are different from those of most gay men.) As in Hay, for example, Clark sees gay love and sexuality, themselves, as one foundation of a new, more caring ethic. Gay identity, for example, is an identity based on the fact of love: "In calling ourselves gay we say that love is central, and after the shame and guilt, and yes after the anger, love remains a word we can speak unabashed while others cringe at its too-telling power."[35] As in Hay, Clark also cites same-sex love as a model of egalitarian relationship: "Our same-sex love at the margins is . . . a balancing, horizontal, mutually relational force in opposition to vertically distributed power."[36]

Clark draws as well on Harry Hay's vision of the margins as a place in which special insights may be developed. He also evokes Robert Bly's belief that a wound can be a blessing and references the spiritual traditions of Judaism and feminist post-Christian theology in which outcasts are embraced and wounding becomes transcendence. Thus, Clark calls on gay men and lesbians both to "express our anger, to grieve our losses, to realize that, as gay people, we have no secured future," but then to "embrace our outcast status, our marginality, our exile" and to move from "passive victimization to an assertive, self-emptying place on the margins."[37] Claiming, with many liberation theologians, a belief that God is on the side of the oppressed, Clark asserts that gays who are sustained by this belief are also able to develop a more inclusive compassion not only for themselves, but for other marginalized and struggling people as well. In the spirit of Harry Hay, gayness becomes "not simply a way of being in bed, but rather a way of being in the world."[38]

Arrival at the train stop of transcendence, however, is far from automatic. Clark never loses sight of the fact that a politics of feeling involves labor, not just the expression of emotion, and he gives a good deal of emphasis to the barriers that gay men may have to address in realizing their full potential for compassion and care. (Although Nimmons also acknowledges that "all too often the shared public habits of gay worlds bristle with attitude and exclusion, loneliness, and looks-ism, defense and disrespect," Clark is more critical, and I think more realistic, about some of the norms of gay male public life.) As in Hay, gay identity is not in itself a guarantee of good politics. According to Clark, for example, gay men do not escape being socialized "in a heterosexist and patriarchal culture."[39] Like heterosexual men, gay men are conditioned to engage in constant self-proving, to experience performance anxiety, to depend on "constant, external approbation or support for our sense of self worth or self-esteem," to engage in competition, and to devalue intimate relation skills.[40]

Gay boys, moreover, fearing that "our emotions and interior life will be derided as sissified," easily become "emotionally constipated." Where heterosexual boys are encouraged to learn some relation skills through adolescent dating, moreover, gay boys, who are (often violently) discouraged from seeking same-sex partners, are thereby also deprived of learning the relation skills that would benefit them the most. When gay boys or men do come out as gay, moreover, they often "come out into a subculture that is immediately sexual, one that devalues romantic emotions, and one that seems to say that relationships have little value."[41]

The low self-esteem that often attends growing up gay in a culture that reviles and punishes gay men and women may be reinforced by the barriers that many gay men face in employment. Despite the "myth of disposable gay income," Clark writes, "far more of us are actually consigned to 'pink-collar' and/or service-related jobs that keep our incomes well below that of the male average." The competitiveness and performance anxiety that gay men are socialized to feel alongside heterosexual men may then be shifted into the sexual arena where "sexual prowess (in terms of both the number of our sexual partners and our sexual 'acrobatic' skills'") as well as having a beautiful body becomes a different form of competition.[42]

Just like heterosexual men, gay men are socialized early on "to devalue or even to despise all things feminine and all those who embody the feminine, whether women themselves, or, stereotypically, effeminate [gay] men." While heterosexual men have to live in a paradoxical love/hate situation with such a cultural message in order to remain masculine in relation to the women they love, gay men are taught to hate themselves as stereotypically effeminate men. Aspects of their own subculture, indeed, "[teach] us to overcompensate for that stereotype by disdaining not only all things feminine but all things feminine or effeminate in ourselves and in our community." Though gay men, not needing women as sexual partners, are freed from the love/hate paradox, "too often a subtle hatred of women has permeated the gay male subculture . . . (creating tensions between 'impressively masculine' gay men and lesbians, transsexuals, and transgenders)."[43] The dynamic is further complicated, Clark writes, when gay men see lesbians as "seemingly or stereotypically masculine while their own masculinity is uncertain." This has fueled "the tension between gay men and lesbians that has so often thwarted our collaborative projects."[44]

For Clark, gay men, like straight, must do their "men's studies homework" by working against their own participation in male dominance. Borrowing from the lesbian writer Carter Heyward, Clark writes that "hearing and learning from criticism—always a painful process for us men" may teach humility and adaptability. Working a twist on Promise Keepers' "not guilt but understanding," Clark calls for a move "not to guilt but to responsibility." According to Clark, more gay men need to do "the work of love" by developing "relational styles which do not imitate patriarchal roles, which renounce male privilege, and which instead humanize sexual sharing with a greater depth, intimacy, and tenderness." Like Hay, Clark writes that "we have an opportunity and a responsibility to relate to one another, even sexually, in mutually subjective, equal, co-sharing, and healing ways, rather than solely as sexual objects, despite our heterosexist enculturation to just such objectification."[45] Citing Mark Justad, Clark also calls on gay men "to relinquish the traditional expectation that we must be ever-strong, objectified, isolated, and autonomous creatures, and to embrace an engaged and relational model for our lives instead." He encourages gay men to "reclaim *inter*dependence and mutuality as (new) values for masculinity, including the related values of 'vulnerability, connection, and empathy,'"[46]

Like Nimmons, Clark sees gay men as having the potential, at least, for more intimate and egalitarian relations with women as well. Nimmons, for example, acknowledges that gay men are socialized as straight, but argues that gay men de-link "gender and genital intimacies" as straight men do not. This permits "a fresh mapping of affection, trust, and power." "If men are from Mars and women are from Venus," Nimmons jokes, "we're the ones who hold dual passports": "We meet women on a turf of greater gender, emotional, and erotic parity."[47] Nimmon's claim certainly resonates with my own experience in a twenty-four-year-long relationship with a mainly gay-identified man who was, until he died, consistently my best friend, as well as, at different times, my lover, husband, potential co-parent, "mother," "father," "brother," roommate, and co-member of a small collective.

Looking back I see that he treated me as an equal even before I understood that I was not so treated in general. He spoiled me for later partners by always doing his share of the housework—and more—and by never having to be asked or reminded. (He was the first man I lived with—little did I know what lay ahead!) He shared many gay men's ability to "laugh at themselves" as well as what Nimmons calls gay men's love of fun. His dry wit and more than occasional silliness made ordinary activities, like walking to the post office with him, an interesting adventure. Holding—and often playfully swinging—his hand as we walked down the street filled me with buoyancy and content. I often reflected that I could go anywhere in the world with him and feel "at home."

QUEER EYE FOR THE STRAIGHT GUY?

Various organized efforts to transform masculine ideals have also called on heterosexual men to do housework and emotion work with their partners in domestic situations. For heterosexual men, however, there have been obstacles that, in many ways, many gay men do not have. Heterosexual men, for example, may be doubly imprinted with the emotional familiarity of being served by women—once by mother and the second time by domestic partners who resemble the mother and who take the mother's place. This emotional familiarity with female service, and the persistence of traditional gender ideology as well, often pave the way for a gendered division of labor in which women do two-thirds more emotion work, housework, and child care than men do. Gay male domestic partners, who may unconsciously wish to be served and mothered, too, cannot as easily fall back emotionally on the notion that caring for others is the work of one gender—that being the gender that is not theirs!

In heterosexual networks such as Promise Keepers, moreover, the call for men to take on housework and emotion work took place in the context of more dominant notions of what it meant to be a man. Much of the energy at Promise Keepers conferences, indeed, was devoted to easing heterosexual men through potential gender vertigo as they were called upon to embrace and commit to these and other untraditional labors. For some gay men, however, the lingering impression that they are seen as effeminate anyway poses another opportunity—that of boldly embracing these feelings and behaviors without fear. Gay men have the potential, at least, for modeling new, more egalitarian ways of partnering, in which decisions about dividing the labor of "giving each other undivided attention," "developing and nurturing shared values," "talking through situations, disagreements, or misunderstandings," "remembering to say 'I love you' in ways other than sex" are no longer determined by old, sometimes unconscious, gender patterns.[48]

Hay, Clark, and Nimmons suggest that heterosexual men might benefit from patterning their behavior after those gays who maintain egalitarian relationships, can share intimate feelings and laugh at themselves, and have a flair for fun. I would support such modeling, although how far this modeling could go remains a question. Given heterosexual men's common fear of being seen as homosexual and given the complexities of their sexual intimacy with women (who tend for most men, consciously or unconsciously, to represent the mother and her power), such patterning would seem a challenge. At the very least, however, many relations between gay men and women and among gay male friends present models of intimacy that could give permission to straight men to, as the historian Martin Duberman puts it, open up some of the "possibilities within themselves that they prefer to keep under lock and key."[49]

BE THE CHANGE YOU WANT TO SEE

The politics of feeling espoused by Clark and Nimmons both is marked by an emphasis upon the actual practice of new forms of attitude and behavior. Nimmons, like the mythopoetics and Radical Faeries, writes of creating new "archetypes" of gay identity and of creating rites of passage for gay men. As the founder of a gay men's network called Manifest Love, Nimmons also advocates weekend and longer retreats during which men evidently employ many of the elements of male romance I found in the groups I studied, such as taking the risk of behaving more openly with each other by engaging in voluntary and nonsexual touching, using the eyes to connect with rather than to objectify or close off other men, and brainstorming new institutions and practices. Men are also encouraged to engage in "Loving Disturbances" once home again. One small group, for example, staged a "gang affection bang" for one friend by teaming up to cook him meals, bake him cookies, clean his house, walk his dog and to generally "celebrate his presence in their lives."[50]

As in Harry Hay, however, personal behaviors are seen as preconditions for progressive structural change. In Nimmons's words, "What is demonstrably different about nurture in gay worlds is the way male caring and service translate in our communal practices, institutions, and rituals." Like the Radical Faeries, Nimmons cites Gandhi as well: "Be the change you wish to see in the world." It is Clark, however, who gives most weight to male–female and cross-race alliance politics. Thus, in Clark, self-love and the entry into a supportive community become the necessary preludes to encompassing "a world of total justice, compassion, beauty, equality, pleasure, and grace where all people come together to actualize our finest potentials" and where all people are free from heterosexist (male) domination."[51] This world, as Clark envisions it, would include "meaningful, cooperative labor for *all* people and non-discrimination for eligibility to all work and activity." It would be marked by "egalitarian rather than hierarchical structures of governance," by "nonviolent conflict resolution," and by "cooperation with, rather than domination/exploitation of, the earth and its resources." It would embrace the development of and respect for the genuine pluralism of a "multi-cultural, multi-ethnic society'" that realizes and embodies the idea that "'unity in diversity is essential for strength.'" It would celebrate "friendship networks or voluntary surrogate families, rather than hierarchal nuclear families," thereby providing "more opportunities therein for men to be nurturers." It would see "the utter demise of gender roles." For Clark, caring on the level of the personal would "[nurture] our sense of accountability, including our commitments to justice for ourselves, for other gay and lesbian people, for women and other oppressed people, and for all nonhuman life, including the earth itself."[52]

MEN FOR A CULTURE OF PEACE

Clark's vision of a brave new world is unabashedly utopian, as is perhaps the chapter I have written. As a friend put it after reading an early draft, "This is beyond utopian . . . but, hey, good for you." Utopian thinking, however, can be a gift. As the late progressive Senator Paul Wellstone once put it, "Politics is what we dare to imagine."[53] What we dare to imagine can have impact on our attitudes and behaviors and on what we are willing to take on. Utopian thinking, moreover, is no stranger to our world. The year 2001, for example, will be remembered for terrorist bombings of the United States and for attempts to ensure the latter's global domination through a strategy of permanent war. The year 2001, however, was also the first year of the United Nation's "decade of peace," a ten-year project devoted to ending violence in every form.

Violence, according to the U.N.'s "Declaration on a Culture of Peace," included war and terrorist attack, but it also included the violence of economic and social inequality along with such personal forms of violence as rape and domestic abuse. Thus, the U.N.'s declaration called for a broad range of efforts: ending discrimination and intolerance in every form, promoting equal rights and opportunities for women and men, promoting the rights of children, eradicating poverty and reducing inequalities within and among nations, acting with full respect for the principles of sovereignty and political independence of states, and achieving freedom of expression, justice, and democracy.[54]

This Culture of Peace, moreover, like the politics of feeling, was linked with the project of transforming masculine ideals and men's actual attitudes and behaviors. Three years earlier, in 1997, in Oslo, Norway, UNESCO's program on "Women and the Culture of Peace" had convened a conference on "Male Roles and Masculinities in the Perspective of a Culture of Peace," which drew feminist men and women from across the globe. Beginning from the perspective that men almost exclusively make the decisions that launch international aggression and civil wars and that men are "responsible for most crimes of violence in private life," the conference posed the question of how men would best be drawn into the making of a culture of peace. One beginning point was that "blaming all men for violence, implying that men are evil, or that women are inherently better people" would lead to "instant alienation of most men from any program of change."[55]

Rather than being shamed, the conference participants concluded, men and boys should be educated about characteristics of "social masculinity" that lead men toward violence and what "institutions and ideologies reinforced aggressive masculinities." Conference participants also promoted the idea of education through practice and advocated finding respectful ways of engaging boys and men in antisexist and antiracist men's groups and in anti-violence efforts such as the White Ribbon campaign. Conference participants also recommended encouraging men to work in child-care centers, working to secure parental leaves for fathers, and developing gender-specific programs for boys that would address issues about masculinity. Conference participants, however, emphasized the point that reeducating boys and men could not work in isolation. It must be supported by action to reduce gender hierarchies and antagonisms in public and private and by efforts to change those economic and social institutions that encouraged violence. Work on men's issue about violence and peace could only be successful in the context of a broad movement toward gender, race, economic, sexual and other forms of equality.

MEN FOR A CULTURE OF WAR?

Efforts to construct ideals and practices that are congruent with a "culture of peace" are all the more crucial these days in the light of current attempts to create a masculine ideal more compatible with war. Deemphasizing the role of "feeling" and relegating even "'compassionate conservativism'" to the past, some proponents of this new ideal emphasize toughness, aggression, and competition as signs of "real" manhood. Some even celebrate the use of force: "Of course, George W. Bush is famous for his 'compassionate conservatism.' . . . But Bush as *hombre* has been the dominant theme of his post–September 11 Presidency. . . . The last couple of years have been replete with Bush toughness—tough talk, tough action, toughness in a tough job."[56] In the words of another advocate: "The use of force, which until recently was passé, has come back."[57]

This celebration of "real" manhood is largely driven by support for the Bush administration's "war on terror." As one proponent put it, "There are many kinds of masculinity. The war on terror, if it is to succeed, will have to mobilize and train some of the less attractive varieties."[58] What proponents of these "less attractive" masculine ideals fail to mention, however, is that 9/11 and the "war on terror" did not originate the plan to launch preemptive military strikes against countries like Iraq. In the words of religion professor Gary Dorrien, "We are told that 9/11 changed everything, and that a preemptive war against Iraq must be waged to defeat terrorism. Even the administration officials who are demanding this war have been calling for it since the mid-1990s and they have no intention of stopping with Iraq."[59]

It was during the first Bush administration, indeed, that a group of neoconservative policy makers and intellectuals began to argue that "the United States needed to expand its military reach to every region of the world."[60] Although the first Bush administration did not finally agree to such a plan, it was revived in 1997 as the Project for a New American Century (PNAC). In the year 2000, the group produced a new position paper that called, once again, for U.S. domination of the world and that espoused the strategies of "unilateral military action and the preemptive use of force." Various proponents of the PNAC endorsed the overthrow not only of Saddam Hussein but also of Palestinian authority and the governments of Syria, Iran, Egypt, Saudi Arabia and Lebanon.[61] After the shocking attacks of 9/11, proponents of PNAC were successful in assuming control of foreign policy in the second Bush administration.

Some advocates of U.S. global domination worried that the U.S. public might not tolerate the empire building strategies of preemptive military force: "The real question is not whether the American military can topple Saddam's regime but whether the American public has the stomach for imperial involvement."[62] The celebration of a masculine ideal based on the necessity of toughness, aggression, competition, and force is clearly one strategy for creating that "stomach." Some proponents of this resuscitated masculine ideal, however, attempt to soften it by implying that elite policy makers bent on global domination through preemptive military strikes may be compared to such ordinary, courageous, and self-sacrificing figures as 9/11 fireman, policeman, and the passengers on Flight 93, or that proponents of permanent war are on a par with foot soldiers in Afghanistan and Iraq: "Now America is embracing a new ethic and a new creed: 'Let's Roll.' (Of course, this is an evocation of the famous words spoken aboard Flight 93 on 9/11.)"[63]

No mention is made of the differences between wealthy policy makers advocating U.S. empire building, at a safe distance from the battlefield, and those who have truly risked, and lost, their lives by following the orders of those in charge or by acting to rescue others from physical harm. There are differences as well in who benefits and who bears the cost of U.S. global policies. As Jim Wallis puts it:

> Clearly the sacrifices for the war in Iraq will be borne by those in most need who will bear the brunt of inevitable spending cuts to vital social programs, and by future generations who will ultimately pay for the beneficiaries of the Bush tax cuts and the recipients of the lucrative contracts for Iraqi reconstruction that are going to carefully selected American corporations. Those who will not sacrifice, in other words, are the wealthy and powerful allies of the Bush administration—and their core constituency. It is not hyperbole to say that those beneficiaries of wartime tax cuts and contract deals should now be called war profiteers.[64]

Citing Episcopal bishop John Chance, Wallis continues, "We've gone from a war on poverty to a war on the poor" in which "Compassionate conservatism is now in grave danger of becoming compassionless conservatism."[65]

These concerted efforts to construct an emotionally tougher, more aggressive, more competitive masculine ideal are one kind of testament to the cultural resonance of the groups I studied. The latter, after all, had focused on the reinvention of ideals of masculinity that, variously, rejected self-making, competition, and economic advance as life's primary goals and promoted nonviolence, altruism, compassion, and care on the part of men. The repetition of these ideals over a period of some forty years, although insufficient as a politics in itself, helped to create the conditions of possibility for imagining a politics that would be adequate to changing the me-first, production-oriented, violence-prone values that undergird the unjust nature of our world.

I would argue that most of the organized efforts to transform masculine ideals that I have written about in this book have produced models of masculinity that would, to varying degrees, serve such efforts. It is a final argument of this book that the groups I studied also produced hundreds of thousands of men who might be drawn upon for such labors but who are uncertain about how best to channel their "feelings of grief, of outrage, of affection for each other, and of longing for lives richer in meaning" into "riskier social action and farther-reaching change."[66]

Pursuing the relation between the performance of altruistic, compassionate, and actively caring masculinities and reducing the violence of economic injustice, of global domination, and of racist, misogynistic, and homophobic structures and regimes is a heroic project, to be sure, but it is one well worth contemplating—for men and women both—in the twenty-first century.

NOTES

1. J. Michael Clark, *A Place to Start: Toward an Unapologetic Gay Liberation* (Dallas: Monument Press, 1989); bell hooks and Cornell West, *Breaking Bread: Insurgent Black Intellectual Life* (Boston: South End Press, 1991); Lawrence A. Chickering, *Beyond Left and Right: Breaking the Political Stalemate* (San Francisco: Institute for Contemporary Studies Press, 1993); Anthony Giddens, *Beyond Left and Right: The Future of Radical Politics* (Cambridge, UK: The Polity Press, 1994); Jim Wallis, *The Soul of Politics: Beyond "Religious Right" and Secular Left"* (New York: Harcourt Brace, 1994).

2. Jim Wallis, *Who Speaks for God? An Alternative to the Religious Right—A New Politics of Compassion, Community, and Civility* (New York: Dell Publishing, 1996); Michael Lerner, *The Politics of Meaning: Restoring Hope and Possibility in an Age of Cynicism* (Reading, Mass.: Addison-Wesley 1996); David Nimmons, *The Soul Beneath the Skin: The Unseen Hearts and Habits of Gay Men* (New York: St. Martin's Press, 2002). Several of these works drew insights from an earlier book, *Habits of the Heart: Individualism and Commitment in American Life,* by Robert N. Bellah, Richard Madsen, William M. Sullivan, Ann Swideler, and Steven Tipton (Berkeley: University of California Press, 1985). This study of individualism and of community in American life reissued with a new introduction in 1996.

3. Chickering, *Beyond Left and Right,* 8; Giddens, *Beyond Left and Right,* 184; Clark, *Place,* 151; hooks and West, *Breaking Bread,* 17.

4. Hooks and West, *Breaking Bread,* 14; Wallis, *Who Speaks?* 363; Clark, *A Place,* 171, 159; Giddens, *Beyond Left and Right,* 10; Nimmons, *Soul,* 190.

5. Hooks and West, *Breaking Bread,* 14; Bellah et al., *Habits,* xxxi; Lerner, *Politics,* 66; Nimmons, *Soul,* citing Malcolm Boyd, 215.

6. Hooks and West, *Breaking Bread,* 17.

7. Lerner, *Politics,* 4; Nimmons, *Soul,* 188.

8. Giddens, *Beyond Left and Right,* 12; Chickering, *Beyond Left and Right,* 171; Lerner, *Politics,* 9, 20; Nimmons, *Soul,* 140; Bellah et al., *Habits,* xxx.

9. Wallis, *Who Speaks?* 85; hooks and West, *Breaking Bread,* 18.

10. Giddens, *Beyond Left and Right,* 3, 4, 247, 169.

11. Hooks and West, *Breaking Bread,* 8; bell hooks, "Love as the Practice of Freedom," in *Outlaw Culture: Resisting Representations* (London: Routledge, 1994), 245.

12. Chickering, *Beyond Left and Right,* 91, 95; Nimmons, *Soul,* 206.

13. William Sullivan, "The Politics of Meaning as a Challenge to Neocapitalism," *tikkun* 11, no. 3 (May–June 1996): 17.

14. Chickering, *Beyond Left and Right,* 163; Lerner, *Politics,* 43.

15. Wallis, *Who Speaks?* 89.

16. Hooks and West, *Breaking Bread,* 13.

17. Chickering, *Beyond Left and Right,* 184, 196.

18. Wallis, *Who Speaks?* 100–101.

19. Wallis, *Who Speaks?* 176; Lerner, *Politics*, 56.

20. Clark, *Place,* 173; hooks, "Love as the Practice of Freedom," 247.

21. Wallis, *Soul,* xiv, xv; Wallis, *Who Speaks?* 4, 153.

22. Giddens, *Beyond Left and Right,* 195.

23. Giddens, *Beyond Left and Right,* 195.

24. Giddens, *Beyond Left and Right,* 190, 240.

25. Wallis, *Soul*, 221, 222.

26. Hooks and West, *Breaking Bread*, 113.

27. Robert F. Reid-Pharr, *Black Gay Man: Essays* (New York: New York University Press, 2001), 4.

28. Giddens, *Beyond Left and Right,* 4, 249; Lerner, *Politics,* 168, 169; hooks and West, *Breaking Bread,* 12.

29. Hooks and West, *Breaking Bread,* 124, 3.

30. Giddens, *Beyond Left and Right,* 240.

31. Nimmons, *Soul,* 219.

32. Nimmons, *Soul,* 42, 44–45, 53.

33. Nimmons, *Soul,* 112, 117; Peter M. Nardi, *Gay Men's Friendships: Invincible Communities* (Chicago: University of Chicago, 1999).

34. Nimmons, *Soul,* 116.

35. Aaron Shurin, "The Truth Come Out," *Gay Spirit: Myth and Meaning,* ed. Mark Thompson (New York: St. Martin's Press, 1987), 259. Cited in Clark, *Place,* 44.

36. Clark, *Place,* 127.

37. Clark, *Place,* 43.

38. I. C. Heyward, *Our Passion for Justice: Images of Power, Sexuality, and Liberation* (New York: Pilgrim, 1984), 82. Cited in Clark, *Place,* 125.

39. Nimmons, *Soul,* 54; J. Michael Clark, "Men's Studies at the Margins: Doing the Work of Love, part 1, *Journal of Men's Studies* 5, no. 4 (May 1997): 315. Online at melvyl@popserv.ucop.edu (page 2 of 17).

40. Clark, "Men's Studies," 8 (online).

41. Clark, "Men's Studies," 7, 4 (online).

42. Clark, "Men's Studies," 8, 9 (online).

43. Clark, "Men's Studies," 6 (online).

44. Clark, "Men's Studies," 6 (online).

45. J. Michael Clark and Bob McNeir, "An Extended Case Study (Doing the Work of Love, part 2)," *Journal of Men's Studies* 5, no. 4 (May 1997), 337; Clark, "Men's Studies," 3 (online); Clark, *Place*, 154.

46. M. J. Justad, "A Transvaluation of Phallic Masculinity: Writing with and through the Male Body," *Journal of Men's Studies* 4: 365 ff., cited in Clark and Mc-Neir, "An Extended Case Study," 333.

47. Nimmons, *Soul,* 143.

48. Clark and McNeir, "An Extended Case Study," 335, 336.

49. Martin Duberman, "Gayness Becomes You," *Nation,* 20 May 2002, 42.

50. Nimmons, *Soul,* 198, 216–17.

51. Clark, *Place,* 151; Clark and McNeir, "An Extended Case Study," 344.

52. Clark and McNeir, "An Extended Case Study," 344.

53. "Paul Wellstone," *Nation* 275, no. 17 (18 November, 2002), 1.

54. UNESCO's Culture of Peace: "A Declaration on a Culture of Peace," www.unesco.org/cpp/uk/declarations/2000htm.

55. Expert Group Meeting on Male Roles and Masculinities in the Perspective of a Culture of Peace: II, Rapporteur's Summary of Issues and Themes. hhtp://www.unesco.org/cpp/uk/declarations/oslorapp.htm

56. Jay Nordlinger, "The Return of Manly Leaders and the Americans Who Love Them," *The American Enterprise* 14, no. 6 (September 2003): 20, 21.

57. "The Kind of Men Society Needs — and Women Want," *The American Enterprise* 14, no. 6 (September 2003): 30.

58. "Men on Men: Intellectual Locker Room Talk," *The American Enterprise* 14, no. 6 (September 2003): 27.

59. Gary Dorrien, "The War against Iraq and the Permanent War," *Electronic Iraq,* 3 March 2003. http://electroniciraq.net/news/203/shtml. First published in *Christian Century,* 8 March 2003.

60. Dorrien, "The War against Iraq."

61. Dorrien, "The War against Iraq."

62. Robert Kaplan, cited in Dorrien, "The War against Iraq."

63. Nordlinger, "Return," 21.

64. Wallis, "War on the Poor," *In These Times* 27, October 2003, 15.

65. Wallis, "War on the Poor," 13, 14.

66. Michael Schwalbe, *Unlocking the Iron Cage: The Men's Movement, Gender, Politics, and American Culture* (New York: Oxford, 1996), 245.

Index

Adams, Malika, 64

African-American gender relations, 64–66, 69–70, 172; black political movements and, 64–66, 69–70, 72–73, 94, 111, 201–2; black women's writing and, 202; critiques of in black political movements, 65–66, 69–70, 201–2; decline of Black Power and, 202; feminisms and, 203; higher cause and, 206; household chores and, 205; impact of economic and social forces on, 188–89, 200–205; magazine literature on, 185–88; male defensive collapse in, 204–5; men's fear of losing centrality in, 203; men's fear of women's control in, 203–4; men's withdrawal in, 203–5; political importance of, 200–202, 205–6; parallels to those of white in, 188, 205; profeminist men and, 206–8; public discourse on, 188–89, 205–6; self-help books on, 187–88. *See also* African-American men, Afrocentric Movement, black feminisms, Black Arts Movement, Black Panther Party, Black Power, United States

African-American men: gay affirmation and, 206–8; male romance and, 27–32, 38–42, 60–61; masculine ideals and, 9, 38–42, 55, 59–61, 66–68, 70–71, 72–74, 206–8; Masonry and, 39–40; profeminism and, 206–8; relation to the feminine and, 47, 207–8. *See also* African American gender relations, Afrocentric Movement, Black Arts Movement, black cultural nationalism, black fathering, Black Panther Party, United States

African-Americans, socioeconomic conditions for, 9, 38–39, 44, 53–54, 72, 188–89, 200–205

African-American women: Afrocentric Movement and, 73; Black Arts Movement and, 70; black cultural nationalism and, 69–70; black film and, 16, 31, 71; Black Panther Party and, 64–66; gangsta rap and, 71; political activism of, 64. *See also* African American gender relations, black feminisms

Afrocentric Movement: critique of gender relations in, 73; masculine ideals in, 72–74

281

About the Author

Judith Newton is professor of women and gender studies at University of California, Davis. She is the author and editor of many books, including *Women, Power, and Subversion: Social Strategies in British Fiction, 1778–1860* and *Starting Over: Feminism and the Politics of Cultural Critique*. She is head of the Consortium for Women and Research at UC Davis.